Foundation Website Creation with CSS, XHTML, and JavaScript

Jonathan Lane
Meitar Moscovitz
Joseph R. Lewis

friendsof

DESIGNER TO DESIGNER™

an Apress® company

Foundation Website Creation with CSS, XHTML, and JavaScript

Distributed to the book trade worldwide by Springer-Verlag New York, Inc., 233 Spring Street, 6th Floor, New York, NY 10013. Phone 1-800-SPRINGER, fax 201-348-4505, e-mail orders-ny@springer-sbm.com, or visit www.springeronline.com.

For information on translations, please contact Apress directly at 2855 Telegraph Avenue, Suite 600, Berkeley, CA 94705. Phone 510-549-5930, fax 510-549-5939, e-mail info@apress.com, or visit www.apress.com.

Apress and friends of ED books may be purchased in bulk for academic, corporate, or promotional use. eBook versions and licenses are also available for most titles. For more information, reference our Special Bulk Sales–eBook Licensing web page at http://www.apress.com/info/bulksales.

The information in this book is distributed on an "as is" basis, without warranty. Although every precaution has been taken in the preparation of this work, neither the author(s) nor Apress shall have any liability to any person or entity with respect to any loss or damage caused or alleged to be caused directly or indirectly by the information contained in this work.

The source code for this book is freely available to readers at www.friendsofed.com in the Downloads section.

Credits

Contributor	**Associate Production Director**
Steve Smith	Kari Brooks-Copony
Lead Editor	**Production Editor**
Clay Andres	Elizabeth Berry
Technical Reviewers	**Compositor**
Meitar Moscovitz, Joseph R. Lewis	Dina Quan
Editorial Board	**Proofreader**
Clay Andres, Steve Anglin, Ewan Buckingham, Tony Campbell, Gary Cornell, Jonathan Gennick, Matthew Moodie, Joseph Ottinger, Jeffrey Pepper, Frank Pohlmann, Ben Renow-Clarke, Dominic Shakeshaft, Matt Wade, Tom Welsh	Dan Shaw
	Indexer
	Beth Palmer
	Cover Image Designer
	Corné van Dooren
Project Manager	**Interior and Cover Designer**
Kylie Johnston	Kurt Krames
Copy Editor	**Manufacturing Director**
Kim Wimpsett	Tom Debolski

*This book is dedicated to the people who currently—
and want to—work to make the Web a better, more
standards-compliant, and more accessible place.
It isn't always easy, but your work really matters.*
—Jonathan Lane

*For Aba, whom most of my work on this book is really for.
Hopefully you'll now feel comfortable using your
editor's Source view.*
—Meitar Moscovitz

To my beautiful wife, whom I love beyond measure.
—Joseph R. Lewis

CONTENTS AT A GLANCE

CONTENTS

ABOUT THE AUTHORS

Jonathan Lane is the president of Industry Interactive, Inc., a Mayne Island, BC, Canada–based web development company. Industry Interactive offers a range of services from hosted web applications to standards-based web application development. Its newest product offering, Mailmanagr, provides an e-mail interface to Basecamp, the popular web-based project management application.

Jonathan started his career working as the web development coordinator for the University of Lethbridge, where he managed the design and development of research, department, and teaching websites, as well as helped move the university's web strategy forward.

Jonathan is married and has a pair of sons, Reilly and Parker, which pretty much occupies all of his nonworking time.

Born and raised in New York City, **Meitar Moscovitz** first touched a computer when he was an infant in 1986 (an Apple Macintosh Plus). At his father's prompting, he created his first website at the age of 12 and through it created the first online community for teenagers and young adults with bipolar disorder. Out of school by 16, he officially joined the workforce as a junior network administrator, and at 18 he started freelancing full time as a web developer. After brief excursions into corporate IT with such companies as Apple and Opsware (now HP), he returned to professional web development and worked on websites for clients including Oxygen Media, Inc., and the Institute of Electrical and Electronics Engineers (IEEE).

He now lives in Sydney, Australia, with his brilliant girlfriend of three years, Sara Hames, and works as the senior front-end web developer and IT director for Digital Eskimo, Pty Ltd. In his rapidly diminishing spare time, Meitar enjoys volunteering his technical talents to nonprofit organizations and other small groups. He's also an avid blogger and juggler, and he has way too many profiles on social networking sites.

Joseph R. Lewis works as a team lead for web development at Sandia National Laboratories in Livermore, California. Joe is a recognized expert in standards-based web development and accessibility, and he has presented and lectured in technology subjects nationwide. Before falling into the obsessive career of web design and development, Joe was a professional musician. He is a classically trained double bassist and graduate of the New England Conservatory of Music, and he has performed with orchestras and chamber groups in major concert halls and festivals across the United States and Europe. When not cranking out code, writing nerd-struck pulp, or practicing music late at night, Joe spends his time with his adorable wife and two crazy kids.

ABOUT THE COVER IMAGE DESIGNER

 **Corné van Dooren** designed the front cover image for this book. Having been given a brief by friends of ED to create a new design for the Foundation series, he was inspired to create this new setup combining technology and organic forms.

With a colorful background as an avid cartoonist, Corné discovered the infinite world of multimedia at the age of 17—a journey of discovery that hasn't stopped since. His mantra has always been "The only limit to multimedia is the imagination," and it's a mantra that is keeping him moving forward constantly.

After enjoying success after success over the past years—working for many international clients, being featured in multimedia magazines, testing software, and working on many other friends of ED books—Corné decided it was time to take another step in his career by launching his own company, Project 79, in March 2005.

You can see more of his work and contact him through www.cornevandooren.com or www.project79.com.

If you like his work, be sure to check out his chapter in *New Masters of Photoshop: Volume 2*, also by friends of ED (ISBN: 1590593154).

ACKNOWLEDGMENTS

I would like to acknowledge Chris Mills for helping get this project started and Clay Andres for taking over and driving things forward after Chris's departure; Kylie Johnston, without whom this book would have earned me my procrastination badge of honor; Steve Smith, Meitar Moscovitz, and Joe Lewis for helping fill in my technical deficiencies; and Kim Wimpsett and Liz Berry for their patience in answering my questions during the production process.

Thanks to my wonderful wife, Rachel, for giving me the time to write, and to my kids, Reilly and Parker, for keeping the noise level to a dull roar (some of the time). Thanks also to my parents: my mom, Cynthia, for the writing genes, and my father, Rick, for that "get it done" attitude. I'm not sure which was used more on this project.

Jonathan Lane

First of all, I'd like to acknowledge the web standards giants who came before me, such as Eric Meyer, Molly Holzschlag, Peter-Paul Koch, Jeffrey Zeldman, and others too numerous to mention, without whom I'd have no shoulders to stand on. I hope my contributions to this book have added some real value to the work they produced before me.

I also want to thank all the people who worked with me on this book: my coauthors and technical reviewers, Jonathan Lane and Joe Lewis, for their very astute observations and suggestions while I was drafting my contributions; the staff at Apress/friends of ED (including but certainly not limited to) Kylie Johnston, Kim Wimpsett, and Liz Berry for their efforts, and very especially Clay Andres, my editor. Clay not only set me the challenge of turning what was originally intended to be a relatively small review task into several months of hard work but, more important, gave me the opportunity to do so in the first place.

Thanks also to the wonderful people with whom I work on website projects every day—the staff of Digital Eskimo in Sydney, Australia, for allowing me to take the time off I needed to focus on this work. Even more important, thanks for providing a really great working environment where I can feel like I'm doing the things I want to do instead of the things I need to do to earn a living.

I would also like to thank my girlfriend, Sara Hames, the writer. Not only does she deserve thanks for helping proofread all of my work before the copy editor saw any of it and for not being upset with me in spite of getting published before her, but also for her immense support and encouragement in many more important ways than words can ever describe.

Finally, I'd like to thank my family for their support years before I knew I'd ever write a book: my brother, Shir, for being the single most resilient, methodical, and authentic person I know; my mom, Rina, for teaching my brother and I how to be the stalwart people we are (whether we make the choices she'd prefer we make or not); and my father, without whose inspiration, insight, and guidance I may never have found the path that led me to where I want to be today.

Meitar Moscovitz

I would like to extend my thanks to the following people:

To Michael Alderete, for introducing me to the idea of a blog so long ago.

To Stephanie Sullivan and Molly Holzschlag, for their sage advice on the matter of writing, among other things.

To Gabriel García Márquez, for writing *One Hundred Years of Solitude*, and to Chris Haag, for giving me a copy.

To Don Palma, for asking me why I wasn't practicing.

To my coauthors and the team at Apress/friends of ED for making this such a positive experience.

And most of all, to Yingwen, because you mean the world to me.

Joseph R. Lewis

INTRODUCTION

Coming to web development with a blank slate can be pretty intimidating. There are a lot of things to learn about the proper construction of a website. The most successful websites have a great deal of thought and work put into them before they're even put into production.

Although it can be scary, there has never been a better time to get started than the present. Web browsers are finally starting to reach a point where they all follow standards (more or less). You have to do less fiddling with things to get them working properly now than ever before. We don't want to jinx it, but we think we can finally start letting our guard down a bit and start trusting browser manufacturers more (yes, even Microsoft).

Who this book is for

This book is intended for people who are new to developing for the Web and those who are interested in overhauling their current work to be standards-compliant. It is relevant to individuals working within companies and institutions, as well as for those who freelance.

How this book is structured

This book offers a brief history of the World Wide Web and then walks the reader through several chapters on each of the areas relevant to developing a website. Each chapter covers a separate process or technology relevant to working with the Web today.

Readers learn about planning a website, managing the design and development process, and developing using web standards; we also provide an overview of server-based technologies.

Layout conventions

To keep this book as clear and easy to follow as possible, the following text conventions are used throughout.

Important words or concepts are normally highlighted on the first appearance in **bold type**.

Code is presented in fixed-width font.

New or changed code is normally presented in **bold fixed-width font**.

Pseudo-code and variable input are written in *italic fixed-width font*.

Menu commands are written in the form Menu ➤ Submenu ➤ Submenu.

Where we want to draw your attention to something, we've highlighted it like this:

> *Ahem, don't say we didn't warn you.*

Sometimes code won't fit on a single line in a book. Where this happens, we use an arrow like this: ➡.

```
This is a very, very long section of code that should be written all on ➡
the same line without a break.
```

Prerequisites

If you've ever used a web browser, you're well-enough equipped to read this book. This book provides a great introduction to standards-based development for a novice audience, as well as covers advanced topics for people who have previously worked with the Web.

Contacting the authors

- Jonathan Lane: You can reach Jonathan at jonathan.lane@gmail.com, http://www.flyingtroll.com/, and http://industryinteractive.net.

- Meitar Moscovitz: For professional queries, you can contact Meitar via any method listed on his professional home page at http://MeitarMoscovitz.com; otherwise, you can find Meitar all over the 'net, but you should probably start at his personal home page at http://maymay.net.

- Joseph R. Lewis: Joseph occasionally writes in his blog at http://www.sanbeiji.com/ and can be contacted via e-mail at joelewis@gmail.com.

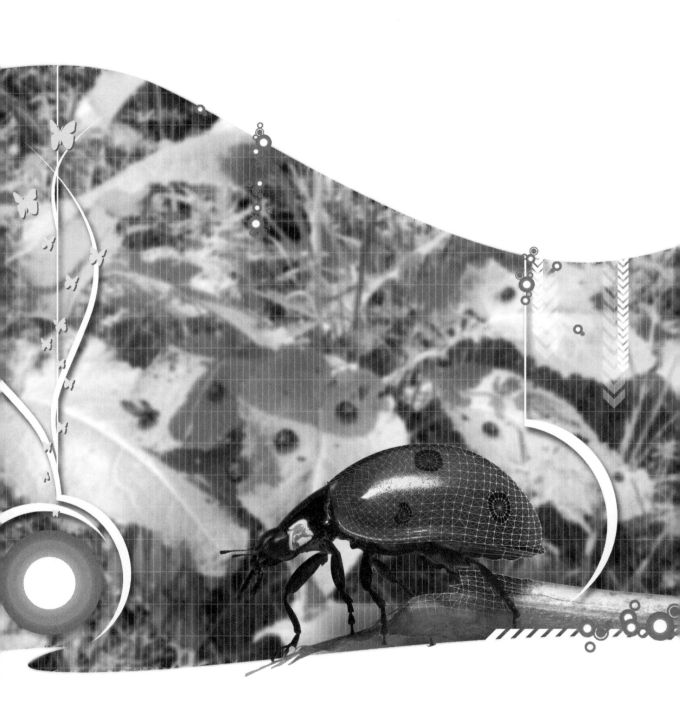

Chapter 1

INTRODUCING THE PAST, PRESENT, AND FUTURE OF THE WEB

Believe it or not, when we were kids, the standard way to send written text to some-one was by mail. Not e-mail, mind you, but the physical kind requiring a stamp on the envelope. Admittedly, this makes us feel incredibly old. Right up until middle school, we would submit handwritten assignments, just like everybody else in our classes. It was the standard.

The Internet is a reasonably new invention, and the World Wide Web is even newer. Yet both have had as profound an impact on civilization as the printing press, the steam engine, or the lightbulb. When we were growing up, we had an impossible time finding good video games for our PCs. Computers were all about business then. We could find six different word processors, but we couldn't find the latest release from Sierra Online (which is owned by Electronic Arts now). These days, if you are looking for a video game, where do you go? The average person will head over to Amazon and preorder their copy of the latest title for next-day shipping. E-commerce has become so ubiquitous that, for certain products, it is preferred over a trip to the local store.

The World Wide Web has made nearly everything near-instantly available to nearly everyone with an Internet connection. Even mega-stores, like Wal-Mart, cannot keep pace with the selection available to consumers online. It used to be incredibly hard to find niche products, such as curling stones, but these days, they're only a mouse click away (http://www.kaysofscotland.co.uk/). In remote communities where there is no Wal-Mart, the Internet has become an essential tool for 21st-century living.

The standard way of doing things

Because of its highly technical childhood, the World Wide Web has a lot of "hacker baggage." When we say that, we don't mean that it's a dangerous place where people roam the wires trying to steal your credit card information (although there is some of that too). We're using the term **hacker** in the classic sense of someone who likes technology and tries to find their own way of solving problems. The Web started off very much from a position of trying to solve a problem, in this case, distributing information. It evolved and gained features out of necessity—people needed to be able to add images and tables to their documents. In the early days of mainstream adoption, when businesses started to move online, there wasn't always a perfect way of doing things, so people came up with their own solutions.

A classic example of this is using a table on a web page to lay it out. At one point, we were guilty of this; but at that point we had no choice. Using a table was the only way you could get two columns of text to display on a page. Today, there are far better options, and that's what this book is about. Web standards have evolved; this isn't 1995 anymore.

Every journey starts with a single step: the Web past

It is hard to find a book about Hypertext Markup Language (HTML) and the Web these days without having it start off with a history section. We used to wonder why that was the case. To understand why the web standards approach to building websites is the best way to go, you have to know about the progression of the World Wide Web as it has evolved to become what it is today. The World Wide Web has very technical roots, and the trouble (or charm) with most techies is that they like to customize— change things until those things are perfect in their minds. They cannot follow what everyone else is doing; they need to add their own flavor to it.

The Web started its life as a research project at CERN (the European Organization for Nuclear Research) in Geneva, Switzerland. At the time, a researcher there by the name of Tim Berners-Lee was looking for a way to quickly and easily share research findings with his peers and organize information in such a way that it would be easy to archive and retrieve. Although the process was started in the early 1980s, it wasn't until 1990 that Berners-Lee produced the first web server and web browser (which was called WorldWideWeb, the origin of the name).

In 1992, the Web began to hit the mainstream when the National Center for Supercomputing Applications (NCSA) in the United States released Mosaic, which was capable of displaying text and graphics simultaneously. Mosaic gave nonscientists easy access over the Internet to documents created using HTML, what we now call **web pages**. Encouraged by this early success, one of Mosaic's creators, Marc Andreesen, left the NCSA and started Mosaic Communications Corporation. This later became Netscape Communications Corporation, creators of Netscape Navigator, which was the first commercial browser and the web standard-bearer through most of the 1990s.

A company called Spyglass licensed NCSA's source code and eventually released Spyglass Mosaic (though on a newly developed code base). This became the basis for Microsoft Internet Explorer and set the stage for the battle for browser supremacy between Netscape and Microsoft.

Just prior to the start of the "browser wars" of the 1990s, Berners-Lee recognized that without some sort of governance, the World Wide Web would experience great challenges as competing web browsers introduced new features. One of the ways to get someone to pick your product over your competition was to offer a bunch of really cool features that the other guy didn't offer. He foresaw compatibility problems emerging as competing companies introduced their own tags in order to add features to the World Wide Web. HTML was the glue binding the Web together, and some central body would need to oversee its evolution in order to maintain a high level of interoperability.

Microsoft gave away Internet Explorer as part of Microsoft Office, bundled it with Windows, and made it available as a free download for all its various operating systems, as well as for Macs. Microsoft was a late starter in the browser market, and by the time it entered the game in 1995, Netscape had an estimated 80 percent market share. The tides rapidly turned, however, and by the time Netscape was acquired by America Online in 1998, Microsoft had approximately half of the web browser market. By 2002, Internet Explorer reached its peak with an estimated 96 percent of web surfers using Internet Explorer. In fact, Microsoft so thoroughly thrashed Netscape in the browser wars that they ended up in a contracted lawsuit that eventually led to a finding of Microsoft's abuse of monopoly power in the marketplace. Figure 1-1 shows a timeline of major browser releases, starting in the early 1990s.

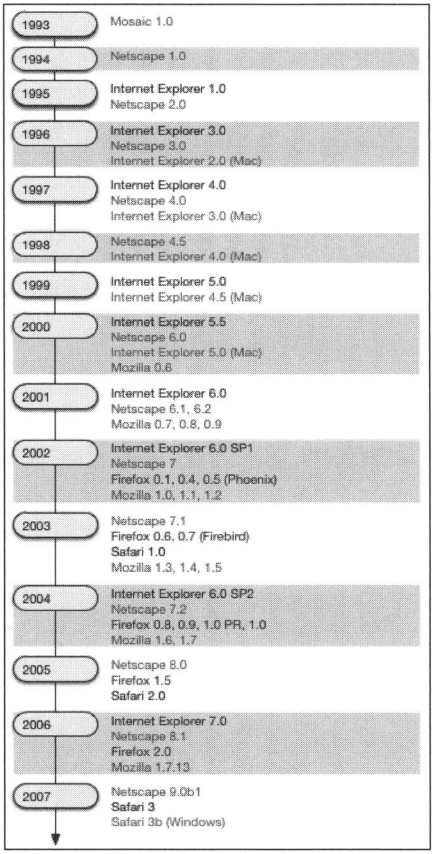

Figure 1-1. Timeline of major browser releases

The browser wars were an incredibly difficult time for web developers as manufacturers raced to do their own thing. Versions 3 and 4 of the major browsers often had developers coding two entirely separate versions of their websites in order to ensure compatibility with both Internet Explorer and

Netscape. Although web standards existed, most browsers only really supported the basics and relied on competing (and incompatible) technology to do anything advanced, which is what web developers wanted to do.

Netscape, although owned by a fairly major company, started to stagnate. Netscape open sourced its code base, and the Mozilla project was born. The Mozilla community took off with the code and started to really implement standards support in a new way through a complete rewrite of the rendering engine. Although Mozilla was, early on, based on Netscape Navigator, the tables rapidly turned, and subsequent releases of Netscape became based on Mozilla.

The Mozilla project has forked into a number of new browsers, most notably Firefox, which has sparked a new browser war with Microsoft. Yet this time, the battle has had a positive effect. Microsoft had all but stopped working on Internet Explorer once it released version 6. When Firefox hit the scene with near-perfect support for web standards, it became an immediate hit and gained a great deal of popularity with both the web cognoscenti and the general public. It seems as though Microsoft had no choice but to improve its web browser, and the result is Internet Explorer 7.

A number of other players emerged in the web browser marketplace, offering competition to the major players. Notably, Opera has always touted excellent support for web standards as one of its major selling features. It has caught on to some degree (2 percent as of January 2008) and is also focusing in a large part on mobile devices.

Safari by Apple Computer hit the scene in 2003 and quickly became one of the most popular choices for Mac users because it integrates well with the operating system and is generally faster than competing browsers on the Mac. Apple introduced a Windows version in 2007, but that product has yet to leave beta. One of the most unique qualities of Safari is that even with its minor updates (so-called point releases), Safari has improved its support of web standards, something that is often relegated to major releases among other browser manufacturers.

Then there were standards: the Web now

Could you imagine if each TV channel was broadcast in either PAL or NTSC in each country, requiring viewers to use a different TV set depending on what they wanted to watch? Similarly, imagine writing a research paper, running a search on Google, and then having to open each of the results returned in a different web browser. The first link is Internet Explorer, the second and third are Netscape . . . OK, now back to Internet Explorer . . . Yet, this is pretty much how things worked in the late 1990s. One of the most common sights on the Web were these wonderful (heavy sarcasm here) graphic badges telling visitors that this website is "Optimized for Internet Explorer" or "Best Viewed with Netscape Navigator" (see Figure 1-2).

Figure 1-2. Internet Explorer and Netscape
Navigation "get it now" buttons

When we talk about web standards, we're generally referring to the big three players on the Web: HTML (or XHTML), Cascading Style Sheets (CSS), and JavaScript. The World Wide Web Consortium (W3C) maintains many other standards, such as Scalable Vector Graphics (SVG) for vector graphic display, Portable Network Graphics (PNG) as a way to compress bitmap graphics, and Extensible Markup Language (XML), which is another markup language, similar in a lot of ways to HTML.

While HTML/XHTML is all about structuring your document, CSS handles formatting and displaying your various page elements. Because they're two separate pieces of technology, you can separate them (by separating content from display). The early versions of HTML (prior to the release of CSS) were intended to be everything to everyone. The ability to specify colors and fonts was built right in by specifying the attributes of various tags. As sites began to grow in size, however, the limitations of going this route quickly became apparent.

Imagine that you have put together a website to promote this book. Throughout the site, which covers all the chapters in detail, there are quotes from the book. To really make these quotes jump off the screen, you are going to put them in red and make them a size bigger. In the good old days, your code would look something like this:

```
<font size="+1" color="red">In the good old days, ➡
your code would look something like this:</font>
```

With a little XHTML and CSS, the code could look like this (note we said "could" because there are multiple ways of doing things—this is a good, structurally relevant example):

```
<blockquote>In the good old days, ➡
your code would look something like this:</blockquote>
```

And then in a separate CSS file (or at the top of your HTML document—but again, that's just another option) that you would import/link to on pages of your website, there would be something like this:

```
blockquote { font-size: 1.5em; color: red; }
```

So what? They both do the same thing. Web browsers will display the quotes in red and make them nice and big. One of the immediate advantages, however, is in making updates. As we mentioned previously, you are liberally quoting the book throughout the entire website, chapter by chapter. By the end of the project, you discover that you have used more than 300 quotes! The only problem is that we, as the authors (and your client), absolutely hate red text. It makes us so angry. So, we're going to ask you to change it everywhere.

What would you rather do: update one line in the CSS file or open every page on the site and change the color attribute to blue? (Blue is much more calming.) Three hundred quotes—you're billing by the hour—so that's not so bad. It's maybe an extra half day of work. Now extrapolate this example to something like the *New York Times* where there are quite likely millions of quotes throughout the entire website. Are you still keen to go change every font tag?

You're thinking to yourself, "My software can do search and replace." This is true. We were once asked to update a department website at an organization where we worked. The website had about 16,000 pages, and by the end of a week, our search and replace still hadn't finished. We're not that patient. Are you?

Additionally, CSS has evolved and is still evolving, allowing designers and developers to do more and more in terms of the layout and appearance of their pages. Using CSS you can position any element anywhere you like on a page. Although you could probably accomplish the same thing with a table-based layout, it would probably take you a considerable chunk of code including setting absolute heights and widths of table cells. One thing you can't do, however, is overlap a pair of table cells, which is something that's extremely easy to do using CSS.

The upcoming release of CSS (version 3) has even more formatting options baked in. You will be able to specify multiple background images for an element, set the transparency of colors, allow certain elements to be resized on the fly, and add drop shadows to text and other elements on the fly. Check out the W3C website or, for a slightly more human-readable form, http://www.css3.info for more information.

The provided example is a pretty simple representation of what you can do using XHTML and CSS. If you head over to the CSS Zen Garden (http://csszengarden.com/) and click through some of the examples there, you can gain an appreciation for the level of control you can have by tweaking the CSS for a website. CSS Zen Garden uses the same markup for every example (the XHTML part stays the same on every page). The only thing that is different on each page is the CSS file that is included, as well as any supporting graphics (see Figure 1-3, Figure 1-4, and Figure 1-5).

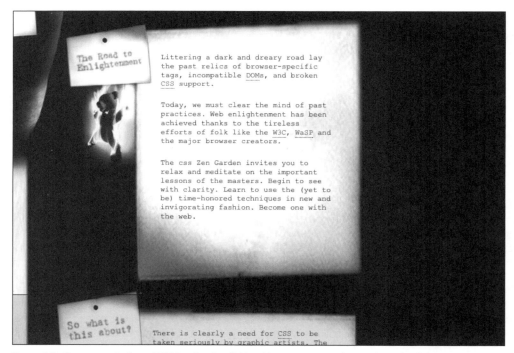

Figure 1-3. One example from CSS Zen Garden (http://www.csszengarden.com). Each of these pages uses the same XHTML markup; each page is just styled differently using CSS and images.

Figure 1-4. This is the same page as shown in Figure 1-3 but styled using an alternate style sheet at the CSS Zen Garden.

Figure 1-5. A final example showing just how powerful CSS can be at changing the look of a page

Imagine not having to touch a single page of markup when redesigning a website and still getting a completely different end result. Properly structured, standards-based pages will let you do it. This could be a major advantage for companies building large-scale content management systems: simply change the style sheet, and the CMS has been tailored to a new customer. Some companies are doing this, but others haven't caught on yet.

A crystal ball: the Web future

The Web is a cool place in many ways, not least because you don't need to be a fortune-teller to see into the future. Because standards take time to develop, we already have an idea of what the future holds. For example, HTML is being reviewed right now (the current W3C Recommendation is for HTML 4.01, which was released in December 1999). A working group has been formed to look at developing an HTML 5 Recommendation in order to clean up some of the loose ends from HTML 4. The group started in 2006 and is aiming to have the Recommendation ready by the end of December 2010 (as you can see, it's a rigorous process that does take some time).

The W3C process for standards approval goes through numerous steps and can easily span several years. The final product of this process is a W3C **Recommendation**. Because the W3C isn't a governing body, all it can do is make a recommendation that software companies can then choose to follow. There are no "laws" of the Web, so if Apple decided to drop HTML support in Safari in favor of its own markup language, Apple could. As you can see from our previous history lesson, this wouldn't have been completely out of the question in the 1990s, but today, it would probably be very self-defeating. The culture of the Web is all about interoperability, and when companies attempt to limit interoperability to gain some sort of competitive advantage, we all lose.

This has led to somewhat mixed results. On one hand, you can go to almost any website and have it work in almost any web browser. There are still some companies that are pulling the old "Please download Internet Explorer" trick, but those companies are few and far between. The fact of the matter is that interoperability, for businesses, means a larger potential customer base. For most Mac users, if they visit a website that is "Internet Explorer–only," they're dead in the water. They could purchase a Windows machine or run some virtualization software in order to run Windows on their Mac, but chances are, if they have the choice (and the Web is all about choices), they just won't bother. They'll go find a competitor that supports Safari or, at the very least, Firefox.

The consultation process for developing new standards and revising old ones is very thorough, and it involves a lot of consultation with the community. Several drafts are developed, a great deal of feedback is collected, and eventually a Recommendation is put forth. We've presented HTML and XHTML almost interchangeably in this first chapter. Although both HTML and XHTML are valid web standards, in this book we'll focus on XHTML, which advances the Web by enforcing that pages be well formed and that pages are marked up in such a way that information about their structure is important.

XHTML is a bit of a hybrid between HTML and XML, which is widely used for data storage. The current version of XHTML in use on the Web today is XHTML 1.01, which is a bit of a stepping-stone in the movement toward complete use of XML in page markup. The reason we say that is because although pages are written in XHTML, they are often still displayed by browsers in a way similar to HTML.

Building on standards for the modern Web

We as people have been building physical spaces for thousands of years. There are a whole host of professions involved in constructing a building: architects, engineers, contractors, plumbers, electricians, carpenters, and so on. Likewise, with the Web, numerous specialists contribute to building a great online space (see Table 1-1). You can build the most beautiful museum in the world, but if the client is asking for a factory, you have not done your job.

Table 1-1. A Comparison Between Traditional Construction Jobs and "Digital Construction" Jobs

Bricks (Buildings)	Bits (World Wide Web)
Architect: Draws up the blueprints; makes sure the only bathroom isn't off the garage.	**Information architect**: Draws up the site map; makes sure site search isn't available only from the "Contact Us" page.
Engineer: Ensures that the building is sound, that the proper materials are being used, and that the wind won't blow it over.	**Technical lead**: Ensures that the systems in place will handle the traffic and that the technology decisions are sound.
General contractor/foreman: Makes sure that everyone shows up to work, that the plans are followed, and that the building gets built.	**Project manager**: Makes sure that the programmers don't spend all their time playing video games and that the project gets done on time.
Interior/exterior designer: Selects the paint colors; what art to hang on the walls; and whether to use carpet, tile, or hardwood. Basically, this person makes sure that things look nice.	**Designer**: Selects the color palette and fonts; develops the graphics. In other words, the designer makes sure that things look nice.
Basement/foundation builders: Pours the concrete for the foundation of the structure.	**System administrators/database administrators**: Creates the infrastructure that supports the website.
Framer/carpenter/drywaller/painter: Builds the structure; turns the architect's vision into reality.	**HTML/CSS developer**: Structures pages properly; puts the designer's vision into practice.
Plumber/electrician: Puts in the pipes and wires to make the house come alive. You can live in a house without plumbing and electricity, but it isn't much fun.	**Programmer/developer**: Adds interactivity to pages through client-side and server-side scripting.

That said, a single person or a small group of people frequently fills a number of these positions. In this industry, being a generalist is a common way to go. As you will learn later in this book, using web standards can give you a leg up in this area by providing you with a foundation of best industry practices. Architects follow the local building code to make sure their projects are safe and constructed in a consistent way. People building for the Web should do the same to ensure their sites are accessible, search engine–friendly, and consistent in modern browsers.

What's inside this book?

Our goal is to take this book beyond web standards to cover the entire process of developing a website based on standards. Believe it or not, there is more to putting together a great website than just knowing a little HTML (or XHTML, as the case may be). This introduction will expose you to different techniques and technologies, and we hope it will encourage you to pursue those areas you find most compelling.

The other day we received a copy of a magazine that has been in print for 29 years. This issue announced that it would no longer be printed and would henceforth be available only online. Increasingly, companies are moving their advertising efforts online, and more and more industries, especially those that target younger markets, are concentrating on communicating with their potential markets through websites and online communities.

Technologies come and go or, as in the case of HTML, evolve. Two years from now, we may have to completely rewrite sections of this book. We will certainly need to add to the history section as new browsers and technologies are introduced into the market and as new trends emerge (during the writing, Safari for Windows was released, and Firefox 3 will likely be released before this book makes it to bookstores). It's exciting to be working with ever-changing Internet and web technologies. We could even be witnessing the beginnings of a great web transformation with the advent of mobile computing. There's no telling what we'll find around the next corner.

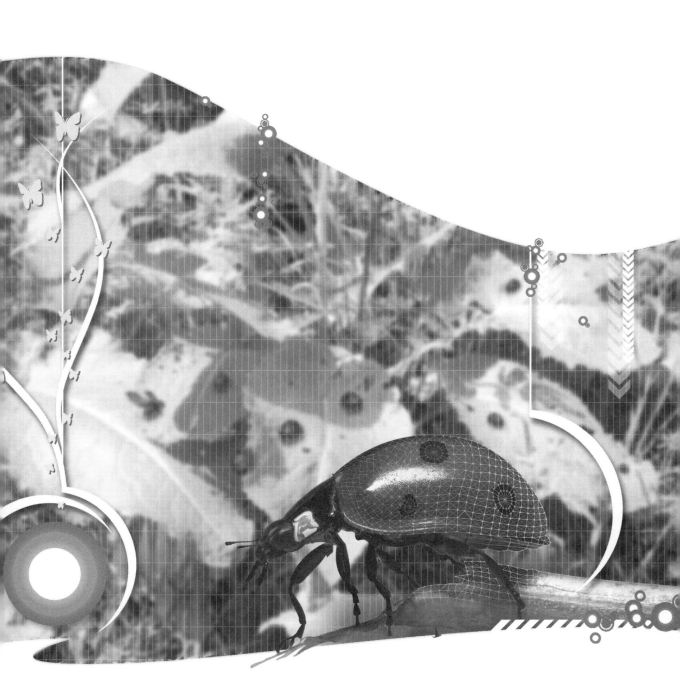

Chapter 2

KEEPING A PROJECT ON TRACK

The topic of project management is often a contentious one (what a weird thing to fight about!). There's usually little disagreement that projects need to be managed—a deadline and a budget have to be set, and something called **scope** needs to be addressed (scope is what you're going to do in a project, like "redesign website X"). Beyond this, there is a great deal of back and forth about how things should proceed. The old-school (and some would say proven) method of project management relies on planning everything in advance and assigning dates (milestones) and people (resources) to each task. Everything is planned and documented in advance, stakeholder sign-off is obtained on the documentation, and then the project proceeds. At that point, a project manager makes sure everything stays on track. They move or add resources to the various tasks identified in order to make sure they stay on time.

The process of web design and development is a unique one, however. The old-school method isn't necessarily the best approach in an industry where new competitors and technologies can emerge during the course of a three-month project. It's reasonably cheap and easy to make changes at any stage of a project. Even though we made the direct comparison of construction work to web work in Chapter 1, we framed it like that in order to give you an idea of what the various roles are on a web project. In reality, building a website isn't like building a house at all; you're not tied to the dimensions after pouring the foundation. The materials used are all digital and for that reason are easy to work with. Deleting something doesn't involve a wrecking ball, and adding something new doesn't require materials to be purchased and brought in from off-site. If you're five days into the project and your client suddenly decides that they would, in fact, like to accept orders online instead of only telephone orders, all you have to do is hand them a revised cost estimate and timeline, if even this. After a website has launched, if you start hearing from visitors that they need to be able to import data in a certain format, you can develop and push that out instantly to your end users by publishing it to the server. No jackhammers . . . no need to make 3 million duplicates. So, why should you set everything in stone on day one?

The project manager doesn't have to be fluent in all development languages, database systems, and server setups (it doesn't hurt to know a little about each, though, just so you can tell whether someone is pulling your leg). The project manager has to know how to deal with people, keep everyone happy (or at least productive), and assure that the project is moving forward. The main goals are to remove any roadblocks to project completion. If your developers' office is under renovation and they can't get any code written because someone is always hammering, then find somewhere quieter for them to work. If your designers' computers are constantly crashing, causing them to have to revisit the same work over and over again, get them new machines.

Stay away from waterfalls: the traditional approach

Project management, in the traditional sense, is often very complex. This single chapter definitely couldn't cover all aspects of it, but we are hoping to share with you some tips and things to look out for along the way. We're strong believers in developing project management skills. And since everyone has their own way of dealing with things and no two projects are the same, we can't give you the perfect road map for getting from x to y to z in every case. The best advice is to go with your experience, and if you really don't know the answer, admit it and then find the answer. Although it's possible that you may be the only person working on any given project, more often than not you will be part of a team. There will always be someone to turn to for advice (or at least their opinion) if you get stuck. If worst comes to worst, there's always the Internet (we hear you can always find someone willing to give you their opinion there).

This traditional approach has its roots in the construction industry. In fact, the U.S. Navy first conceived of it in order to get better control over the process of building ships. When materials need to be ordered, parts manufactured off-site, and specialized labor brought in, there is a big advantage in trying to plan things in advance. Having software specialists sitting around before the computers used for targeting enemies have been installed is a huge waste of time and money. Having a master plan that lets you see, in advance, whether things are ahead of or behind schedule gives you that ability to contact subcontractors in advance and either delay or move up their participation in a project.

When we mention the traditional approach to project management, we're referring to the formal process taught by the Project Management Institute (http://www.pmi.org/). This process is sometimes referred to as the **Waterfall model**; with this method, a project is planned as much as possible up front. Planning continues until a consensus on "perfection" is reached, and then work commences. There is a lot of criticism of this way of doing things, particularly in software and web development projects, because there is no feedback and evaluation built in until the end of the project. We hope we've made the argument that this method does have its place in certain industries, however. For example, in large-scale construction projects, you need to have a plan in place before you start. It would be foolish to start building a high-rise floor by floor, not knowing how many stories it will have until you're done. You can't just leave some "feature" of the building (such as electricity) until the last minute. You can do precisely that in web development projects, however. The rigidity and linear nature of the Waterfall model just doesn't suit web development. The upfront costs in both time and money associated with this type of planning are out of scale with most web work.

Another consideration is that with the pace at which various technologies progress, taking three months to plan a project up front may, in fact, put you three months "behind the curve" in terms of the technology available. A different way to think about this is the following: say you're spending a week at the beginning of the planning stage of your project in order to do an analysis of the various database systems available in order to determine which one is fastest for implementing a new short text-messaging application. You look at three different products and decide on Product A because it's definitely the fastest in database inserts (adding records) and selects (querying data out of the database). You finish planning and begin development. After one week developing your application, Product B releases a new version that is 100 times faster at doing selects (which makes it about 20 times faster than Product A that you're currently using). Do you switch? Well, you're already falling down the waterfall; there's no turning back now. Your entire timeline will fall apart, and things will need to be replanned if you switch at this stage.

The nine knowledge areas

Nine knowledge areas are covered in the Project Management Body of Knowledge (PMBOK), published by the Project Management Institute (see Figure 2-1). These nine areas cover every possible aspect of project planning and management. We have space in this book only for a quick overview of each, but if you want to learn more, we encourage you to take a look at some of the publications put out by the Project Management Institute.

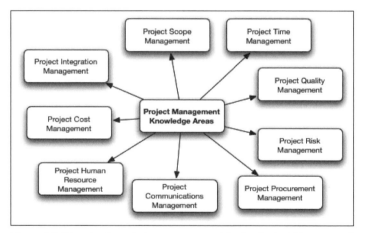

Figure 2-1. The nine knowledge areas covered by the Project Management Institute

Here is a brief description of each of the areas:

- *Project Integration Management*: This area looks at planning and integrating all the various parts of the project. It talks about developing a project charter (a document that summarizes what the project will accomplish and why it's needed), developing a plan for the project (how you're going to do what you've outlined in the charter), and how everything is going to be communicated between the team and the client or stakeholder(s).

- *Project Scope Management*: This area outlines, specifically, what work has to be done to complete the project and how that work is going to be broken down between the various "resources." It also identifies how any changes will be handled during the project.

- *Project Time Management*: This area defines how long a project is going to take and identifies how many people, including the specific skills and at what times, will be needed in order to complete the defined project.

- *Project Cost Management*: Money is another important factor. This area defines the budget for the project and how things will be controlled to stay within that budget.

- *Project Quality Management*: How will you make sure that what you produce works and does what it's supposed to do? What kind of testing will be done, and what test results are acceptable?

- *Project Human Resource Management*: Where are you going to get your team members? What skills do they need? Do you need to train anyone? How will the team be managed?

- *Project Communications Management*: This area covers how things will be shared amongst the project team and the stakeholder(s), how progress will be communicated and tracked, and how things will be documented.

- *Project Risk Management*: This area looks mostly at the risks involved if the project fails (or succeeds; there may be risks either way). It attempts to anticipate any problems that may emerge at various points in the project and plan ways to minimize or eliminate those risks.

- *Project Procurement Management*: How/where will products or services be acquired when needed, and how will subcontractors be managed (if applicable)?

Although we don't advocate going the PMI route on web development projects, your client/employer may have different ideas (and hey, it's their money). If you're required to go this route, do yourself a favor and find somebody with the project management professional (PMP) designation to bring on board. It's a fairly expensive process, in both time and money, to obtain this designation, but if your client is a stickler for the Waterfall method, having a PMI-accredited project manager on board will save you hours of time. Be aware, however, that these individuals don't come cheap. You will want to contact them at the very start of a project before the budget is set so that they can get involved immediately.

Web project management: the power of iteration

As we mentioned previously, the Web is an inexpensive medium. Making mistakes during development is OK, and they are usually easy to fix. Because of this, web project management can be more relaxed, allowing for feedback and change at any stage. The heavy-handed "scope management" system imposed in the traditional method of project management can be relaxed, and a more collaborative development process can be pursued. The gist of this is "Let's just start building this thing; we can make changes as we discover the need for changes." The reason this is the opposite of traditional project management is that the traditional approach aims to control change very tightly (some might say discourage change, but that's not necessarily true). This approach encourages it (within the limits of time and budget) so that everyone is happy with the end product because they've all been deeply involved in shaping it from the beginning.

When it comes to developing web projects, you'll hear a lot of different terms thrown around. **Agile development** is commonly used, and it describes a number of development processes that involve multiple iterations and working closely with stakeholders until everybody agrees that an end result has been reached. If you were working for a client, you would build something and show it to them at a very early stage. The client could try it, react to it, and tell you that changes need to be made or that something is missing; then you could make those changes right away. Working this way, you would step, piece by piece, through a project adding all of the functionality that is necessary.

An agile example of planning

Agile project management is better illustrated through example. Say you're building a news website for a client, a television network launching an on-air news program incorporating citizen journalism. They tell you they need a site that will allow their viewers to submit news stories and categorize them. Everyone should then be able to vote on which stories they like the best, and those will be the ones that make it on air. They want the entire program to be about news as it happens from the perspective of those who are "at ground zero." You chat a bit with the client, and you both throw together a one-page document that outlines the general idea of what you're going to try to accomplish. You work through a schedule and a budget for the project, and then you get started on building a submission page.

The news website absolutely cannot exist without a place for viewers to submit stories and a place for those stories to be displayed. It's always a good idea to identify the core of a website (or most "inner" page of a website) and start there, because the only thing limiting your work is time and money. Think about it: if your time runs out and you've spent all of it developing a viewer-to-viewer messaging system, the website doesn't accomplish what it needs to be able to do.

The submission page asks the visitor to enter their e-mail address, enter a link to the story, select which categories it belongs to, and enter a brief synopsis. You then build a news display page that groups everything by category (picture something similar to Digg.com or Slashdot.org). Your designer puts together a mock-up, and you paste in the graphics and CSS so that your client can get an idea of what the end product will look like.

Your client takes a look at what you've done so far, and they comment that they can't have people submitting news stories with only an e-mail address. The station needs to know more. OK, so we'll need to flush this part out into a user management piece with usernames and passwords (who wants to reenter all their contact information every time they submit a story?). You throw together a few more pages exhibiting this functionality and again have your client take a look.

At this point, the client remarks that the news network has finished developing the "look" of the show: the set design is complete, and the show's introduction is done. Understandably, they want the website to have a similar aesthetic. You get your designer in contact with the network's in-house marketing and design staff, they begin working through the visual details of the website, and you continue with development.

The client thinks it looks great and functions really well. The network's sales staff has decided that the website is going to make money and support itself by selling advertising targeted toward each of the different categories of news. So if there's a food category, maybe restaurants or specialty food shops will be approached to advertise, for example. You start building a component that displays ads based on the category, as well as some reporting on how many times those ads are being clicked and viewed so the advertisers can be billed fairly. You think it would be pretty neat to build a "this section sponsored by" function so that each category can have a major advertiser. You throw together a quick mock-up of how this would look and again have your client visit. They are completely thrilled with the idea.

Development continues back and forth like this until something is produced that's good enough to make public. At that point, it may be released with the word *beta* attached to it, and news junkies (aka early adopters) are invited to come participate. Changes continue to be made (RSS feeds are added a day after the site goes live, user comments two weeks later, and so on) until the client calls it quits and declares the project complete. The on-air show premieres a month later and is a huge success.

Taking the agile approach here allowed the requirements of the project to be discovered based on the best and most up-to-date information. If you had taken the traditional approach, you may have missed certain pieces of functionality that became apparent while you were using and interacting with early versions of your news website. You may have missed the user management part altogether and then, once you launched, had your users complaining that you're completely out of touch with their needs. You might have missed the opportunity for the additional revenue stream from on-site advertising or missed the user comments section, which is something that has contributed greatly to the website's success.

Achieving the goal: identifying doneness

If there's a single practical bone in your body, you're probably thinking to yourself, "Boy, that sounds great, but how do you really know when it's done and when to call it quits?" As we hinted at it in the previous example, you can keep an eye on three elements to determine when a project is done and when it's time to stop working. Usually it's a combination of all three; however, occasionally one factor will override the others.

These three things relate to the traditional approach to project management. The success of all projects boils down to time, budget, and scope, and a project manager's job is to balance these three qualities in order to produce a high-quality product within the time and budget allotted. These three factors are often represented as the points of a triangle, and your goal is to try to get each of the sides to be the same length (to achieve balance). More often than not, if you're doing client work, the client will have a deadline for when they want to (or have to) launch their website. Most clients will have a budget, which is some amount of money that they've allocated to complete the project. And usually there will be some definition of what is needed functionally (they need a website to show off their new line of hair products).

Focus on time

Working with your client, you should decide on a realistic timeline for completion. Clients will often have some sort of date in their mind that corresponds to some event, such as the end of a financial quarter, a particular board meeting, or the launch of a new product. When the client says, "We need that news website online in time for the premiere of our new citizen-journalist TV program," then you know you have a drop-dead date. Time is frequently one of those things that is fixed; you can't ask the company to reschedule a board meeting or ask people to put off launching that new product because the website won't be done in time. The trick is keeping a handle on the work that needs to be done so that it can be done before that defined date.

Once you identify this fixed point in time, you just work backward. A good word to learn now, one that makes every project manager happy, is the word **contingency**. Contingency is your secret reserve of time and/or money that you can use at your discretion to keep everyone happy. In the case of time, building some padding into your estimate is a good way to assure some breathing room. If your lead developer gets the flu and doesn't show up for three days, you can't ask your client to delay the launch by three days. Don't go overboard, but do build in a little slack time, especially if you're working on multiple projects at the same time or if you're freelancing. Besides, because you're following an agile approach, you don't know exactly what the end product will look like, so it's impossible for you to dictate exactly how long it will take to develop. Identifying the drop-dead date, as well as a soft-launch date (a date slightly in advance of the drop-dead date where all new development will stop and your team will focus on testing and making sure everything is ready for launch) may be the best you can do.

The traditional approach requires a project plan at the outset, where you identify a number of milestones in advance (like "Visual Design complete"). You can see how this would be impossible on a project where the design will evolve throughout the entire project life span. Figure 2-2 compares the traditional and agile approaches.

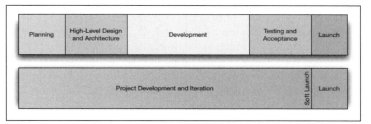

Figure 2-2. Comparing traditional time management to agile time management. The traditional approach divides a project into phases; the agile approach does not limit activities to any one period of time.

Focus on budget

Another great way to keep a project on track and to determine when it's complete is the project budget. You're not likely to find a client with an unlimited budget (and if you do, make sure you keep them close to your heart, because you and Scarlet O'Hara will never go hungry again!). With this in mind, the economics of a project can be kept really simple. As a freelancer, you are normally asked to bid on a project. This is a funny little guessing game that you play with your client where you try to come up with a number that will allow you to make money on the project and allow you not go over the number that they have in mind. Developing a budget is one of the most important areas for you to work collaboratively with a client.

Despite this long-established practice of just taking a shot in the dark, we have had far more success with asking clients up front if they have a budget in mind. If they do (and they're willing to tell you), sit down with them and reciprocate their willingness to share information. If your client tells you that they have $5,000 to spend on a project, tell them that you charge $100 per hour (insert your own numbers here). Based on those numbers, you can spend 50 hours working on their project. By this point, you've heard what they have in mind, and you can tell them up front either that their project is completely realistic and you would be happy to take care of it for them or that perhaps they should consider scaling back their idea somewhat. If you can't reach an agreement on either budget or what they want done, then you need to decide whether you're going to walk away or take a pay cut. Bear in mind that if you plan on subcontracting some of the work out, you have to know in advance what those individuals charge and whether they would be willing to work for any less.

You may think that this number of hours (50) would dictate the project timeline; that's not necessarily true. Let's pretend you're going to be working solo on this project. You could be done with the project in a week and a half working full-time, or you could be done in six and a half weeks, working one day per week on it. This factor may also have an effect on whether you're willing to take a bit of a pay cut (work a few extra hours).

If you find that it's really hard to keep your hourly wage at a level you're comfortable with, try working with your client on the timeline. Are there ways you can save time on a project so that your part is finished faster? Can someone within your client's organization take on some of the workload (writing/editing some of the page content, for example)? Can you compress the entire project by getting the client to commit to calling it finished (within reason) in one month? If you think about it, $5,000 for a single month of work isn't bad.

This may sound like a harsh way of putting it, but it's really the truth. If you consider that you value your services at $20 per hour and a client has a $200 budget (it's a really small project), they get 10 hours of your time. If you give them 20 hours, you've just devalued yourself to $10 per hour (and so on). We're not saying that you should never do this, but be sure you're in control of it. Maybe you're working for a nonprofit organization, so you give that client a break—that's fine. That Fortune 500 client can afford to pay your rate, though. It doesn't need charity. This is precisely the reason why the "shot-in-the-dark" quoting system is so flawed. It removes all of your flexibility and usually ends up with the client bearing the brunt of it as you try to build in padding.

When you use an agile approach, make sure your client understands the mathematics of the situation. Let them know that they have X hours, and they are free to ask you to use them in any way they see fit. If they want to build in a search engine that will take 100 hours, that's fine, but that's 100 hours you can't spend on anything else. It's really easy to think big at the outset of a project when none of the hours has been eaten up and none of the budget has been used. So, your best bet at this point is to identify the single most important thing and to do that first. What would a news website be without a news page? What's a search engine without a database to search? How good is a financial management application without the ability to track expenses? Everything else is peripheral to the project and can be added if time permits.

Finally, there is the debate over hourly and fixed-price quotes. Most clients want you to commit to doing some piece of work for some set cost. They're trying to minimize their exposure on a project and prevent it from going over budget. Most freelancers aren't completely comfortable with that approach because they know that changes can happen throughout a project, and committing to a fixed price limits what they can and can't do. They'll either push for hourly billing or give a fixed-price quote with a lot of contingency built-in.

It's pretty easy to see that this situation puts you at odds with your client right out of the gates. It seems like you're fighting a struggle to make money vs. their attempts to save money. Again, why not try to work with your client and tell them that you're billing them for the time you put in? You think that what they have budgeted is realistic, and you won't leave them high and dry (that's why you always start with the core of the project), but if they start to ask for bells and whistles at the end of the project when time is running out, they're going to have to come up with additional funds.

That might be a little vague, so suggest to your client that you'll give them weekly updates on time and money and that when there's only 10 hours left in the budget (adjust accordingly based on length/complexity), you'll have a quick conversation on wrapping things up.

Focus on scope

And that leads us into our final factor, scope. In casual conversation, you'll frequently hear the term **scope creep** thrown around when people are discussing project management. Scope creep is a dirty term in traditional project management; it means that the "perfect" project plan conceived at the outset is out of control and that the expectations are changing (another good reason not to plan everything up front).

Now, we'll make the argument that scope creep is, in fact, the single greatest thing that can happen on a web project (within reason). As long as you have the time and the budget for it, you want change. You want your client to tell you that Screen A looks horrible and the average user would never be able to figure it out. Why do you want this? The answer is easy: if your client is telling you, then the eventual end user of your website is not. This means you're producing a better, more intuitive product. That's a good thing!

On the other hand, scope has a funny way of creeping out in a different direction, like your client coming back to you midway through the project and telling you about how they were at this great website the other day that let people chat with each other in real time and share photos and that third parties could develop little applications that would plug in to the website and do different things. "Can we make our news site work like that?" they ask.

There is a bit of an assumption being made here that between you and your client you can come up with what's best for the end user. Make sure you're never just accepting things because your client asks for it—it has to make sense. If there's ever conflict, go to a neutral third party (ask an end user). This can be a formal process involving in-depth user testing and focus groups, or it can be as simple as asking your brother or sister (assuming one of them is the target audience of the website). You can do this at any stage of a project life cycle, whenever you're not sure what the answer is (or just want to make sure you're heading in the right direction). If you're considering adding a new feature to an existing website but you're just not sure if it's the right idea, ask your current users (run a short survey).

Let's hope that at this point in your project, you're comfortable speaking frankly with your client. Chances are, they've been involved in the project from day one and have bought in to what the vision is. Sure, what they're describing sounds great, but it's not what you're working toward. Websites don't need to remain static once they've launched (in fact, it's better if they don't!), and you would be pleased to work with them to develop these features for their "version 2." If, however, your client has decided that this website just won't be as good without all this other stuff, feel free to take an hour, sit down, and work the numbers with them. Tell them that you need to finish the project core first, and then you'll be happy to move on to some of these other features. Live chat? That sounds great! It will take 150 hours and will push the launch back two weeks. The idea of third-party apps? That's a great idea too: 300 hours on your end and probably a couple of months. Don't overinflate these numbers—just be honest and ask them whether they're willing to increase their budget and push back their launch date. Pragmatism is important when it comes to project management.

One of our favorite quotes, one that tends to surface at times like this, comes from a company based in Chicago called 37signals. They say that it's always better to build half a product than a half-assed product. What they mean is that it's better to build something that's really simple that doesn't have a ton of features, when the features that it does have are really well implemented. Spend a little extra time on your forms to figure out whether what you're asking makes sense. Take the extra time to implement Ajax where it makes sense. Your customers will thank you for it, and it's less likely that you'll hear, "Gee, this news site is really informative and well built. Too bad I can't use it because it doesn't have live, real-time chat." On the other hand, if you rush through building things, you're likely to hear about how ugly, how complicated, or how many errors people are getting.

"But the PMI covers nine areas; you've talked about only three!"

Hey, we warned you that the PMI approach to project management is more complex than what's necessary in your average web project. That said, there are a few more lessons to extract from the traditional approach to project management.

Communication is paramount

Clients love to see progress. If you could e-mail them every day showing them some really cool new piece of functionality or some neat new design element, you would probably have the happiest client in the world. The flip side is true too: if you've run into some major roadblock, it's better to get it out in the open early and explain what you're going to do to handle it.

The agile approach is very powerful, if everyone is along for the ride. One of the reasons the traditional approach is still hanging in there is that a whole pile of documentation is created at the outset and then handed to the client to sign off on. The client feels good about things because they know what the plan is and can see how it's going to go off without a hitch (and then reality sets in). Taking the agile approach, you have to be diligent about talking with your client, forwarding changes to them, and actively seeking their feedback. With the agile approach, you can't just accept a project, walk away for two weeks, and come back saying "Here you go!" It's a very interactive process.

Chances are, you'll never hear a single complaint if you're overcommunicating with your client, within reason. (Remember, they have a job to do too!) From our experience, however, the single greatest factor leading to a project's failure is a breakdown in communication. If one party stops talking to the other, you have a serious problem that needs to be resolved immediately.

An excellent strategy is that as soon as you can, give your client access to your development (staging) server where they can see the project progressing and start working with it immediately. Set some sort of informal policy in place about how they are looking at a work in progress and how things may break for a short period of time as things change. Send them messages periodically highlighting various features and areas that you want them to play with in depth. Encourage them to send you their impressions and any bugs they might find.

Quality and testing

As we touched on earlier, your goal on any project should be to build as high a quality product as possible. If you have the option of adding just one more feature or spending the time getting the existing features working perfectly, do the latter. It's pretty hard to launch a product and have absolutely no problems with it, whether they're technical, functional, or even a pesky cross-browser bug or two. Try to allocate at least 10 percent of the time you spend on a project to testing it and using it yourself. Encourage as many other people on your team to do the same. Different people look at problems in unique ways; although you may have absolutely no trouble filling in that news submission form in the previous example, a different visitor may look at it and freeze because they don't have a URL to submit with the news story. Maybe it's something they saw on TV or read in a magazine. What then?

The issue of quality also brings up another concern: who will be responsible for maintaining the website once it's launched? If a bug is discovered, do you and your team fix it, or does your client have someone in-house? How will that cost be handled?

Procurement and contracting

A lot of projects will require you to seek external service providers. Chances are you aren't a project manager, designer, developer, database administrator, information architect, and systems administrator all rolled into one. Unless your client plans to host on their own servers or already has a host in place, it may fall to you to at least find secure hosting for your project.

Although outsourcing parts of the project can be a life-saver, you need to keep a few things in mind: First, be sure to know how much it's going to cost you up front. If you don't know how much that hotshot designer is going to run and you quote some hourly amount to your client, you might find yourself working quite a few hours for free. Second, make sure you know the quality of their work and you're comfortable handing control of a certain part over to them. If there is some highly technical aspect to your project that falls outside your skill set, it's OK to admit it and find someone who can do it. Heavy preference here should be on someone you've worked with before or someone you know by reputation.

The next thing to consider is that a subcontractor is just that. They work for you, not for your client. You don't need to worry about whether you let them communicate with your client (in fact, I'd encourage that they do), but you do have to establish that any major changes to the scope of the work they're going to do has to run through you. Also, you're on the hook to pay them. They aren't your partner; they're more like your employee. If your client fails to pay you, you're still on the hook to pay your subcontractors.

Last, but certainly not least, you're on the hook for the quality of their work/service. One of the most common requests during new site development is for you to handle the logistics of where the website will be hosted. This is a positive thing in that you have control over what host you choose, and what features they offer, enabling you to get exactly what's needed. The downside is that you will likely be the point of contact for both your client and the host. So if the host suffers a major outage, you can count on getting angry phone calls from your client. Just as you wouldn't hire a designer who has never done web design before, you shouldn't engage a hosting company unless you're sure about the quality of the service they offer.

Tools available

We're quite fortunate, for this part, because it has been only in the past five years or so that the tools in the project management space have evolved to the point where they're usable by mere mortals. Imagine what kind of a tool professional project managers (PMI-trained) use. If you guessed a complex application that involves a great deal of abstract lines and symbols, you're right! Up until a few years ago, your choices for managing projects were either to use Microsoft Project, as shown in Figure 2-3 (or a similar product), or to just fly by the seat of your pants and handle everything with a calendar and e-mail.

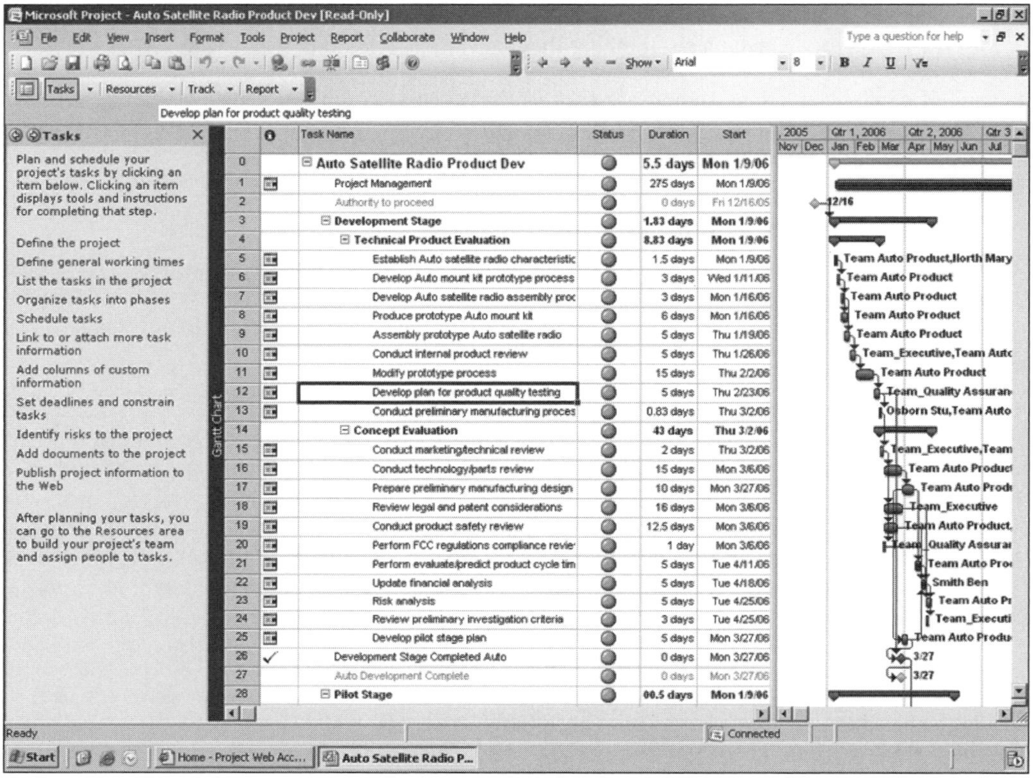

Figure 2-3. A Gantt chart view in Microsoft Project. Sure, there's a lot of information packed in there, but is any of it really useful?

We don't mean to come down on Microsoft Project; it's a brilliant tool for managing Waterfall projects. It will automatically calculate dates and schedules based on the parameters you lay out. But, similar to the discussion of the Waterfall model in general, it's just not appropriate for a web project. Planning a project using a Gantt chart locks you in to a number of things up front, when you have the least amount of information with which to make an informed decision. Gantt charts plot out the sequence and dependencies between tasks. They remove so much flexibility from your scheduling, so why do we use them?

Again, we'll issue the same words of warning here: some organizations will be using Microsoft Project and require you to do the same. If that's the case, go register yourself in a course (yes, there are entire courses on how to use Microsoft Project), or at the very least, go buy yourself a good book on the topic. It's a pretty complex piece of software, and it really pays off to know how to use it properly.

The alternatives

This section started off hinting that there are some much better alternatives that definitely bear consideration.

Basecamp

The trailblazer in this arena is a service called Basecamp (http://www.basecamphq.com/), shown in Figure 2-4. It's a little unique in that it's a web-based hosted application that you subscribe to; there's nothing to install. It offers a free trial that gives you access to the majority of features.

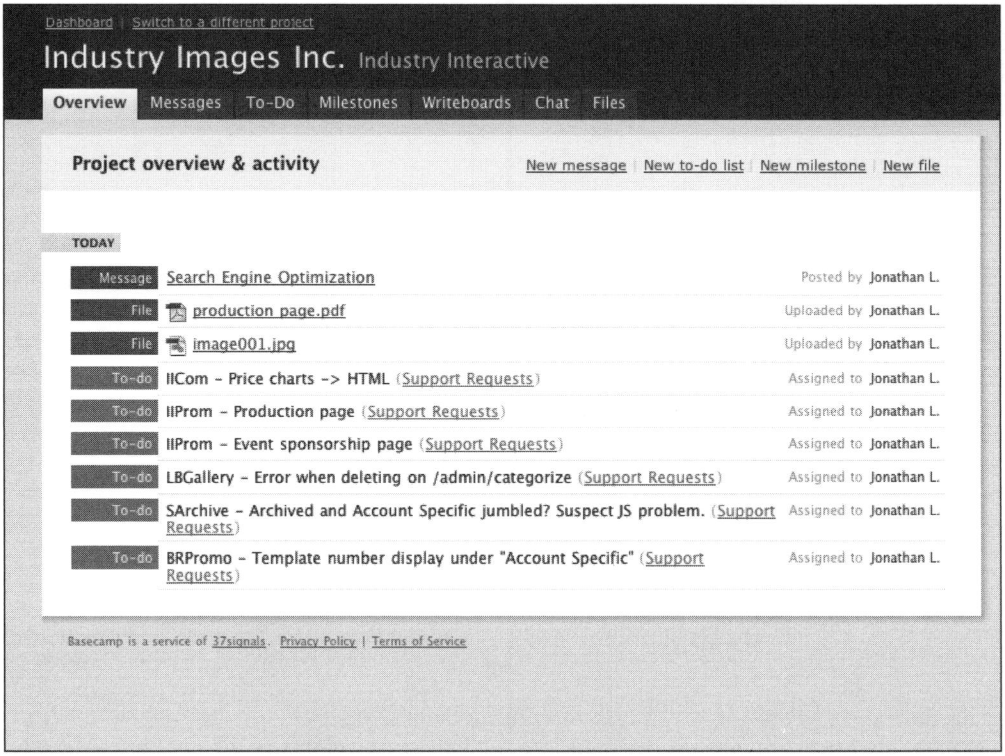

Figure 2-4. Basecamp is web-based (no software to install) and provides a clean, easy-to-use interface.

What makes Basecamp different from Microsoft Project? Basecamp represents a fundamental shift in thinking about project management. Similar to the earlier discussion about agile development, Basecamp takes the stance that project management is more about communication and collaboration than it is about reporting and control. Basecamp provides a simple set of tools that you can use to work with your clients and to communicate progress to them. Instead of producing a complex chart at the beginning of the project, you identify a series of milestones to work toward.

With its easy-to-use tools and clear interface, we strongly recommend you take a look at Basecamp to help you keep on top of client projects.

Trac

Trac (http://trac.edgewall.org/) is an open source project management application. It's a little more technical than Basecamp because you need to download and install it on a server of your own, but the advantage is that you don't have to pay a monthly fee to use it. Trac is another simple tool that provides you with the ability to keep your project team on track. Most notably, it integrates well with

Subversion (as shown in Figure 2-5), which is open source version control software that keeps a record of changes you make to files so that if you make a mistake, you can easily "roll back" to a previous version.

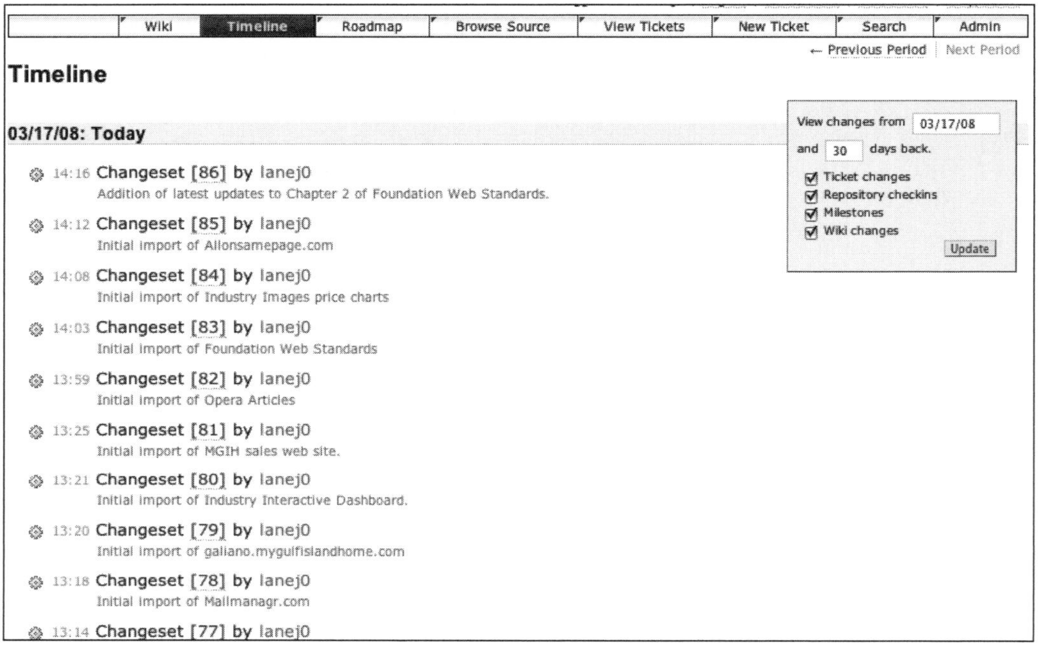

Figure 2-5. Trac is also web-based but must be installed on your own server. It's a little more technical, so unless your client is a technical individual/organization, you might be best saving it for internal team collaboration.

Trac also provides a great wiki that is extremely helpful in making notes for yourself and other team members as the project progresses. The interface for Trac isn't as simple as the one for Basecamp, so personally, we use Trac as an internal tool amongst technical team members, and we use Basecamp in order to collaborate with clients.

Others

There are a million (give or take a few hundred thousand) project management applications out there. Some are web-based, and others are installed on your local machine. What you use will depend in large part on what you need and what you and your client feel comfortable with. Don't feel pressured into using a project management application that produces charts, figures, and graphs galore. The fact of the matter is, long project reports rarely ever get read. Keep things short, simple, and to the point in order to avoid misunderstandings.

Summary: the best advice

The best advice for project management is the best advice for the actual development of the project itself: keep it simple. If you have a schedule in hand, a budget, and a rough idea of what needs developing, you're all ready to go. There is no reason why projects need to get blown out of proportion. Keeping things simple will free you up to concentrate on what's important: delivering the best possible product for your clients.

The greatest single skill in project management is experience. It's one of those things that really does get easier as you go along. You not only become more confident in what you're saying and doing, but you're also able to do more things "off the top of your head." It's really handy to be able to sit down with a client in that initial meeting and be able to give them some ballpark estimates on time and cost. Early on, you'll want to put heavy disclaimers on them and say that you're going to need more time to "crunch the numbers." After a while, though, your ballparks come pretty close to the actual, and you can drop the disclaimers.

You won't always find clients who can agree with keeping things light and agile. At that point, you have a decision to make. If you're in a position where you can pick and choose your clients, I strongly urge you to do so. Honestly, the best projects are those that don't have to fall down over a waterfall. If you're not in a position to turn down any client work, know what you're getting into. Plan for a good deal of time and money contingency to account for all of the (unnecessary) planning and controlling you'll be doing. Plan to keep a tight handle on things as far as changes once development has started and try to complete the website as quickly as you can. The longer a project goes, the more likely it is that it will fail.

Additionally, if you're able to, hire a PMP to oversee things, or at the very least, plan to devote as little as 50 percent of your time to just managing the project. It's pretty onerous keeping tight control on things and making sure that the project is proceeding in lockstep with the plan.

Being agile and standard: there's a good combination

Web standards complement the agile development process well. We briefly discussed in Chapter 1 that separating your content from your design is great for making widespread updates at any stage. Placing the style definition for your website in a separate file that is linked to every page allows you to modify things in one place and have it change everywhere. This is incredibly useful throughout your iterations, because functional changes later in a project will often affect the visual appearance of a website. In the previous example, changing the website to accommodate marketing's request could have been a complex and annoying process, but because of our separation of content and formatting, it was a breeze.

Profiling professions: Jason Fried

Jason Fried is one of the founders and is CEO of 37signals LLC, a Chicago-based former web development consultancy turned web application product provider. 37signals offers a number of excellent products, from its flagship Basecamp project management software to its latest offering, a CRM-like tool called Highrise.

In addition to having a great deal of expertise working with large-scale applications, Jason and his team are also pioneers in the field of "getting real," a variation of the agile development practices we discussed earlier in this chapter. The people at 37signals believe that more software isn't necessarily better software and that keeping things small and simple is always the best way to go.

Lane: What's your role at 37signals, and what does that translate to in terms of day-to-day activities?

Fried: My role is pretty varied. I'm one of the founders, and technically the CEO, although we don't tend to use titles like that. I'm in charge of running the company, coming up with new products, and guiding the company in terms of strategy, as well as guiding the overall design and look and feel of the products.

So, I do a little design, although not as much as I used to; we have another person who does the lead design now, but I set up the overarching look and feel and the corporate identity of the products. I tend to do a lot of writing as well, but most of all these days it's marketing and strategy, coming up with new products, keeping an eye on everything, and guiding the products in the right direction.

Lane: Tell me a bit about your background working with computers, things like education and previous work experience, that led you to what you're doing today.

Fried: I'm not actually technical, so I don't do any programming. My expertise with computers revolves around design: HTML, CSS, graphic design, that sort of thing. My background is actually not related to that whatsoever. I've got a degree in finance, but I've always been interested in design, and I've always been designing stuff ever since I got a computer in junior high—just kind of messing around and learning how to design things.

Around 1996 when the Web hit, I was just getting out of college, and I always wanted to start my own business, so it was a great opportunity to do that and design stuff, which is what I always wanted to do. I started learning how to design websites, and nobody else knew how to do it at the time, so I was on equal footing, and it just took off from there.

Lane: 37signals started out as a web design company, working on projects for clients, and you've now transitioned into creating products of your own that you now resell to customers. Could you talk a bit about how that transition happened?

Fried: It was kind of by accident. We were a web design firm, and we started getting really busy doing a lot of client work. We were managing our projects basically like most people do, sending e-mails back and forth, and it was really messy. It wasn't a good way to stay organized, and it showed. I think clients didn't feel particularly comfortable working with us in that way because they didn't know what was going on with their projects all the time.

We realized that we needed something to keep track of this sort of thing and have clients be able to give us feedback and to follow along in a project. We looked around for some tools and didn't like what we saw, so we decided to build our own, and as we started using it (it took about three months or so to build), our clients were saying "Hey, you know I could use something just like this too. This is really handy, and I could use it for projects with my own company." Some of our colleagues that we showed it to said, "I need this for my own business," so we decided that there might be a product there.

We polished it up a bit and gave it a name, Basecamp, and put some prices on it and put it out on the market, and that's how it all got started. About a year later Basecamp was generating more revenue than our consulting business was, so we stopped doing client work, and we focused exclusively on building our web-based applications.

Lane: One of the things you're most famous for, aside from your great products, is your philosophy of "getting real." Could you briefly talk about what that means and how someone would go about "getting real"?

Fried: The whole "getting real" philosophy is basically about just what it says: doing the real work and not talking about it or writing it down; just doing and figuring things out as you go. Our feeling is that you never really know what you're doing until you're doing it. You can write about it all day long, you can think about it all day long, and you can plan it out all day long, but until you're actually doing the work, you don't know how it's going to turn out and whether it's any good.

So, we get rid of all those abstractions—things like documentation and information architecture diagrams and functional specification documents—and we just dive right in. It's about iteration: putting our heads down, doing a bit of work, lifting our heads up looking around. Where do we need to go next? What do we need to do next? And we follow that reality instead of following a plan we wrote six months ago or a functional specifications document that we wrote before we even knew what we were actually building. That's the overarching philosophy of "getting real."

Lane: In terms of actually developing a project, what's the process? Where do your product ideas come from?

Fried: We always scratch our own itch. Every product we've built, we've built for ourselves first because we had a need; it just comes to a point where you realize that you have a need. There's no science behind it; it's just a moment where you think "Gosh, I've been doing this wrong for so long that there must be a simpler way" and that's where the genesis of a new product idea comes from.

So, for example, Highrise, our most recent product, is a contact manager and simple CRM tool, and it came about because we were talking to a lot of people in the press and doing a lot of interviews, and we weren't really keeping track of who we were talking to and what we said to them and articles they'd published and their contact information. So if someone at 37signals needed to talk to one of these people again, we didn't know what had been said before or when the last time we talked to them was, and it was just a mess, so we needed something like that.

Again, we looked around for stuff because it's hard to build things, so if we could find something that we thought worked well, we would use that, but we just really couldn't, so we decided to build our own. That's how all of the products have started. It just comes from a need, and then what we do is if we decide to go forward with it, we don't need to make a huge commitment to it. If we start on it and then three weeks later we don't like it, we stop, unlike traditional process where you make a commitment, you write a functional specifications document, and you spend a lot of time doing a lot of things first before you know if it's any good.

Then we start with the interface; we start designing what the thing is going to look like first. That dictates the rest of the project; the programming is then plugged into the interface, so it's not the other way around. It's not the programming first and the interface second. Once we've got the basic screens done, we hand them over to the programmers, and they hook it up; and then we start using it, and we go back and forth: Does this make sense? Is this too slow? How does this feel? And we just keep tweaking it until we find that we're really satisfied with what we have for an initial version, and then we put it out on the market. We'll then continue to tweak it over time based on people's feedback.

A lot of people talk about engineering when it comes to software, but we don't like that word. Engineers are people who build bridges. We're software programmers, and I think that when you start thinking about them as engineers, you start falling into that trap of "what is an engineer?" An engineer is someone who makes these big, important decisions that are long-term, and I just think that that's the wrong mind-set.

Lane: What advice do you have for people who are just starting out in working with the Web?

Fried: My suggestion for everything is to start with as simple a version as possible, not only with software but with business. If you're going to start a business, start as simple a business as you can, which is probably just you or maybe another person if you need to. Whatever business structures are available to you in whatever country you're in, start with the simplest possible form. In the United States, the LLC is pretty much the simplest structure there is, so start there.

Don't make any huge decisions up front. Just start working on something, see if it works, and start using it as you're building it. You'll know pretty quickly if it's going to be any good or not, and if it is, hopefully other people will like it and just take it from there.

Definitely don't go out and get funding; don't go out and feel like you have to have a big business attitude or image. I think a lot of small companies try to act big for some reason, and you really don't need to. Just act your size and be who you are, and things will probably work out if you have a good product and you know how to pay attention to the right things. Running a business isn't all that hard; nothing is that hard unless you make it complicated. Most things are pretty simple and pretty easy as long as you take the easy route and build things as simply as you possibly can, to start at least.

Every mistake we've ever made as a business is because we've tried to do something too complex or too hard. It wasn't because we tried to do something too simple. Whatever you're going to do, take the easy way first and see if it's worth putting more time into it afterward. If so, then maybe you can make it more robust, but don't go there at first. Start as simple as you can.

Lane: 37signals has never used traditional advertising for any of its products (paid advertising). What can people who are just starting out do to get their names out there, get some customers, and spread the word about the work they're doing?

Fried: My suggestion is to be as public as you can. The best example of this is a guy named Gary Vaynerchuk of Wine Library TV. He is, to me, the perfect example of how to do it right. He's incredibly passionate, and let's say you're not good on video; let's say you write instead, but I'm going to use him as an example. He came out of nowhere about a year ago, out of complete nowhere, and now he's an Internet celebrity, and a lot of people know about him. He's been on many TV shows, he's gotten tons of press, and he hasn't spent a single penny on PR.

What he does is he shares. He shared his passion; he goes out there and tells people what he loves and helps them out. Whenever you share and teach, people pay attention, and they will begin promoting for you. It's really a great model, and Gary is spot on when it comes to that sort of thing.

I think that that's how we built it. We share a lot. We share a lot about our business, about what we do and why we do it, about what works, and about what doesn't work. We have strong opinions, and we're not afraid to share them, and I think that when you go out there and share your heart and whatever it is that you're doing, I think that people pay attention, and it's a great way of getting the word out.

Also, when you're a teacher, people pay more attention to your actual words, and I think that they appreciate what you're doing more. It's not just about trying to sell someone something; it's actually trying to help someone learn something, and that has a lot of weight to it as well.

My suggestion would be to find out what you really love to do and tell people about it every opportunity that you get. If it's a video blog, like Gary started out with, or if it's just writing a weblog or if it's writing articles in a magazine or writing a book, or whatever it might be, figure out what you can do to share what you know.

Lane: One of the things you talk about in your book, *Getting Real*, is choosing the right customers. How do you go about finding good customers? How do you avoid bad ones?

Fried: I think it's the same way you recognize a good friend compared to a bad friend or someone you wouldn't be friends with at all. Customers are people, and if you don't want to hang out with them or be around them, then they're probably not going to be good clients. You look for those sorts of matches on a personal level I think.

You have to respect the other person and appreciate who they are and enjoy them as a human being. That's really the best way to find great customers or great clients. If you go to a meeting with somebody and they're rude or they're dismissive or they're impossible to deal with for whatever reason, they're not going to be a good client. If the initial meeting is bad, the client is going to be bad. If the request for proposals is bad, the client is going to be bad. You have to look for those signs just like you would with a friend. That's the best way we've found to do it.

I also think that the way you present yourself on your own website will hopefully attract the right kind of people. There are lots of people who wouldn't work with us when we were doing website design because we didn't have a traditional website with a portfolio section like a typical web design firm website would. Our initial site was simply text, black-and-white text, which no one was doing at the time. When we launched in 2000, everyone was doing really colorful stuff and animated stuff, and we were just doing plain text. We were telling a story; this is what we thought was important. The kind of clients who read that and could relate to that and thought "We like these people," those were the kind of clients we found. The potential clients who said "This is ridiculous, I don't get it" were the people who wouldn't work with us. So I think your site has a lot to do with self-selection, and I would recommend that you stick to your point of view early on, because that's a great way to find the right kind of people who will work with you.

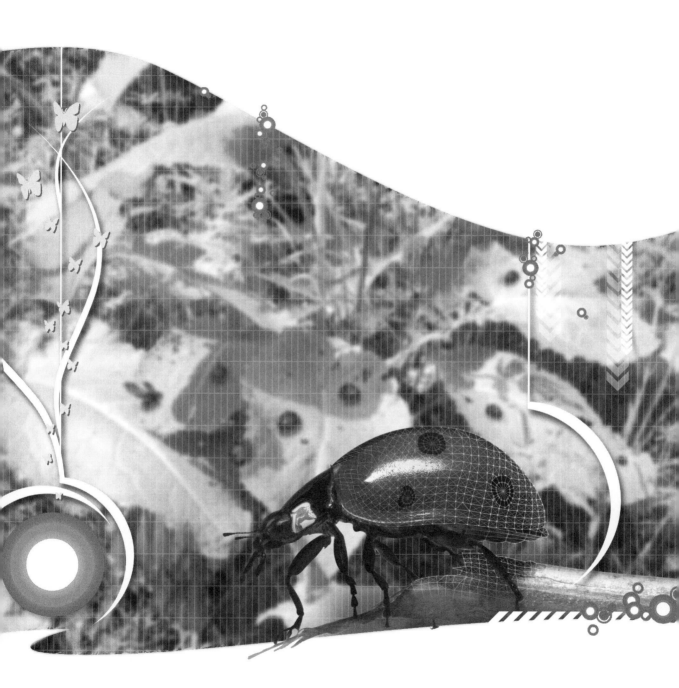

Chapter 3

PLANNING AND HIGH-LEVEL DESIGN

It's entirely by design that we spent the better part of the previous chapter discouraging too much up-front planning. Don't call us hypocrites now that we're offering you an entire chapter covering the planning and pre-project process. The reality of the situation is that it can be to your advantage to do a little work up front before digging into the development stage. Every project you embark on isn't going to be crystal clear; you will more than likely end up working outside your comfort zone on more than one occasion. Although it's easy to get a general feel for most projects, there will undoubtedly be specialized areas in which you will need to consult a subject-matter expert. Your clients may or may not have some idea of what they're looking for, and even then, after talking it over with them, you may come to the realization that their vision of what they want makes absolutely no sense for their end users. Although the temptation is there to simply do what the client wants, collect your paycheck, and walk away, it's far more fulfilling to work on projects where you can see the value that will be produced and where people will actual use the product you produce.

Disagreement with your client, particularly in the early stages of a project, can be really stressful. You want to get along and work collaboratively to produce something great, not just to have to fight over every point. The tools and exercises we'll present to you in this chapter will help you strike that collaborative note with your clients. We hope that by working through some of these sections together, you can draw similar conclusions and move forward as a united front. And remember, although you're an expert in your field and your instincts for what's good and what's bad are probably better than the average Joe, your clients are the experts in their field. They know their customers, employees, partners, and business processes better than you, so if they're adamant about a particular point, don't automatically assume they're wrong. Arrogance is not a productive working methodology.

If you happen to find yourself working as part of a larger team, as opposed to freelancing, it's likely that a number of the activities described in this chapter will be done by the person responsible for client relations. That individual could hold any number of titles; on very large teams, they're either the producer, the account manager, or occasionally the project manager. In smaller groups, it may be a designer or developer (or a designer/developer) who works closely with the client. Regardless, it never hurts to have an understanding of how things work, even if you aren't directly involved in them.

The toolbox

All the activities described in this chapter are optional. Just like our discussion of project management in the previous chapter, you have to do what feels right for you and your client. We suggest that the only activity that isn't optional is the first one; you need to have a discussion with the stakeholders on a project in order to determine your starting point. Most important, you need to know and agree upon what that finish line looks like.

If you need to get things straight in your head, you can do some of these activities without your client. Others are better to work through with your client so that you're both on the same page. If you feel strongly about something, be prepared to defend your position. If your client insists on using the Comic Sans font throughout their entire website, you're going to need a better argument than "No, it's ugly and unprofessional" to dissuade them (even though we all agree with you). Just consider this a little advance warning.

Goals and objectives discussion

The first order of business, once you've landed a project, is to sit down with everybody involved and have a quick discussion about some of the basics of the project. This is often called the **project kick-off meeting**. In addition to hashing out the details of a timeline and a budget, there are a few key questions that are helpful to have answered. A lot of these questions overlap in some way; that's OK. Sometimes it helps if people think about them differently and phrase their answers accordingly. You can handle this step remotely if you need to by forwarding a "questionnaire" to your clients, but it's generally faster and easier to schedule a one-hour meeting with everyone involved in order to answer these questions:

- *What is the goal of this project?* The answer to this question should be a little more specific than "to build a website." Why are you building a website? What is the purpose of the website? Are you trying to sell something? Are you trying to provide better customer/technical support to your customers? Goals are often difficult to identify because they're sometimes really nebulous. Another good way to phrase this question is, "If I told you that no matter what your budget and no matter what your timeline, I can build only one thing for you, what would that be? Would it be a set of pages where products can be purchased? Would it be a blog?" This generally gets people focusing on what the biggest problem is that you're trying to solve by building this website. Most websites should have no more than one or two goals; anything more, and you're probably looking at something that's too complex for a single project.

- *What are the objectives of this project?* Again, keep it general. (Note there is a difference between general and vague; these objectives will help you define scope, so lay them out in such a way as to be able to "check them off" a list. Try to identify specific user groups for each.) Things like "Give the media a place to get information about our company" and "Provide our agency with a professional online presence" are the level you want to stay at. If you're meeting with a group from your client's company, this is the stage where every department can have their say. Sales, PR, customer support, and even the CEO may have some input as to what objectives they want to accomplish. Again, to re-phrase the question, try asking "What sorts of things can we do to accomplish the goal we've identified?"

- *Can you provide a short description of this project?* This should be a couple of lines long, maximum. Ideally this is the answer you would give if the company CEO ambushes you in the elevator and she asks you what you're working on. You get bonus points if the answer is in language that's simple enough for you to use to explain to your family at reunions. Wouldn't it be nice, for once, to be able to explain to your Uncle Irv that you do something more than just "make websites?"

- *What are the benefits of doing this project?* Will it save the organization money in the long run? Is it a good recruiting tool for prospective employees? Will it help the sales team move more products? This is the "dream big" section where everyone can pitch in their two cents about their biggest problems and how they're hoping this project will solve them.

- *What's the scope of this project?* This is usually one of the hardest questions to answer, because it's not entirely clear at the outset. Regardless, everyone will have some idea of what the end product will look like; it's good to get that out here.

- *What are the deliverables?* This can also be phrased as "How will we measure success?" The answer to this question may be as simple as "a completed website with supporting documentation," or it might be something a little more abstract like "an increase in our Google search ranking." Make sure that what emerges from this question is something realistic and attainable. If your client responds "to improve customer satisfaction," don't accept that at face value. How is customer satisfaction currently measured? Maybe it's the number of phone calls to customer support. If you decrease that number, have you improved customer satisfaction? How much does that number need to decrease? By at least 25 percent? If there's no existing measure of customer satisfaction, suggest coming up with some way to assess that before your project launches and then after. Maybe a customer survey is a good way to go.

We suggest sending these questions out a week in advance of your scheduled meeting. That gives everyone a chance to think about and jot down their ideas so that you can have a really productive discussion. It's OK to have debates and disagreements at the project kickoff meeting, and they may turn ugly, but it's better to get it out of the way at this point rather than on the day you go to launch. Your role at this meeting will be to mediate it. Draw on your background, and try to propose solutions that will accommodate everybody.

Brainstorming

The term **brainstorming** is often abused in the business community and has gotten a pretty bad reputation as a result. There is a right and a wrong way to brainstorm, though, and doing it properly is an extremely useful tool for getting a flood of ideas. To brainstorm properly, you'll need a few things: a bunch of sticky notes (or index cards), some pencils or pens, and a countdown timer (Figure 3-1).

Figure 3-1. Pile of index cards generated from a brainstorming session on "ways to sell more widgets." This pile now gets organized and grouped.

Clearly outline what you're working on so that everyone is on the same page. It may be a broad topic such as "technical/functional features of our new website," or it might be something specific such as "ways we can promote the launch of our new service." Tell everyone in the group that the next minute is just about getting ideas out there; it's not about discussion (that will follow). Everyone should write their idea on a sticky note (one idea per note) and call it out as they are writing it. No idea is stupid at this point, and it doesn't have to be completely clear what the idea is—just something memorable so that the thought won't be lost.

Set the timer for one minute, and tell everyone to start. As the leader of this activity, you shouldn't participate; rather, you should "police" the activity. Make sure people don't start talking about the merits of an idea while the timer is running. There should not be any judgments being made on ideas at this stage, so "That's dumb" or "Forget about that" should be strongly discouraged.

Calling out ideas will reduce the amount of duplication you get out of this activity, but inevitably you'll still get some duplicate ideas. It also serves to spark ideas in others, so if one person calls out "professional product photos," then that may spark the idea of "multiple product angles" in someone else. Once the timer runs out, get everyone to sit back, and collect all of the index cards. Read each idea to the group while you have everyone's undivided attention, and if anything is a little ambiguous, ask the contributor of that idea to clarify their thinking (write it down). At this stage, weed out any duplication of ideas that may have occurred as well.

Once the list has been pared down, start grouping ideas. So if you look at our "ways to promote our new service" topic, you might group the ideas by "cost money" and "free." Then you might further break them down into "online" and "offline" media. It's at this stage that ideas can be discussed and the advantages and disadvantages of each can be explored (see Figure 3-2).

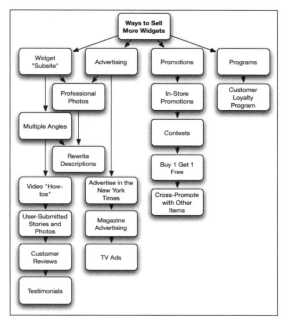

Figure 3-2. Once the brainstorming session is complete, take some time to group similar ideas together and give them some structure. Eliminate any ideas that are clearly bad (as a group, make a judgment call) or impossible to implement, and feel free to add anything new that comes up.

User stories and user personas

User stories and user personas are similar in that they call for you to get inside the head of your end user and describe what they need or what they're thinking or doing at any given moment. A **user persona** involves creating a fictional character, which you envision is one of the target users of your website. You then create a profile and background information for this person, describing their age, occupation, technical background, and likes and dislikes. The biggest benefit to developing user personas is that they're great at serving as a reminder that you're not (necessarily) developing a particular website for yourself. Because of this, create your personas in such as way that they can serve as a constant reminder to the project team throughout the entire design and development phase. If you construct personas and then file them away, they aren't going to do anyone any good.

We think that there's a fundamental problem with personas, though, in that you're inventing a fictional character to deal with a real-world situation. If you're a 29-year-old male, you probably can't imagine what on Earth an 18-year-old female would think of a website you created. If you have a background in computers, you might have a tough time seeing what a website would look like to someone with little or no computer experience (such as your grandmother). Trying to determine fact based on fiction just seems counterintuitive. If the target user group of your product will be someone outside your realm of understanding, then we recommend involving someone from that target market in your project team. You don't have to bring them in immediately, but once you have something they can interact with, if even in a limited capacity, have them take a spin around your website and give you some feedback.

User stories (sometimes called **use cases**) look at individual needs of a user or features of the website you intend to produce. This is another great activity to complete as a group, and it's an even better activity if you can involve individuals from your target audience.

Start with a stack of index cards and ask everyone to start writing down features or functions of the website that they see as essential. They need to be really concrete, such as "a five-star product rating system" or "people who purchased product X also bought product Y." Things such as "an easy-to-navigate website" are too broad. If the title alone isn't sufficient, ask people to write a short paragraph of what they mean/envision; drawing diagrams is OK too. The real purpose is to clearly capture any and all ideas.

Give your group 20 minutes or so to produce their stack of cards and then come together as a group to discuss what everyone has come up with. Eliminate duplicates (if applicable), and then discuss the priority of each story (high, medium, or low). If there are disagreements over the priority of a particular story, the person who wrote the story gets to decide.

After you leave the meeting, assign an ID number to each story, and estimate how long it would take to develop this feature (see Figure 3-3). It could be something like three days or one hour. You can now look through your stack of stories and quickly see what's really important but really easy to do, what's really important but really hard to do, and what's not so important but easy or hard to do.

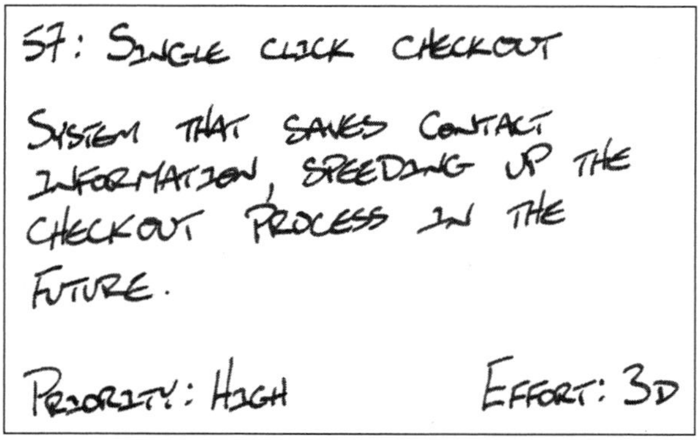

Figure 3-3. Completed user story indicating ID number (57), priority (high), and effort (3 days)

We find that user stories help us answer the question of "What's next?" We talked about taking care of the core of the website first; that is the single thing that the website needs in order to function. What do you work on after that? Start tackling your high-priority stories, starting with the least time-consuming ones and proceeding through to the more time-consuming. Then attack the medium-priority stuff and finally the low-priority stuff.

It's normal to add user stories throughout the life of an agile project or to make revisions to the priority or effort (maybe implementing the user database for the forums has made single-click checkout really easy to implement). Feel free to keep revisiting your stack and making additions and updates as required.

Feature/unfeature list

Brainstorming and user stories are a great way to get the creative juices flowing with everyone, but all of the ideas generated may not be what's best for your website. Also, although it's important to know what the competition is doing, you shouldn't let it dictate your work. Just because your biggest competitor has introduced live video chat on its website doesn't mean you should do the same. Heck, let your competition do the market research on it and spend the money figuring out whether it's a killer feature. What you're producing should stay focused on your end user and what they need. Keep it simple; you can always add things later.

The feature/unfeature list is exactly that: a list of what you must include in your project to make it useful and successful and a list of what you aren't going to include. Although that seems like a silly notion, why should you bother creating a list of what you're not going to do? It can really help to define what you're working toward. It can also really help with scope definition and in determining the budget and timeline for a website. If you can get everyone to agree up front that you're not looking to develop a music player, when that pesky VP of marketing all of a sudden decides to get involved with your project and asks where the music playback controls are, you'll be able to point to your unfeature list and say that it hasn't been overlooked but was discounted earlier in the process.

For example, say you've been asked to create a social application that focuses on music. Your feature/unfeature list might look like Table 3-1.

Table 3-1. Example Feature/Unfeature List

This project is...	This project is not...
A stand-alone web application	A Facebook application
A place where fans can come to discuss their favorite bands	A place where fans can come to trade audio files of their favorite bands
A news resource for upcoming CD releases and concert dates	A news site providing interviews and general information about bands
Meant for individuals who are at least 18 years of age	Meant to be a hangout for pre-teens to discuss the latest *American Idol*
About the music, the artists, and the fans	About the money (as long as we break even)
A place for discussion	A file-sharing outlet

This list gives you some clear direction as to what the project team wants to avoid and what it expects the end product to look like.

Wireframes

You can think of **wireframes** as the thumbnail sketches of the web world. Wireframes are outlines of your pages using lines and boxes to represent where various elements will be placed (see Figure 3-4). Their primary purpose is to get the team focusing on content, functionality, and navigation (or flow), not on appearance. They are extremely quick to construct; in fact, a number of designers we know don't even bother using a computer. They'll simply sketch them on a piece of paper, which they will then scan and send off to a client for feedback.

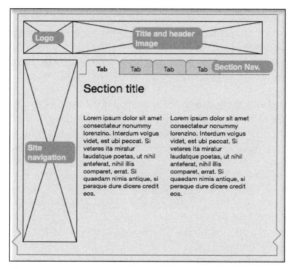

Figure 3-4. Basic wireframe showing the various parts of a page. A number of great templates are available on the Web for constructing wireframes.

If you mock up a page in Adobe Photoshop using stock photos and placeholder graphics, we guarantee you that the majority of the comments you will receive will focus on the images you selected or the shade of yellow you used for your highlights. We once did a mockup using "Lorum Ipsum" text, only to have it returned from the client with the comment that their website will need to be in English. Go ahead and roll your eyes, we did. It can be really frustrating when, despite your best efforts, your client still focuses on the wrong thing entirely. Do what you need to do to center their attention. If it means removing all text and replacing it with dashes, or replacing images with gray boxes, do it.

In removing graphics, colors, and text, you force individuals to focus on the layout and content of a page. This activity is designed to get people thinking about what placement leads to the best interface for your pages and the nature of the content they will contain. Questions such as "Does it really make a lot of sense to split the navigation between a horizontal bar along the top and several vertical columns of links?" will come up at this stage. It's also common to hear remarks that the company's logo isn't prominent enough or that the content area doesn't have enough space.

The biggest drawback to producing wireframes is that it's difficult to display interactive elements. If you have a box that will expand and collapse, it's tough to represent that in a simple sketch. As Ajax becomes used in more and more places online, the notion of a "static mockup" of a page will be less and less useful.

Wireframes are really only useful in larger groups where you're trying to get everyone to focus on one thing at a time. If you're working one on one with a client, don't even bother with wireframes; cut right to the prototype. Let them see and work with the website in a browser; they'll be able to gain a deeper understanding of the right way of doing things.

Mock-ups

Several designers will still produce Photoshop mock-ups of a website for their client ahead of time. Some will even produce two or three variations so that their client can pick the one they like best. As you may have gathered, we think this is largely a waste of time.

For starters, only one of the variations you've produced will be selected, and then all the time and effort you put into the others will go into the great digital landfill. Why divide your time amongst several options? Produce one design, and make it the absolute best you can. Get everything pixel-perfect!

And then present it to your client in XHTML/CSS. We understand that Photoshop is ingrained in the designer's thought process. If you're one of those folks who need to start with a blank canvas in order to get your creative juices flowing, so be it. But take it only as far as you need. As soon as you have that vision in your head, start realizing it in a real-life web page.

Similar to wireframes, Photoshop is terrible at exhibiting dynamic content. You can flip layers on and off, we guess, but why spend the time? It's just as fast to code it and then make small changes to the code as needed. Going to code gets you thinking about the best way to produce a page, instead of the best way to replicate your Photoshop mock-up.

The best-case scenario is that designers can write code and coders can design like artists, but that's rarely ever the case. Chances are that if you're working in an organization that's big enough to have both designers and developers, the existing workflow will incorporate mock-ups. In cases like that, just make sure that once you have the mockups "converted" to something interactive that you work closely with your designer to review what you've done and whether it matches the direction they had envisioned.

Information architecture

Your goal with this activity is to lay out the **site map** of the website and also to come up with the nomenclature and taxonomy you'll be using (you haven't suddenly slipped into a biology textbook, don't worry). Will you be calling the page containing company "Contact Information," "Contact Us," or simply "Contact"? Maybe you'll go with the more casual "Drop Us a Line" or perhaps "Feedback." There's no right answer here; it depends on a number of factors.

If you're developing a new website, your best bet may be to surf around a bit and see what other people are using for their naming. Go to some of the biggest websites and try to draw parallels between their pages and yours. We're not suggesting here that "the big players" are always right; it's just that a great deal of people have been exposed to those websites before, so their naming schemes have caught on.

If you're redesigning an existing website, it might make sense to keep the existing labels for things. The existing user base has already invested the time to learn that when they click "Dude, hook me up," it means take them to the online store. It's a judgment call that will be guided by the goals and objectives of the website. If your client is hoping to rope in new customers, it might be smart to rename your links in order to lower the bar for entry. Deciding on navigation is one of the key decisions for the success of your website. Once you think you have it figured out, ask a neutral third party to see whether they "get it" too. On the other hand, if the main goal is simply an update in the look along with a dose of increasing sales to existing users, don't go hog-wild. Existing users are existing users because they like the site as it is. Don't risk alienating them with sweeping changes for the sake of change.

A typical site map is just a series of boxes labeled with page names (see Figure 3-5). If you find that your website is oozing Web 2.0 machismo and you have more Ajax than you have images, then number each of the pages on your site map and provide a paragraph or two describing some of the functionality and interactions on that page.

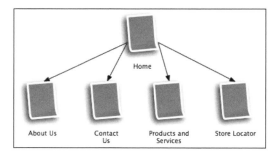

Figure 3-5. A typical site map showing the names of pages and their relationship to one another

Prototype

But that's not a tool, that's actual production work! It's crazy, we know, but getting to a working product is the single best design tool available. In a working product, there are no miscommunications or misconceptions. It's just the first step toward finishing a project. Sure, you may get absolutely everything wrong in the first version and have to change it all, but at least you know what not to do now. We want to pause for a second and just remind you that we're not presenting these tools to you in a particular order, but rather, as a collection from which you can pick and choose. The reason you should have this thought current in your mind is because skipping every step except the prototype can produce a successful project. We've launched a lot of wildly successful projects that had no up-front planning except for preliminary discussions and a prototype that eventually evolved into the final deliverable.

Start simple; don't even worry about the design for the first little while. White backgrounds and black text with simple text links are just fine for laying out a product and getting a feel for how things go together. Create some basic pages with titles (and content if available), and start building the hierarchy (see Figure 3-6).

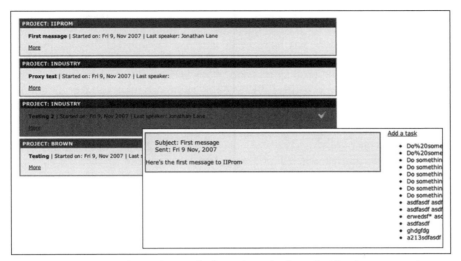

Figure 3-6. A prototype doesn't have to be fancy. Start simple, and add to it as you go along. Separating presentation from content (using XHTML and CSS) will let you make changes to the look quickly.

Elaborate as you go along. Drop the company logo into the corner of the page; let your client tell you whether it's too big, too small, or the wrong shade of purple. Keep a list of the changes requested so that you don't let anything slip through the cracks. Better yet, let your client make the list for you. Tools such as Basecamp or Trac (which we discussed in the previous chapter) will let you add to-dos or tickets to keep track of what has been requested and what has been accomplished.

Let's go to an example

Hey, congratulations! We heard you just landed a contract with this hot new startup in Silicon Valley to produce a sales website for its hot new Web 2.0 product that it's launching in a couple of months. That's awesome!

You're a little freaked out? This is your first major project besides that softball website you put together for your Uncle in Cleveland last month? Don't worry about it; let's walk through the initial stages together.

OK, so you already know that the startup has scheduled the launch of its service to take place in two months (60 days). Being the entrepreneurs that they are, they're still on a bit of a tight budget, but they've managed to scrape together $2,000 for the project. You're just starting out in your career anyhow, so you're charging your standard rate of $20 an hour. You're reasonably confident that you're going to be the only one working on this project, and it doesn't sound like they need anything too complex (in fact, "simple" came up 35 times in your initial conversation with them!).

So, where do you start? Well, this book you read once suggested that the best way to start a project is with a project kickoff meeting. It's lucky for you that you're taking a vacation to the Silicon Valley area next week, and you've already set up a time to swing by their offices. (Man, this project is just one lucky coincidence after another!) What on Earth will you talk about, though?

First things first. You've been talking exclusively with the CEO and VP of marketing. You fire off a quick message to them thanking them for their business and confirming the date and time of the meeting. In this message, ask them who you will be meeting with, and suggest that they include anyone who may have a stake in the project. At this stage, leave it wide open; it may be useful to have some of the folks who actually developed the product on hand. Along with this e-mail, you forward the six questions outlined in the "Goals and objectives discussion" section. Ask them to take some time to think about them in advance and jot down a few ideas. Also request that they forward these questions to anyone who will be in attendance.

Fast-forward one week, and you're on-site with your clients. After brief introductions, you jump right into the meeting. Luckily, everyone is well prepared, and you're able to zip through the six questions with little disagreement or conflict. Something interesting does emerge from the discussion, however. The management team is concerned about how they are going to receive feedback from their customers and suggestions for improvement so that they can continue to improve their product.

It's the perfect time to break out the second weapon from your arsenal and engage everyone in a brainstorming session. You set your timer for one minute, hand out a pad of sticky notes and a pen to everyone in the room, and remind them to focus on their customers. Who are they? What is their level of expertise? And go!

Ideas start flying back and forth, and everything from "a toll-free hotline" to "a user discussion forum" to "a wiki" are tossed onto the table. Time runs out, and you collect all the notes and head over to the wall to start grouping them.

One by one, you read each idea aloud, asking for clarification when necessary. You group them by level of technical knowledge required, ranging from "little to none," as is the case with the toll-free phone number, to "advanced," as with the wiki.

There is something intriguing about the wiki idea, however. People in the room start to talk about it and thinking out loud that it could enable the company to drastically reduce support costs, allowing "pro" users to help out new customers. Company staff would need to swing by only occasionally to answer the "dead-end" questions.

You sit back for a minute and reflect that it's not completely unreasonable to include this in the original project. There's already a bunch of really great wikis out there; it would really just be a few hours of work to integrate one into your client's website. You know that they have a hard $2,000 budget limit, but you're pretty sure that you can shuffle some things around. You pipe up telling them that you'll take care of it, no additional cost.

You've set the right tone for the project. You've established that you care about your client and their success and that you're willing to do what needs doing to produce the best possible finished product. You leave the meeting feeling great about the way things went and with a promise to get back to your client soon with something for them to see.

Two weeks later (remember, you were on vacation), you send your client a link to a prototype you've put up on your testing server. They immediately start clicking through it and sending you comments about what they like and dislike.

Summary: achieving balance

Your goal in the planning stage is to get a better idea of what the finished product will look like. Don't expect a photograph right out of the gates, but an abstract sketch is a good objective. The tools outlined earlier are really nothing more than a few standard ways of communicating with clients that may help you to get thoughts across. If you feel the need, you can repeat any of these exercises at any point during project development. It may prove interesting to see how things have progressed over the course of a project.

Don't feel obliged to run through everything outlined here as if it's a road map to project bliss. Before you begin any of these activities, ask yourself whether you (or anyone on the project team) will ever look at the output of these activities ever again. What is the point of developing an information architecture/site map if it's going to be completely ignored when you produce your prototype?

A really important point to note is that none of the output of these activities should be considered "locked-in" material. The agile project dictates iterations and changes once more information has been discovered. If someone creates a user story outlining the need for a discussion forum and it later becomes evident that nobody is interested in using a discussion forum, ax it.

Profiling Professions: Daniel Burka

Daniel Burka is well known throughout the web community as a pioneer in Web 2.0 design. His exceptional implementation of a clean and simple design for the wildly popular community news website, Digg.com, as well as his ongoing efforts to incorporate community feedback in order to constantly improve and evolve Digg, have made him a sought-after designer and speaker.

His latest endeavor, Pownce, is another hit by offering users an extremely easy-to-use interface to share files, links, and events within a network of friends.

Lane: Give us a rundown of what you're working on these days.

Burka: By day, I'm the creative director at Digg, and by night (and in all my spare time) I design the user interface for Pownce. Being the creative director at Digg means that I manage a small team of designers who handle all of the user interface tasks on the site. I work closely with Kevin Rose, Digg's founder, to spec out concepts, determine how features will be incorporated into the interface, and generally defend all things related to the user experience. The role I play at Pownce is similar, though we have a tiny little team, and I spend a lot more time developing new things than refining existing features.

Lane: Tell us a bit about your background: things like education and work experience that led you to your work in web design.

Burka: I luckily stumbled into web design when I was in high school. My twin brother and some friends were experimenting with graphic design tools, and I joined in. We then discovered we could make some easy money in the summers doing government-sponsored web projects through a Canadian government program. Over a few years, that group of friends coalesced, and we formed a company called silverorange that eventually evolved into a very strong web development shop. I actually studied history at university and eventually (eight years in!) got a BA with a minor in art history. I think this academic education helped me in many ways, but I learned most practical design practices through trial and error with my friends at silver-orange.

Lane: Step us through the process you went through when you were designing Digg.com. Where did your initial ideas come from?

Burka: Starting Digg was actually somewhat intimidating because it was a very large project already at the outset. Instead of tackling the whole thing at the beginning, I tried to identify the core component that made Digg unique, which were the story items on the home page. I isolated that one part and spent several days breaking it down, reorganizing the pieces, and developing a visual language. This groundwork established many ideas that percolated through the rest of the site as we increased our scope.

Lane: What are some of your favorite websites and why?

Burka: A List Apart: fantastic content that's well organized in a layout that happens to be very attractive. Those attributes are important in precisely that order. Apple: Apple's ability to keep the home page as a single focused element is impressive. CNN: I don't agree with every design decision on CNN's site, but the evolution of the CNN website has been impressive over time.

Lane: What advice do you have for people just getting started in working with the Web today?

Burka: I'd advise people to find a tight group of like-minded people to work with. Whether you're attending a design school or starting out with a small business, finding a group of people that you can bounce ideas off of, receive critiques on your work, and generally have fun learning together is an invaluable resource. It's certainly possible to learn web design on your own, but I doubt it's as productive or as much fun. Oh, and take Jeffrey Zeldman's advice—get half your money up front.

Lane: What tools do you use when designing a website?

Burka: Start with a whiteboard, move on to Photoshop, jump into the code in Coda. I can't draw with a pen and paper to save my life.

Lane: Web technology progresses pretty quickly. What are some of the ways you use to keep up on the latest trends in design and technology?

Burka: RSS feeds and talking to the right people. One of the great things about working on the Web is that almost all of the discussions happen online. I spent the first seven years of my web design career in eastern Canada, and we had no trouble keeping up with changes in the industry. Bloggers and sites like A List Apart really keep you in the loop.

Lane: If there were one thing you could completely change about the Web (or add/get rid of), what would it be?

Burka: Obviously, it'd be a fundamental shift, but getting rid of the statelessness of the Web would make a huge difference. Being able to haphazardly jump back and forth through a website using browser controls makes us do all kinds of weird design decisions that we don't even think about much of the time.

Lane: Where do you see things going with the Web in the next couple of years? What are you excited about?

Burka: I'm excited about the renewed potential of the mobile Web. People have been predicting the rise of mobile for years, and it's finally starting to show some promise. And, the best part is that, with devices like the iPhone, the gap between mobile and standard web experiences is narrowed.

Lane: What can new web designers/developers do to get their names out there and get noticed?

Burka: Seriously, the first thing is just to do really good work. A long time ago, I was speaking to one of the best graphic designers no one has ever heard of, and he told me that if you do good work, everything else will work itself out. It was very good advice.

Better short-term advice is that you shouldn't sit around waiting for good work to arrive. If you have any extra time, develop fictional projects and experiments. The 37signals early conceptual redesigns of banking, shipping, and payment sites are great examples. This will help you build out an impressive portfolio even if you don't have impressive clients yet.

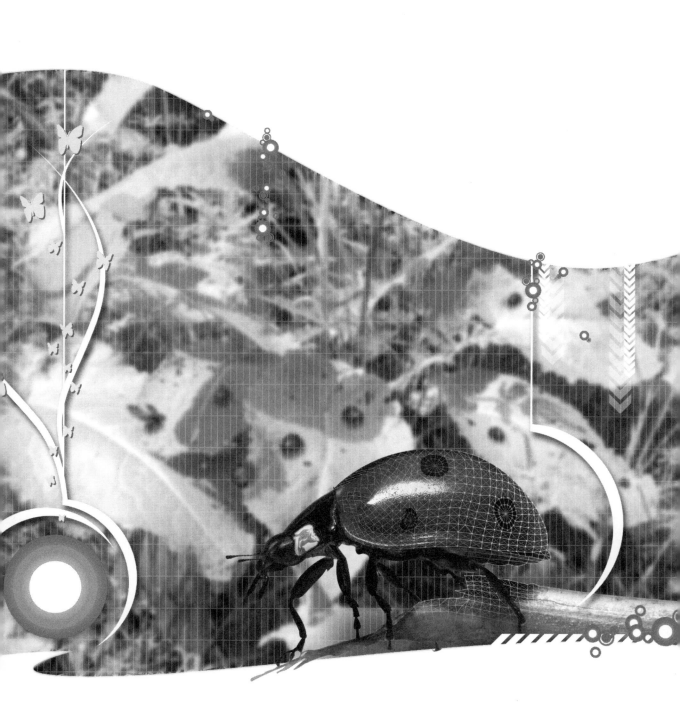

Chapter 4

WRITING MARKUP WITH HTML AND XHTML

What would the Web be without web pages? What *are* web pages, anyway? It's obvious that web pages have a lot of *stuff* in them and that they consist of a variety of different kinds of this stuff. For instance, lots of web pages have text, and lots also have images. Some web pages have videos. Yet others have tables full of price lists or comparison charts.

All this stuff that's in web pages consists of, like the Lego sets you may have played with as a child, lots of different pieces, called **elements**, that when put together in a certain way result in the page you see. Thus, a single web page can really be broken down into many different individual elements. In fact, that's exactly what web developers do when they build web pages—they put lots of different pieces together in a certain way.

Before we show how to start building whole web pages, though, we'll first talk about these individual elements and show how they fit together.

What are web pages, really?

It may take you by surprise that even though the web pages you look at are full of pictures and videos and things like that, underneath it all every page is just a single (albeit possibly very long) string of text. Not all of it is in English, of course, because computer programs such as your web browser don't actually speak or understand

English. Nevertheless, your web browser does understand a kind of language, the Hypertext Markup Language (HTML).

When you go to a website in your web browser, you're actually telling your web browser to download a file. This file, called an **HTML document**, is nothing more complicated than a bunch of text that's written in this HTML that your web browser knows how to read. The HTML you download is then interpreted by your web browser and displayed to you as a web page.

If it's all just a single string of text, you might be wondering, how does the web browser know that a picture should go in the top-left corner or that these two pieces of text are in different paragraphs? The answer is that in addition to all the *content* that's in the HTML document (such as the text of the two paragraphs), there's also information about the content. This information about the content isn't actually visible on the web page, but trust us. It's there.

It's all that extra information, called **markup**, that tells the web browser what kinds of things the content pieces are, where they begin and where they end in that long string of text, and what they are called.

If you think about it for a moment, you'll realize that this isn't so different from what you do whenever you write a letter or talk to your friends on the phone. When you write a letter, you usually end it with your name on a line of its own, and readers can recognize that part of the letter as identifying the sender. Similarly, you don't say "period" at the end of every sentence when you talk to your friends; you just kind of lower your tone a little. Your friends know that this means you're done talking.

Web browsers do the same thing, only they don't have tone of voice or lines of text in specific places (like the end) to go by to get these hints about what the content they have is. Instead, they use all that invisible markup to figure it out.

The basics of markup

Everything that ends up on a web page has to be specifically prepared to go there. As much as you might wish it so, you can't just copy everything in a Microsoft Word document and paste it into an empty text file and call that a web page. If you did that, your page would be missing all the important markup your web browser needs to understand what you've given it. Thankfully, preparing a document for the Web—or **marking up** a document—is actually a simple process that involves working within a set of tools and using them for the right purpose. The rest of this chapter will outline how those tools came about, what they are meant for, and how best to use them. By the end of this chapter, you'll be able to understand that long string of HTML text just as well as your web browser does.

Where computer markup languages came from

As explained earlier, a **markup language** simply consists of specific kinds of annotations that identify the components of a document. This identification allows the content to be interpreted in a meaningful manner by any machine, user, or system, such as the hundreds of different kinds of web browsers used today. Markup languages date back to the 1960s, having been used to define and identify data for decades. One of the earliest standardized markup languages is called, very simply, Standard Generalized Markup Language (SGML).

SGML was originally created for use in governmental, legal, and other complex, structured documents that needed to be read and "understood" by computers. To this day, the Oxford English Dictionary remains completely marked up in SGML. The language has many features and is very flexible, but ultimately it remains too burdensome for most of today's simple uses (such as displaying web pages). Instead, several derivatives of SGML have become popular, such as HTML and Extensible Markup Language (XML).

Since web pages didn't need to be as complicated as government documents, HTML was conceived of as a simpler and more limited derivative of SGML. However, as the Web evolved from an academic document linking system to what it is today, it became clear that HTML was, at times, *too* limited. Rather than return to the complicated all-or-nothing approach mandated by SGML, XML was developed to create a modular markup language that would be the foundation on top of which anyone could create their own *custom* markup language. Since anyone could extend this language in any way they chose, this new specification was called the Extensible Markup Language.

Thanks to its explicit design as a modular and extensible language, XML is one of the most flexible markup languages in use today. There are extensions to XML for all sorts of content ranging across everything from computer configuration files to vector-based graphics and, of course, web pages. The specific application of XML to web pages is called Extensible Hypertext Markup Language (XHTML).

Like HTML, XML uses a subset of SGML's properties. Unlike HTML, XML defines a much more rigid syntax and grammar for the markup language. This makes it easier to learn and easier to read for both people and machines. Despite the rigidity in syntax, it remains flexible and open, even for storing the most versatile data.

Elements (and tags)

So, how does all this markup work? Let's closely examine some example XML markup to find out.

Recall that the core purpose of markup is to organize content into related pieces and identify them explicitly. These pieces of content are grouped into sections, called **elements**. The start and end annotations of elements are commonly referred to as **tags**.

An element is nothing more than text wrapped between a pair of tags. Angle brackets, the < and > characters, delimit the beginning and end of a tag. Take for instance, this piece of text:

    Where the Streets Have No Name

You might easily identify this text as a song title written by the band U2. However, someone else might not be able to recognize this song title, so you need to indicate what it is in proper markup form. Well, let's label what it is and identify it as a title, like so:

    <title>Where the Streets Have No Name

So, you've now identified where the title starts by annotating the beginning of the song title with the `<title>` tag, but in XML, that's not enough. You also have to identify where this title ends. To do that, you simply use the same tag again and include a forward slash directly after the left angle bracket:

    <title>Where the Streets Have No Name</title>

Now you have successfully marked up the title of this song by annotating its beginning and its end explicitly using opening `<title>` and closing `</title>` tags. What you've created is a `<title>` element that, in this case, is nothing more than the text of the song. In XML and all its specific applications—including XHTML—all elements with any kind of content (either text or other elements) begin and end with a pair of tags like this.

Let's add the artist information next so that readers of the XML document know what band wrote the song. All you have to do is mark up the text U2 as a similarly obvious element. Let's call it `<artist>` and add that directly after the title:

```
<title>Where the Streets Have No Name</title>
<artist>U2</artist>
```

You can continue adding information about the song in this way and include all sorts of information. For instance, this song came out on the album titled *The Joshua Tree* in 1987. You can add that to your list of information, marked up as follows:

```
<title>Where the Streets Have No Name</title>
<artist>U2</artist>
<album>The Joshua Tree</album>
<released>1987</released>
```

By now you have a good deal of information encoded in the XML document about this song. Let's now take this one step further and encode information about many songs in the same document. To do this, you need a way of grouping all the elements related to a single song together so you can clearly delineate where the information about one song ends and the next one begins.

In XML and most other markup languages, elements can be **nested** (placed inside one another) if the information can be grouped together in a meaningful way. So, you could take all the markup you have already defined for your single song and put it inside a `<song>` element, like this:

```
<song>
    <title>Where the Streets Have No Name</title>
    <artist>U2</artist>
    <album>The Joshua Tree</album>
    <released>1987</released>
</song>
```

Now, you have defined one `<song>` element in your document. Since that `<song>` element encloses four other elements, it is said to have four **children** and is itself called the **parent** element of those child elements.

> *You can see a common convention of an SGML-derived markup language here. Any element that is nested inside another element is typically indented, and the enclosing element's start and end tags are on their own lines. This is done purely for ease of reading and editing by humans. Software programs written to interpret this markup will typically ignore all this whitespace between the tags (including the indentation, the line breaks, and so on), as well as any extra whitespace inside elements or an element's content, so technically all these tags could be right next to each other and still be just as meaningful. The browser simply interprets any number of consecutive spaces or tabs as a single space. Nevertheless, it's good practice to keep to this style of indentation since it's much easier to edit the markup when its structure is visually obvious.*

Now that your song's information is properly grouped, it's easy to expand this document to include other songs. For instance, you might want to have a document with information that encodes one of your favorite mixes. You can duplicate your single song markup and simply change the information held in the child elements for the different songs, as shown here:

```
<song>
    <title>Where the Streets Have No Name</title>
    <artist>U2</artist>
    <album>The Joshua Tree</album>
    <released>1987</released>
</song>
<song>
    <title>Hungry Like the Wolf</title>
    <artist>Duran Duran</artist>
    <album>Rio</album>
    <released>1982</released>
</song>
<song>
    <title>More Than a Feeling</title>
    <artist>Boston</artist>
    <album>Boston</album>
    <released>1986</released>
</song>
<song>
    <title>Dream On</title>
    <artist>Aerosmith</artist>
    <album>Aerosmith</album>
    <released>1973</released>
</song>
```

This isn't right quite yet, because all you have now is a bunch of individual songs, not a playlist for your mix. You still need to group these songs together in some way. Let's use a <playlist> element for that purpose:

```
<playlist>
    <song>
        <title>Where the Streets Have No Name</title>
        <artist>U2</artist>
        <album>The Joshua Tree</album>
        <released>1987</released>
    </song>
    <song>
        <title>Hungry Like the Wolf</title>
        <artist>Duran Duran</artist>
        <album>Rio</album>
        <released>1982</released>
    </song>
    <song>
        <title>More Than a Feeling</title>
        <artist>Boston</artist>
        <album>Boston</album>
        <released>1986</released>
    </song>
    <song>
        <title>Dream On</title>
        <artist>Aerosmith</artist>
        <album>Aerosmith</album>
        <released>1973</released>
    </song>
</playlist>
```

Finally, you have a complete playlist of four songs that's been properly marked up in XML. Using just the very basic building block of XML, elements, you can create arbitrarily complex documents that encode information about whatever topic you like in a hierarchical fashion. This hierarchical structure is known as a **tree**. However, if all you had to work with were elements, your tree would grow very big very quickly, and it could quickly become unwieldy. So in addition to elements, there are two more very important parts of the XML markup language that allow you to add extra information about your data: attributes and values.

Attributes and their values

As mentioned, **attributes** are a means of adding extra information to elements in an XML document. Attributes always specify some value, so you'll always see attributes and values together in the form of attribute-name="attribute-value". Generally in XML, each element can have an unlimited number of attributes, though in practice each specific application of XML has a certain set of valid attributes and valid values for those attributes. Part of learning any dialect of XML is learning which elements can have which attributes and what the allowed values for those attributes are.

Attributes and their values are specified by adding their name and value inside the opening tag for the element to which they apply. For instance, you can include the date this playlist was created as an attribute of the <playlist> tag. For example, let's specify that your playlist was created on May 28, 2006. You could add this data to the <playlist> tag as follows:

```
<playlist created="May 28, 2006">
```

Alternatively, if you wanted to specify the author of the playlist, you might add that data like so:

```
<playlist author="johndoe">
```

To include both the author of the playlist and the date it was created, you simply include multiple attributes in the same element:

```
<playlist author="johndoe" created="May 28, 2006">
```

This brings up an interesting question: what data should be marked up as an element, and what data should be marked up as an attribute/value pair? You could have just as easily created an <author> element and defined johndoe as its content inside the playlist tag or a <created> element in the same way. Although there is no real right or wrong answer here, it's generally considered best practice to use attributes and values for **metadata** (or data about data) and to use elements for everything else.

In other words, if it's data that's meant to be seen by the end user, it's best to mark it up in an element. If it's data that describes some other data in the document, it's best to use an attribute/value pair. This is often a confusing topic, so don't think you have to get it perfect right away. Oftentimes you just have to step back and take a look at how you're intending to use the data and determine the best solution for your markup based on its application.

Empty elements

There's one other way you might encode information inside an XML document, and that is through the use of an **empty** element. Empty elements are just like regular elements except that they don't contain any content, neither text nor other elements, inside them. Such elements are well suited for things such as embedding pointers to other documents or objects (such as pictures) inside an XML document or storing important "yes/no" (Boolean) values about the document.

For example, if you wanted to use your playlist document in an automated CD-burning application, you might embed an empty element inside the <playlist> element called <burn>, which could have an attribute called format and whose value would indicate the kind of CD format to use when ripping the mix:

```
<burn format="music" />
```

Notice that empty elements, like their nonempty counterparts, are both opened and closed. In the case of empty elements, however, the closing tag *is* the opening tag and is denoted simply by including the closing forward slash right before the right angle bracket.

Document types

When marking up a document, you must conform to some kind of standard of what elements, attributes, and values are allowed to appear in the document, as well as where they are allowed appear and what content they are allowed to contain. If web developers didn't conform to these standards, every website in the world might use a different set of elements, attributes, and values, and no web browser (much less any human!) would be guaranteed to be able to interpret the content on the web page correctly. For example, where you used a <playlist> element to enclose your favorite mix in the previous example, someone else might have used a <favorite-mix> element.

Lucky for us, the standards that web pages and most other kinds of XML documents use are published publicly and are known as **document types**. Every XML document declares itself as a specific type of document by including a special <!DOCTYPE> tag with the appropriate attributes that refer to a specific Document Type Definition before anything else. A Document Type Definition, in turn, is itself a marked-up document that defines the rules, or **grammar**, of the specific document type.

DTDs are intended to be read by machines, not humans, so they can get pretty complicated. The important thing for you as a web developer to understand is that it's the document type that determines exactly how you can use elements, attributes, and values to build your web page. In practice, there are only a couple different types of DTDs that web pages actually reference, so you'll need to become familiar with the rules of only those types.

As a brief exercise, let's figure out what elements, attributes, and values are allowed in the simple earlier example. First, you need to allow for the existence of the following elements: <playlist>, <burn>, <song>, <title>, <artist>, <album>, and <released>. Next, you need to specify that the attributes called created and author are permitted to be attached only to the <playlist> element and that the format attribute can be attached to the <burn> element. You can say that any values are valid for these attributes, or you can say that only "date" values are permitted for the created attribute and only "text" values are permitted for the author and format attributes. If you do that, you'll also have to explicitly define what "date values" and "text values" are.

Document Type Definitions are useful not only so *you* can understand how to formulate your markup properly but also so that your markup can actually be checked by a computer. Software programs called **validators** can read a document of markup and its corresponding DTD, and they can alert you to any inconsistencies between the two. Using your example, your DTD could alert you if you accidentally mistyped and created a <spong> element or tried to specify the author attribute on a <title> element instead of <playlist>.

Starting with XHTML

There are several flavors of both HTML and XHTML that have been specified over the years. As the benefits of a standards-compliant Internet began to be more widely accepted and the transition from HTML to XML-based XHTML began, two types of XHTML were created. One of them is called XHTML 1.0 Transitional, and the other is XHTML 1.0 Strict. As the name implies, the transitional document type (or **doctype** for short) was meant to be more flexible and forgiving than its Strict counterpart and was intended to be an intermediate step for developers who were used to the looser grammar and syntax of HTML.

Because this transition should in most cases be over already and, more important, because you most likely do not fit into the aforementioned category of developers, you will simply jump in to learning XHTML 1.0 Strict.

Document shell

When creating a new XHTML document, it's easiest to start with a basic template because there are several elements, attributes, and values you'll always need, and most of them are difficult to remember. First, create a new folder on your computer called html, and inside it create a new blank document saved as index.html. Open index.html, and inside it, put the following code:

```
<!DOCTYPE html PUBLIC "-//W3C//DTD XHTML 1.0 Strict//EN"
    "http://www.w3.org/TR/xhtml1/DTD/xhtml1-strict.dtd">
<html xmlns="http://www.w3.org/1999/xhtml" xml:lang="en" lang="en">
<head>
    <meta http-equiv="Content-Type" content="text/html; ➥
charset=utf-8"/>
    <title>New Document</title>
</head>
<body>

</body>
</html>
```

Before moving on, let's examine what this markup actually means, piece by piece.

This is the code to identify the doctype of this document:

```
<!DOCTYPE html PUBLIC "-//W3C//DTD XHTML 1.0 Strict//EN"
    "http://www.w3.org/TR/xhtml1/DTD/xhtml1-strict.dtd">
```

What this says is you're using the XHTML 1.0 Strict definition published by the W3C, and the DTD is online at http://www.w3.org/TR/xhtml1/DTD/xhtml1-strict.dtd. That's it. It seems complicated, but it's going to be the same in every XHTML 1.0 Strict document and can simply be copied and pasted in place every time.

This is the opening tag of the <html> element:

```
<html xmlns="http://www.w3.org/1999/xhtml" xml:lang="en" lang="en">
```

Doctype excluded, everything else in the document will be inside this "root" element. The attributes and values here specify the XML namespace (xmlns) as XHTML, the XML language as English, and the document language also as English. Like the <!DOCTYPE> declaration, the opening of the <html> element can also be copied and pasted to every (English) XHTML document. (For XHTML documents whose content is not English, simply change the value of the lang attribute.)

The head

This is the <head> of the document:

```
<head>
    <meta http-equiv="Content-Type" content="text/html; ➥
charset=utf-8"/>
    <title>New Document</title>
</head>
```

A large portion of information goes into the <head>, much more than you have right now. The important distinction here is that none of the information in the <head> of the document actually displays in the web browser window (except for the information in the <title>). The browser will, however, read some of the information and use it in a wide variety of ways.

61

The first element you see inside the <head> element is the (empty) <meta> element. As mentioned earlier, *meta*data is data about data, and this element is used to provide information about the document itself. In this case, it says that the content inside is text/HTML and all the text is encoded using the UTF-8 character set.

> *Is this document XHTML, or is it HTML? Even though the doctype specifies that this is an XHTML document, the <meta> element is telling the browser that it's an HTML document. So, who does the browser listen to? In reality, most of the time the browser doesn't listen to either of these and instead trusts the web server to set the appropriate HTTP headers. If set, most browsers disregard both the doctype declaration and any value set in a <meta> element and parse the markup as whatever the server says it is. Since most web servers are configured to incorrectly tell browsers that XHTML documents are really HTML documents, the designers of XHTML ensured that the markup was entirely compatible with HTML to avoid problems that may arise from this inconsistency.*

The next element is quite possibly one of the most important in the document: the <title> element. It is simply a place to name the content of your document. The content inside the <title> element is normally shown in the title bar of the web browser's window or on the browser tab where the page is being viewed. To change the value of the <title> element, simply change New Document to whatever is most accurate and descriptive of your page content.

The title is also commonly used as the headline in search results from search engines such as Google and Yahoo. When people are searching for content that is on your page and search engines find and show your page as a result, the title of your page is often the only thing they have to decide whether your page is what they want. If you intend your page to be found by people using search engines, pay close attention to the <title> element.

The body

The body is where the meat of your document goes. It's currently empty, but you'll be filling it with the content for your page soon enough.

```
<body>

</body>
```

Lastly, you need to end the <html> element you opened back near the top of the document:

```
</html>
```

Marking up content

Now that you have the shell of your document in place, it's time to start adding real content. There are many elements at your disposal in XHTML, and all of them serve a different purpose. Let's walk through some of the most important, starting with headlines.

As you start adding marked-up content to your XHTML document, pay close attention to the names of the elements you use. Since the purpose of markup is to explicitly label the content to define what kind of building block it is intended to be in the document, all the elements in XHTML are designed to be **semantically rich**, or in other words, to provide *meaning* to the content they define.

Headlines

In almost any document you create, you're going to come across the need for headlines to introduce the sections of text or other content in the document. If you've dealt with any form of publishing in the past, you'll understand that there are different levels of headlines: primary, secondary, tertiary, and so forth. In XHTML, you can use six levels of headlines, and the elements are called <h1> to <h6>. The <h1> tag is for the most important headline in a document, and <h2>, <h3>, and so on, decrease in importance until you get to <h6>, the least important (or most esoteric) headline in the document. Let's take a look at an example:

```
<h1>How I Learned to Ride a Bike</h1>
```

Headlines, as you would expect, cannot be nested *inside* each other, but they can be right next to each other:

```
<h1>Overview of How I Learned to Ride a Bike</h1>
<h2>Step 1: Practice with Training Wheels</h2>
<h2>Step 2: Practice Balancing Without Support</h2>
```

In essence, headlines create an outline for your content, so when you mark up a document with headlines, be sure to think about what kind of outline makes the most sense.

Blocks of text

Most likely, a majority of your document will simply be blocks of text such as paragraphs, block quotations, and other such things. XHTML has elements specifically meant for each of these items. Most are just as easy to apply as headlines. Let's look at an example with a few paragraphs:

```
William Shakespeare was an English poet and playwright. He is widely
regarded as the greatest writer of the English language and the world's
pre-eminent dramatist. His surviving works include approximately
38 plays and 154 sonnets, as well as a variety of other poems.
Shakespeare was also respectively modest about his innovative works,
never truly boasting about his tremendous ability. He is often called
England's national poet and the "Bard of Avon" (or simply "The Bard").

Shakespeare was born and raised in Stratford-upon-Avon, and at age
eighteen married Anne Hathaway, with whom he had three children.
Sometime between 1585 and 1592 Shakespeare moved to London,
where he was an actor, writer, and part-owner of the playing company
the Lord Chamberlain's Men (later known as the King's Men), with which
he found financial success. Shakespeare appears to have retired to
Stratford in 1613, where he passed away three years later at the
age of 52.
```

Shakespeare produced most of his known work between 1590
and 1612. He is one of the few playwrights of his time considered
to have excelled in both tragedy and comedy, and many of his dramas,
including Macbeth, Hamlet and King Lear, are ranked among
the greatest plays of Western literature. His works have greatly
influenced subsequent theatre and literature, through their
innovative use of plot, language, and genre.

You specify to the web browser that these blocks of text are paragraphs by marking them up with the element designed for such content. Since paragraphs of text are such a common occurrence on web pages, the element for them is given the shorthand name <p>:

<p>William Shakespeare was an English poet and playwright. He is widely
regarded as the greatest writer of the English language and the world's
pre-eminent dramatist. His surviving works include approximately 38
plays and 154 sonnets, as well as a variety of other poems. Shakespeare
was also respectively modest about his innovative works, never truly
boasting about his tremendous ability. He is often called England's
national poet and the "Bard of Avon" (or simply "The Bard").</p>

<p>Shakespeare was born and raised in Stratford-upon-Avon, and at age
eighteen married Anne Hathaway, with whom he had three children.
Sometime between 1585 and 1592 Shakespeare moved to London,
where he was an actor, writer, and part-owner of the playing company
the Lord Chamberlain's Men (later known as the King's Men), with which
he found financial success. Shakespeare appears to have retired to
Stratford in 1613, where he passed away three years later at the age of
52.</p>

<p>Shakespeare produced most of his known work between 1590 and 1612.
He is one of the few playwrights of his time considered to have
excelled in both tragedy and comedy, and many of his dramas, including
Macbeth, Hamlet and King Lear, are ranked among the greatest plays of
Western literature. His works have greatly influenced subsequent
theatre and literature, through their innovative use of plot,
language, and genre.</p>

Again, there's nothing complicated here. Simply start the paragraph with the open paragraph tag (<p>) and end it with the close paragraph tag (</p>).

In addition to paragraphs, you can indicate that a selection of text is quoted from another source by using the <blockquote> element (an abbreviation of *block quotation*). Since the only thing that the <blockquote> element indicates is that its content was sourced from somewhere else, inside each <blockquote> element you will still need to use elements such as headlines and paragraphs to mark up the quotation's content. It is by nesting elements in this way that you begin to provide rich meaning to your content. Here's an example of a block quotation that quotes a couple of paragraphs:

```
<blockquote>
    <p>Through the release of atomic energy, your generation has
        brought into the world the most revolutionary force since
        prehistoric man's discovery of fire. This basic force
        of the universe cannot be fitted into the outmoded
        concept of narrow nationalisms.</p>
    <p>For there is no secret and there is no defense; there is no
        possibility of control except through the aroused
        understanding and insistence of the peoples of
        the world. We scientists recognize your inescapable
        responsibility to carry to your fellow citizens an
        understanding of atomic energy and its implication
        for society. In this lies your only security and your
        only hope - you believe that an informed
        citizenry will act for life and not for death.</p>
</blockquote>
```

Most of the time when you're quoting an outside source, you want to cite that source along with the quote. As you might have guessed, there's another XHTML element designed to do just that: the <cite> element. Unlike the <blockquote> element that contains other blocks of text, however, the <cite> element is permitted to contain only other text (and not *blocks* of text). This is what it looks like when you cite the previous quote:

```
<blockquote>
<p>Through the release of atomic energy, your generation has
        brought into the world the most revolutionary force since
        prehistoric man's discovery of fire. This basic force
        of the universe cannot be fitted into the outmoded
        concept of narrow nationalisms.</p>
 <p>For there is no secret and there is no defense; there is no
        possibility of control except through the aroused
        understanding and insistence of the peoples of the
        world. We scientists recognise your inescapable
        responsibility to carry to your fellow citizens an
        understanding of atomic energy and its implication
        for society. In this lies your only security and your
        only hope - you believe that an informed
        citizenry will act for life and not for death.</p>
    <p><cite>Albert Einstein</cite></p>
</blockquote>
```

One good reason why the <cite> element must be placed inside the paragraph here is so that you can more accurately indicate the cited reference. Say, for example, the content you wanted in that last paragraph is "Original Quote by Albert Einstein." Rather than citing that whole sentence, which wouldn't make much sense, you can mark up the reference as such:

```
<p>Original Quote by <cite>Albert Einstein</cite></p>
```

This is much more accurate because it specifically and explicitly isolates the cited reference, Albert Einstein in this example, and thus provides far more meaningful markup.

In a way similar to the way that the <blockquote> element is used, two additional common elements are used to mark up specific blocks of content. First is the code element, and it indicates the enclosed text is, as you would guess, computer code of some sort. (What sort of code isn't typically specified, although you can do so using certain attributes if you'd like.) The code element can be used to mark up large blocks of content or just a single piece of code, or word in a sentence, much like the <cite> tag.

Then there is the <pre> tag, which indicates that the content inside it is *pre*formatted with line breaks, whitespace, tabs, and so on, and it should be rendered the same way in the browser window as it appears in the actual physical markup. The <pre> tag is most often used in combination with the <code> tag to show computer language excerpts or to display certain kinds of formatted text such as poetry.

Grouping content

When marking up a page of content, you will always have groups of elements that are related to each other in some way. Whether it's a headline and a couple paragraphs, a set of lists, or branding and navigation, it makes sense to group and identify these elements together. You can do this using the <div> element, short for *division*. The <div> element is simply a way to group content into related chunks and provides no further semantic meaning (or default visual appearance) to the content.

For example, if you have a headline followed by a few paragraphs of information relating to the headline, you can nest this content inside a <div> element to indicate that form of relationship. It's a very loose relationship, mind you, but it can be an important and useful tool when marking up entire pages of content. The <div> element can also be nested within itself to form more specific associations, using one <div> element to relate content already grouped inside other <div> elements.

```
<div>
    <h1>Overview of How I Learned to Ride a Bike</h1>
    <p>In this short excerpt, I'll describe the various steps I needed to
    take to learn how to ride a bicycle when I was but a young
    lad.</p>
</div>
```

By grouping content into logical chunks like this, you can then effect changes and work with the entire chunk at the same time. But, how do you identify which chunk you want to work with? For that, you need to provide descriptive names to these chunks using the common attributes described in the next section.

Identifying content

There are two **core** attributes defined by the XHTML DTD that can be used to give elements names that you can refer to later (mostly in Cascading Style Sheets, described later in this book). These attributes are id and class, and they can both be used on any element. The id attribute is simply a way to give a unique identity to an element. The class attribute serves a similar purpose, but instead of being unique throughout the document, the same class can be specified any number of times.

A common example of this is to set the id attribute on particular <div> elements to provide a little more meaning to the group. For example, say you have a headline and a paragraph about a featured product on your website:

```
<h1>Swingline Stapler</h1>
<p>This workhorse stapler brings you a solid and consistent performance
that makes it an industry standard. An all-metal die-cast base for
years of durability. A performance driven mechanism with an inner
rail for long-term stapling integrity. Ease of use, refined design,
time-tested features: exactly what you'd expect from America's
#1 stapler.</p>
```

Let's nest these two elements inside a `<div>` element to group them together:

```
<div>
    <h1>Swingline Stapler</h1>
    <p>This workhorse stapler brings you a solid and consistent
        performance that makes it an industry standard. An all-metal
        die-cast base for years of durability. A performance driven
        mechanism with an inner rail for long-term stapling integrity.
        Ease of use, refined design, time-tested features:
        exactly what you'd expect from America's #1 stapler.</p>
</div>
```

Now you can identify that `<div>` element as a "feature" on your web page by using the id attribute:

```
<div id="feature">
    <h1>Swingline Stapler</h1>
    <p>This workhorse stapler brings you a solid and consistent
        performance that makes it an industry standard. An all-metal
        die-cast base for years of durability. A performance driven
        mechanism with an inner rail for long-term stapling integrity.
        Ease of use, refined design, time-tested features:
        exactly what you'd expect from America's #1 stapler.</p>
</div>
```

Since you've used the id attribute, you've also implied that you'll have only one "feature" on your web page at any given time. If this isn't true, and you'll in fact have multiple "features," then you need to use the class attribute instead. You can still use unique values in id attributes to identify individual features if you like.

```
<div class="feature" id="feature-1">
    <h1>Swingline Stapler</h1>
    <p>This workhorse stapler brings you a solid and consistent
        performance that makes it an industry standard. An all-metal
        die-cast base for years of durability. A performance driven
        mechanism with an inner rail for long-term stapling integrity.
        Ease of use, refined design, time-tested features:
        exactly what you'd expect from America's #1 stapler.</p>
</div>
<div class="feature" id="feature-2">
    <h1>Black Standard Stapler</h1>
    <p>Not as exciting as the Swingline Stapler, but a classic stapler
        nonetheless! </p>
</div>
```

Most important, id and class attributes should add meaning to the markup and describe what the content *is*. Avoid id values that are presentational in nature, such as left-column or blue-box. Presentation and styling will be completely handled using CSS, so your markup should remain as semantic as possible.

Links

Of course, the breakthrough that HTML introduced was the ability to allow page authors to create links from one document to another by marking up specific text with an element that created a reference (also called a **pointer** or a **hyperlink**) to another page. The element that was created for this purpose is simply called the <a> element, which stands for the *anchor* element. Authors would place anchors in their pages that each linked to some other page, and those pages in turn would provide their own anchors that pointed at other pages; this was the beginning of hypertextual navigation, or **web surfing**.

Like the <cite> element, anchors are typically parts of a sentence. To actually create a link, the anchor needs to do two things. First, it needs to designate something to be the link itself. This is what the user ends up being able to click. Second, it needs to specify the destination to which the link points. This is where the web browser will take the user when the user clicks the link.

The link itself is created just like any other element, by enclosing a word or phrase (or other item) within the <a> element. The resulting content of the link is referred to as the **anchor text**. Since the destination at which the link points is metadata, it is specified in an attribute of the <a> element. This attribute is called the **hyperlink reference** and is abbreviated to href for short. You can set the href attribute to any URL on the Internet or to any local page on the current site. Let's take the following sentence as an example:

> For more information, visit Wikipedia, the free online encyclopedia.

It would make sense to link part of this sentence to Wikipedia, located online at http://wikipedia.org/. So, use the <a> element, and set the href attribute to the Wikipedia website:

> For more information, visit <a href="http://wikipedia.org/">Wikipedia
> </a>, the free online encyclopedia.

From a technical perspective, this is absolutely correct. The element is in the right place, it's wrapped around the right word, and the attribute is valid. However, there's something more you should think about whenever you create links from one page to another. Forgetting to think about it is one of the most common mistakes that web developers make. What you need to remember to think about is how you can link up as much relevant text as possible.

There are several reasons why this is an important thing to do. First, it provides a larger clickable area for the visitor of the website. Rather than having to hover over a single word, multiple words together provide more room to click, and that makes it easier to use (see Figure 4-1). Second, it creates more descriptive anchor text, and that can help a person decide whether that link is really what they want to visit.

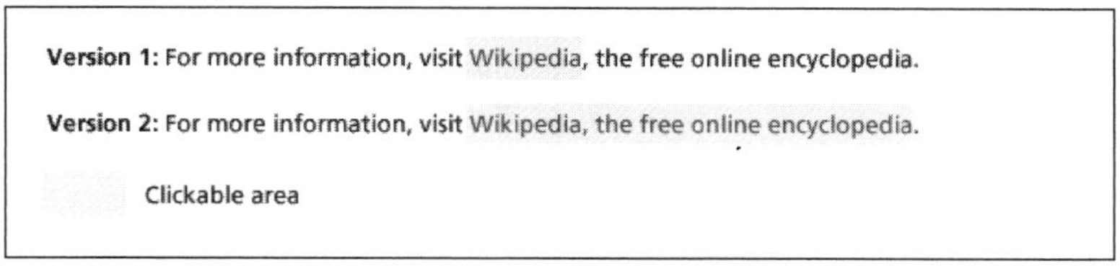

Figure 4-1. An illustration of the clickable area provided by a multiword link compared to linking a single word. Using multiple words gives a visitor a larger "target" on the page for them to click.

How do you know whether the anchor text you've provided is good enough? A good rule of thumb that you can use to test it is that you should always be able to extract all the anchor text of all the links on your page, and without any supporting context, the links should clearly imply their destination. Avoid linking words that have nothing to do with where you're linking to, such as "click here," or just "here." These types of links aren't helpful to anyone. So again, the more descriptive a link's anchor text is, the better.

The href attribute, URLs, and web page addresses

Without links, the Web wouldn't be the Web, so it behooves you to pay a little more attention to the href attribute and the values it can take.

For obvious reasons, the href attribute is always going to contain a hyperlink reference, which is really just a fancy way of saying a web page address or, more formally, a URL. The acronym URL stands for Uniform Resource Locator. For the purposes of this chapter, a **URL** is just a way to generalize the kinds of resources that you can request through a web browser. A web page is one kind of resource, an image is another, and a video is yet another. Most of the time, hyperlink references refer only to web pages. All URLs, including those that specify web page addresses, can be written in three distinct ways. Each of these ways is a valid value for the href attribute.

The most verbose form of a web page address is called a **fully qualified URL**. Fully qualified URLs are so named because they are composed of all three pieces of a URL: the **scheme** (also called the **protocol**), the **domain name** (also called the **host name**), and the **path**. In the example link to Wikipedia in the previous section, the scheme was http:, the domain name was //wikipedia.org, and the path was the trailing / (which means "the home page").

Some parts of URLs are considered optional, which means that if they are omitted, they're filled in according to the current context. For instance, in fully qualified URLs, the scheme portion is optional and is filled in with whatever scheme the current page uses. So if your web page, like most of the web pages out there, uses the http: scheme and you link to Wikipedia, then http://wikipedia.org/ and //wikipedia.org/ are identical. On the other hand, if your web page uses the https: scheme, then a link to //wikipedia.org/ will end up linking to https://wikipedia.org/ instead.

Another way to specify a URL is called an **absolute** link. Absolute links require that only the path portion of the address is to be placed in the href value but that the path begins with the website's root, or initial forward slash (/). These are called absolute links because they specify the web page's full path from the root of the website (typically the home page) to their current location.

69

The final method is called a **relative** link, and like absolute links, relative links also require that only the path portion of the address be present. Unlike an absolute link, however, a relative link *must not* begin with an initial forward slash. Relative links *always* use the context of the current location of your web page to infer the complete URL, so they are by definition restricted to always link to pages hosted at the same domain name. Relative links can be a little harder to grasp, so let's look at a few examples.

A website's structure is just like the files and folders on your computer, such as the structure shown in Figure 4-2. If you're currently viewing a file called overview.html and you wanted to link to messages.html, you could simply place messages.html in the href value like this:

```
<a href="messages.html">Messages</a>
```

Figure 4-2. The file/folder hierarchy of a website is just like the file/folder hierarchy on your computer. Similar pages can be grouped together into folders, and linking can occur between files and across folder levels.

If you wanted to link to john.html in the people folder, you would have to add the folder (also called the **directory**) before the file, with a forward slash between the folder name and file name:

```
<a href="people/john.html">Messages</a>
```

Both of these are relative links that link to different pages on the same website, relative to their own positions. Relative links are handy because they don't need to be updated if the structure of some part of your website changes. They need to be updated only if the file that they reference (or if they themselves) moves.

What if you're currently looking at john.html in the people folder and you want to link back to the overview.html page above it? In this instance, you need to use a special symbol to indicate you want to move up one folder level before looking for a particular file. That symbol is two periods, which just means "the folder above me." Like all folders, you then follow this symbol with a forward slash:

```
<a href="../overview.html">Messages</a>
```

This would tell the browser to go up one level in the website tree and then load the overview.html page. This ../ sequence can be used multiple times if you need to go two or more levels up.

It's almost always best to link to files on your own site with relative or absolute links as opposed to fully qualified ones. This saves you from having to type your own domain name over and over again (which makes your HTML files that much shorter), and it makes your site more portable in case your domain name changes in the future.

Emphasis

When working with almost any kind of content, some parts of that content will need to be emphasized more than others. For instance, many times when marking up a document, you need to make words **bold** or *italic*. Back in the old days before web developers realized the importance of having semantically rich and meaningful HTML documents, this was most commonly done using the <b> and <i> elements. Wrap a word or phrase in the <b> element, and it would render as bold in the browser window. That seems simple enough, right? But let's analyze this for a minute.

What does "bolding" some part of a sentence really mean? It *doesn't* mean "make it bigger"—that's just how it ends up looking. What it means is "make it stand out." The key concept, of course, is that when you think of making something bold, all you really want to change is its presentation, or how it looks. Well, as you and I know, thanks to being the enlightened semantic web developer that you are, markup should be about what the content *means* and not what it looks like.

In modern HTML and XHTML, you typically replace all occurrences of the <b> element with the <strong> element, which simply means "strong emphasis." Similarly, you replace all occurrences of the <i> element with the <em> element, meaning simply "emphasis." When you enclose words or phrases inside the <em> element, the browser automatically defaults to italicizing the text. Similarly, the browser defaults to bolding words or phrases inside the <strong> element.

Be sure to use the <em> and <strong> tags only when you mean to emphasize text. If you're looking to achieve italic or bold on text without meaning to emphasize it, say a book title, stylize the text appropriately using CSS (discussed in future chapters). Don't put <em> or <strong> tags around text *just* because you want it to be italicized or bold. Be sure to keep your markup meaningful and accurate.

Lists

Lists are another common item in publishing. Using XHTML, you have three different kinds of lists: ordered, unordered, and definition lists. Ordered lists are meant to itemize sequential items and so are prefixed by numbers, in order, by default, whereas items in an unordered list are meant to itemize things that don't imply a sequence, so they're prefixed by bullets by default. Definition lists are meant to hold glossary terms or other title and description items in a list, so they're not prefixed by anything at all by default.

The elements you use to define these lists are <ol> for ordered lists, <ul> for unordered lists, and <dl> for definition lists. In each case, the only children these elements are allowed to have are the appropriate list items. So, let's start building a list.

Unordered and ordered lists

For this example, let's mark up a grocery list:

```
Milk
Eggs
Butter
Flour
Sugar
Chocolate Chips
```

Here, an unordered list makes perfect sense because the order you buy these items in really makes no difference. If this were not a shopping list but, say, a list of directions for making chocolate brownies, then perhaps the order you add these items to your mixing bowl would matter, and an ordered list would be more appropriate. But let's stick with your shopping example and add the <ul> element to your list:

```
<ul>
    Milk
    Eggs
    Butter
    Flour
    Sugar
    Chocolate Chips
</ul>
```

So, you have all the items in your list inside the appropriate element. Next, each item of an unordered (or ordered) list must be contained within a list item element, defined with <li>. Let's insert the <li> elements into your unordered list:

```
<ul>
    <li>Milk</li>
    <li>Eggs</li>
    <li>Butter</li>
    <li>Flour</li>
    <li>Sugar</li>
    <li>Chocolate Chips</li>
</ul>
```

Now your list is complete. If you were to look at this in a browser, it would look something like Figure 4-3.

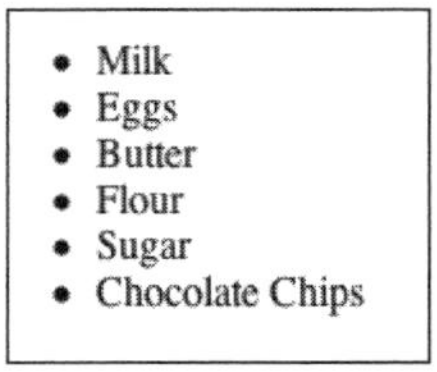

- Milk
- Eggs
- Butter
- Flour
- Sugar
- Chocolate Chips

Figure 4-3. A simple example of an unordered list

Great! Aided by your shopping list, you go out and gather your ingredients for chocolate brownies. When you are ready to mark up your brownie recipe, however, you find out that these were actually put in this order for a reason (that's the order you need to add them to the mixing bowl). Marking that up is as simple as replacing your <ul> element with an <ol> element. The <li> elements work inside both ordered and unordered lists, and the browser will render the appropriate prefix to each list item.

So, let's see the markup for your newly ordered list:

```
<ol>
    <li>Milk</li>
    <li>Eggs</li>
    <li>Butter</li>
    <li>Flour</li>
    <li>Sugar</li>
    <li>Chocolate Chips</li>
</ol>
```

And in a browser it looks like Figure 4-4.

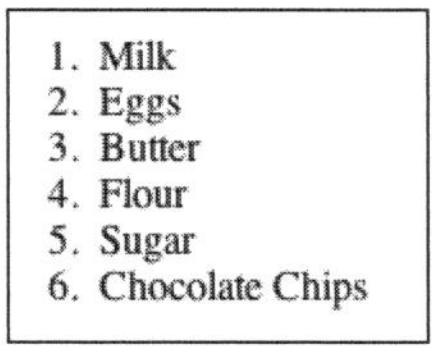

1. Milk
2. Eggs
3. Butter
4. Flour
5. Sugar
6. Chocolate Chips

Figure 4-4. An ordered list displayed in a web browser

Notice that you didn't need to put the numbers in the list at all. The browser does that on its own. This turns out to be especially convenient when you need to add items to the top or middle of an ordered list. There is no need to redo the numbering yourself, because it's handled automatically. This is one example of the power that can be harnessed by using semantic, meaningful markup.

It's interesting to see how you can start to use multiple elements in concert, if needed, to continue encoding semantic meaning to your list's content. For instance, if you wanted to emphasize the text inside a particular list item, you could nest the <em> element inside the <li> element like this:

```
<li><em>Chocolate Chips</em></li>
```

Similarly, you could link a particular list item to another page on the Internet:

```
<li><a href="http://www.aeb.org/">Eggs</a></li>
```

You could even, if you wanted, emphasize the text that's being linked:

```
<li><em><a href="http://www.aeb.org/">Eggs</a></em></li>
```

Lists are also able to be nested *inside* each other to create a list of lists. For example, you could expand your shopping list into item categories and their actual ingredients:

```
<ul>
    <li>Baking Ingredients
        <ul>
            <li>Milk</li>
            <li>Eggs</li>
            <li>Butter</li>
            <li>Flour</li>
            <li>Sugar</li>
            <li>Chocolate Chips</li>
        </ul>
    </li>
    <li>Cereal
        <ul>
            <li>Fruity Pebbles</li>
            <li>Cheerios</li>
            <li>Cinnamon Toast Crunch</li>
        </ul>
    </li>
</ul>
```

What you have here is an unordered list nested inside a list item of another unordered list. When viewed in a browser, you see the results look something like Figure 4-5.

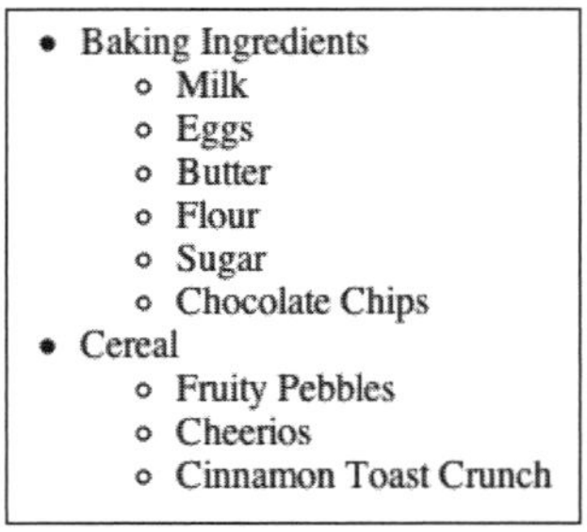

- Baking Ingredients
  - Milk
  - Eggs
  - Butter
  - Flour
  - Sugar
  - Chocolate Chips
- Cereal
  - Fruity Pebbles
  - Cheerios
  - Cinnamon Toast Crunch

Figure 4-5. Lists can be nested within one another in order to create different levels of organization.

By default, most web browsers will automatically switch the bullet styles of the inner lists for you when you create nested lists to make it easier to tell them apart.

Many elements in XHTML can be nested inside the same elements (like these lists). Some, however, cannot. These rules are all defined in XHTML's Document Type Definition, although oftentimes the best rule of thumb is just to think about whether it makes sense for the element to be found inside another element of the same kind. Lists, as you can see, make perfect sense. Paragraphs, however, do not. What sense would it make to put a paragraph inside another paragraph? Not very much at all. (But you can certainly put a paragraph inside a list item.)

Definition lists

Let's quickly examine how to mark up definition lists, because they are slightly different from ordered and unordered lists. Instead of the single `<li>` element for the list items, you have two elements to work with inside definition lists. These are `<dt>` for the definition's title and `<dd>` for the definition's description.

```
<dl>
    <dt>body</dt>
    <dd>Holds content of the document</dd>
    <dt>head</dt>
    <dd>Holds additional information about the document</dd>
    <dt>html</dt>
    <dd>Root element of the document</dd>
</dl>
```

You can see the basic premise is what you're already used to: a `<dt>` element wrapping the definition's title followed by a `<dd>` element wrapping the description, all held together by being enclosed inside a definition list. Browsers will render this markup to look something like Figure 4-6.

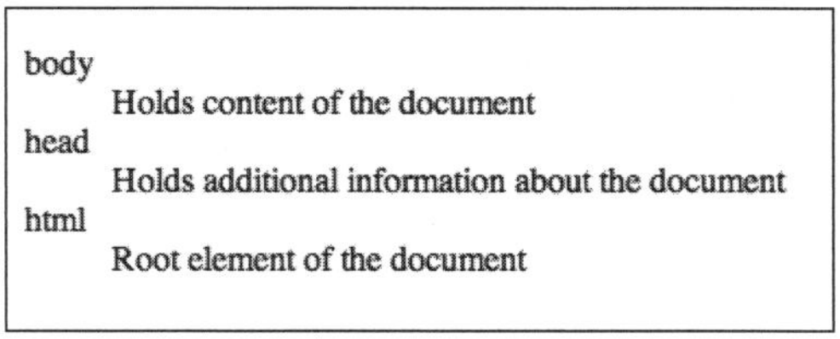

```
body
        Holds content of the document
head
        Holds additional information about the document
html
        Root element of the document
```

Figure 4-6. The definition list groups definition terms (<dt>) and definition descriptions (<dd>) together through indenting.

Images

So far, you've explored various kinds of elements that deal solely with text. However, web pages can be a lot more interesting than that. Let's find out how you can add images to your pages next.

When placing images in a document, you use the <img> element. Image elements are empty elements because they will be replaced with the image you're referencing. However, to work properly, you need to tell the web browser where to find the image you'd like to insert, as well as give it a brief textual description of what the image is.

These two pieces of metadata are specified inside the two required attributes that <img> elements hold. First, the src attribute points to the actual image file to be loaded in place of the <img> element. The same rules apply to the src attribute here as the href attribute on the <a> element. Relative or absolute, the src attribute gives the browser the URL of where to look for the image.

The second attribute is alt, short for the *alternate text* for the image. (You might also hear people calling this the image's **alternative text** or **alt text**.) It's used to describe what the image is and what meaning it has in the document. Here's an example (as displayed in Figure 4-7):

```
<img src="/images/moose.jpg" alt="The Majestic Moose" />
```

Figure 4-7. Although the content of your images may vary, we can probably all agree that being able to add images to pages is an important feature.

Recall that since this is an empty element, it contains no other content and thus is opened and closed with a single tag. The attributes here indicate that you want to load in the moose.jpg file found in the images folder relative to the website's root and that you want to provide the alternate text of "The Majestic Moose."

The src attribute's purpose is obvious, but the alt attribute's purpose isn't. Usually, the alternate text doesn't even show up on the page when you look at it in your web browser. So, what's it there for?

The alternate text actually provides several very important features. First, in keeping with the semantic importance of markup, it's what lets the image provide some meaning to the document. In the previous example, if this were a page about wildlife, then the picture of the moose would likely be considered part of the content of the page. Without the alternate text in the <img> element, the image would be essentially "meaningless," and the document would lose some of its semantic value.

On the other hand, if the rest of the page was about grocery shopping and the picture of the moose was just there for visual ambiance, then the image is probably superfluous and might be considered "not content." In this case, you would leave the alternate text completely blank to indicate that the image is used only for visual reasons and shouldn't be considered an important part of the content of the page:

```
<img src="/images/moose.jpg" alt="" />
```

Note that you still need to include the alt attribute in the <img> element code but that the value of the alt attribute is missing (or **null**). Determining what images on your page should be "real content" and which ones shouldn't is part of the *art* of web development. There often isn't a clear or right answer, so you simply need to use your best judgment.

Assuming the picture does add some value to the page, then the alternate text also helps out in a few additional concrete ways. First, even though it does not show up on the page in the normal sense, many web browsers will show the alternate text for an image if you hover your cursor over the image for a few seconds or if you give the image keyboard focus. You can think of it like a transient caption; it's there if the visitor to your web page requests to see it, but it's otherwise hidden.

Of course, some visitors to your website won't be able to *see* at all. These visitors might be humans with visual impairments or they might be machines, such as Google's search engine spider (googlebot). For these visitors, the presence (or absence) of the alternate text is more important than the image itself.

Visually impaired people browsing the Web often do so with a special kind of web browser that reads the content of web pages aloud to them. These programs are called **screen readers**. When a screen reader happens upon an image in your document, it uses the alternate text to describe what the image shows. Providing good alternate text for your images is crucial to making your web pages accessible and understandable to these visitors.

Similarly, when Google or Yahoo is reading the markup of your page, good alternate text in your <img> elements can help them make sense of what the purpose and content of the image is, allowing them to be more effective in ranking your web pages appropriately in their search result listings. Generally, the better your alternate text describes the content in your images, the higher your search result rankings will be.

Finally, if for any reason the image you've told the web browser to include in the page can't be found (the image file itself) or loaded, most web browsers will replace the <img> element with the text of the alt attribute. This provides a sort of contingency plan to help ensure that visitors to your website get what they came for, even if they can't get it in the preferred form. Similar techniques are used all the time in web development, and they're collectively called **graceful degradation**.

When using images on your sites, be mindful of how many you have put on each page, how big they are, and what purpose they serve. Excessive use of images will make a page slow to load, and it might also be visually disruptive. Compared to XHTML, images are extremely large. On most pages, the bulk of time it takes to download that page is caused by its images.

Tables

When you have to mark up data that is best presented in rows and columns (**tabular data**), it calls for the <table> element. Some common examples of tabular data are calendars (where rows are weeks and columns are the different days of the week) or comparison charts. When you think of tabular data like this, you often think of spreadsheets and all the riveting data that goes along with them.

Fortunately, marking up tabular data is relatively easy, and XHTML gives you plenty of semantic elements to organize your data appropriately. Let's start with some example data and walk through the process of marking it up with semantic XHTML elements (see Table 4-1).

Table 4-1. Simple Table Example

First Name	Last Name	Birthday
George	Washington	February 22, 1732
Abraham	Lincoln	February 12, 1809

Table 4-1 shows the first and last names of two American presidents, George Washington and Abraham Lincoln, along with their birthdays. First things first: let's create a table in your XHTML document to contain this data. You do this with open and close <table> tags to create the containing <table> element:

```
<table>
</table>
```

Next, let's add the first row. Table rows are defined with the <tr> element:

```
<table>
    <tr>
    </tr>
</table>
```

This row has three distinct cells. XHTML table cells are marked up using the <td> element, which stands for *table data*:

```
<table>
    <tr>
        <td>First Name</td>
        <td>Last Name</td>
        <td>Birthday</td>
    </tr>
</table>
```

You now have a table with one row and three cells in that row. But you can do even better, since this row is obviously a header that introduces what data you'll find in the rows that follow. Using XHTML, you can use the <thead> element to mark up your header data and indicate that this row has this special purpose:

```
<table>
    <thead>
        <tr>
            <td>First Name</td>
            <td>Last Name</td>
            <td>Birthday</td>
        </tr>
    </thead>
</table>
```

Just as this introductory row is special, if you look closely, you'll notice that each of these three cells are special: they are column headings, not ordinary table data. To indicate this in your markup, you'll replace the <td> elements with <th> elements, meaning table heading. The <th> element is used for any table cell that is a heading for either a column or a row (column in your case) to differentiate it from regular table data.

```
<table>
    <thead>
        <tr>
            <th>First Name</th>
            <th>Last Name</th>
            <th>Birthday</th>
        </tr>
    </thead>
</table>
```

Now that your header is in place, you can start adding the bulk of the table's data. Just like your header data was enclosed in a <thead> element, you will wrap your body data in a <tbody> element.

```
<table>
    <thead>
        <tr>
            <th>First Name</th>
            <th>Last Name</th>
            <th>Birthday</th>
        </tr>
    </thead>
    <tbody>
    </tbody>
</table>
```

To insert your individual data cells, you use the <td> element, with each row put inside a separate <tr> element as before:

```
<table>
    <thead>
        <tr>
            <th>First Name</th>
            <th>Last Name</th>
            <th>Birthday</th>
        </tr>
    </thead>
    <tbody>
        <tr>
            <td>George</td>
            <td>Washington</td>
            <td>February 22, 1732</td>
        </tr>
        <tr>
            <td>Abraham</td>
            <td>Lincoln</td>
            <td>February 12, 1809</td>
        </tr>
    </tbody>
</table>
```

When viewed in a browser, this XHTML table will look something like Figure 4-8.

First Name	Last Name	Birthday
George	Washington	February 22, 1732
Abraham	Lincoln	February 12, 1809

Figure 4-8. A minimal table with column headings rendered in a web browser

An important thing to note about XHTML tables is that using this minimal markup, columns are created by implication based upon the number of individual table data cells that exist in each row. With three table data cells per table row element, you create a three-column table. If you add a table data cell to the rows, you'll have made a table with four columns, and so on. Using certain attributes described in just a moment, you can modify this behavior slightly, but the important thing to remember is that (in most cases), only table *rows* are structurally grouped together in the markup, whereas the columns are usually *implied*.

> *Astute readers will point out that there is, in fact, a way to explicitly label columns using XHTML markup. The way this is done is by defining a set of <col> elements, optionally contained within one or more colgroup elements before the start of the table data. Although semantically rich and mostly harmless to old browsers, these elements aren't widely implemented in the real world and so are considered to be outside the scope of this book. Implementing them in this example is left as an exercise to the reader.*

Before you call your table complete, however, you'll add a few more things that will make it truly exemplary of semantic XHTML markup. By design, a data table is a very visual element that relates data in columns and rows so a viewer can grasp a complicated concept or more easily understand a large data set. For much the same reasons that you added the alt attribute to the <img> element, you'll provide some additional data about this table in text form.

First, you'll add a <caption> element, which is (obviously) meant to be a caption for the table. You can use this to provide a title for the table or perhaps an overview of its purpose. In this example, you could use "American Presidents" as the caption. Next, you'll add a summary attribute on the <table> element. A table's summary attribute is meant to hold more detail about what information is actually displayed in the table, and, just like the alt attribute on <img> elements, the summary is read aloud to visually impaired users who are browsing your web page with the aid of a screen reader. Let's see this in code:

```
<table summary="This table compares the first name, last name, and
        birth date of George Washington and
        Abraham Lincoln.">
    <caption>American Presidents</caption>
    <thead>
        <tr>
            <th>First Name</th>
            <th>Last Name</th>
            <th>Birthday</th>
        </tr>
    </thead>
    <tbody>
        <tr>
            <td>George</td>
            <td>Washington</td>
            <td>February 22, 1732</td>
        </tr>
        <tr>
            <td>Abraham</td>
            <td>Lincoln</td>
            <td>February 12, 1809</td>
        </tr>
    </tbody>
</table>
```

Tables can have as many rows and columns as you'd like. As mentioned earlier, the number of <th> or <td> elements inside the <tr> element(s) dictates the number of columns in the table, and the number of <tr> elements dictates the number of rows.

Both <th> and <td> elements accept attributes called rowspan and colspan. These attributes indicate how many rows or columns this particular cell spans. The rowspan attribute, as you can infer, describes how many rows the particular cell spans, and colspan defines how many columns the cell spans. Let's take a look at an example using your "American Presidents" table.

Instead of having the individual header cells for the first name and the last name, let's merge those into one title cell called Name. Similarly, let's take both birthday cells and merge them into one with new content that merely states "A long time ago":

```
<table summary="This table compares the first name, last name,
        and birth date of George Washington and Abraham Lincoln.">
    <caption>American Presidents</caption>
    <thead>
        <tr>
            <th colspan="2">Name</th>
            <th>Birthday</th>
        </tr>
    </thead>
    <tbody>
        <tr>
            <td>George</td>
            <td>Washington</td>
            <td rowspan="2">A long time ago</td>
        </tr>
        <tr>
            <td>Abraham</td>
            <td>Lincoln</td>
        </tr>
    </tbody>
</table>
```

You'll notice in the markup that you need only two <th> elements now because the first one is taking the place of two of them. Similarly, you don't need the third <td> for the birthday column in the last row because it's being filled by the <td> from the previous row by the rowspan value.

Let's see what this looks like in the markup. As shown in Figure 4-9, we shaded the two cell groups you modified so you can see what change took place, though the shade wouldn't show up in the actual browser window.

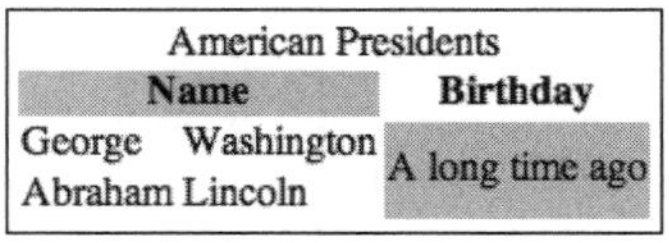

Figure 4-9. Cells in a table can be merged together to span multiple rows or columns.

As you can see, tables provide a lot of flexibility and can be a great way to display certain kinds of data. Before the advent of Cascading Style Sheets in modern web development, however, tables were more often used to control the visual layout of a web page, which polluted the document's semantics and made web designers bend over backward to try to find clever ways of making their designs fit into the grid-like structure dictated by tables.

Even today, some websites that simply *have* to look right in old browsers use tables for this purpose. If you can avoid doing this, great, but if not, then remember this if you remember nothing else: include an empty summary attribute on the <table> element. Just as you would provide an empty alt attribute value on an image that serves no semantic purpose, so too must you declare a meaningless table if you use one!

Forms

Filling out forms online is a great way to glean information from your visitors or provide enhanced service to them. Although the scripts that actually receive and process such form data are beyond the scope of this book, we'll next discuss how some of the various form elements work in XHTML markup.

The first thing you'll need in any form you create is the <form> element:

```
<form>
</form>
```

<form> elements accept many attributes, but only one, the action attribute, is required. The action attribute is similar to the href attribute in the <a> element. It specifies a particular URL where the script that processes the form data can be found. Let's set your example form to be processed at /path/to/script:

```
<form action="/path/to/script">
</form>
```

When this form is submitted, it will send the browser to the /path/to/script page along with all the data from your form. Right now, however, there's no data to be sent because you haven't defined any fields to fill in. So, let's add some fields to this form.

A <form> element is a lot like a <blockquote> in the sense that it can have only certain child elements. For simple forms, you can use the <p> or <div> elements that you've already seen used before, and you can place all the form's controls into these elements. However, since you're about to build a relatively complex form, you'll use the XHTML element specifically designed to group form controls into groups: the <fieldset> element.

The <fieldset> element, which (as you might expect) defines a set of related form fields, is a lot like the <div> element. Both elements are used to group related elements together in a single chunk of code. Unlike <div>s, however, <fieldset> elements can contain a special element, called legend, that gives the <fieldset> element a name that is visible to your web page's visitors. You might do well to think of this element in the same way you might think of the <caption> element for tables.

With the <fieldset> element and its legend in your form, your markup now looks like this:

```
<form action="/path/to/script">
    <fieldset>
        <legend>Personal Information</legend>
    </fieldset>
</form>
```

The most common kind of form field is a simple text field where users can type something. These, and most other kinds of form fields, are added to forms by defining <input> elements. Form <input> elements can be of a number of different types, such as text fields, check boxes, or radio buttons. The kind of form control any particular <input> element becomes is specified by the value of its type attribute.

If a type attribute isn't specified, the default of type="text" is inferred. For example, this is how you might ask for the visitor's e-mail address using a text input field inside your form:

```
<form action="/path/to/script">
    <fieldset>
        <legend>Personal Information</legend>
        <input type="text" name="email" />
    </fieldset>
</form>
```

There are two things you should notice about the <input> element used here. First, it's an empty element, like an <img>. Second, you've also included an attribute called name, and you've given it a value of email. All form elements that need to provide some data to processing scripts need to have a name attribute with a value. This is the name that the processing script will use to refer to the data in this <form> element after the form has been submitted. If you don't provide a name, then the processing script won't be able to see any of the data in the form element.

A form like the one in the previous code listing might look like Figure 4-10 in a web browser.

Figure 4-10. A very simple form example using a field set and a single text input box

You can see that the name attribute isn't displayed anywhere (nor should it be), so there's currently no easy way for the visitor to know what they're expected to type into that text field. To give the text field a name that human visitors can use to refer to it, you have to use the <label> element.

You can place <label> elements anywhere in the form—they don't have to appear right next to the input field that they label. For this reason, each <label> element needs to be uniquely associated with an input field in some way other than proximity. You've already learned how to uniquely identify elements on a web page using the id attribute, so let's first uniquely identify this form field with the name email_field:

```
<input type="text" name="email" id="email_field" />
```

Now that you have a unique identifier to refer to this input field with, you can add the <label> element to your form. You'll add it directly in front of the <input> element for simplicity's sake, but again, you technically could have placed it anywhere inside the <form> element. When using a <label> element, the text inside the element should describe the field that the element labels (like the anchor text does for links), and the value of the for attribute should match the id of the field being labeled. In code, that might look something like this:

```
<label for="email_field">Email Address</label>
<input type="text" name="email" id="email_field" />
```

If you look at this in a browser window, you see that you now have something usable by a visitor (see Figure 4-11).

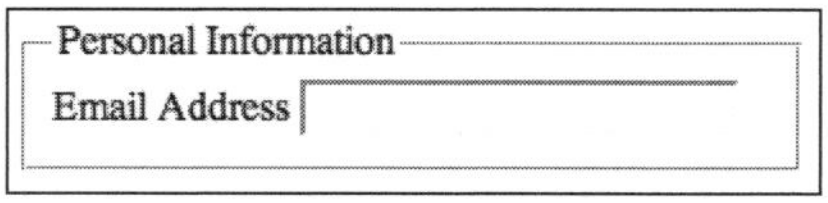

Figure 4-11. We've added a label here so that the user actually knows what's being requested (an e-mail address).

Another possible type value for the <input> element is checkbox. A check box is a simple "yes or no" input, and it is nearly the same as the text field's <input> element in code. Let's use a check box to ask somebody whether they are currently enrolled in a college or university. You'll simply add the check box and all its attributes, as well as a descriptive label for what your check box is asking, after the text field for the visitor's e-mail address:

```
<form action="/path/to/script">
    <fieldset>
        <legend>Personal Information</legend>
        <label for="email_field">Email Address</label>
        <input type="text" name="email" id="email_field" />
        <input type="checkbox" name="enrolled" id="enrolled_field" ➥
value="1" />
        <label for="enrolled_field">I am currently enrolled in a
        college or university</label>
    </fieldset>
</form>
```

One of the attributes you've added to the check box is the value attribute (careful, this is an *attribute* named value). The value of the value attribute will be sent to the processing script *only* if the box is checked. Here you've used 1, a simple approach to indicate that "yes, this box was checked on the form."

Now that you've added the check box and its appropriate label, take a look in the browser to see how that would look (see Figure 4-12).

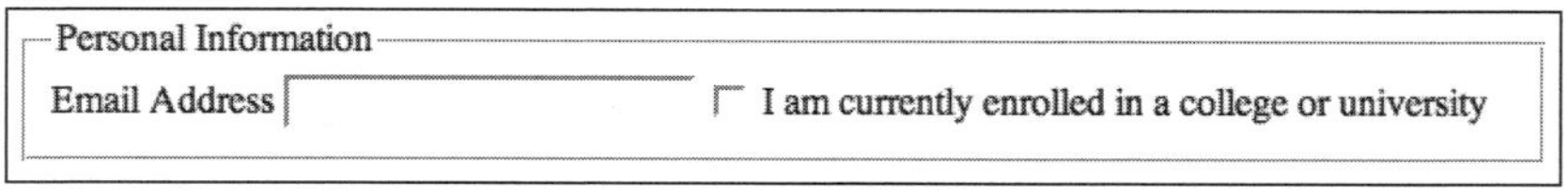

Figure 4-12. The revised form with a check box added

It's certainly a start. Next, you'd probably need some way to separate these elements so the browser knows to show them on different lines. If you think about it, what you're beginning to create is a list of inputs for the user to fill out. In this case, these inputs are in a particular order. It sounds like an ordered list fits this scenario perfectly. Let's nest the inputs and labels in list items and nest the list items in an ordered list element:

```
<form action="/path/to/script">
    <fieldset>
        <legend>Personal Information</legend>
        <ol>
            <li>
                <label for="email_field">Email Address</label>
                <input type="text" name="email" id="email_field" />
            </li>
            <li>
                <input type="checkbox" name="enrolled" ➥
                    id="enrolled_field" value="1" />
                    <label for="enrolled_field">I am currently
                        enrolled in a college or university</label>
            </li>
        </ol>
    </fieldset>
</form>
```

There's one other attribute that you can use for a check box, should you want it to be checked when the visitor first loads the form. In this case, perhaps a majority of your visitors *will* be enrolled in some college or university. All you need to do to make this happen is specify a checked attribute with a value of checked. (That's not a typo. The name of the attribute and the value it expects is supposed to be the same.) The visitor can still uncheck the box, but in some situations it might prove easier to have the field checked in the first place. Let's see the markup for the check box when it's checked by default.

```
<input type="checkbox" name="enrolled" id="enrolled_field"
            value="1" checked="checked" />
<label for="enrolled_field">I am currently enrolled in a
                            college or university</label>
```

Another input type that XHTML forms permit you to use are radio buttons. A radio button is similar to a check box except there are multiple options from which a user can choose, and only one can ultimately be selected. Radio buttons are thus almost always found in sets that ask the user to select one of a small number of items.

Each radio button is represented as an <input> element with its type set to radio. You associate multiple radio buttons as belonging to the same set by giving each one the same value in its name attribute. Each radio button's value attribute, however, should be unique among the radio buttons in the set. Like check boxes, each radio button needs a label, so each radio button's id attribute should also be unique (in the entire document, not just the set of radio buttons or even just the <form> element they're in).

To put this into the example, let's ask the visitor their favorite color. You'll give them four colors to select from: blue, red, yellow, and green. While marking up this question for your form, you can immediately notice that you have yet another list. This time, though, the items are not in any particular order, so you'll use an unordered list.

You will also need to introduce the question, because now your <label> elements are labeling the actual choices instead of the question at hand. You'll simply do that with some text before you start the unordered list.

```
<form action="/path/to/script">
    <fieldset>
        <legend>Personal Information</legend>
        <ol>
            <li>
                <label for="email_field">Email Address</label>
                <input type="text" name="email" id="email_field" />
            </li>
            <li>
                <input type="checkbox" name="enrolled" ➥
                    id="enrolled_field" value="1" ➥
                    checked="checked" />
                <label for="enrolled_field">I am currently enrolled in
                    a college or university</label>
            </li>
            <li>What is your favorite color?
                <ul>
                    <li>
                        <input type="radio" name="favorite_color"
                            id="favorite_color_blue" value="blue" />
                        <label for="favorite_color_blue">Blue</label>
                    </li>
                    <li>
                        <input type="radio" name="favorite_color"
                            id="favorite_color_red" value="red" />
                        <label for="favorite_color_red">Red</label>
                    </li>
                    <li>
                        <input type="radio" name="favorite_color"
                            id="favorite_color_yellow" value="yellow" />
                        <label for="favorite_color_yellow">Yellow
                            </label>
                    </li>
                    <li>
                        <input type="radio" name="favorite_color"
                            id="favorite_color_green" value="green" />
                        <label for="favorite_color_green">Green</label>
                    </li>
                </ul>
            </li>
        </ol>
    </fieldset>
</form>
```

Looking at the browser again, you can see that your form is working as expected (see Figure 4-13).

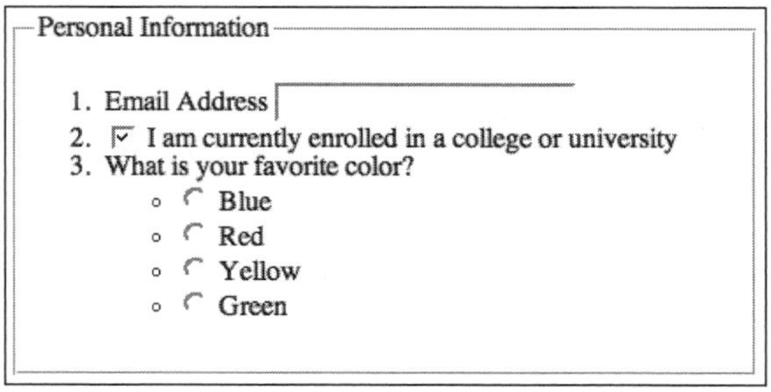

Figure 4-13. The radio buttons you've added provide your visitor with a set of four options from which they can pick only one.

Next, let's add two more form fields asking for input from your web page's visitors. For these last two datum, let's ask for your visitor's time zone and provide a free-form area in which they can type whatever text they like. Since these two items are somewhat unrelated to the previous three questions, let's group them separately from the previous form items by using a new `<fieldset>` element.

To let the visitor select their time zone, you could display a set of radio buttons in a list just as you've done for their favorite color. However, radio buttons take up a lot of space. Furthermore, there are dozens of time zones in the world. If you used radio buttons again, your form would be gigantic.

Instead, let's use a different form control that XHTML makes available: a drop-down list. This control is defined by the `<select>` element and the `<option>` element in tandem, much like a regular ordered or unordered list.

```
<label for="timezone_field">Time zone</label>
<select name="timezone" id="timezone_field">
    <option>-5</option>
    <option>-6</option>
    <option>-7</option>
    <option>-8</option>
</select>
```

With this markup, the user is given four options to select their time zone from: –5, –6, –7, or –8. These are actually the number of hours offset from UTC time of the eastern United States through to the Pacific coast. It's how computers most often tell time (by keeping track of everything in UTC time and then calculating offsets per time zone), but it's not how people think of their time zones. So, using the value attribute for each option element, let's give the computers what they expect *and* show the human visitors values that are more comfortable for them to read:

```
<label for="timezone_field">Time zone</label>
<select name="timezone" id="timezone_field">
    <option value="-5">Eastern</option>
    <option value="-6">Central</option>
    <option value="-7">Mountain</option>
    <option value="-8">Pacific</option>
</select>
```

87

Now, when the user selects Eastern as their time zone, the processing script that sees this form will see the value −5.

You can place as many <option> elements inside <select> elements as you like. However, when there are a lot of options, or the options are representative of different categories, it makes sense to group these options. For that, you use the <optgroup> element, just as if you were using <div> or <fieldset>. Let's add more time zones to your list, but let's organize them inside <optgroup> elements so that the categorization is clearly obvious:

```
<label for="timezone_field">Time zone</label>
<select name="timezone" id="timezone_field">
    <optgroup label="Mainland America">
        <option value="-5">Eastern</option>
        <option value="-6">Central</option>
        <option value="-7">Mountain</option>
        <option value="-8">Pacific</option>
    </optgroup>
    <optgroup label="Outlying States">
        <option value="-9">Alaskan</option>
        <option value="-10">Hawaiian</option>
    </optgroup>
</select>
```

Notice that here inside the <optgroup> element you're using a label *attribute* to give a name to your group of <option> elements. Be careful not to confuse this with the <label> *element* used to label the entire <select> element.

As a final touch, let's add that free-form area of text where you encourage your visitors to send you their comments. This is accomplished with a <textarea> element and is one of the simplest form controls to use. It has just two differences. First, unlike most of the other form controls you've seen, the <textarea> element does not need a value attribute because its content becomes its value. Second, it requires two new attributes, rows and cols, to indicate its default height and width, respectively. (This sizing can later be overridden with CSS.) A <textarea>'s markup might look like this:

```
<label for="comments_field">Comments</label>
<textarea name="comments" id="comments_field" rows="6"
    cols="65"></textarea>
```

At long last you have your form controls all set up to collect input from the user. There's only one thing you're missing: a way for the visitor to actually submit the form to the processing script. For that, you need to use one more type of <input> element: the submit type. This type of <input> element will create a button that the user can activate that submits the form.

Typically, when using elements that create form controls that operate on the form (such as a submit button), you can skip specifying a label for that element since the form control itself effectively serves that purpose. Since you're not using a <label> element for your submit button, you don't have to use an id attribute either, so your element is really quite simple.

```
<input type="submit" value="Submit this Form" />
```

Now your visitors will be able to click the Submit this Form button to send the form to the processing script.

With the markup shown in the next code listing, you have a fully functional form in the web page. The user can provide input using the form controls you've defined and can submit the form, which will pass the values of the <form> elements to the processing script.

When viewing the web page, your form will now look something like what is shown in Figure 4-14.

```
<form action="/path/to/script">
    <fieldset>
        <legend>Personal Information</legend>
        <ol>
            <li>
                <label for="email_field">Email Address</label>
                <input type="text" name="email" id="email_field" />
            </li>
            <li>
                <input type="checkbox" name="enrolled" ➡
                    id="enrolled_field" value="1" ➡
                    checked="checked" />
                <label for="enrolled_field">I am currently enrolled in
                    a college or university</label>
            </li>
            <li>What is your favorite color?
                <ul>
                    <li>
                        <input type="radio" name="favorite_color" ➡
                            id="favorite_color_blue" value="blue" />
                        <label for="favorite_color_blue">Blue</label>
                    </li>
                    <li>
                        <input type="radio" name="favorite_color" ➡
                            id="favorite_color_red" value="red" />
                        <label for="favorite_color_red">Red</label>
                    </li>
                    <li>
                        <input type="radio" name="favorite_color" ➡
                            id="favorite_color_yellow" value="yellow" />
                        <label for="favorite_color_yellow">Yellow
                </label>
                    </li>
                    <li>
                        <input type="radio" name="favorite_color" ➡
                            id="favorite_color_green" value="green" />
                        <label for="favorite_color_green">Green</label>
                    </li>
                </ul>
            </li>
        </ol>
```

89

```
        </fieldset>
        <fieldset>
            <legend>Application Information</legend>
            <ol>
                <li>
                    <label for="timezone_field">Time zone</label>
                    <select name="timezone" id="timezone_field">
                        <optgroup label="Mainland America">
                            <option value="-5">Eastern</option>
                            <option value="-6">Central</option>
                            <option value="-7">Mountain</option>
                            <option value="-8">Pacific</option>
                        </optgroup>
                        <optgroup label="Outlying States">
                            <option value="-9">Alaskan</option>
                            <option value="-10">Hawaiian</option>
                        </optgroup>
                    </select>
                </li>
                <li>
                    <label for="comments_field">Comments</label>
                    <textarea name="comments" id="comments_field" ➥
                        rows="6" cols="65"></textarea>
                </li>
            </ol>
        </fieldset>
        <input type="submit" value="Submit this Form" />
</form>
```

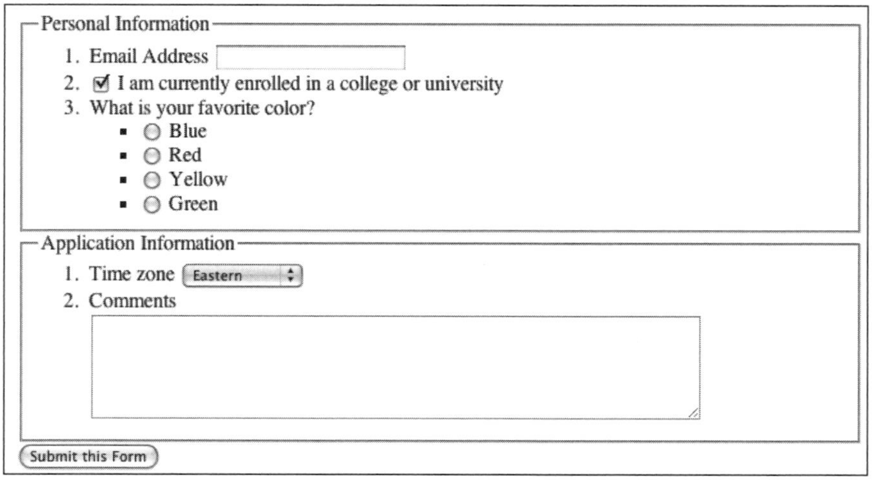

Figure 4-14. The completed form including a text input, check box, radio buttons, a selection list, and a text area input all grouped together into field sets

Of course, there's even more you can do with XHTML forms. For instance, there are a few more options for the `type` attribute that you can specify on `<input>` elements. An important one to know about is the `password` type, which creates an element that is identical to the `text` type except that it renders every character that the user types into it as asterisks (*) or bullets (•) instead of actual text. The text that's typed is, in fact, unchanged, but it doesn't show up on screen that way for security purposes. There's also the `file` type, which allows the visitor to select a file from their computer to upload through the form using their operating system's native file selection dialog box.

There are also a few more kinds of buttons that are similar to the `submit` type of input. There's a `button` type that displays a button whose behavior you can control through JavaScript, though it won't do anything at all by default. There's also a button *element*, which can be used to turn certain other elements (such as an `<img>`) into a button. (These kinds of buttons will, by default, submit the form.) There's also the `image` type of `<input>` element, which is another way to turn an image into a button, and it takes a `src` attribute just like the `<img>` tag.

Finally, there's also a `reset` type of the `<input>` element that also creates a button, only instead of submitting the form, this kind of button will put the form in its original state, removing any input the user may have entered. There's rarely any real need for this kind of button (especially on longer forms), but it's there if you ever do need it.

As you can see, designing forms can be quite an undertaking on the Web. They introduce a kind of interactivity that you can't get from other kinds of media like television or magazines. Forms, and the capabilities they provide to enable two-way communication between the website creator and the website visitor, are what makes the Web a truly unique publishing platform.

Special characters

When marking up content, you're bound to notice that there are certain characters that just don't display properly when you put them directly in your markup. Perhaps the most obvious of these would be the less-than and greater-than symbols, also called **left and right angle brackets** (< and >). Instead of treating these like angle brackets, the browser assumes these are the beginnings and ends of tags.

Because of the double duty these characters serve, if you actually wanted to use < or > in your content, you would need to use special codes called **entity references** to refer to them. In computer speak, this is called **escaping** the characters. Escaping characters in XHTML is achieved simply by replacing the character you intended to type with a combination of other characters that represent it. In every case, **escape sequences** such as these begin with an ampersand (&) and end with a semicolon (;).

The entity references for the less-than and greater-than symbols are < and >, respectively. This, however, poses a new problem. How do you mark up an ampersand symbol? The answer is the same: you escape it by using its entity reference. The entity reference for an ampersand is &.

Table 4-2 lists a few of the most common characters and their corresponding entity references.

Table 4-2. A Listing of Useful HTML Character Entities

Character	Character Entity Reference for HTML and XHTML
<	&lt;
>	&gt;
"	&ldquo;
"	&rdquo;
'	&lsquo;
'	&rsquo;
&	&amp;
Nonbreaking space	
— (em dash)	&mdash;
?	&larr;
?	&uarr;
?	&rarr;
?	&darr;
®	&reg;
™	&trade;
©	&copy;

There are hundreds of different entity references, and an exhaustive glossary would be superfluous in this book. However, keep these in mind when marking up your content, because they will probably prove very useful. For example, what if you wanted to have the following sentence on your page?

```
I'm sure that using the <div> tag
is more professional than "faking a layout" using tables.
```

First, you see we'll need to replace the angle brackets with their entity references. Don't forget to mark up the XHTML tag as computer code, either:

```
I'm sure that using the <code>&lt;div&gt;</code> element
is more professional than "faking a layout" using tables.
```

Then there's also the curly quotes around the words *faking a layout*. Let's replace those:

```
I'm sure that using the <code>&lt;div&gt;</code> tag
is more professional than &ldquo;faking a layout&rdquo; using tables.
```

And lastly, the curly apostrophe in the word *I'm:*

```
I&rsquo;m sure that using the <code>&lt;div&gt;</code> tag
is more professional than &ldquo;faking a layout&rdquo; using tables.
```

When you view this in a browser, it will look like your original sentence (see Figure 4-15).

I'm sure that using the <div> tag is more helpful than "faking a layout" using tables.

Figure 4-15. Replacing certain punctuation with HTML entities will allow you to preserve the formatting of your sentences.

Using entity references is quite simple because you're simply replacing one character with a short sequence of others. They're helpful in keeping your markup portable across browsers, and they keep your content looking and acting properly. You can get a complete list of entity references at http://www.webstandards.org/learn/reference/charts/entities/.

All together now: creating real pages

Now that you know the basics of marking up different kinds of content, you'll learn how to put a whole page together to view it in a browser.

Starting with your index.html file that you created a few sections ago, the first thing you'll do is begin filling in some more details for your specific page. Let's make a home page for Papa Pepperoncini's Pizza.

Recall that your document shell looks like this:

```
<!DOCTYPE html PUBLIC "-//W3C//DTD XHTML 1.0 Strict//EN"
    "http://www.w3.org/TR/xhtml1/DTD/xhtml1-strict.dtd">
<html xmlns="http://www.w3.org/1999/xhtml" xml:lang="en" lang="en">
<head>
    <meta http-equiv="Content-Type" content="text/html; ➥
      charset=utf-8"/>
    <title>New Document</title>
</head>
<body>

</body>
</html>
```

First, let's change the title of your page to "Welcome to Papa Pepperoncini's Pizza":

```
<!DOCTYPE html PUBLIC "-//W3C//DTD XHTML 1.0 Strict//EN"
    "http://www.w3.org/TR/xhtml1/DTD/xhtml1-strict.dtd">
<html xmlns="http://www.w3.org/1999/xhtml" xml:lang="en" lang="en">
<head>
    <meta http-equiv="Content-Type" content="text/html; ➥
      charset=utf-8"/>
    <title>Welcome to Papa Pepperoncini's Pizza</title>
</head>
<body>

</body>
</html>
```

Next, let's add some content into the <body> of the page. You'll need to add four main sections to the page: a header to proudly display Papa Pepperoncini's name as well as to contain the main navigation for the site, a place for a welcome message, an area to showcase weekly specials, and finally a footer for your copyright information. The most logical way to differentiate these sections is to create <div> elements that will group each one individually and then give each <div> element a descriptive id value to uniquely identify them:

```
<!DOCTYPE html PUBLIC "-//W3C//DTD XHTML 1.0 Strict//EN"
    "http://www.w3.org/TR/xhtml1/DTD/xhtml1-strict.dtd">
<html xmlns="http://www.w3.org/1999/xhtml" xml:lang="en" lang="en">
<head>
    <meta http-equiv="Content-Type" content="text/html; ➥
      charset=utf-8"/>
    <title>Welcome to Papa Pepperoncini's Pizza</title>
</head>
<body>
    <div id="header">
    </div>
    <div id="welcome">
    </div>
    <div id="specials">
    </div>
    <div id="footer">
    </div>
</body>
</html>
```

Now, the content for the footer is easy, so let's add that quickly:

```
<!DOCTYPE html PUBLIC "-//W3C//DTD XHTML 1.0 Strict//EN"
    "http://www.w3.org/TR/xhtml1/DTD/xhtml1-strict.dtd">
<html xmlns="http://www.w3.org/1999/xhtml" xml:lang="en" lang="en">
<head>
    <meta http-equiv="Content-Type" content="text/html; ➥
      charset=utf-8"/>
```

```
        <title>Welcome to Papa Pepperoncini's Pizza</title>
    </head>
    <body>
        <div id="header">
        </div>
        <div id="welcome">
        </div>
        <div id="specials">
        </div>
        <div id="footer">
            <p>Copyright &copy; 2008 Papa Pepperoncini's Pizza &mdash;
          All rights reserved.</p>
        </div>
    </body>
    </html>
```

Note the use of entity references for the copyright symbol and the dash.

In the header, you'll want the name of the restaurant to be a headline because it's a crucially important piece of your page. You'll also turn this headline into a link to the home page so that no matter where visitors are on your website, it will be easy for them to return to the home page.

For your navigation menu, you always want to have a link to the home page, a link to a page that displays the restaurant's menu, a link to a page that lists all the locations for Papa Pepperoncini's Pizza (maybe it's a chain, or even if it's not, this list will still have at least the one location in it!), and some general information about how Papa Pepperoncini works his magic. Since this navigation menu is really just a list of links to different pages, you'll put all these links inside an unordered list and link them to pages that you'll create later.

```
    <!DOCTYPE html PUBLIC "-//W3C//DTD XHTML 1.0 Strict//EN"
        "http://www.w3.org/TR/xhtml1/DTD/xhtml1-strict.dtd">
    <html xmlns="http://www.w3.org/1999/xhtml" xml:lang="en" lang="en">
    <head>
        <meta http-equiv="Content-Type" content="text/html; ➥
          charset=utf-8"/>
        <title>Welcome to Papa Pepperoncini's Pizza</title>
    </head>
    <body>
        <div id="header">
            <h3><a href="index.html">Papa Pepperoncini&rsquo;s Pizza</a> ➥
          </h3>
            <ul>
                <li><a href="index.html">Home</a></li>
                <li><a href="menu.html">Our Menu</a></li>
                <li><a href="locations.html">Locations</a></li>
                <li><a href="about.html">About Us</a></li>
            </ul>
        </div>
        <div id="welcome"></div>
        <div id="specials"></div>
```

```
        <div id="footer">
            <p>Copyright &copy; 2008 Papa Pepperoncini's Pizza &mdash;
                All rights reserved.</p>
        </div>
    </body>
</html>
```

Notice the use of an <h3> element for the restaurant title. You might choose an <h3> here because even though the company name is important on this page, it might not be quite as important as the welcome message, which Papa Pepperoncini has decided earlier is to be the main goal of the home page. As a result, you'll save your <h1> for the headline inside the welcome section.

Deciding which pieces of content are the most important parts of a page and how to mark them up is part of the *art* of web development. Another way to do this would have been to have multiple <h1>s on this page, but some might argue that this would dilute their importance. Really, there's no right answer here. This example just goes to show that you don't actually have to place <h1> elements before <h2> elements, and so on. Regardless of how you choose to mark up content like this, the important thing is to have a reason that makes sense and to stick to whatever method you choose consistently throughout the entire process of creating pages for the website.

Next, let's move on to the welcome message. Papa Pepperoncini sent you some text that he wanted to use for this section, so you'll mark it up properly by making sure his content is placed inside appropriate elements and that any special characters (like quotation marks or ampersands) are replaced with their proper entity references:

```
<!DOCTYPE html PUBLIC "-//W3C//DTD XHTML 1.0 Strict//EN"
    "http://www.w3.org/TR/xhtml1/DTD/xhtml1-strict.dtd">
<html xmlns="http://www.w3.org/1999/xhtml" xml:lang="en" lang="en">
<head>
    <meta http-equiv="Content-Type" content="text/html; ➥
     charset=utf-8"/>
    <title>Welcome to Papa Pepperoncini's Pizza</title>
</head>
<body>
    <div id="header">
        <h3><a href="index.html">Papa Pepperoncini&rsquo;s Pizza</a> ➥
        </h3>
        <ul>
            <li><a href="index.html">Home</a></li>
            <li><a href="menu.html">Our Menu</a></li>
            <li><a href="locations.html">Locations</a></li>
            <li><a href="about.html">About Us</a></li>
        </ul>
    </div>
    <div id="welcome">
        <h1>Welcome to Papa Pepperoncini&rsquo;s!</h1>
        <p>Please, sit down! Papa Pepperoncini&rsquo;s Pizza is the
            finest Italian Eatery this side of the Atlantic, and
            we&rsquo;re glad you&rsquo;ve come to visit.  Feel free
to look at the menu, browse through our  locations, or
```

```
            read about our history.  And if you need anything,
        just let us know.
                        Grazzi!</p>
        </div>
        <div id="specials">
        </div>
        <div id="footer">
            <p>Copyright &copy; 2008 Papa Pepperoncini's Pizza &mdash;
                    All rights reserved.</p>
        </div>
    </body>
</html>
```

The last piece is your display of the weekly specials. These are clearly another list, so you'll put them in an <ul> and add a headline to introduce them:

```
<!DOCTYPE html PUBLIC "-//W3C//DTD XHTML 1.0 Strict//EN"
    "http://www.w3.org/TR/xhtml1/DTD/xhtml1-strict.dtd">
<html xmlns="http://www.w3.org/1999/xhtml" xml:lang="en" lang="en">
<head>
    <meta http-equiv="Content-Type" content="text/html; ➥
      charset=utf-8"/>
    <title>Welcome to Papa Pepperoncini's Pizza</title>
</head>
<body>
    <div id="header">
        <h3><a href="index.html">Papa Pepperoncini&rsquo;s Pizza</a> ➥
        </h3>
        <ul>
            <li><a href="index.html">Home</a></li>
            <li><a href="menu.html">Our Menu</a></li>
            <li><a href="locations.html">Locations</a></li>
            <li><a href="about.html">About Us</a></li>
        </ul>
    </div>
    <div id="welcome">
        <h1>Welcome to Papa Pepperoncini&rsquo;s!</h1>
        <p>Please, sit down! Papa Pepperoncini&rsquo;s Pizza is the
                finest Italian Eatery this side of the Atlantic, and
                we&rsquo;re glad you&rsquo;ve come to visit.  Feel free
            to look at the menu, browse through our locations, or
    read about our history.  And if you need anything,
                just let us know.
                        Grazzi!</p>
    </div>
    <div id="specials">
        <h2>Weekly Specials</h2>
        <ul>
            <li>Monday: Small Caesar Salad and Eggplant Rollatini</li>
```

```
            <li>Tuesday: Pasta Gagioli and Gnocchi in a Pesto Cream
                    Sauce</li>
            <li>Wednesday: Spiedini alla Romano with Marinara
                    Sauce</li>
            <li>Thursday: New England Clam Chowder and Grilled Shrimp
                    Kabob over Rice</li>
            <li>Friday: Tracciatella a la Romano and 7" Italian Combo
                    Hero</li>
        </ul>
    </div>
    <div id="footer">
        <p>Copyright &copy; 2008 Papa Pepperoncini's Pizza &mdash;
                All rights reserved.</p>
    </div>
</body>
</html>
```

This is a great start. Before you get ahead of yourself, though, let's make sure you haven't made any typos or forgot to close any elements by running your markup through the online validator at http://validator.w3.org, which will ensure you don't have any errors.

"Congratulations," the validator tells you; this code indeed validates as XHTML 1.0 Strict markup. You should now see something like Figure 4-16 in the browser window.

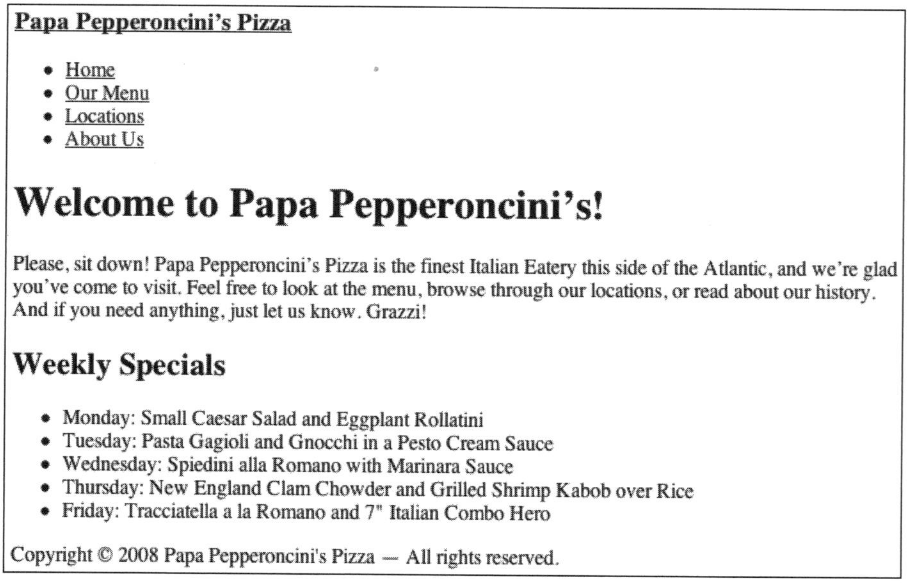

Figure 4-16. A shot of the completed page. It's perfectly presentable, even without any styling applied (but where's the fun in that?).

Wonderful! All your content is in place and fully understood by the web browser. OK, so it's not very pretty quite yet. All in due time. When you continue to develop this page in the upcoming chapters, you'll use CSS to give the humble but meaningful markup some visual pizzazz.

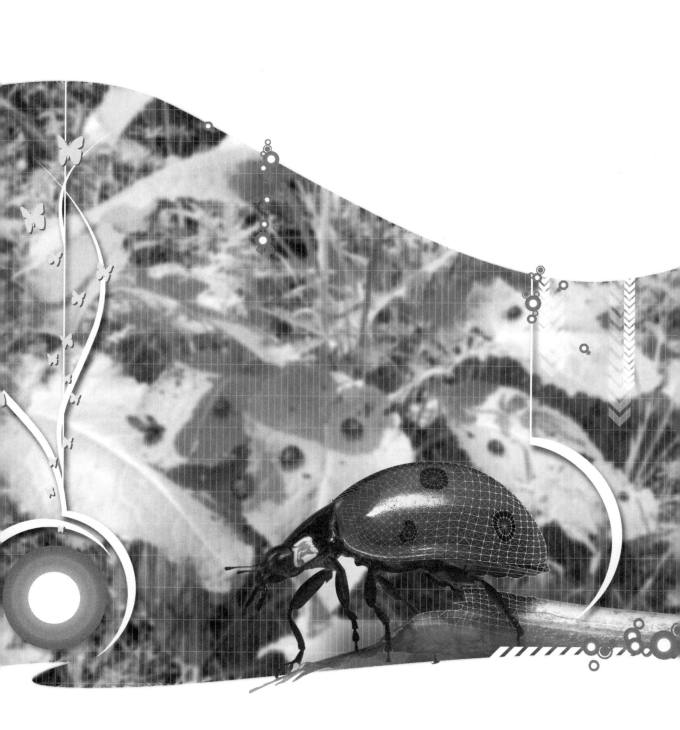

Chapter 5

EXPLORING FUNDAMENTAL CONCEPTS OF CSS

By now, you should have a solid understanding of how to create web pages using HTML or XHTML markup. You should understand how to encode semantic meaning into your page content. You should be familiar with the concept of page elements and how these elements can be nested inside one another to give a page an orderly structure. Finally, you should also understand the basics of how a web browser interprets your (X)HTML source code and determines its rendering. All of these topics were covered in the previous chapter, and all the concepts in this chapter will build on them.

In this chapter, you'll take a much closer look at how the web browser actually displays elements inside its window, and we'll discuss the specifics of how you can control this behavior. Of course, this means you're going to dive into the world of Cascading Style Sheets (CSS). Before you get carried away writing code, however, we'll first explain where CSS came from and why it's such a powerful tool for web designers.

The origins and evolution of Cascading Style Sheets

Many web designers are surprised to learn that style sheets have existed in some form or another since the inception of HTML's ancestor, the Standard Generalized

Markup Language (SGML), back in the 1970s. This is because even before the Web was born, documents marked up in SGML needed some way to encode formatting information in addition to their semantic meaning. In the early days of HTML, both this visual formatting information (called **presentational style**) as well as the semantic meaning were encoded directly inside the markup of each element. Over time, as discussed in earlier chapters of this book, this proved problematic for many reasons.

It was clear that the Web needed a better way to encode formatting information both to ease the development and maintenance of content already published on the Web as well as to increase the capabilities of web browsers. What you know today as Cascading Style Sheets was first formalized in 1994 by the joint efforts of Bert Bos and Håkon Wium Lie, two developers involved in the World Wide Web Consortium's (W3C's) presentational style debates. Together with the support of the W3C's HTML editorial review board, the CSS level 1 (more simply called CSS1) specification was officially published at the end of 1996.

Even then, CSS boasted some special features that made it especially well suited as a generalized presentation language. For example, CSS was not limited to applying stylistic information to web pages marked up in HTML. It could be just as easily applied to any other markup language. Today, CSS can be applied to such XML dialects as SVG (a markup language for describing vector-based artwork) and XUL (a cross-platform user interface language). Indeed, it's this ability to separate the information about specific content from the information about how that content is displayed that gives CSS its power.

Another advantage that CSS held over other display languages was its ability to apply multiple style sheets to a single document. This allowed one document to "inherit" the declarations of all the styles in each style sheet it referenced, each successive style sheet "cascading" on top of the others. This cascading effect—the fact that later declarations about certain styles could overrule earlier declarations about the same styles—is part of what gave CSS its name. Later in this chapter, you'll see how this capability directly benefits web developers like you.

Best of all, CSS had an incredibly simple syntax that made extensive use of English keywords. This makes it easy to read and understand. For the same reason, as you'll see here, it's also easy to learn.

Even though the benefits of CSS were very quickly realized by the W3C and it took only another two years for CSS level 2 (CSS2) to become an official Recommendation in 1998, it wasn't until very recently that reliable, widespread support for CSS in web browsers have given it a prominent place in the tool sets of web designers and developers. We know what you're thinking: if CSS was this good this fast, why did it take so long to make it into mainstream web browsers?

For many years after the original release of CSS, it was difficult for web developers to make full use of this technology. Thanks to competition between the major browser vendors to one-up each other on features, differing opinions regarding what the standards should actually be, and in the worst cases the complete failure to even approach support for said standards, it became nearly impossible for a professional web developer to be able to rely on the use of CSS for web design. At the time, web developers used a patchwork of techniques that relied upon nested table layouts, presentational HTML markup, and the implementation of proprietary browser features that required developers to write browser-specific code or else completely abandon support for certain browsers.

Eventually, with the numbers of different browsers on the Web rising and the seemingly endless browser wars causing developers even more grief, it was the release of Internet Explorer 5.0 for Mac OS 9 on March 27, 2000, that finally gave everyone a way to move toward standards compliance.

Specifically, the new version of the web browser from Microsoft, written partly under the direction of Tantek Çelic, implemented a rendering engine (called Tasman) that provided a means for web developers to explicitly choose one of a number of possible "rendering modes." Developers writing new code that conformed to the W3C's published standards could then switch the web browser into a "standards rendering mode." Older pages that would likely be incompatible with standards mode, however, would use a different rendering mode that became widely known as **quirks mode**.

The new browser set a new precedent, one that emphasized standards while simultaneously showcasing new capabilities. Web developers started to develop for the new browser and over time grew more insistent on the use of standards-based code in the industry. Web standards evangelists such as Jeffrey Zeldman, Molly Holzschlag, and Eric Meyer—who each pressured browser manufacturers to increase their support for web standards and CSS in particular—began making headway. At the same time, web developers such as Peter-Paul Koch were calling for greater compatibility between differing browsers' implementations of JavaScript, and usability experts such as Jakob Nielsen and accessibility experts such as Joe Clark each made strong cases for web standards in their respective areas. Slowly, the tables began to turn.

Work on CSS level 3, which began immediately after the release of CSS level 2 in 1998, is still ongoing as of this writing. Thankfully, the push toward standards in the web development community and the support of this movement by large businesses that have reaped economic benefits from these standards makes the future of CSS seem very bright. Increasingly widespread support for CSS in all kinds of network-enabled devices is also pushing the language to ever-greater heights. These days, CSS can be used to control not only the visual presentation of content in a web page but all sorts of other things, such as the rate that text on a page should be read aloud by screen readers.

How CSS works

To a lot of people, CSS often looks like magic. Admittedly, it's not easy to wrap your head around the idea that with two simple text files, one with HTML markup (that gives a page's content meaning and structure) and a completely separate one with CSS rules (that define the layout and presentation of this content), you can end up with a visual display that looks nothing like the original. How can a humble text file full of CSS rules change so much about a web page so dramatically? Let's find out.

Default browser styles

A **style sheet** is actually a pretty simple construct. Like (X)HTML markup, a style sheet is just a plain-text file, but unlike markup it contains no content of its own. A CSS style sheet is *always* applied to the content of some other document. It's this other content that the CSS declarations affect. By itself, a CSS file can't do anything.

Recall that in the previous chapter you developed a web page for Papa Pepperoncini's Pizza restaurant using XHTML markup. You'll use the content of that page and apply the styles to it. Right now, that web page looks rather plain—but it's not *entirely* devoid of formatting, as shown in Figure 5-1.

Figure 5-1. Content displayed with only simple, default presentation styles

As you can see, you have a link at the top of the page ("Papa Pepperoncini's Pizza"), and the text of this link is blue and underlined. Beneath that, you have a list of links, with each list item clearly displaying a bullet point. Then you have the text of a large headline, much larger than the rest of the text on the page. You also have a paragraph of text that has a decent amount of whitespace between itself and the headlines that surround it. The same is true of the rest of the elements of the page.

So if this is the page supposedly without any styling information, how come the page is showing off some smarts about how you might envision these elements to look? In fact, it's not your page at all but rather a style sheet that is built right into the web browser. Using the excellent Web Developer Toolbar add-on for the Firefox web browser (discussed in more detail in Chapter 8), you can disable these built-in styles. Figure 5-2 shows how the web page *really* looks with no style sheets at all, not even the browser's built-in one.

As you can see from this example, most of the styling is now gone. The links are still blue, and the headlines are still bold, but that's about all that remains. The important thing to understand from this example is that when you begin to add your own styling information to your web pages, you're actually overriding styles that already exist in a style sheet that's baked right into your visitor's web browser.

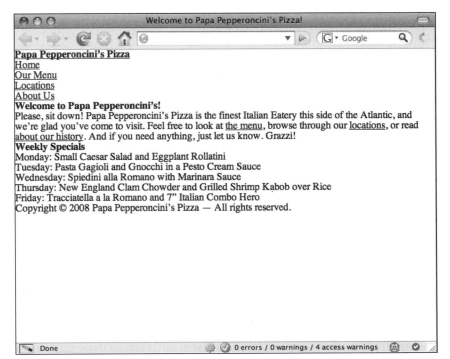

Figure 5-2. Papa Pepperoncini's Pizza web page with Firefox's built-in style sheet disabled

Unfortunately, not all web browsers come with the same style sheet baked into them, which means that different browsers will display the same elements in different ways unless you define your own rules and override all the default ones.

Even though Cascading Style Sheets brings with it incredible flexibility of presentation, the style sheets themselves must be constructed in a certain way, just like the XHTML page you created in the previous chapter had to be written using restricted syntax and grammars. We'll use the default browser styles you just discovered to explain the syntax CSS uses and to show how style sheets are constructed.

Anatomy of a CSS style sheet

A single CSS style sheet can contain a theoretically endless amount of presentational information. This information is organized into a sequence of **statements**, each of which specifies one **rule** (sometimes also called a **ruleset**). Rules do all of the heavy lifting in CSS; they determine what stylistic information to apply where. When you create a style sheet, you spend most of your time writing these rules.

Each of these rules can be expressed in plain English, and in fact you've already done so in the example of the default styles. For example, "A link's text should be blue and underlined" is something a CSS rule might specify. A following rule might specify that "Paragraphs should have a decent amount of whitespace between whatever is above and whatever is below it." In CSS, you might write these rules like this:

```
a:link {
    color: blue;
    text-decoration: underline;
}
p {
    margin-top: 25px;
    margin-bottom: 25px;
}
```

This snippet of CSS is, itself, a valid style sheet. If you apply these styles to a web page, all links will turn blue and will have underlined text, and all paragraphs will have exactly 25 pixels of spacing above and beneath them. Of course, that's already similar to how most browsers display links and paragraphs by default, so this isn't very exciting. However, what is exciting is that it's probably not very hard to figure out which parts you need to change to make all your links, say, green, and how to change the number of pixels above or below your paragraphs. For instance:

```
a:link {
    color: green;
    text-decoration: underline;
}
p {
    margin-top: 50px;
    margin-bottom: 50px;
}
```

Now all your links will be green and underlined, and each paragraph will have exactly 50 pixels of empty whitespace above and below it. With the previous example, it's also easy to see how to change the elements in your page to which the declared styles are applying. For example, instead of making links underlined and green, let's make your top headline element (<h1>) show up that way:

```
h1 {
    color: green;
    text-decoration: underline;
}
p {
    margin-top: 50px;
    margin-bottom: 50px;
}
```

Now, links will revert to showing up in whatever way the browser's default style sheet says they should appear, but your top-level headline will be green and underlined, as shown in Figure 5-3.

Figure 5-3. Overriding default styles for `<h1>` and `<p>` elements on a web page

You can even change *all* your headlines so that they look like your top-level headline. You simply add the other headline elements to the first rule, separating each element name with a comma:

```
h1, h2, h3, h4, h5, h6 {
    color: green;
    text-decoration: underline;
}
p {
    margin-top: 50px;
    margin-bottom: 50px;
}
```

This results in the appearance shown in Figure 5-4.

107

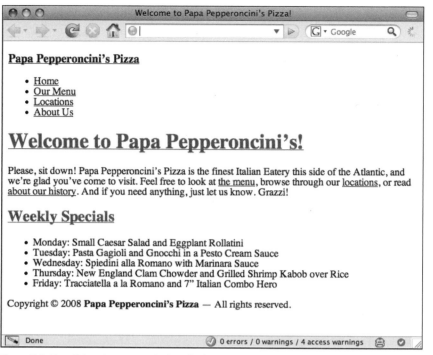

Figure 5-4. Specifying the same rule for all of your headlines

Wait a minute. This worked for two of your headlines, but not the one at the top of your page ("Papa Pepperoncini's Pizza"), which is still blue and underlined. Don't worry, it's not a mistake; it's CSS in action. So, what's going on here?

Recall that this headline is actually a link. You specified your XHTML for that headline like this:

```
<h3><a href="index.html">Papa Pepperoncini&rsquo;s Pizza</a></h3>
```

The <h3> element's only content is itself another element, specifically the <a> (anchor) element. Additionally, recall that the web browser already has a default style for all links, specifically, that they should be blue and underlined. So, the web browser isn't actually ignoring you; it's just applying *all* the style rules it has loaded in *all* of its style sheets one after the other to your page elements. Since the <a> element is nested within the <h3> element, the text inside that headline is *really* a link, and since the browser has a rule specifying all links should be colored blue, that's what the browser has done.

To prove that this is indeed what is happening, add some more text to the headline element but not to the link:

```
<h3><a href="index.html">Papa Pepperoncini&rsquo;s Pizza</a>
        &mdash; The Best Pizza in Town!</h3>
```

Now, a reload of your web page shows you a blue link ("Papa Pepperoncini's Pizza") and a green headline ("— The Best Pizza in Town"), as shown in Figure 5-5.

Figure 5-5. The part of the headline not affected by the CSS rule for link styling is green just like the other headlines.

This example showcases the importance of understanding the markup underlying your page. If you don't understand the structure of your markup, you can't accurately determine what pieces of your page are which elements, and therefore you won't be able to understand how your style rules are getting applied to the page.

These examples also showcase a number of discrete chunks that compose a CSS rule. At the beginning of each line, you have a **selector**, which in these examples matched the element to which you were applying the rest of the rule. Changing the selector changed what element was *selected* by the rule. You could specify multiple elements as the target of a single rule by writing them in a comma-separated list.

After the selector, there was a chunk of text between open and closing curly braces ({ and }). These braces mark the beginning and end of a **declaration block**, similar to how XHTML elements have open and close tags. Inside the declaration block of your rule, you specified two individual **declarations**, although you could have specified any number of declarations (there is no limit to the number of declarations that can be written inside a declaration block). Each declaration ended with a semicolon (;).

In the case of the rule selecting (or targeting) the headlines, these declarations specified values for the color and text-decoration **properties**. The properties were separated from the values with colons (:). Inside the declaration block and between the two rules, all whitespace was ignored. Figure 5-6 details the syntax of a CSS rule.

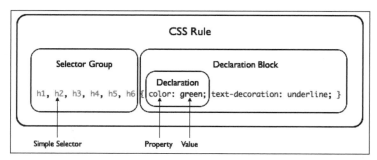

Figure 5-6. The components of a CSS rule

The CSS2 specification defines hundreds of properties for which you can set values. When it is finally implemented, CSS3 will add even more properties. Some properties can apply to every kind of element, such as headlines, links, paragraphs, tables, images, and so on. Other properties can apply only to certain kinds of elements, and they won't work if you apply them to others. Learning which properties you can apply to which elements and learning what kinds of values each property can set are part of the process of becoming proficient with CSS.

For now, let's be content with the knowledge that there is more to learn and move onward. Later in this book, you'll revisit the topic of CSS properties and values and examine what options CSS2 gives you. In the meantime, however, you'll learn more about how CSS can be integrated with a web page.

Applying styles to web page elements

So, you now understand what CSS is, you know what it looks like, and you know what it can do and how it does it. It's almost time to write some new CSS rules to make Papa Pepperoncini's Pizza page sparkle. But first, you need to figure out how to attach a CSS style sheet to an HTML or XHTML web page so that the styles you write will actually be shown.

You can apply CSS rules to page elements in three ways. You can embed a CSS rule directly into an element, you can embed a whole style sheet inside the HTML or XHTML page itself, or you can link a style sheet from an entirely separate file to your HTML or XHTML page. Let's examine all three possibilities in detail.

Inline styles

Perhaps the simplest and most familiar way of applying CSS styles to web page elements would be through the use of **inline styles**, or styles written directly into the element. Since an inline style by definition applies only to the element in which it is placed, there is no need to use a CSS selector in the rule, and since the style is already enclosed inside the element, a declaration block's curly braces aren't needed either. All you need to specify for an inline style to work is the property and value you want to set on the element.

Inline styles are written into the value of the `style` attribute of an element, like so:

```
<p style="color: purple;">Look ma, I&rsquo;m purple!</p>
```

Naturally, inline styles don't give you much flexibility since they can't use the power of CSS selectors to target multiple elements of the same type on a page as your previous examples have done. Worse, inline styles embed presentational information directly into your document, which is exactly what CSS was developed to avoid. In general practice, inline styles really aren't a good solution for applying styles to elements.

Nevertheless, there are some cases where inline styles are useful. For instance, they make it easy to experiment with particular elements and to test what different values of different properties will do to an element. While you're learning about what CSS properties exist and what they can do, feel free to use inline styles to try them. In an actual project deliverable, however, you shouldn't leave any presentational data inside your markup, so you should pull these inline styles out and place them in either embedded style sheets or external style sheets.

Embedded style sheets

Embedding a CSS style sheet inside an HTML or XHTML file enables you to use every feature of CSS without limitation, but only with the single document that contains the embedded style sheet. By placing CSS rules in a <style> element, you're effectively creating a small area inside your markup where you can safely put CSS rules. When the browser encounters this special area, it stops interpreting your source code as (X)HTML markup and begins to interpret the code as CSS rules. Let's see how this might work in practice.

In your example web page for Papa Pepperoncini's Pizza, you have an XHTML document shell that looks like this:

```
<!DOCTYPE html PUBLIC "-//W3C//DTD XHTML 1.0 Strict//EN"
    "http://www.w3.org/TR/xhtml1/DTD/xhtml1-strict.dtd">
<html xmlns="http://www.w3.org/1999/xhtml" xml:lang="en" lang="en">
<head>
    <meta http-equiv="Content-Type" content="text/html; charset=utf-8"/>
    <title>Welcome to Papa Pepperoncini&rsquo;s Pizza</title>
</head>
<body>
    <!-- XHTML content goes here -->
</body>
</html>
```

In this shell, you have two main elements nested within the root <html> element: <head> and <body>. The <body> is where your XHTML content goes. The <head>, you might remember, is where the majority of the metadata about your document goes. Since CSS defines the presentation of content, it's considered a form of this metadata, and you need to place it inside the <head> element. You do this by defining a <style> element and giving this element a type of text/css to specify to the browser what style language the content of the element contains. For CSS, you will always use the text/css type.

The document shell with an embedded style sheet would then look like this:

```
<!DOCTYPE html PUBLIC "-//W3C//DTD XHTML 1.0 Strict//EN"
    "http://www.w3.org/TR/xhtml1/DTD/xhtml1-strict.dtd">
<html xmlns="http://www.w3.org/1999/xhtml" xml:lang="en" lang="en">
```

```
<head>
    <meta http-equiv="Content-Type" content="text/html; charset=utf-8"/>
    <title>Welcome to Papa Pepperoncini's Pizza</title>
    <style type="text/css">
        /* CSS content goes here */
    </style>
</head>
<body>
    <!-- XHTML content goes here -->
</body>
</html>
```

You can embed as many style sheets as you like (or need) into a single document in this way. By way of example, let's split the rule where you specified two declarations to apply to the <h1> element earlier into two style sheets with one CSS rule each:

```
<!DOCTYPE html PUBLIC "-//W3C//DTD XHTML 1.0 Strict//EN"
    "http://www.w3.org/TR/xhtml1/DTD/xhtml1-strict.dtd">
<html xmlns="http://www.w3.org/1999/xhtml" xml:lang="en" lang="en">
<head>
    <meta http-equiv="Content-Type" content="text/html; charset=utf-8"/>
    <title>Welcome to Papa Pepperoncini&rsquo;s Pizza</title>
    <style type="text/css">
        h1 {
            color: green;
        }
    </style>
    <style type="text/css">
        h1 {
            text-decoration: underline;
        }
    </style>
</head>
<body>
    <!-- XHTML content goes here -->
</body>
</html>
```

Placing CSS rules inside embedded style sheets in this manner clearly gives you more flexibility regarding what you'd like your CSS rules to accomplish, but it's still limited to applying the rules to a single page. The greatest benefits of CSS can be seen when you use a single style sheet to define the presentation not of a single web page but of an entire website that may have 10, 20, 100, 1,000, or more individual pages.

To accomplish this feat, you must completely separate the CSS styling from the HTML or XHTML markup by placing it into a separate file.

External style sheets

The most common—and most efficient—way to apply CSS to a web page and indeed to an entire website is via the use of entirely separate files that are linked to a web page with a special reference element, much like the way the <img> element references an external image file. These separate files with CSS rules in them are called **external style sheets**, because they are placed outside of any containing markup. Even though these CSS rules are separated from the actual web page document, they still behave the same way as if they were written in an embedded style sheet.

To reference an external style sheet from an HTML or XHTML page, you use the <link> element to—you guessed it—link your CSS file to your markup. Since you can link many different kinds of things into a web page, the link needs to be of a certain relationship, specifically, a style sheet relationship. This is specified in the rel attribute. Like an <img> element, you also need to tell the browser where to find this external style sheet. You can do this with the href attribute, and as you have probably already guessed, its value is any valid URL. Finally, just like an embedded style sheet, you need to tell the browser that this style sheet is written in CSS, so you specify a type of text/css.

All together, the <link> element might look like this:

```
<link rel="stylesheet" href="css/basic.css" type="text/css" />
```

This (empty) element specifies that an external CSS style sheet can be found inside the css folder and that its file name is basic.css. Inside the basic.css file, you simply write CSS rules as you normally would. Since this entire file is going to be interpreted by the browser as CSS, there's no need to enclose the CSS rules within a <style> element.

Web pages can be linked to any number of external style sheets. There's really no technical limit, although in practice the more CSS files you link to, the longer it will take for your browser to go and fetch all of them. Of course, the benefit of an external style sheet is that more than one *web page* can be linked to *it*, which means you can reuse the style rules you write for one web page across an unlimited number of other web pages. This is what makes CSS so outrageously scalable. It doesn't matter whether your site has one page or one million pages; as long as these pages have the basic elements that need to be styled in the same way, a single CSS file can be used to style them all.

Let's take Papa Pepperoncini's Pizza restaurant website as an example. Recall that your navigation menu for this website has four links in it:

```
<ul>
    <li><a href="index.html">Home</a></li>
    <li><a href="menu.html">Our Menu</a></li>
    <li><a href="locations.html">Locations</a></li>
    <li><a href="about.html">About Us</a></li>
</ul>
```

Each of these four pages will contain the same navigation menu, marked up in the same way. Thanks to this consistency and thanks to CSS's ability to create one set of rules that can be reused across any number of pages, you can write a set of rules that will style these links in any way you want, and then, merely by linking each of these four pages to the same external style sheet, the navigation menu's links on all of the pages will look the same.

Let's give each of the four links a nice teal color. Since these links are obviously a navigational element, let's also remove the underline from each of them. Finally, since you want them to stand out a little bit more prominently on your page, let's make them just a touch bigger than normal text. You can accomplish all of this with a single CSS rule that includes just three declarations:

```
ul a {
    color: teal;
    text-decoration: none;
    font-size: larger;
}
```

All you need to do is place this CSS rule into the basic.css file in your css folder and then link each web page you create to this external style sheet using the <link> element. As long as your markup remains consistent on all the pages you create for Papa Pepperoncini's Pizza restaurant website, the style rules you've just written for the main navigation will automatically be applied.

This method is obviously much better than having to write (or copy and paste) the same set of stylistic information to each of the four pages because it's faster to implement. It's also easier to maintain. Let's say that after you show Papa Pepperoncini your design concepts, he tells you that he thinks the navigation menu is too small. He wants to make all the navigation links across the entire site even bigger than they are. Since you've managed to successfully separate the main navigation links themselves from the visual style you've given them, this update isn't a problem. To accommodate Papa Pepperoncini's request, all you need to do is open your basic.css file and change your CSS rule, perhaps to something like this:

```
ul a {
    color: teal;
    text-decoration: none;
    font-size: xx-large;
}
```

Now, any web page that you've previously linked to this style sheet is instantly updated, just like that. But hold on, what is this ul a selector? Surely there's no ul a element, you might be saying to yourself, and of course (since element names in HTML or XHTML cannot contain spaces) you'd be correct. In fact, this is a new kind of CSS selector, one that targets anchors only when they are nested inside an unordered list.

More CSS selectors: targeting page elements with surgical precision

So far, you've seen how to apply CSS rules to specific types of page elements. Of course, specifying style rules based on element types is handy, but ultimately its usefulness goes only so far. For example, what if you wanted *some* links to look one way and some *other* links to look some other way. Obviously, basing all your styles solely on the element type (<a>, or anchor, in this case) isn't going to cut it. You need a more precise way to select elements. That's where the different kinds of CSS selectors step in to help you.

As you already know, CSS selectors allow you to *target* elements in your markup to which you want to apply certain styles. You already know how to use one kind of CSS selector, the type selector, which (as its name implies) selects elements based on their type (or name). For example, a selector that reads as h1 will apply to all <h1> elements. Similarly, a selector that reads as h1, h2, h3 will target all <h1>, <h2>, and <h3> elements in the page.

To be more precise, the type selectors that you have used so far are called **simple selectors** because they are, well, pretty simple. To construct more complex CSS selectors, you combine, or **chain**, multiple simple selectors together in specific ways. These more intricate patterns enable you to target elements on your page with surgical precision. Let's take a brief look at what other kinds of selectors you can avail yourself of when using CSS.

ID selectors

Another kind of simple selector is the **ID selector**. As you might expect, this selector targets an element whose id attribute has been given the specified value. For instance, on Papa Pepperoncini's page, you've previously defined a <div> element with an id of header to group all the elements that are part of the website's masthead:

```
<div id="header">
    <h3><a href="index.html">Papa Pepperoncini&rsquo;s Pizza</a></h3>
    <ul>
        <li><a href="index.html">Home</a></li>
        <li><a href="menu.html">Our Menu</a></li>
        <li><a href="locations.html">Locations</a></li>
        <li><a href="about.html">About Us</a></li>
    </ul>
</div>
```

Now, by using the ID selector, you can select this entire group of elements and, for instance, make all the text inside them bold and rendered in a specific font with a single CSS rule. You might think a nice, snazzy font like Zapfino would look nice, but since that font is not guaranteed to be installed on all (or even most) computers, you'll just say that any serif font will suffice in case that one is not available for some reason:

```
#header {
    font-weight: bold;
    font-family: Zapfino, serif;
}
```

ID selectors always begin with an octothorpe (#) and then are immediately followed by the id value of the element you want to target. In the previous example, since the <div> element's id attribute value was header, that's what goes after the octothorpe. This will have the same target as an ID selector that explicitly specifies the <div> element, like this:

```
div#header {
    font-weight: bold;
    font-family: Zapfino, serif;
}
```

However, the first selector is more *generic*. It doesn't care what type of element the header is, as long as that element has header as its id attribute value. The second selector does care, and it will target the header element only if that element is a <div>. Since id attribute values must be unique across a web page, most of the time you can be assured that these two selectors are entirely interchangeable. In some cases, however, you need the more specific selector to override another style. We'll cover selector specificity a little later in this chapter.

As you can see in Figure 5-7, both the third-level headline and the links in the main navigation list were affected by your CSS rule implicitly, since they are both contained within the header <div> (and because both the font-weight and font-family properties are inherited, a topic we'll cover in just a short while).

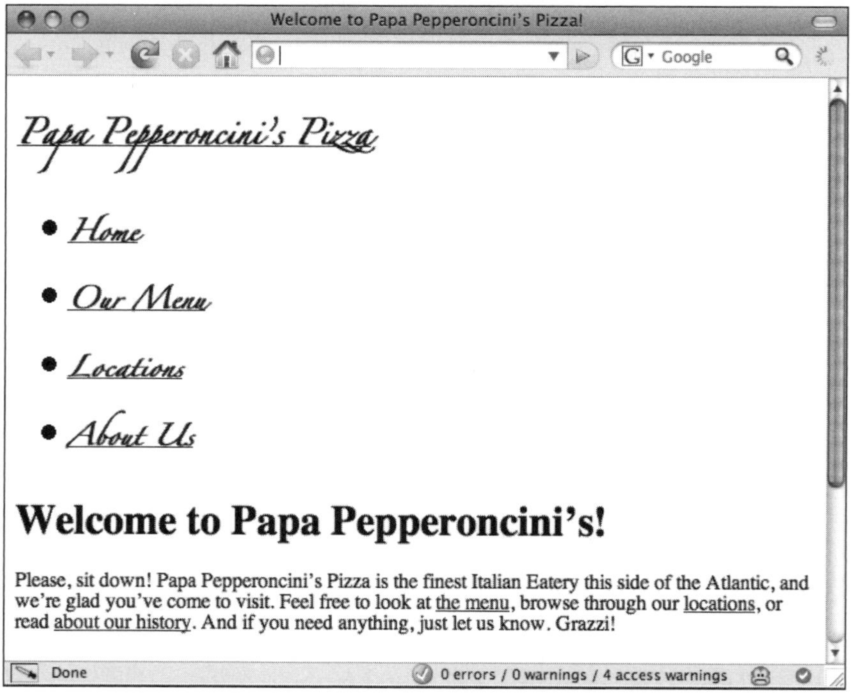

Figure 5-7. Using the ID selector applied CSS styles to a group of elements with a single rule

The important take-away from this example is that using the ID selector allows you to target elements that have been given a unique id value, and this is handy for applying styles to the groups of elements nested within that particular element.

Class selectors

Class selectors are yet another kind of simple selector. These selectors function in the same way as ID selectors, except instead of targeting elements with an ID value, they target elements that have been given a particular class value. In the previous chapter, you gave a class of feature to two <div> elements on your page.

```
<div class="feature" id="feature-1">
    <h1>Swingline Stapler</h1>
    <p>This workhorse stapler brings you a solid and consistent ➥
            performance that makes it an industry standard. An ➥
            all-metal die-cast base for years of durability. ➥
            A performance-driven mechanism with an inner rail for ➥
            long-term stapling integrity. Ease of use, refined design, ➥
            time-tested features: exactly what you'd expect from ➥
            America's #1 stapler.</p>
</div>
<div class="feature" id="feature-2">
    <h1>Black Standard Stapler</h1>
    <p>Not as exciting as the Swingline Stapler but a classic ➥
            stapler nonetheless!</p>
</div>
```

Recall that you've grouped the headlines and paragraphs that relate to featured products into a logical grouping named feature. Now, using the CSS class selector, you can style all these features consistently throughout your entire website. Let's say each of them should be inside a 250-pixel box with a slim, 1-pixel-wide silver-lined border. Each of the squares should be spaced about 10 pixels apart, but they should line up with one another. Once again, all it takes is one single CSS rule to accomplish all of this:

```
.feature {
    width: 250px;
    height: 250px;
    border: 1px solid silver;
    padding: 15px;
    margin-right: 10px;
    margin-bottom: 10px;
    float: left;
}
```

Figure 5-8 shows the result. Like ID selectors, class selectors also begin with a special symbol, in this case a dot (.), and are then immediately followed by the class value of the element(s) you want to target.

Figure 5-8. A class selector used to style a group of similar page elements

The real magic, however, happens when you want to add feature boxes to your web page. Since you've already declared what a feature looks like, you merely need to add the marked-up content to your page and class it appropriately. The CSS rules you've already written will take care of the rest. Figure 5-9 shows the result with two additional <div> elements added to the XHTML markup and *no* changes to the CSS rule.

```
<div class="feature" id="feature-1">
    <h1>Swingline Stapler</h1>
    <p>This workhorse stapler brings you a solid and consistent ➥
            performance that makes it an industry standard. An ➥
            all-metal die-cast base for years of durability. ➥
            A performance-driven mechanism with an inner rail for ➥
            long-term stapling integrity. Ease of use, refined design, ➥
            time-tested features: exactly what you'd expect from ➥
            America's #1 stapler.</p>
</div>
<div class="feature" id="feature-2">
    <h1>Bronze Stapler</h1>
```

```
        <p>For the classiest look, go for the polished style of bronze. ➥
            With our Bronze Stapler, you can be assured of ➥
            reliability, quality without sacrificing looks! Our ➥
            patented bronze-casting technology ensures this ➥
            stapler will look fantastic on any wooden or metallic ➥
            surface.</p>
    </div>
    <div class="feature" id="feature-3">
        <h1>Black Standard Stapler</h1>
        <p>Not as exciting as the Swingline Stapler, but a classic ➥
            stapler nonetheless!</p>
    </div>
    <div class="feature" id="feature-4">
        <h1>Silver Polished Stapler</h1>
        <p>Nothing says productivity quite like the polished look of silver ➥
            and chrome. With our Silver Polished Stapler, we ➥
            guarantee you&rsquo;ll enjoy paperwork again!</p>
    </div>
```

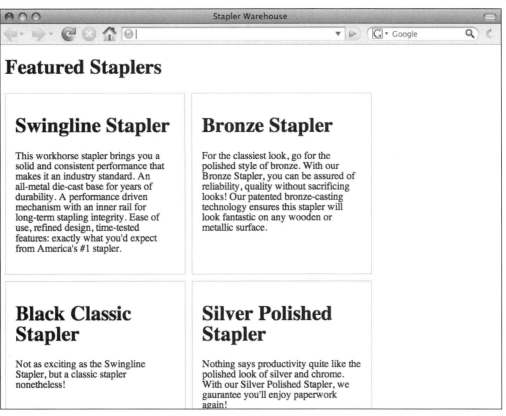

Figure 5-9. Adding classed elements requires no additional styles.

This example highlights the importance of semantic markup. It's only thanks to the sound semantic markup that underpins your web pages that enabled you to leverage the benefits of CSS in this way.

Pseudo-class selectors

We introduced a pseudo-class silently way back when we began talking about the syntax of CSS rules. That rule looked like this:

```
a:link {
    color: blue;
    text-decoration: underline;
}
```

The selector in this instance is a:link. Here, the type selector is simply a, and the pseudo-class is :link. Pseudo-classes will be discussed in more detail in the next chapter, so for now it's simply important to be aware of their existence and to recognize them as another kind of simple CSS selector.

Yet more simple selectors

If you thought type, ID, class, and pseudo-class selectors weren't enough, there are still more kinds of simple selectors that we haven't touched upon. These include attribute selectors and the universal type selector. In fact, both the ID and class selectors are a shorthand form for an attribute selector (because they select elements based on a particular attribute value, such as ID or class). Since these two simple selectors are rarely used, they won't be discussed here.

Once again, the important point is that all of these kinds of simple selectors are merely building blocks for creating more complex patterns with which to target specific elements in a web page.

Descendant selectors

The other CSS selector we introduced earlier is known as a **descendant selector**. This selector consists of two type selectors separated by whitespace, and as its name also implies, it targets elements of the specified type that are descendants of another element of the specified type. CSS rules with descendant selectors look like this:

```
ul a {
    color: teal;
    text-decoration: none;
}
```

This CSS rule says, "Target all a elements that are nested within <ul> elements, color them teal, and remove any underline they may have." In this example, the whitespace in the CSS selector is called a **combinator** because it combines two simple selectors. You can use the whitespace combinator to chain any number of simple selectors together in order to create more complex descendant selectors. For example, if you wanted to select all links in a document that are inside paragraphs that were grouped with other elements inside <div> elements, you would use the following CSS selector:

```
div p a {
    color: teal;
    text-decoration: none;
}
```

Once again, this says, "Target all <a> elements that are nested within <p> elements, if those <p> elements are nested within <div> elements." So, the previous CSS rule would affect the links in a markup structure like this:

```
<div>
    <p><strong>We appreciate your ➡
            <a href="buy.html">patronage</a></strong>, and encourage your ➡
            <a href="contact.html">feedback</a>.</p>
</div>
```

However, such a CSS selector would *not* affect links in a markup structure like this:

```
<div>
    <h3><a href="index.html">Papa Pepperoncini&rsquo;s Pizza</a></h3>
</div>
```

Note that in the first example the selector matches *both* of the links even though one link is inside a <strong> element and one isn't. The descendant selector matches elements regardless of how deeply nested they are. Its only requirement is that the markup's tree structure matches the chain of simple selectors at any given point.

Child selectors

If you did want to target elements that are nested only one level down from another element (the child elements of that element), you could use the **child selector** to accomplish that. Like descendant selectors, child selectors are composed of at least two simple selectors and the greater-than symbol, which is the combinator. For example, to target all links that are placed directly inside list items (and are *not* nested inside any other element between the list item and themselves), you could use the following child selector:

```
li > a { ... }
```

Note that any whitespace between the simple selectors and the combinators is ignored, unless the only combinator between simple selectors is, itself, whitespace (that is, a descendant combinator). That is to say that this CSS selector—which reads "li type selector, space, child combinator, space, a type selector"—is *not* a CSS selector with descendant combinators even though it includes spaces.

Unfortunately, Internet Explorer versions prior to version 7 don't support child selectors, so they aren't commonly used in CSS style sheets today except as a way to get around bugs in those browsers. The technique of hiding certain CSS declaration blocks from certain browsers behind specially crafted CSS selectors is called a **CSS hack** and is discussed further in the next chapter.

Adjacent sibling selectors

The final kind of combinator that CSS2 provides is the **adjacent sibling selector**. This selector is again composed of at least two simple selectors and a combinator, which in this case is the plus sign (+). This selector gives you the ability to select a specific element only if that element is a sibling of another specific element that comes immediately before it in the markup.

Recall that a nested element in your markup is called a **child**, and the element that it is nested within is called a **parent**. A **sibling** is thus an element that is also a child of this parent element.

For example, in the navigation menu for Papa Pepperoncini's Pizza website, all the list items are siblings because they are all children of the unordered list:

```
<ul>
        <li><a href="index.html">Home</a></li>
        <li><a href="menu.html">Our Menu</a></li>
        <li><a href="locations.html">Locations</a></li>
        <li><a href="about.html">About Us</a></li>
</ul>
```

Obviously, the unordered list is the parent of the list items. It is also the **ancestor** (grandparent) of the links. The links are themselves children of the list items, but none of the links is a sibling of any other links, because each has different parents (that just happen to all be list items).

In the previous list, each list item child follows another list item sibling except the first (which can't follow anything, since it is, of course, first). Using the adjacent sibling selector, you could write a rule to select all but the first list items in lists and make them just a bit smaller, like this:

```
li + li { font-size: x-small; }
```

If you used this CSS rule on Papa Pepperoncini's Pizza website, the navigation menu's Home link would be bigger than the rest of the links in the menu, as Figure 5-10 shows.

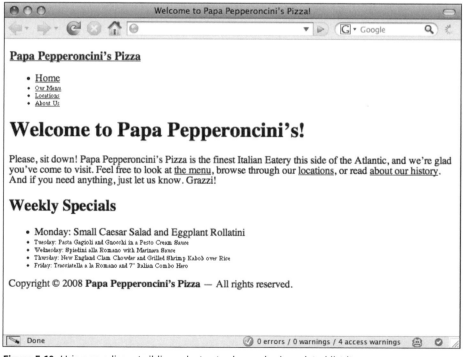

Figure 5-10. Using an adjacent sibling selector to de-emphasize related list items

In Figure 5-10, you can also see an unintended side effect of the previous CSS rule. Specifically, both of your lists, the main navigation menu *and* the list of weekly specials, have had the previous style rule applied to them. Thankfully, because you have well-structured markup, you can use a combination of all the different kinds of selectors you've just learned about to pinpoint the elements you'd like to style.

Combining multiple CSS selectors in a single rule

Now that you understand the building blocks of CSS selectors, what kinds of simple selectors are available to you, and how to chain them using specific combinators, you can take a quick look at a few complex examples. First, it's helpful to note that there is no law that says you can use only one kind of combinator in a CSS selector. This means you can use any combination of simple selectors and combinators to create arbitrarily complex selection patterns.

Let's amend the rule you used in the previous section so that it will apply only to the main navigation list. Currently, your rule looks like this:

```
li + li { font-size: x-small; }
```

It is affecting list items in every list on the entire page, and that's too broad for your tastes. So, let's narrow its subjects down to only the list items that are descended from the header <div>. To do this, you simply add an ID selector targeting the header <div> and use a descendant combinator to chain it to your existing selector. The new CSS rule looks like this:

```
#header li + li { font-size: x-small; }
```

This returns Papa Pepperoncini's list of weekly specials to the proper size. As another example, the following CSS selector is also perfectly valid:

```
#header li > a { ... }
```

This selector is composed of three simple selectors and two combinators, and it says, "Target all <a> elements that are children of <li> elements, when those <li> elements are descended from an element with an id of header." Here are some more examples of complex selectors. See whether you can work out what they mean.

```
div#header h1 { ... }
#specials .feature p { ... }
.feature > h1 em { ... }
.feature h1 + p { ... }
```

As you can now see, CSS selectors give you enormous power to target the elements you want—and only the elements you want.

CSS inheritance: making the general case work in your favor

As we talked about earlier, using properly structured markup and identifying the groups of those elements using IDs and class names gives you the ability to apply certain styles to a big chunk of the elements in your web page using a single CSS rule. You've already seen one example of this in practice, where you styled all the text in Papa Pepperoncini's website header in one fell swoop. Recall that the XHTML markup you developed for the website header looks like this:

```
<div id="header">
    <h3><a href="index.html">Papa Pepperoncini&rsquo;s Pizza</a></h3>
    <ul>
        <li><a href="index.html">Home</a></li>
        <li><a href="menu.html">Our Menu</a></li>
        <li><a href="locations.html">Locations</a></li>
        <li><a href="about.html">About Us</a></li>
    </ul>
</div>
```

The CSS rule you used to style all the text in the header with a particular font was this one:

```
#header {
    font-weight: bold;
    font-family: Zapfino, serif;
}
```

As you can see, you never explicitly selected any of the links, list items, or headlines inside the header <div>. Nevertheless, the text of each of these elements has been given the style you declared in the CSS rule selecting the header <div>. How did this happen? It's not magic; it's another feature of the CSS specification that the designers of CSS were clever enough to create.

This behavior is called **inheritance**, so named because of the way child elements acquire certain CSS properties that their parents also have just by virtue of being that parent element's child. Another way to say this is that children **inherit** CSS properties from their parents and ancestors. This automatic inheritance saves web developers like you from the tedious task of explicitly defining CSS properties for every single element on a web page. Can you imagine what a nightmare that would be? There are 12 elements in just the previous HTML snippet! You'd be no better off with CSS than you were without it!

Another way to think about inheritance and how it works is to think of your XHTML elements as steps, each nested element another step down from its parent element. When you apply a CSS property to one of the steps, it "cascades down all the steps" beneath it and gets applied to those elements, too.

As we remarked earlier, some CSS properties display this inherited behavior, and others do not. As a general rule, most of the properties that replace HTML elements for styling (such as text properties like font and color) and that you've already seen used in this chapter, are inherited properties and behave in this way. However, a number of properties are not inherited because it would make little sense for them to be, such as width and height. These properties, and others that affect the layout of the web page (discussed later in this chapter), are specific to the elements on which they are applied.

CSS inheritance is ultimately a way to allow you to get the biggest effect with the least amount of work, but it's not too wide a brush. At any point, you can specify another, more *specific* CSS rule to override an earlier rule. For instance, using the previous example, you could give the text within the list a plainer font with the following CSS rule:

```
#header ul { font-family: Verdana, sans-serif; }
```

Doing this is like pouring a new CSS property on your steps at the point of the unordered list so that this new property cascades down on top of the one that was applied to the step above it, the header <div>.

The CSS cascade and rules of specificity

What happens when the declarations of two or more CSS rules conflict with one another? Far from being a one-off occurrence, these situations are actually at the core of how CSS works and are referred to as the **cascade**. Learning how the cascade works is fundamental to learning CSS.

The CSS cascade is just a fancy name given to a set of rules that define how conflicts among different CSS declarations should be resolved. These rules are based on the concept that more *specific* rules should override more *general* rules. Each CSS rule that applies to an element is examined and sorted based on its **specificity**. The most general rules are applied first, then the next most general rule, and so on, until the browser reaches the most specific rule, each successive rule overriding the previous rule's declarations for the element's properties.

So, what makes one CSS rule "more specific" than another? It depends on a number of factors, such as where it was written in the source code (its **source order**) and the specificity of the CSS selector used. (There are other things that determine the specificity of a rule, such as its origin and its weight, but these are advanced topics that you will not likely encounter in the day-to-day web development process.)

These days, a number of tools are available that can help you visualize the cascade. Adobe Dreamweaver is one such tool, which has a good visualization feature for specificity in its CSS panel, and the TopStyle and CSSEdit applications are also good tools to consider for getting on top of the cascade. Additionally, both the Firebug add-on for Firefox and the Element Inspector in Safari 3 can show you inheritance results and the cascade order, too. These two tools are especially convenient since they are embedded directly into their respective host browsers.

CSS selector specificity

The selector you use as part of your CSS rule determines a great deal about how specific your rule is. In most cases, it's really easy to determine which selectors are more specific than others, since CSS selectors translate to English quite easily. For example, it's easy to see that a selector with multiple combinators will be more specific than a selector without any of them. This:

```
#header a { ... }
```

is more specific than this:

```
a { ... }
```

because the first reads as "all links descended from the header," whereas the second simply says "all links." Clearly, links that are specifically inside the header are a more specific target than links that can be anywhere on a page.

As a general rule of thumb, the more simple selectors and combinators a CSS selector has, the more specific it is. Some simple selectors are more specific than others, however, and so are some combinators. For example, a type selector is more general than a class selector, which is more general than an ID selector.

If you think about it, this is all simply common sense at work. You can have `<div>` elements all over your page, but a much smaller number of them might be classed as "features," and only one of them might be given the `feature-1` unique identifier. What this means is that given an element—for instance, `<div class="feature" id="feature-1">`—the following three CSS rules will all match, but the rule that uses the ID selector will actually be the one that the visitor sees applied.

```
.feature { color: green; }
#feature-1 { color: red; }
div { color: black; }
```

Of course, the result here is that this feature's text will be colored red. It doesn't matter in what order these three CSS rules are written down in the CSS file or even if they're not in the same style sheet at all. Since selector specificity is the primary sorting method the browser will use to determine the cascading order of an element's CSS properties, the most specific selector will always win.

Source order cascading

If two or more CSS rules conflict with one another but their selectors have an equal specificity, then their source order is used to determine which rule actually gets applied. This can often happen in complex style sheets that have many levels of cascading rules.

For instance, you may choose to make all the text in your feature boxes green by default, so you place the following CSS rule in an external style sheet:

```
.feature { color: green; }
```

You then link this style sheet to your web page, so the `<head>` portion of your document might look something like this:

```
<head>
    <title>Fantastic Staplers: Home Page</title>
    <link rel="stylesheet" type="text/css" href="css/global.css" />
</head>
```

Now, every page on your website that has been linked to this external style sheet will show feature boxes with green text. However, say that in the special Sales section of your website you want feature box text to be red, not green. How might you go about overriding the earlier rule you've written?

One possibility is to use a more specific CSS selector. For instance, perhaps each web page that is in the Sales section of your site has a `<body>` element with the id of `sale-section`. In that case, you can just add this rule anywhere in your style sheet:

```
#sale-section .feature { color: red; }
```

However, this requires changing the XHTML markup, even if only a little bit. There are some situations when this isn't possible or, more to the point, isn't advisable. Recall that CSS was invented to separate style from content, so it should be possible to make this change without affecting the XHTML content at all, and of course, it is. By adding a new style sheet to your page, re-declaring the feature box text as red, and inserting this new style sheet closer to the `<body>` element, you can use the CSS cascade's source order sorting to effect the change. Using this method, the `<head>` section of your document would now look something like this:

```
<head>
    <title>Fantastic Staplers: Sale Page</title>
    <link rel="stylesheet" type="text/css" href="css/global.css" />
    <style type="text/css">
        .feature { color: red; }
    </style>
</head>
```

Notice that this example is using an embedded style sheet to define the style sheet with the overriding rule, but it doesn't have to be an embedded style sheet. In fact, if the Sales section of your website is more than a single page, it behooves you to create a new external style sheet and link that in after the initial style sheet, like this:

```
<head>
    <title>Fantastic Staplers: Sale Page</title>
    <link rel="stylesheet" type="text/css" href="css/global.css" />
    <link rel="stylesheet" type="text/css" href="css/sale-section.css" />
</head>
```

In both examples, however, the concept is the same: style sheets defined further down the page (closer to the <body> element) will override ("cascade on top of") the styles defined further up the page (closer to the start of the <head> element) when the CSS rules that conflict have the same specificity.

It's also interesting to note that this is the same behavior you observed much earlier, when you overruled the browser's default styling with a style sheet of your own. Since the browser's default styles are defined "first" (they are at the earliest point of the cascade), any conflicting styles you define later overrule the browser's styling.

Visual rendering: document flow and the CSS box model

There are two final concepts to understand about CSS before you can honestly say that you know enough CSS to be dangerous. These are the CSS box model and how it relates to document flow. It's these two fundamental concepts that make designing for web pages radically different than designing for printed media. If you really want to become proficient with CSS-based designs, and especially if you're coming from a print design background, these are the concepts you absolutely need to nail.

Computer screens are not magazine pages, and at least for the foreseeable future, they won't ever be exactly like them. When you design for the printed page, you make certain assumptions about what kinds of designs might work based on facts that you understand about how printed media works. For example, you know that a standard printed page is a rectangle about 8.5 inches wide by 11 inches high, so you don't put a picture that is 10 inches wide or 13 inches high on the page because it just wouldn't fit. On the other hand, you know that you can put high-resolution images on the page because such images look really good when printed on paper (though they may not look so great on a computer monitor).

The web page, like the printed page, also has certain constraints, weaknesses, and advantages. For example, a web page can have a link or can change some of its content dynamically in response to user actions, such as hovering their cursor over a certain area. For obvious reasons, this is something a printed page couldn't dream of doing.

First, we'll quickly explain what document flow is. Then we'll briefly introduce the CSS box model. After that, we'll discuss how the two concepts are intricately related, and finally, we'll show you some of the ways that you can use CSS declarations to alter these two things at will.

What is document flow?

Document flow is a fundamental concept to CSS designers. In fact, the concept of document flow (or just **flow** for short) predates CSS considerably. So, what is it?

Document flow is a system by which a renderer (such as a web browser) lays out pieces of visible content on a screen so that they *flow* one after the other in predictable ways. Every element on a web page, every headline, every list item, every paragraph, and even every line of text and each individual character within every paragraph follow the rules of flow to determine where they end up on the screen.

For the most part, document flow just mimics what you would expect to see on a printed page. For example, while reading this book, you're looking at large chunks of text (paragraphs), each of which have a number of lines. These lines have printed characters on them that start from the left side and end at the right side. When you read the full paragraph, you're reading from the top-left corner of the paragraph, horizontally across each line, and ending at the bottom-right corner of the same paragraph.

This is the normal direction in which content flows in the English language. However, this is not true for all languages. Hebrew is an example of a language that reverses the direction of flow so that it begins from the top-right corner and ends at the bottom-left corner. Arabic does this, too. As described in the previous chapter, since web pages are really just long strings of sequential characters that a web browser sees one after the other, it needs some way to know how to order these characters and elements on the screen. It uses the rules of flow to do this.

It's easy enough to see how flow affects characters in a paragraph. Based on the language specified in the web page's <html> element, the web browser simply places the first character at either the top-left or top-right corner of the paragraph and then places each successive character it sees to the right or left of the one before it. Recall that your <html> element for Papa Pepperoncini's Pizza website began like this:

```
<html xmlns="http://www.w3.org/1999/xhtml" xml:lang="en" lang="en">
```

Since you've defined that this web page is written in English by specifying the xml:lang="en" and lang="en" attributes, the web browser will assume a normal flow for what is expected in English, specifically a direction of left-to-right text. If you're feeling experimental, go ahead and add the dir attribute with a value of rtl (short for right-to-left) to the <html> element, and you'll see that now every headline and paragraph is right-aligned (instead of how it was previously left-aligned) and the punctuation marks are all on the "wrong side" of the words.

So, parts of the rules of flow control things like the direction of text and where the beginning of an element's content should be placed, but as you'll see next, there's much more to flow than that.

What is the CSS box model?

You'll hear the term **box** used a lot when talking about CSS. The first question you need to ask yourself then is, quite obviously, what is a box?

In CSS, a box is simply a rectangular region that represents the physical space that a certain thing takes up. Typically, for web pages, this space is a group of pixels on a computer screen. For example, for every <p> element you define in your web page, you create a rectangle inside of which the content of that paragraph is displayed, or *flows into*. You can use tools such as Firebug or the Web Developer Toolbar add-on for Firefox to see these boxes, as shown in Figure 5-11.

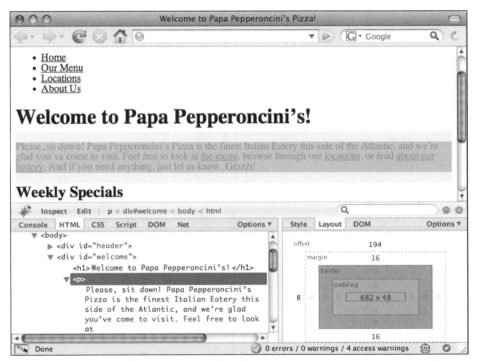

Figure 5-11. Firebug highlights the CSS box of an element when you hover your cursor over it.

Notice how the CSS boxes of the paragraphs always extend to the paragraph's edges, even though the last line of text inside the paragraph may not. This is because it's not only XHTML elements like the <p> element that create CSS boxes. Indeed, *everything* on a web page that is visible creates a box of a certain type, including strings of text content.

However, not all CSS boxes are created equally. These characters inside paragraphs do not create the same kinds of boxes that the <p> element does. This is very deliberate, and as you're about to see, it's a very important distinction.

Inline-level vs. block-level boxes

The <p> elements create what are known as **block-level** boxes, whereas the strings of text within them create **inline-level** boxes. These two different kinds of CSS boxes flow onto the screen in very different ways.

Block-level boxes always flow onto the page *one on top of another*, like boxes (or bricks) in a vertical stack. Since paragraphs are declared by all web browsers' default style sheets to be block-level boxes, each time you define a new <p> element (and thereby generate a new block-level CSS box), the browser places that paragraph underneath any block-level boxes that came before it. This is why two paragraphs next to one another always create two distinct chunks of text, one atop the other, by default. Other elements that create block-level boxes are headlines, <div> elements, and lists (not list items, but the list items' containing elements, <ul>, <ol>, and <dl>).

Inline boxes are almost always inside some containing block-level box, but instead of flowing one after the other in a vertical stack like the way block-level boxes do, they flow one after the other *horizontally*. Each character of text (or **glyph**) that the browser sees is thus placed *in the same horizontal line* with any inline-level elements that came before it. It's only if there's not enough horizontal space for things to fit on the same line that inline-level boxes get bumped down to the next line. Some examples of web page elements that create inline-level boxes by default are images, links, and emphasized text (the <em> and <strong> elements, for instance).

Runs of text that aren't nested within any of these inline-level elements also create inline boxes implicitly. These implicit inline-level boxes are called **anonymous** inline boxes because they don't have an element that is specifically associated with them.

For instance, the following XHTML markup you used for the paragraph of text on Papa Pepperoncini's website footer creates *two* CSS boxes (not one), one of which is a block-level box and one of which is an inline-level box:

```
<p>Copyright &copy; 2008 Papa Pepperoncini&rsquo;s ➥
    Pizza &mdash; All rights reserved.</p>
```

The <p> element is the one that creates the block-level box. All the text inside the <p> element creates the anonymous inline-level box. If you then added another inline-level element into this paragraph, say a <strong> element for some additional emphasis on Papa Pepperoncini's name, you'd suddenly have *four* CSS boxes.

```
<p>Copyright &copy; 2008 <strong>Papa Pepperoncini&rsquo;s ➥
    Pizza</strong> &mdash; All rights reserved.</p>
```

In this paragraph, the <p> element still creates the block-level box, but the text "Copyright © 2008 " creates the first anonymous inline box. Next, the <strong> element creates a second inline-level box (whose contents is "Papa Pepperoncini's Pizza"). Finally, the text " — All rights reserved." creates the second anonymous inline-level box. So in total, one block-level box plus two anonymous inline boxes plus another (nonanonymous) inline-level box equals a total of four CSS boxes.

The kind of CSS box that an element generates (inline-level or block-level box, for example) can be controlled with CSS. Specifically, the value of an element's display property determines what kind of box it will generate. Here's an example of what the default CSS rules that web browsers use to make <p> elements block-level and <strong> elements inline-level might look like:

```
p { display: block; }
strong { display: inline; }
```

Of course, you can override these default styles and make any element generate any kind of box you want—something that was flat-out impossible before the advent of CSS. For example, you could add a CSS rule that makes <strong> elements generate block-level boxes instead of inline-level boxes, like this:

```
strong { display: block; }
```

If you add that CSS rule to the style sheets for Papa Pepperoncini's web pages, you'll see that you now have three lines of text inside the one paragraph and that the words "Papa Pepperoncini's Pizza" will be on their own line. This is because, as you now know, the rules of flow dictate that block-level boxes be stacked vertically. Since the <strong> element is now generating a block-level CSS box, it must be placed on its own line, so you end up splitting the footer sentence across three lines.

In this state, you still have four CSS boxes, but instead of having three inline boxes all within a block-level box, you now have two inline boxes and two block-level boxes. One of the block-level boxes (the one generated by the <strong> element) is *overlapping* the one generated by the <p> element. You can make this more obvious by adding background colors to your <p> and <strong> elements:

```
p { background-color: blue; }
strong {
    display: block;
    background-color: red;
}
```

In Figure 5-12, your three lines of text are now striped blue, red, and then blue again.

Figure 5-12. Background colors reveal that the paragraph has been split by the insertion of a new block-level box.

There's another thing worth pointing out about this picture, too. Notice that each stripe goes all the way to the edge of the browser window. At first, you might be tempted to assume that all CSS boxes are just always going to be as wide as they can be, but this is not true, and this fact highlights another important difference between inline-level and block-level boxes.

Block-level boxes that have no specific width declared (such as the ones generated by both your <p> and <strong> elements) do, indeed, grow as wide as they can, while still fitting inside their containing

131

element's CSS box. In this case, all the block-level CSS boxes are as wide as the browser window, or **viewport**, because none of them has an explicit width, so they all grow to be as wide as they can be inside the web browser.

Inline-level boxes, however, grow only as wide as they need to be to make their content fit within them. Inline boxes are like shrink-wrap that surrounds whatever content they have. You can make this more obvious by giving a background color to your two remaining inline boxes.

First, since both of your remaining inline boxes are anonymous, you need to use an element you haven't seen before—the <span> element—so that you can target them with CSS. The <span> element is just like the <div> element except instead of generating a block-level box, by default it generates an inline-level box. The XHTML paragraph looks like this with the <span> elements added:

```
<p><span>Copyright &copy; 2008 </span><strong>Papa Pepperoncini&rsquo;s ➥
        Pizza</strong><span>&mdash; All rights reserved.</span></p>
```

The CSS now looks like this with the background colors applied to the <span> elements:

```
p { background-color: blue; }
span { background-color: green; }
strong {
    display: block;
    background-color: red;
}
```

Figure 5-13 shows the result.

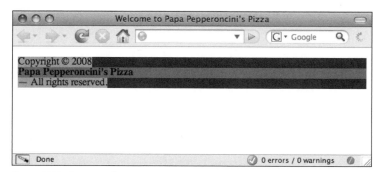

Figure 5-13. Four CSS boxes revealed using background colors. The inline-level boxes are shrink-wrapped to fit their contents, but the block-level boxes are as wide as their container lets them be.

The two inline-level boxes (colored green) shrink to the width of their content, but the block-level boxes (colored blue and red) extend to be as wide as they can.

Changing CSS box properties: the CSS box model explained

Every CSS box, whether inline-level or block-level, has four distinct areas within it. These are, from the "inside out," the **content** area, the **padding** area, the **border** area, and the **margin** area. The content area is one you are already familiar with. It is the rectangular area inside of which an element's content, whether plain text or other nested elements, is placed. The padding area is a transparent space around the content where only the background properties of an element (if any) will show. The border area frames the padding and the content, much like a picture frame. Finally, the margin area defines the amount of whitespace the CSS box should have around it.

Even though all of these areas always exist for all CSS boxes, much of the time, all of them except the content area is not shown because they have zero width and zero height. That is, they take up no space in the layout of a page whatsoever. However, with CSS, you can make each of these areas larger so that they will show up and thus affect the layout of the elements on your web page.

Firebug has a great Layout tab that lets you see exactly what the dimensions of each of these areas are for any given element. Let's start by examining the content area more closely and then do the same for each of the other three areas that the CSS box model defines.

Content area: defining the dimensions of content boxes

As you saw in the previous section, the content area of a CSS box behaves differently depending on the type of box being generated. For block-level boxes, the content area grows as wide as it can within the confines of its containing block or the browser viewport in the absence of such a container. For inline-level boxes, the content area shrinks so that it is only as wide as the widest part of its content. Both block-level and inline-level boxes grow as high as their tallest content, and no higher. This can be summed up in CSS with the following declarations:

```
width: auto; height: auto;
```

As you've probably guessed by now, changing the values of the width and height properties change the content area's width and height, respectively. Say, for instance, that you want the footer for Papa Pepperoncini's Pizza website to be exactly 300 pixels wide. No problem.

```
#footer { width: 300px; }
```

The width property (and any property that accepts a length value, such as the height property) can take as its value a number followed by an abbreviation (px in this example) that indicates the unit of measurement. The abbreviation px is short for pixels.

In this example, you're setting the width of the element with the ID of footer to exactly 300 pixels, no more and no less. Obviously, pixels make sense only for designs that are going to be displayed on a device that measures distances in pixels (like a computer monitor, and decidedly *not* a printed page). There are other *length units* that CSS will allow you to use, and we'll talk about one other unit a bit later.

So, with the earlier CSS rule applied to Papa Pepperoncini's footer, your footer text is now exactly 300 pixels wide all the time. Resizing the window will not change the width of your footer, and neither will adding more text content into it. The footer will remain at a fixed width because you've told it to do exactly that.

Note that even though this example *appears* to be using CSS inheritance, it's actually not. The <p> element inside the footer <div> still has a width value set to auto, since the width property is not inherited. However, since the <p> element is nested inside the footer <div> (the footer <div>'s CSS box is the paragraph element's *containing block*), and since the footer <div> is constrained to be only 300 pixels wide, the paragraph inside the footer can also be a maximum of only 300 pixels wide.

Since an inline-level box's width is defined by its content, the width property does not apply to these types of CSS boxes.

Padding area: giving backgrounds the floor

The padding area of a CSS box is the area immediately surrounding the content area. Padding is used to space the content of a box away from its edges. This helps a design look less cramped.

By default, most elements will not have any padding. The noteworthy exceptions are typically lists of some kind (unordered, ordered, or definition lists), whose child list item elements receive their indentation in some browsers through the application of a default padding value. (In other browsers, this same indentation effect is achieved with a default margin value. Margins are described later in the chapter.) In CSS, a box with no padding at all might be declared by using the following declaration:

```
padding: 0;
```

Notice that there is no unit abbreviation, such as px, after the 0 in the value of the padding property. Since 0 is the same value whether it is specified in pixels or in inches (or any other length unit), no unit abbreviation at all is needed.

Of course, all you need to do to give an element's box some visible padding area is to increase the amount from zero to some noticeable value. Let's give Papa Pepperoncini's footer 10 pixels of padding:

```
#footer {
    width: 300px;
    padding: 10px;
}
```

This change is subtle, but using Firebug you can clearly see that you now have 10 pixels of padding surrounding the content of the footer, as shown in Figure 5-14. Any background properties you specify on a box, such as a background color or background image, will "shine through" the invisible padding area because a box's backgrounds, unlike its contents, start at the edge between a box's padding and its border, *not* inside the box's content area.

You can see from this example that, in fact, you've applied 10 pixels of padding to *all four sides* of the content area. You have 10 pixels on the top, the right, the bottom, and the left sides of the footer <div>'s content. Also notice that the width of your content area is still 300 pixels, just as you left it.

The important thing to infer from this is that any space you give the padding, border, or margin areas of a CSS box get *added* to any size you might specify for the box's width (or height) property. In effect, your 300-pixel-wide CSS block-level box is now a 320-pixel-wide CSS box, because we've just added 10 pixels of padding to both the left and right sides of the box.

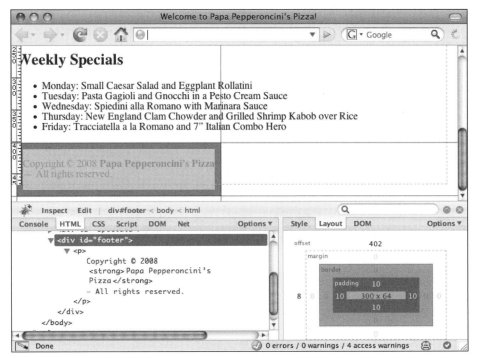

Figure 5-14. Firebug highlights different areas of a CSS box with different colors, making it plainly visible that your footer now has some padding applied to it.

With CSS, you have the flexibility to define different sizes for each of the four individual sides of a box. The padding property I used in the earlier CSS rule is just *shorthand* that expands to the following four declarations:

```
padding-top: 10px;
padding-right: 10px;
padding-bottom: 10px;
padding-left: 10px;
```

Every time you simply declare a value for a box's padding area with the padding property, you're really declaring each of those four specific padding properties with the same value applied to each property. CSS is full of shorthand properties like this, and it's important to be aware of them and what they expand to. When declaring rules generally, shorthand properties can save you quite a bit of typing (and quite a bit of bandwidth when downloading the finished CSS style sheet, too), but when you're declaring rules to override other rules, it pays to be as explicit as possible.

A CSS box's padding area behaves slightly differently based on whether the box is an inline-level box or a block-level box. The padding area of a block-level box behaves as you would expect, causing the content area to move both vertically and horizontally to accommodate the additional padding. However, while the *horizontal* padding of an inline box (that is, the right and left sides) behaves that way too, the *vertical* padding (the top and bottom sides) does not. Specifically, an inline box's vertical padding will increase the area available for the box's backgrounds, but *no other boxes will be affected by the inline box's occupation of the additional space.*

This is most easily illustrated with an example, so let's experiment with the introductory paragraph on Papa Pepperoncini's home page, since it's a paragraph that spans more than a single line. The XHTML for that paragraph looks like this:

```
<p>Please, sit down! Papa Pepperoncini&rsquo;s Pizza is the finest ➥
    Italian Eatery this side of the Atlantic, and we&rsquo;re glad ➥
    you&rsquo;ve come to visit. Feel free to look at the menu, ➥
    browse through our  your locations, or read about our  history. ➥
    And if you need anything, just let us know. Grazzi!</p>
```

Now, let's use a <span> element to create an inline box that you can target somewhere in the middle of the paragraph:

```
<p>Please, sit down! Papa Pepperoncini&rsquo;s Pizza is the finest ➥
    Italian Eatery this side of the Atlantic, and we&rsquo;re ➥
    glad you&rsquo;ve come to visit. <span>Feel free to look at ➥
    the menu</span>, browse through our locations, or read about ➥
    our history. And if you need anything, just let us know. ➥
    Grazzi!</p>
```

Finally, let's add a CSS rule to add a background color to the <span> element so you can easily see the content and padding areas of the inline box the element generates. You'll also increase the element's default amount of zero padding significantly. Figure 5-15 shows the result.

```
span {
    background-color: green;
    padding: 10px;
}
```

As you can see, the green background of the CSS box *overflows* beyond the confines of the line, sliding behind the line of text beneath it and obscuring the line of text above it. The vertical padding applies but does not affect the surrounding CSS boxes in any way. The text on either side of the green-colored inline box, however, is pushed 10 pixels further away, because the horizontal padding of the inline box does affect its surroundings.

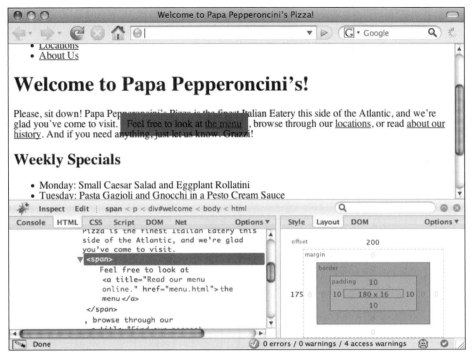

Figure 5-15. The vertical padding of an inline box does not affect the layout of other boxes on the page.

Border area: drawing borders and outlines

The border area is, as its name implies, a space to define a border (or outline) for a CSS box. The edge between a box's padding and its border is where any background stops being visible. A CSS box's four borders (top, right, bottom, and left sides as usual) have a number of different possible looks. Let's use a border to outline the footer on Papa Pepperoncini's website.

```
#footer {
    width: 300px;
    padding: 10px;
    border: 1px solid black;
}
```

Figure 5-16 shows the result of this addition.

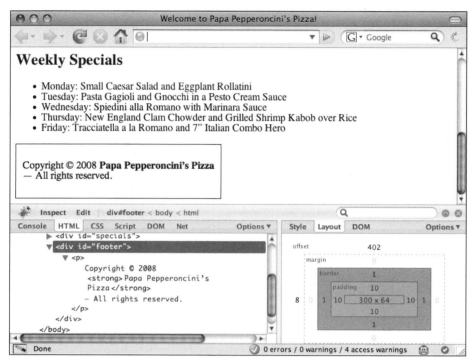

Figure 5-16. A border applied to a CSS box frames the padding and content areas of the box.

Borders behave in the same way as padding does. On a block-level box, all four sides affect their neighbors, but on an inline box, only the horizontal borders affect the layout of neighboring boxes.

The border property is another shorthand property. It sets a border width, style, and color for all four sides of a box. The example border declaration shown earlier expands to the following 12 declarations listed here, each of which can be set with a different value:

```
border-width-top: 1px;
border-width-right: 1px;
border-width-bottom: 1px;
border-width-left: 1px;
border-style-top: solid;
border-style-right: solid;
border-style-bottom: solid;
border-style-left: solid;
border-color-top: black;
border-color-right: black;
border-color-bottom: black;
border-color-left: black;
```

Borders have a lot of options, too many to go into at length in this chapter, so we encourage you to explore some of the other possible values for these properties on your own.

Margin area: defining whitespace and centering

The margin area of a CSS box defines whitespace that surrounds the box's other areas. Most of the spacing of elements on web pages is accomplished with clever combinations of margins and padding. Like the padding and border areas, CSS allows you to specify different amounts of whitespace (margin sizes) on each of the four sides of a CSS box, or you can use the margin shorthand property to set the margins of all four sides in one declaration.

Margins can be thought of as a way for an element's CSS box to invisibly "push against" any other boxes next to it in exactly the same way as you've seen happen with padding. Like padding and borders, all four sides of block-level box's margins affect the layout of its neighboring CSS boxes, but only the horizontal margins of an inline box do.

Typically, headlines, paragraphs, lists, and many other elements have a certain amount of vertical margins defined by the browser's default style sheet. This CSS rules could look like this:

```
h1, h2, h3, h4, h5, h6, p, ul, ol, dl { margin: 1em 0; }
```

The selector for this rule is simply a group of individual type selectors that matches all possible headline levels, paragraphs, unordered lists, ordered lists, and definition lists. The declaration uses the margin shorthand property. With two values, such as that shown earlier, the margin shorthand property expands to the following four CSS declarations:

```
margin-top: 1em;
margin-right: 0;
margin-bottom: 1em;
margin-left: 0;
```

That is, the first value sets the values for the vertical (top and bottom) sides, and the second value sets the values for the horizontal (right and left) sides.

The length unit being used here is an **em**. One em is the same length of whatever the length of the element's current font's lowercase letter m happens to be. Since the lowercase letter m is a different size in different fonts (and different font sizes), this unit is referred to as a **relative length unit** because the actual computed value is relative to another value that may change. Contrast this with an **absolute length unit**, such as pixels, which are always the same size no matter what. When working with text on a web page, it often pays to set sizes using a unit that is measured relative to a font size.

Why might the CSS rule for a margin use a relative unit that is defined by font sizes? If you think about it, the font size of an <h1> element is drastically different from the font size of an <h6> element and similarly different from the size of regular body text such as the contents of <p> elements. It makes sense, then, that the amount of whitespace (margins) on top of and below the CSS box for each of these elements is different.

It would look a little weird if you had a huge level-one headline but only had a few pixels distance between it and the introductory paragraph that came next, wouldn't it? Using relative units allows you to be consistent in your declarations and yet apply different actual values to CSS properties based on the values of other CSS properties. This is the basis for creating what is known as an **elastic layout**, an advanced implementation of designs that results in the ability to "zoom in" on a page by increasing the text size in the browser.

The margins of a box are also often used to center a block-level element horizontally within its containing block. Centering blocks is accomplished by setting both the right and left margins of the CSS box to the special value auto. You'll recall that this value simply means something like "automatically adjust this value based on the available space." Let's center the footer of Papa Pepperoncini's website as an example:

```
#footer {
    width: 300px;
    padding: 10px;
    border: 1px solid black;
    margin: 0 auto;
}
```

Again, the margin shorthand property is used to set the margins for all sides of the footer <div>. The vertical sides are both given margin values of 0 (meaning, no extra whitespace at all), and the horizontal sides are both set to auto. Figure 5-17 shows the result of adding the margin rule that centers the footer.

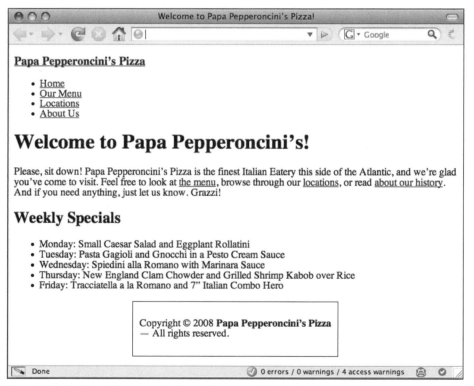

Figure 5-17. Block-level boxes are horizontally centered in the document flow by declaring a specific width and horizontal margins set to auto.

The footer is centered within the browser viewport because its right and left margins are each automatically adjusting their size to an equal share of the available horizontal space. To create available space in the first place, a width value other than the default of auto and less than the width of the footer's containing block (the browser window, in this case) must be specified so that the element appears centered in this way.

Margins have one other interesting property that can at first be confusing but quickly becomes indispensable. When the bottom margin of one element is directly next to the top margin of another with no intervening areas (no padding or border areas separating them), then the two margins combine to form a single margin equal to the size of the larger margin. This peculiar behavior, called **collapsing margins**, occurs only for vertical margins and never for horizontal ones.

This behavior is handy because it prevents you from needing to specify a multitude of additional CSS rules in the common case where two block-level boxes follow one another in the document flow, such as a sequence of multiple consecutive paragraphs. In that case, setting a top and bottom margin of, say 1em, on each paragraph will result in exactly 1em of whitespace between each paragraph (*not* 2em). If vertical margins didn't collapse, you'd instead have to specify something like 1em of bottom margin and *zero* top margin on every paragraph *except* the first in the series.

It can take a bit of time to get comfortable with the notion of declaring the sizes of what are essentially invisible areas of a page in order to define the layout of elements. This method of designing runs counter to the natural feel of directly manipulating the object itself. Nevertheless, you'll find that if you "go with the flow" of a web page, you'll end up creating designs that are far more flexible and far more maintainable.

Summary

This chapter covered an immense amount of technical material and a lot of theoretical ground. Don't feel discouraged if you think you may need to return to this chapter to get a handle on everything we've discussed. Thanks to its flexibility, power, and unfortunately spotty browser implementations, actually creating complex designs with CSS can be tricky, but knowing the foundations will prove invaluable just a short ways down the line.

In this chapter, we introduced the majority of foundational concepts that explain how CSS actually works inside the web browser, such as the cascade, inheritance, document flow, and the box model. We also introduced a great deal of practical information regarding how to use CSS, such as how to apply CSS styles to a web page by using external or embedded style sheets and individual inline styles. We also covered the syntax and terminology of CSS rules, distinguishing between properties, values, declarations, declaration blocks, selectors, and rules. We explored many possible CSS selectors and observed how you can have incredible flexibility over how you apply styles to elements by chaining simple selectors together with combinators. Finally, we introduced a plethora of CSS properties, including shorthand properties, that each changed the way an element is displayed visually.

Armed with this knowledge, you'll next take a look at a real design and dissect it to discover how it was implemented. You'll then use this experience to help you implement a simple design for Papa Pepperoncini's website. Along the way, we'll introduce you to some additional CSS concepts and properties that will give you yet another layer of appreciation for the power and flexibility of web standards.

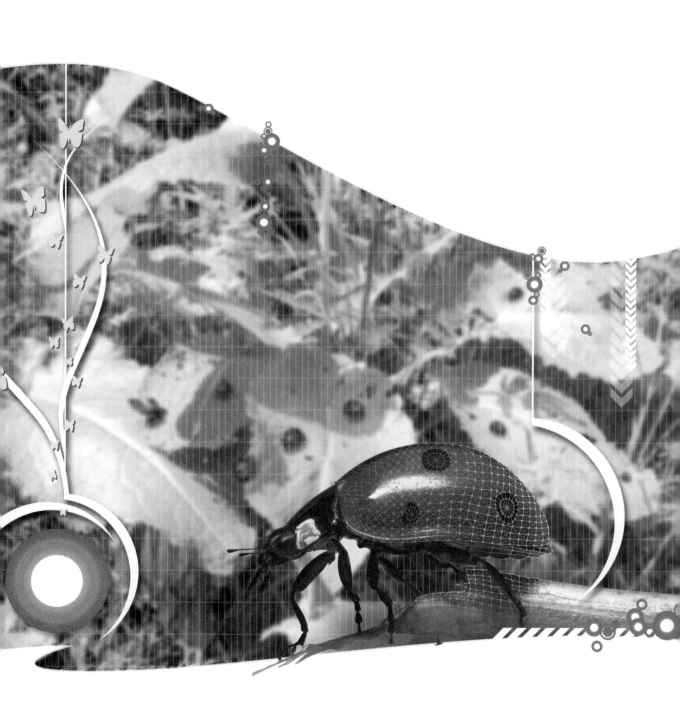

Chapter 6

DEVELOPING CSS IN PRACTICE: FROM DESIGN TO DEPLOYMENT

In the previous two chapters, we talked a lot about the theory and concepts behind standards-based front-end web development. You learned why and how to create structured, semantically meaningful XHTML markup. You learned how Cascading Style Sheets work, how web browsers display XHTML content by default, and how to apply your own CSS rules to web pages. It's finally time to bring all your newfound knowledge to bear on a real project and turn your bland, unstyled web page into a beautiful, professionally implemented CSS design.

Since the easiest way to learn CSS-based design techniques is arguably to simply dive right into them, we invite you to think about this chapter as though you were looking over our shoulders while we show how to implement this design in code. We'll be carrying through the execution of the earlier examples in this book, the Papa Pepperoncini's Pizza website. Throughout this chapter, we'll be making references to topics covered in the previous two chapters, so we strongly urge you to read those chapters before beginning this one.

The visual source: understanding design documents

In any website design process, there always comes a point at which the developer (that's you) needs to turn a visually presented layout into a real web page. The designs for websites are typically created in programs such as Adobe Photoshop or GIMP. These programs are photo manipulation applications, so they produce raster graphics that can't be used on web pages. However, these files contain all the specific information about what a design looks like, including what fonts are used for each text element, the physical dimensions of all the items in the design, and the raw assets for each graphic.

As a front-end web developer, you are tasked with translating this design file into XHTML and CSS code to make your web page's look and feel match the look and feel of the design document as closely as possible. This is easier said than done because design files aren't constrained by the same limitations that web browsers are. Many times, design elements may need to be modified in some way so that they are suitable for the web pages for which they're destined. For this reason, it really pays off to be familiar with one of these image-editing applications. Such software is beyond the scope of this book, however, so you'll be focusing solely on implementing a design in CSS in this chapter.

Diving into code: advanced CSS concepts applied

To refresh your memory, Figure 6-1 shows you what the Papa Pepperoncini's Pizza website looks like without any styles applied to it.

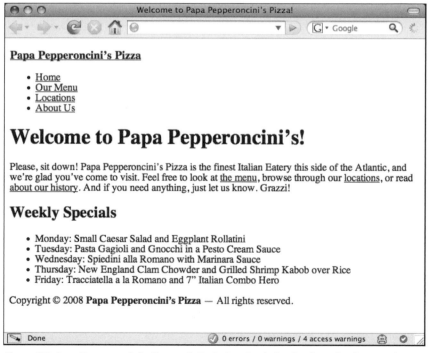

Figure 6-1. Papa Pepperoncini's Pizza website before its design has been implemented

In this chapter, you'll turn that web page into one that looks like the Photoshop design document shown in Figure 6-2.

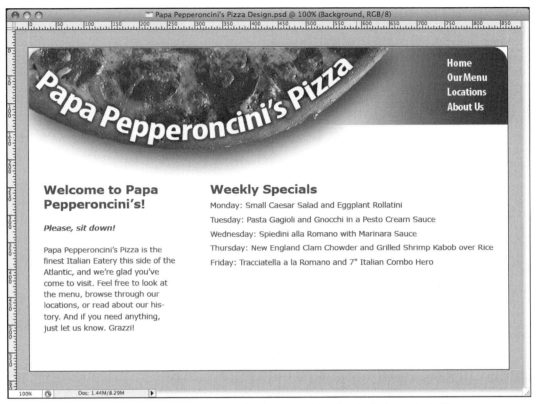

Figure 6-2. The original Photoshop PSD shows you the designer's vision for the look and feel of Papa Pepperoncini's website.

As you can see by comparing the design document to the current version of the web page, the designer's vision is radically different from the original, default styling. Using CSS, however, you'll make it happen.

The CSS development workflow

When developing any website design with CSS, you can follow some well-established best practices. Following these guidelines will make your life a lot easier, and they will ensure you end up with well-tested, standards-based code. One of the most important guidelines is to develop your style sheet in whatever browser most strictly adheres to the W3C's published standards. Since we're showing how to develop CSS now, we'll use the most popular browser that conforms to the W3C's CSS standards. As of this writing, that browser is Mozilla's Firefox web browser, currently at version 2.0.0.14 (though soon to be Firefox 3, because it is in the final stages of beta at this time), so whenever we refer to "our web browser" for the time being, that's the browser we mean. Although it's a good idea to occasionally check your progress in other browsers, for the sake of clarity in this text we'll refrain from mentioning other browsers and how to deal with their bugs until after the CSS design is completely implemented.

First things first: let's set up the source code file. In Chapter 4, you developed a basic XHTML template for the home page of Papa Pepperoncini's Pizza website. You saved this template as a plain-text file named index.html. The content of this file is as follows:

```
<!DOCTYPE html PUBLIC "-//W3C//DTD XHTML 1.0 Strict//EN"
    "http://www.w3.org/TR/xhtml1/DTD/xhtml1-strict.dtd">
<html xmlns="http://www.w3.org/1999/xhtml" xml:lang="en" lang="en">
<head>
    <meta http-equiv="Content-Type" content="text/html; ➥
        charset=utf-8" />
    <title>Welcome to Papa Pepperoncini&rsquo;s Pizza!</title>
</head>
<body>
    <div id="header">
        <h3>
            <a href="index.html">Papa Pepperoncini&rsquo;s Pizza</a>
        </h3>
        <ul>
            <li><a href="index.html">Home</a></li>
            <li><a href="menu.html">Our Menu</a></li>
            <li><a href="locations.html">Locations</a></li>
            <li><a href="about.html">About Us</a></li>
        </ul>
    </div>
    <div id="welcome">
        <h1>Welcome to Papa Pepperoncini&rsquo;s!</h1>
        <p>
                Please, sit down! Papa Pepperoncini&rsquo;s Pizza ➥
                is the finest Italian Eatery this side of the ➥
                Atlantic, and we&rsquo;re glad you&rsquo;ve come to ➥
                visit. Feel free to look at the menu, browse through ➥
                our locations, or read about our history. And if ➥
                you need anything, just let us know. Grazzi!
        </p>
    </div>
    <div id="specials">
        <h2>Weekly Specials</h2>
        <ul>
            <li>Monday: Small Caesar Salad and Eggplant Rollatini</li>
            <li>Tuesday: Pasta Gagioli and Gnocchi in a Pesto Cream ➥
                Sauce</li>
            <li>Wednesday: Spiedini alla Romano with Marinara Sauce ➥
                </li>
            <li>Thursday: New England Clam Chowder and ➥
                Grilled Shrimp Kabob over Rice</li>
            <li>Friday: Tracciatella a la Romano and ➥
                7&rdquo; Italian Combo Hero</li>
        </ul>
    </div>
```

```
        <div id="footer">
            <p>Copyright &copy; 2008 <strong>Papa Pepperoncini&rsquo;s ➡
                Pizza</strong> &mdash; All rights reserved.</p>
        </div>
    </body>
</html>
```

When you begin to add CSS rules to your page, you'll do so inside an embedded style sheet. The reasons you use an embedded style sheet over an external style sheet during development is twofold. First, it's far easier to keep a single file open in your favorite text editor than it is to switch between two files. Second, putting all your CSS rules in an embedded style sheet while you write them ensures that a single reload of the web page in your browser will apply the new rules, regardless of how your web browser may be configured. If you were to use an external style sheet, you may run into issues caused by the browser's attempts to cache your external CSS style sheet.

The first thing you need to do is create the style element in which you'll write your CSS styles. For the moment, you'll simply create an empty embedded style sheet with a single comment. Comments in CSS behave the same way comments in (X)HTML do; they let you write notes in plain English to yourself that the browser simply ignores. Unlike comments in (X)HTML, however, CSS comments begin with the two-character sequence /* and end with the two-character sequence */.

```
<!DOCTYPE html PUBLIC "-//W3C//DTD XHTML 1.0 Strict//EN"
    "http://www.w3.org/TR/xhtml1/DTD/xhtml1-strict.dtd">
<html xmlns="http://www.w3.org/1999/xhtml" xml:lang="en" lang="en">
<head>
    <meta http-equiv="Content-Type" ➡
                content="text/html; charset=utf-8" />
    <title>Welcome to Papa Pepperoncini&rsquo;s Pizza!</title>
    <style type="text/css">
        /* CSS rules for Papa Pepperoncini's Pizza will go here */
    </style>
</head>
```

Now that you have a place to start defining CSS rules, you'll next define some global styles to make sure all web browsers will use your own defaults instead of their own:

```
<style type="text/css">
html, body {
    margin: 0;
    padding: 0;
    border: none;
    background: white;
}
</style>
```

These CSS rules "zero out" any margins, padding, and borders that browsers may give the page by default by setting all these attributes to explicit initial values. Doing this ensures that you have a common starting point for each browser.

Now that you've made a change to the CSS rules in your style sheet, you can view the change by reloading the index.html page in your web browser. Each time you save a new change, you'll typically check to see whether it got applied properly by reloading the web page in the browser. Then, you'll continue by saving another change, and you'll repeat the process all over again. You simply lather, rinse, and repeat until the entire design is complete.

This is a good start so far. Let's begin defining the CSS rules specific to this design.

Typography: text colors, fonts, and font sizes

With CSS, you get the most benefit by defining the most common design properties first. These will be encoded with CSS rules with very general selectors and will rely on CSS inheritance to cascade all the way down to your page elements. By defining the similar design elements in this general way first, you save time and ensure that the most basic parts of the design are applied consistently to the whole website in one fell swoop.

In this design, the colors are simplistic: a tomato red with orange and white highlights—the colors of Papa Pepperoncini's signature product, the classic Italian pizza. Almost all the text in the web page is this same tomato red color, so let's define that globally by applying it to the <body> element:

```
<style type="text/css">
html, body {
    margin: 0;
    padding: 0;
    border: none;
    background: white;
}
body {
    color: #993333;
}
</style>
```

The value for the color property used here merits some explanation. Up until now, you've used only keywords as values for the color property, such as white or black. However, the CSS specification defines only 16 standard color keywords (based on the Windows VGA color palette), which is obviously somewhat limiting. This is why CSS also lets you specify a color that is defined by numeric value, called a **numeric RGB specification**, which lets you define any combination of red, green, and blue colors individually in order to compose the exact color you want to use.

> It might be interesting to note that the CSS3 specification defines 140 or so color keywords that you can use in your style sheets. Many of these are already supported in browsers, so you may find that you can safely use them today. However, if you do, your CSS code will not be able to validate as a CSS2 style sheet because the CSS2 specification does not include those keyword values. Instead, either validate your CSS code against the CSS3 specification or use a different method to define your colors, such as an RGB triplet.

Theoretically, using an RGB specification for your color increases your choice of possible color values into the millions. Modern displays that can support more than 256 colors can safely take advantage of these additional color values; however, websites that still need to support older display technologies most commonly use a subset of these colors called **web-safe colors** (or sometimes just **web colors** for short). This is a specific set of about 216 colors that are guaranteed to display in almost the same way across a number of computing platforms that have limited capabilities. The tomato red value used earlier is one of these web colors.

You can write the CSS color units in numeric RGB specification in one of two notations. The more common notation is the one used previously and is called **hexadecimal notation** (or more simply, **hex**) because it uses hexadecimal digits to define the values of each of the three colors. A hexadecimal color unit always begins with an octothorpe (#) and is then followed by hexadecimal digits, called a **hex triplet** (it's a triplet because of the set of the three RGB colors—red, green, and blue). The first two digits of the hex triplet are the value for red, the next two are the value for green, and the final two are the value for blue.

In the example CSS rule, this means 99 is the value for the red channel, 33 is the value for the green channel, and 33 is the value for the blue channel. There's also a noteworthy shortcut that you can use to specify hex values for web-safe colors, such as this one, where each of the color channels has the same hex digit. Instead of using a six-digit hex number, you can specify each color channel as a single hex digit, which the web browser will duplicate on its own. So, in this case, the following two CSS declarations are identical:

```
color: #993333;
color: #933;
```

There's nothing magic about this expansion. The browser simply sees that the hex value is specified with a mere three digits instead of six and duplicates the digit from each color channel to complete the set. Here's another set of CSS declarations that are identical:

```
color: white;
color: #FFFFFF;
color: #FFF;
```

Knowing this, you can shorten your CSS rules like so:

```
<style type="text/css">
html, body {
    margin: 0;
    padding: 0;
    border: none;
    background: #FFF;
}
body {
    color: #933;
}
</style>
```

Keeping CSS style sheets short is one way to make your website load faster, since the smaller the size of your files, the less time it takes a browser to download and parse them.

The other, less common notation for CSS color units lets you use a comma-separated list of either three decimal numbers (between 0, which is equivalent to #00, and 255, which is equivalent to #FF) or percentages (where 0.0% is equivalent to #00 and 100% is equivalent to #FF). As an example, these color declarations that set the property to green are also all identical:

```
color: green;
color: #0F0;
color: #00FF00;
color: rgb(0, 255, 0);
color: rgb(0%, 100%, 0%);
```

Moving on, you can next notice that the majority of the text on your web page is displayed using the Verdana font face. This is a common font for web pages because it's installed by default on almost every standard personal computer available today. Other common fonts include Arial, Helvetica, and Times, as well as most of the variations of these font families. Since you as a web developer cannot guarantee the existence of a particular installed font on a visitor's computer, it's safest to use the most common fonts, but the cost of this safety is that these fonts don't always look very nice on every design. With CSS, you can actually specify a list of fonts that you want the browser to try and apply, in order. This way, anyone with the nicer fonts installed will see them, and the visitors without them will get the generic fonts.

Since the design you have specifically calls for Verdana, let's list that font first:

```
<style type="text/css">
html, body {
    margin: 0;
    padding: 0;
    border: none;
    background: #FFF;
}
body {
    color: #933;
    font-family: Verdana;
}
</style>
```

Of course, there's still a chance (however slim) that the visitor viewing your page doesn't have Verdana installed on their computer. In that case, let's list another similar and common font choice, say Arial, followed in turn by the generic sans-serif font keyword:

```
body {
    color: #933;
    font-family: Verdana, Arial, sans-serif;
}
```

As you can see, fonts are listed in a comma-separated list, one after the other in the order you want the browser to try to apply them. In this case, you're telling the browser to "use the Verdana font if available, but if not, then try Arial. If that's not available either, just pick any font that doesn't have serifs in it." If a font name contains spaces, it needs to be quoted so the browser knows that the space is part of the font name. For instance, a common font that has spaces in its name is Times New Roman. To use that font in the list of font-family values, you'd need to write it like this:

```
font-family: "Times New Roman", Helvetica, serif;
```

In this example, you're telling the browser to "use the Times New Roman font if it is installed; otherwise try using Helvetica, and if that isn't available, just use any font with serifs." Note that Times New Roman is quoted and that the comma that delimits it from Helvetica is *outside* the quotation marks. In addition to the sans-serif and serif generic font families that CSS lets you specify, you can also declare cursive, fantasy, and (much more commonly used than the previous two) monospace.

You've now completed the very basic text coloring and font choices for your page, but there's more you need to do in regard to your text. You need to set a default size for the text on your page.

Sizes, as you'll recall from the previous chapter, can be specified in any of a number of CSS units. For a web page that will be viewed on a computer monitor, sizing fonts by specifying pixel lengths might seem like the most natural choice. However, since pixels are an absolute unit, they actually impose undesirable constraints on the visitor. Specifically, in Internet Explorer 5 and 6, text with a font-size property that uses a pixel value *can't be resized* at all!

To avoid this accessibility concern, you'll use a percentage value to specify the text's default size. Let's specify this value as 62.5%, since that gives you a default font size of 10 pixels, which seems like a nice round number. (Text that is 10 pixels in size is still a bit too small for your design, but you'll hold off specifying exact sizes until you get a little further along.) This way, the text in every browser remains resizable while still being declared as the same size.

```
body {
    color: #933;
    font-family: Verdana, Arial, sans-serif;
    font-size: 62.5%;
}
```

In addition to the font-family and font-size properties, another property that's worth mentioning as it relates to font sizes is the line-height property. You can use this property, which determines the height of each line inside an inline CSS box, to great effect. Most commonly, this property allows you to add a bit of spacing between the bottom of one line and the top of the one that follows it. For instance, here's how you could easily create double-spaced paragraphs in your page:

```
p { line-height: 200%; }
```

Of course, unless you're writing an academic paper, double-spaced lines are probably too far apart from one another. Most often, the most you need is a half line of whitespace between the lines of your text. In that case, a value of 150% will give you the result you want. That is, a value of 100% is the current height of the line, so 150% is the current height plus half its height, or one-and-a-half lines high, which results in a half line of whitespace between each line.

Now that you've defined both font-family and font-size, you can actually take advantage of another one of CSS's shorthand properties, the font property. This property allows you to set (almost) every property that applies to text in one declaration. At a minimum, it requires that you specify a font-size and font-family, though it also allows you to specify the font-style, font-variant, font-weight, and line-height properties in addition to these two required properties. Let's use it to quickly add in the default text's line height, too:

```
body {
    color: #933;
    font: 62.5%/1.3em Verdana, Arial, sans-serif;
}
```

The syntax of the font property can be a little tricky. As you can see here, you specify the font-size first. This value is then followed by a forward slash (/), and after that you specify the line-height value as another length unit. We used the em length unit here, but you could just as well have used a percentage. In fact, when it comes to font sizing, ems and percentages are interchangeable: 100% is equivalent to 1em, so 1.3em is equivalent to 130%.

Finally, the font property ends with the font-family property's list of your chosen fonts. What this says to the web browser is that you want to "set all the text inside the body to 62.5% of its default size, increase each line's height by an additional 0.3em (that is, by an additional 30%), and use the Verdana font to display text or Arial if Verdana isn't available or any other sans-serif font if Arial isn't available either."

Since the font property is so chock-full of options, let's take a look at some more examples:

```
font: italic 200% Zapfino, cursive;
```

This declaration sets the targeted text to a font-style of italic, a font-size of 200% (which means double whatever it was before), and a font-family list of Zapfino, cursive. Notice that you didn't specify a line-height property, since that is one of the optional properties. Here's another example:

```
font: small-caps bold 16pt "Helvetica", serif;
```

This time, you've set the font-variant property to small-caps (which turns text into uppercase lettering, with capital letters in the XHTML source code sized slightly larger than lowercase ones), the font-weight to bold, the font-size to 16pt (pt is short for points, a length unit traditionally used to size text for printing), and the font-family list to Helvetica, serif.

As a final example, these two CSS rules are identical:

```
h2 {
    font: inherit small-caps bold larger/150% Helvetica, serif;
}
h2 {
    font-style: inherit;
    font-variant: small-caps;
    font-weight: bold;
    font-size: larger;
    line-height: 150%;
    font-family: Helvetica, serif;
}
```

The interesting value in this example is inherit, which you've set on the font-style property. This special value just means "Use whatever the target element's parent's value for this CSS property is." Nearly all CSS properties can take an inherit value.

At this point, Papa Pepperoncini's website is looking a bit more stylish, but not by much. Figure 6-3 shows what you have so far. Next, since you've finished writing the CSS rules specifying the generalities, let's tackle that fancy header with the image of a big pizza pie in it.

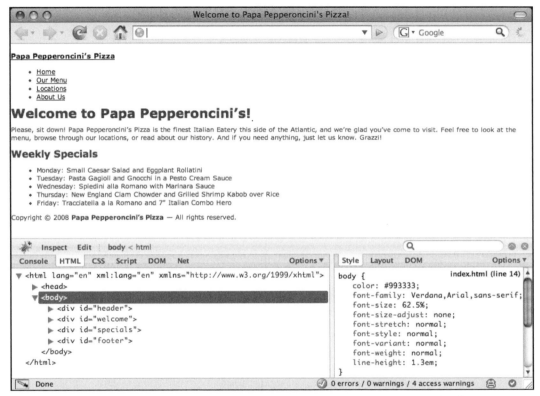

Figure 6-3. The text of Papa Pepperoncini's Pizza website is beginning to show some color and styling.

Implementing the header: images and backgrounds

In this design, you have a large image of a pizza pie in the top-left corner that overlaps a red stripe. The red stripe has a gradient that goes from white under the pizza to red at its edge. Both the top-left and top-right corners are curved. In the original design file you got from your designer, the width of their canvas was 863 pixels. Furthermore, the designer's canvas couldn't accommodate any resizing that your web page must accommodate, so it doesn't make sense to try to replicate the design as though it were set in stone.

Instead, you'll use the design document as a *guideline* for the final look of the web page. Specifically, you can tell from looking at the design that the designer clearly intended the masthead to stretch from the one edge of the browser window to the other. If you implement this design with a fixed width, however, you'll end up with a design that can't accommodate a resized window. On the other hand, if you design the page in a way that allows the width of the header to be the same as the width of the browser window at any given point, you need to ensure that the gradient on the red stripe turns into a solid color before the point at which the design can stretch.

As you can imagine, in a much more complex design, there are many more complex issues such as this to consider. However, even with this simplistic example, you can clearly begin to see just how different designing for a web page is than designing for print. A lot of the design decisions that may seem great for print turn out to be really challenging when it comes time to implement the design in XHTML and CSS code.

Additionally, there is usually a point in any design where you simply have to allow for some distortion. Few layouts are resilient enough to accommodate everything from a 128-pixel-wide viewport, such as those commonly found on cheap mobile phones and PDAs, to a 2560-pixel-wide viewport, such as that provided by a 30-inch Apple Cinema Display, or even just text at the smallest or largest sizes possible. Thinking about how a design will stretch and how the text in a layout will flow is critical to creating good designs for web pages, but few print designers are used to this sort of thing.

In this case, you need to make a few changes to your design document in order to accommodate the variable-width layout you want. First, you need to move the end of the gradient past the point where the curve on the top-right corner of the design begins. It's at that point, 835 pixels to the right of the left edge of the browser window, where you'll be "stretching" the banner image. Second, you need to split the banner background into two separate images: one that includes the pizza and the curved text "Papa Pepperoncini's Pizza" on top of it for the left side of the banner and one that includes the curved corner for the right side of the banner.

> *When designing web pages, it's important to consider your target audience's likely screen resolution. At the time of this writing, most users have computer monitors that are at least 1024 pixels wide by default, but there are still some users (estimated at about 8 percent) with displays set to a resolution of 800 by 600 pixels. In those cases, a design that is wider than the width of their screen, such as this 835-pixel-wide design, will always cause a horizontal scroll bar to appear. To ensure you avoid this, you need to slim the design down to some width that is narrower than their browser window is likely to be. In the case of a monitor set to a resolution of 800 by 600, the safest bet is to keep your design less than 760 pixels wide.*

Figure 6-4 shows the image of the pizza you'll use, which also includes the entire gradient on the red-dish stripe, and Figure 6-5 shows the image of the curved corner on the right side of the page.

There are some interesting things to note about these images. Note that the image with the pizza, drop shadow, curved text, and gradient is saved as a JPG file. This is because the JPG image file format is a far superior image file format for encoding complex imagery that doesn't have clearly identifiable geometric shapes, such as straight lines. On the other hand, the other image that consists almost entirely of two solid colors (a reddish stripe and white stripe underneath it) is saved as a GIF file for the same reason. The GIF image file format compresses very nicely when the image's contents are primarily straight lines or other geometric shapes.

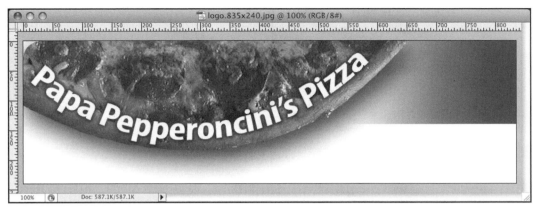

Figure 6-4. The banner image will be an 835-pixel-wide JPG image created by flattening several layers of the designer's original PSD document.

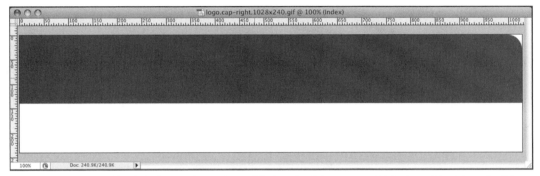

Figure 6-5. The right side of the banner image is modified so that it becomes a 1028-pixel-wide stripe of solid colors. This extra width is necessary to accommodate resizing the browser window.

Another thing to notice about these images is their file names. Though purely a stylistic choice, we called the one with the pizza logo.835x240.jpg because this is an image of Papa Pepperoncini's logo, and it is 835 pixels wide by 240 pixels high. Embedding the image's dimensions into the file name like this helps us remember what we're working with when all we're looking at is the text of a CSS style sheet. The multiple dots in the file name let us create a customized name space for each of our images. For instance, we named the other image file logo.cap-right.1028x240.gif. Among other things, this naming scheme makes sure that both images will show up next to each other in alphabetized file listings, such as those that FTP client programs produce, and that images with a similar purpose are grouped automatically. You'll see us use this convention throughout the rest of this chapter.

Finally, there are two more noteworthy things to pay attention to in the image of the curved top-right corner of the banner. First, it's extremely wide—1028 pixels wide to be precise. We made sure it was so wide because it's this extra width that will be visible when the visitor resizes their browser window. This extra width ensures that you can accommodate a browser viewport that is a total of 1863 pixels wide (835 pixels + 1028 pixels = 1863 pixels). It's very unlikely that most visitors will resize their browser window beyond this width, so this should be sufficient.

With the images sliced out of the design document and saved as files suitable for display on the Web inside a directory (let's call it images) in the same directory as your XHTML file, you can now write the CSS that attaches your images to your XHTML header. First, let's attach the header's background image, which will be the GIF image of the top-right corner of the banner:

```
<style type="text/css">
html, body {
    margin: 0;
    padding: 0;
    border: none;
    background: #FFF;
}
body {
    color: #933;
    font: 62.5%/1.3em Verdana, Arial, sans-serif;
}
#header {
    background-image: url(images/logo.cap-right.1028x240.gif);
}
</style>
```

This is another property and value you haven't seen before, so let's examine it a bit closer. The background-image property is pretty self-explanatory. It's used to apply an image to the background of an element. However, the value is a bit more complex. Since images are always separate files, they need to be referenced in CSS with a URL, just like they need to be referenced with a URL from the XHTML <img ... /> element. There's nothing special about this URL either. It simply states that the image you're referencing can be found at the relative URL specified between the parentheses of the CSS property's value. Figure 6-6 shows the result of the CSS rules thus far.

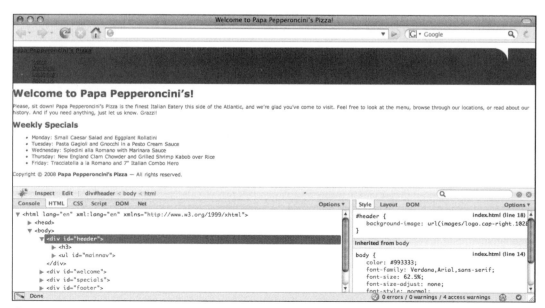

Figure 6-6. Applying a background image tiles the background image by default.

This looks mostly OK, but as you can see, there's a problem at the top-right corner of the viewport, where the curve ends and the stripe seems to repeat itself. Indeed, it does, because by default any background image applied to an XHTML element is **tiled**, or repeated, both vertically and horizontally. To avoid this, you need to specify a value of no-repeat on the background-repeat property:

```
#header {
    background-image: url(images/logo.cap-right.1028x240.gif);
    background-repeat: no-repeat;
}
```

Figure 6-7 shows that the background image is now no longer tiling.

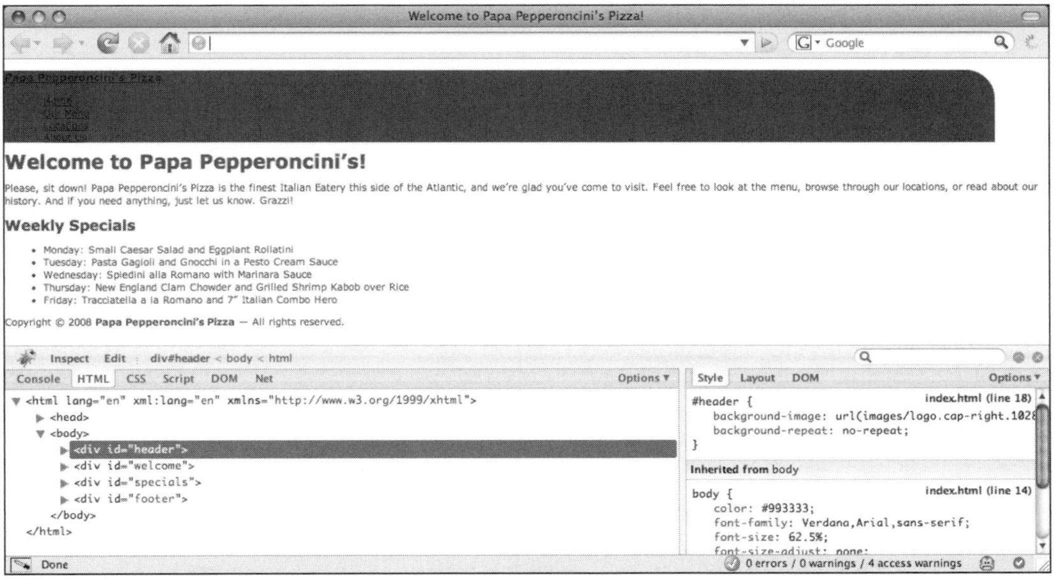

Figure 6-7. The header's background image no longer tiles but still needs to be placed in the right spot.

This is getting better, though you still need to ensure that this image is actually on the *right* side of the header, not the left. You'll need to use the background-position property to do this:

```
#header {
    background-image: url(images/logo.cap-right.1028x240.gif);
    background-repeat: no-repeat;
    background-position: right top;
}
```

The background-position property specifies exactly where inside the CSS box's padding and content areas the background image is first displayed. The property takes two values, the first of which specifies a horizontal offset from the padding area's left or right edge and the second of which specifies a vertical offset from either the padding area's top or bottom edge. Notice that this is not the same as the CSS box model properties such as padding or margin for which values are declared in a clockwise rotation. That is, first top, then right, then bottom, and finally left. This is often abbreviated to TRBL and memorized with the mnemonic "Don't get into TRouBLe."

157

For simplicity's sake, you used the keywords right and top previously, which simply means "Align the right edge of the background image with the right edge of the CSS box's padding area, and align the top edge of the background image with the top edge of the CSS box's padding area."

In addition to keywords (which can also be left, bottom, and center), you can also use any length unit or a percentage value for the background-position property. For example, another way to write the same declaration used earlier would be to use the values 100% 0% (that is, offset 100 percent horizontally and 0 percent vertically). This method of defining positions of properties as horizontal and vertical offsets from another specific point is common in CSS, and you'll be using it much more later in this chapter.

Similar to the way you used the font shorthand property before to shorten your CSS declaration block to a single declaration that dealt with fonts, let's use the background shorthand property to do the same thing with these three background properties:

```
#header {
    background: url(images/logo.cap-right.1028x240.gif) ➥
                              no-repeat right top;
}
```

All the background shorthand property requires is either a background-color (which you have not specified) or a background-image (which you have). Since you haven't specified a value for background-color, the rule *effectively* looks like this:

```
#header {
    background-color: transparent;
    background-image: url(images/logo.cap-right.1028x240.gif)
    background-repeat: no-repeat
    background-attachment: scroll
    background-position: right top;
}
```

That is to say, without a color specified, the background shorthand property uses a value of transparent for the background-color property. Backgrounds that are transparent have no color, which is equivalent to saying that they have "no fill" in a graphics-editing application such as Adobe Photoshop or Adobe Illustrator. This lets whatever is behind the background "shine through." In this case, what's behind the header's background is just the page's background. Since you defined that background in an earlier CSS rule to be the color white, that color is what shines through.

The other property that the background shorthand property expands with is the background-attachment property. This property defines what happens to the background image when you scroll down on the page. You'll explore this property a little later, so for now you merely need to be aware that the possible values for this property are either scroll or fixed (or, naturally, inherit) and that, by default, this value is set to scroll, which just scrolls the background image along with the page as you would expect.

With the first image implemented, it's time to add the second, more prominent image. This time, however, you'll apply it to the <h3> element instead of the header <div>. You do this for three good reasons.

First, you can't give any element more than one background image, and you've already given the header <div> its background image. Second, the words "Papa Pepperoncini's Pizza" are actually in the <h3> element, so it makes sense that this element would be the one to house the graphical version of the headline, too. Finally, since the <h3> element is nested inside the <div> element, it will be displayed "on top of" (that is, closer to the viewer's eyes, or "on a higher layer than") the <div> element.

This may sound a bit confusing, so add the image to the header and see what this means in practice:

```
<style type="text/css">
html, body {
    margin: 0;
    padding: 0;
    border: none;
    background: #FFF;
}
body {
    color: #933;
    font: 62.5%/1.3em Verdana, Arial, sans-serif;
}
#header {
    background: url(images/logo.cap-right.1028x240.gif) ➡
                            no-repeat right top;
}
#header h3 {
    background: url(images/logo.835x240.jpg) no-repeat;
}
</style>
```

Once again, you're using the background shorthand property to declare a bunch of properties related to the <h3> element's background in one declaration. This time, however, you can omit the values that relate to background-color, background-attachment, and background-position, since the defaults (transparent, scroll, and left top) are exactly what you want. As Figure 6-8 shows, the result of adding these last few CSS rules may not have been what was expected.

So, what's going on here? Recall from the discussions in the previous chapter that the CSS box model defines four distinct areas that a CSS box generates. The innermost of these areas is the content area, which is what contains the text and child elements of an element. The area that surrounds the content is the padding. Both the content and padding areas display a CSS box's background, such as the background images you've given the <h3> element.

You'll also recall that the type of CSS box an <h3> element generates by default is a block-level box. Block-level boxes grow as wide as they can, so in this case that means the <h3> element is as wide as the browser viewport. Their height, however, is determined by their content by default. In this case, since the <h3> element contains only a single line of text, it is exactly that high and no higher. The background image you've applied to this element is, in fact, taller than the height of the element, and as a result, it gets *clipped* at the bottom. What you may not have noticed before that you might realize now is that the background image for the <div> element was also getting clipped.

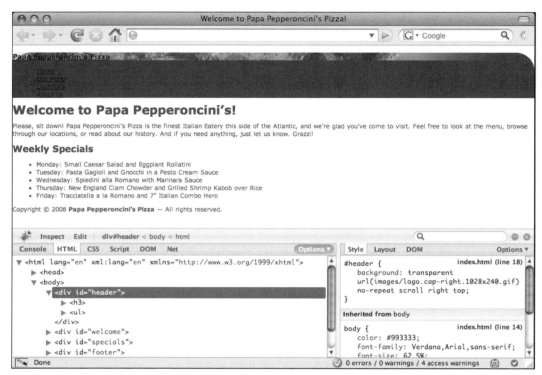

Figure 6-8. Adding the headline's background image on top of the header's background image begins to create the layered effect you want.

Clearly, you need to make these elements higher somehow. This is straightforward enough, of course. You'll simply add a declaration to the rule that targets the <h3> element in the header that sets its height property to be the height of the banner images, which are each 240 pixels tall:

```
#header h3 {
    background: url(images/logo.835x240.jpg) no-repeat;
    height: 240px;
}
```

In addition to increasing the height of the <h3> element, this declaration *also* increases the height of the header <div> element because the <h3> element is part of the <div>'s content area. Furthermore, because the <h3> element is a child of the <div>, the <h3> element's background image is overlaid on top of the <div>'s background image, as Figure 6-9 clearly shows.

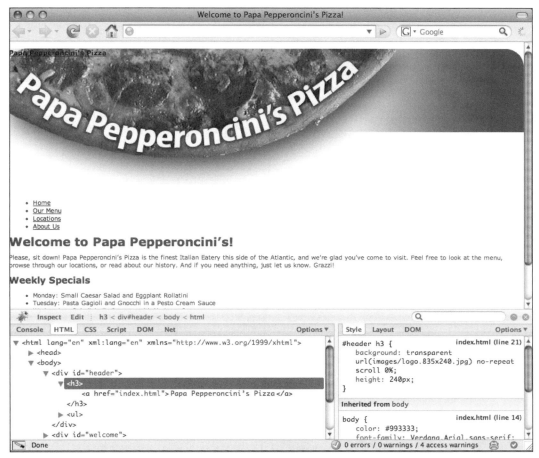

Figure 6-9. Background images get clipped if they are larger than the element's CSS box, so applying a height to the headline is necessary to display the full image of the pizza.

What this demonstrates is that each CSS box that is generated within the content area of another CSS box is actually being stacked on top of it, like a collage made with construction paper. As you continue nesting XHTML elements, you continue to stack CSS boxes one on top of another in an endless (and often invisible) tower. It's for this reason why any background applied to the <body> element always appears to be behind any other element on the web page and why the most deeply nested XHTML elements always appear to be in front of all their parent elements.

This stacking or layering behavior has a name. It's called the **stack level** or **z-axis**, which refers to the depth axis of a three-dimensional graph. Indeed, you can think of the web browser's viewport as one of these three-dimensional graphs. Depending on a web page's direction of flow (discussed in the previous chapter), the top-left corner of the browser viewport (or the top-right corner in right-to-left flows) can be said to be at position 0,0, meaning it is 0 pixels offset from the left edge of the viewport and 0 pixels offset from the top edge of the viewport. Each CSS box on a web page is positioned somewhere along the x-, y-, and z-axes on this imaginary graph. Figure 6-10 shows what this graph might look like from a web browser's point of view.

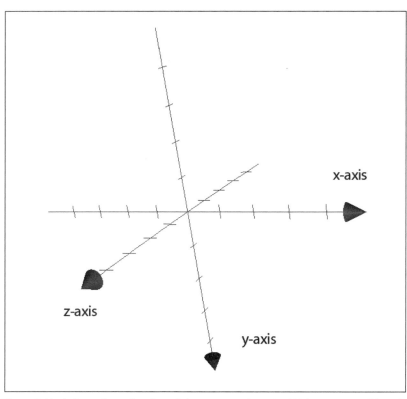

Figure 6-10. A three-dimensional graph has x-, y-, and z-axes. CSS boxes are positioned somewhere along each of these three axes, which is why they sometimes appear to be in front of one another, closer to the viewer's eyes facing the screen.

Moreover, exactly where a CSS box is placed along this z-axis by the browser can be controlled with CSS using the z-index property, which specifies a number that represents a point along this z-axis. For now, it's important to be aware only of the existence of this stacking behavior and its default behavior.

You need to make a few final modifications to the <h3> element in the header before you can call it complete. Obviously, since you're using the <h3> element's background to display the text "Papa Pepperoncini's Pizza," you no longer need to show the text in the <h3> element itself. However, you can't just get rid of that element. You can, however, move the inline box that its text content creates using the text-indent property. By setting a negative value on this property, you move the inline box toward the left edge of the viewport. By setting this value significantly high enough, you can actually move the text beyond the left edge of the viewport, effectively hiding it from view.

```
#header h3 {
    background: url(images/logo.835x240.jpg) no-repeat;
    height: 240px;
    text-indent: -999px;
}
```

This removes the text from the screen successfully, but since it doesn't do anything at all to the <h3> element's block-level box, there's still a gap between the top edge of the viewport and the image of the pizza logo. This gap is caused by the <h3> element's default top margin, so we'll zero it out (along with all its other margins).

```
#header h3 {
    background: url(images/logo.835x240.jpg) no-repeat;
    height: 240px;
    text-indent: -999px;
    margin: 0;
}
```

In the original unstyled page, the headline that read "Papa Pepperoncini's Pizza" was a link. However, when you moved the inline box with that text out of view, you also moved the link that text was contained within out of view. For the finishing touch on the masthead, you'll have to move the link back but keep the text hidden.

All you need to do to return the link is make the link's anchor element a block-level box. Doing this removes the effect of the text-indent declaration from the <a> *element itself, but not for the anchor text*. Since it's in fact the anchor elements that provide the clickable functionality of links and not the text they contain, this turns the one-line sliver of the top of the banner into the link you lost. To give the illusion that the logo image of the pizza itself is the link, you just need to set a specific width and height on the <a> element.

```
#header h3 {
    background: url(images/logo.835x240.jpg) no-repeat;
    height: 240px;
    text-indent: -999px;
    margin: 0;
}
#header h3 a {
    display: block;
    width: 835px;
    height: 100%;
}
</style>
```

The width is set to be equal to the width of the logo image of the pizza itself, and the height is set to 100%, which means "as tall as the containing block." In this case, the containing block of the <a> element is the <h3> element, so this ensures that the link is exactly as tall as the headline.

At this point, you have the masthead design fully implemented, without losing any of the semantic richness that the XHTML document contains. Even better, you've given it a lot of flexibility so that it can accommodate a browser window being resized to a significant degree, and you've also increased the usability of the header by greatly enhancing the clickable area of the link to the home page. Figure 6-11 shows the completed header implementation.

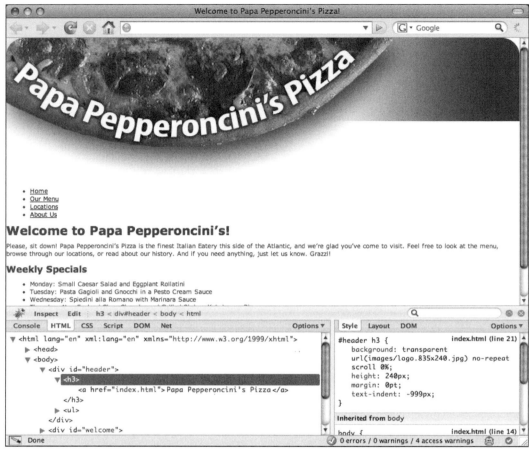

Figure 6-11. The completed header

The web page is now beginning to look like something you can be proud of, so without further ado, you'll continue working your way down the source code of your XHTML document. It's time to dive into styling the main navigation list.

The main navigation menu: absolute and relative CSS positioning

As you can see from looking at the design document, the main navigation menu is a vertical list of four text items in a larger font size, bold, and colored white; the list is positioned at the top right of the web page's masthead. Additionally, there is an orange icon that resembles a slice of pizza pointing at the currently selected menu item. This means that when the visitor is viewing the home page, the pizza slice icon needs to be visible next to the Home menu item, but when they are reading the online menu, the pizza slice icon needs to be visible next to the Our Menu menu item.

Let's begin by putting the navigation menu in the correct spot on the page. Right now, because the `<ul>` element that contains the navigation menu list items is generating a block-level CSS box in the normal flow of the web page, it is being rendered on its own line underneath the block-level CSS box generated by the 240-pixel-tall <h3> element. To move it to the top-right corner of the page, you first need to remove the <ul> element from the page's normal document flow so that you can control its positioning yourself. You do this by changing the element's position property:

```
#header ul {
    position: absolute;
}
</style>
```

When you save your changes and then reload the page to view the effect of this change, the result (shown in Figure 6-12) might be startling.

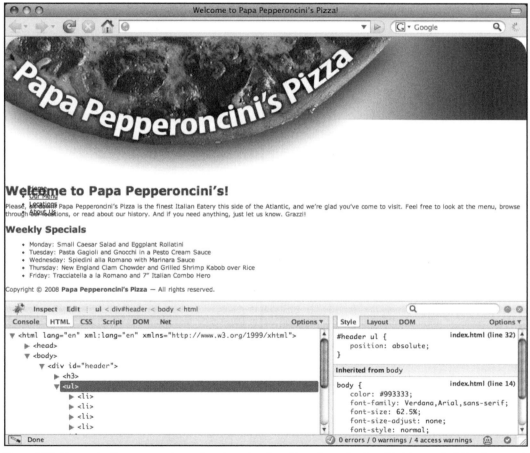

Figure 6-12. The navigation menu gets rendered overlapping other elements when it's taken out of the document flow and positioned absolutely.

As you can see, the headline and paragraph that used to be underneath the navigation menu appears to have slid upward on the page, and the navigation menu is now being displayed directly on top of those elements. What's happening here is actually simple: all you've done is remove the effect of the block-level CSS box generated by the <ul> element so that no other CSS boxes on the page are affected by its presence. This has the effect of making all the other CSS boxes completely ignore that it even exists, so as a result, the headline that reads "Welcome to Papa Pepperoncini's!" as well as the paragraph that follows it behave as though the navigation list isn't there.

Of course, the navigation menu certainly still exists; however, it exists in its own *rendering context*, which is akin to its own private document flow, completely unaffected by the flow or layout of other elements' CSS boxes. In a designer's terminology, you've effectively "created a new visual layer on top of the background layer" that contains only the navigation menu. In this state, you can move the navigation menu anywhere you want. Since you want to pin it to the top-right corner of the page, you'll use the top and right properties, which specify offsets from the top and right edges of (in this case) the viewport, each with a value of 0.

```
#header ul {
    position: absolute;
    top: 0;
    right: 0;
}
</style>
```

A reload of the web page now will show you that the navigation menu is indeed pinned to the top-right corner of the browser window and stays there while you resize the window. The position property is one of the most important properties to understand, so let's take a brief detour to discuss some of its other possible values.

The four values of the position property

When laying out designs with CSS2, CSS developers have a number of paths they can take. For the majority of them, the different possible values of the position property are used. The position property of an element can have one of four possible values. These are scroll, absolute, fixed, and relative. Each of them makes the element behave slightly differently, so let's examine each in turn.

The scroll value is the default value. If you never write a CSS style sheet with a position declaration in it, all of your elements will effectively be set to use the scroll value for this property. This value is easy to understand since you've been using it all along; it's the default behavior of document flow that we've become accustomed to whereby scrolling the page scrolls all of the elements on the page. Each CSS box is effectively cemented at whatever point it initially appeared.

The absolute value is probably the most frequently used value for this property. As shown, it completely removes the element from the normal document flow and allows you to use additional CSS properties (that is, the top, right, bottom, and left offset properties) to explicitly specify offset coordinates along the browser's x- and y-axes for the new position of the element on the page. This flexibility is incredibly powerful because it means you can specify a precise pixel location at which the element's CSS box appears. However, the offset coordinates are not always the edges of the browser viewport. To be precise, the absolute value sets the offset properties to values relative to the element's nearest positioned ancestor.

An element's **nearest positioned ancestor** is whatever ancestor element has already been given a position value other than scroll. In a typical left-to-right flow, that element's top-left corner then becomes the descendant element's 0,0 coordinate. To illustrate this, let's position the header <div> element absolutely as well and give the navigation menu's <ul> element a bright yellow background so you can clearly see its edges. Figure 6-13 shows the (rather odd-looking) result.

```css
#header {
    background: url(images/logo.cap-right.1028x240.gif) ➥
                             no-repeat right top;
    position: absolute;
}
/* other CSS rules... */
#header ul {
    position: absolute;
    top: 0;
    right: 0;
    background-color: yellow;
}
</style>
```

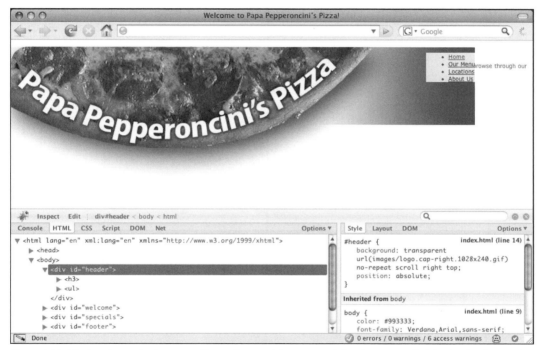

Figure 6-13. Moving the navigation menu list to the top-right corner of the viewport and giving it a background color for spotting it easily

There are probably a number of surprises shown here. First, it appears as though all the text has suddenly vanished. In fact, it hasn't vanished; it has just slid all the way to the top of the page and is being hidden by the tall banner images. Recall that the banner images actually contain white pixels in them, so what appears to be just the background of the white-colored web page underneath the banner images is actually part of the image and is thus obscuring the text that is now behind them. You can actually see this by noticing the slight outcropping of text at the top right of the viewport that reads, just barely, "browse through our."

Another apparent oddity is that the banner image's right side, the one with the rounded top-right corner, has also seemingly disappeared. This, too, has not actually disappeared but is instead also hidden underneath the <h3> element's background image of the large pizza pie and gradient stripe. On a related note, the entire banner's width has shrunk slightly and is no longer stretching across the entire viewport. This is because, despite that the header <div> is still a block-level element, it is no longer within the document's normal flow and so it has no containing block that it can reference to determine its total allowable width. As a result, its width is defined by its content, which in this case happens to be the 835-pixel-wide <a> element inside the <h3> element.

Finally, notice also that the navigation menu's absolutely positioned <ul> element is displaying the same width-shrinking behavior as the <div> element, which you now know to be because it is being rendered in its own visual context as well. However, instead of being pinned at the top-right corner of the browser's viewport as before, it is now pinned at the top-right corner of the header <div>. This is because the header <div> element is now the <ul> element's nearest positioned ancestor, so when you absolutely positioned it 0 pixels offset from the right edge and 0 pixels offset from the top edge of its containing block, that containing block now refers to the header <div>'s CSS box instead of the browser viewport.

On the other hand, the fixed value for the position property, which behaves the same way as the absolute value, will always use the browser's viewport as the offset reference. This has the important side effect of effectively pinning a CSS box at a certain point *on the screen*, regardless of whether a visitor scrolls the page. Unfortunately, neither Internet Explorer 5 nor 6 supports the fixed position, so this effect is not widely used.

The final possible value for the position property is relative. This value behaves similarly to the absolute value, but unlike the absolute value, setting an element's position property to relative does not remove it from the document's normal flow. Like the absolute value, however, it does create a positioned ancestor for any child elements. Let's switch the absolute value set on the header <div>'s position property to relative.

```
#header {
    background: url(images/logo.cap-right.1028x240.gif) ➥
                            no-repeat right top;
    position: relative;
}
```

This restores the original layout you had before, with one important and very subtle distinction: the navigation menu is no longer pinned to the top-right corner of the browser viewport; instead, it is pinned to the top-right corner of the header <div>. Now, if you move the header <div> itself, the navigation menu will come along for the ride with it because you've effectively grouped all the elements inside of it into one self-contained layer.

Another way to think about the relative value for the position property is to say that it positions a CSS box at a certain offset relative to whatever its offsets would have been had the position value been scroll. For example, if you wanted to move the welcome <div> upward toward the banner image, you could give it a relative position with a negative top offset:

```
#welcome {
    position: relative;
    top: -70px;
}
```

Doing this will *not* cause the section of content that lists the weekly specials to "slide up on the page" as it would have done had you used an absolute value, because the relatively positioned CSS boxes retain the same layout effects as CSS boxes positioned with the scroll (default) value.

So as you can see, the relative value can serve two distinct purposes. First, with no associated offset properties declared, you can use it to create a positioned ancestor in order to position another element on the page. Second, you can use it to nudge CSS boxes around without affecting the position of their neighbors.

Positioning elements with the CSS position property and the related offset properties is among the most advanced CSS technique available to front-end web developers today, so it can take a lot of experimentation and practice to feel completely confident in using it. That said, spending a good deal of time experimenting with CSS-based positioning will undoubtedly pay huge dividends, so the investment is well worth it.

Now that you have a handle on how to position elements on the page using CSS-based positioning, we'll show how you can use the CSS box model in combination with this technique to skin your navigation menu.

Skinning the navigation menu: styling lists with CSS

At this point, the header is nearly complete. All that remains is to skin the navigation menu so that it has the look and feel the designer envisioned. To accomplish this, you'll need to learn about the various CSS properties you can use to manipulate the display of lists.

Because you're about to write a lot of CSS rules that target your navigation menu's <ul> element, it now makes sense for you to give that element an id attribute with a unique value so that you can select it more simply from your style sheet. Let's call it mainnav since it is the containing element of the main navigation elements.

```
<div id="header">
    <h3><a href="index.html">Papa Pepperoncini&rsquo;s Pizza</a></h3>
    <ul id="mainnav">
        <li><a href="index.html">Home</a></li>
        <li><a href="menu.html">Our Menu</a></li>
        <li><a href="locations.html">Locations</a></li>
        <li><a href="about.html">About Us</a></li>
    </ul>
</div>
```

You can now also change the CSS selectors from #header ul to #mainnav. Since list elements, such as the <ul> element that the navigation menu uses, typically have some amount of margins or padding applied to them by default via the browser's built-in style sheets that you don't need right now, ensure you remove any of these that may exist as well.

```
#mainnav {
    position: absolute;
    top: 0;
    right: 0;
    margin: 0;
```

```
        padding: 0;
    }
</style>
```

There's nothing inherently special about a list element such as this. It simply generates a regular block-level CSS box. However, the same cannot be said of the `<li>` elements that lists generally contain.

By default, `<li>` elements generate a whole new kind of CSS box that is called a **list-item box**. List-item boxes behave similarly to the block-level boxes you're already accustomed to, with one important difference. In addition to generating a standard block-level CSS box, list-item boxes also generate a secondary **marker box** inside of which a special decorating **marker** is drawn. Typically, these markers are bullets (•) for li elements that are children of `<ul>` elements and are numbered (1., 2., 3., and so on) for `<li>` elements that are children of `<ol>` elements.

As with most things in CSS, certain properties give you more control over what kinds of markers are drawn, as well as where to draw these markers. For this design, you don't actually want to use these markers since you're not displaying the navigation menu in the traditional style of a list. This is actually quite typical of most designs for navigational menus on websites today. Despite that navigation menus are, in fact, logically and semantically represented as lists, their visual presentation is often quite different.

You have a number of options to choose from for making the list look less like a list. Most simply, you could set each list item's display property to block. Doing so will cause the `<li>` elements to generate normal block-level boxes instead of list-item boxes, effectively making the markers (the bullets) disappear. Another option is to leave the list-item boxes alone and just remove the marker boxes they generate. You'll do this by declaring the list-style-type property, which defines what kind of markers to display.

```
#mainnav {
    position: absolute;
    top: 0;
    right: 0;
    margin: 0;
    padding: 0;
    list-style-type: none;
}
</style>
```

Declaring a value of none indicates that no marker boxes should be generated. Instead of writing a new CSS rule, you've added this declaration to the declaration block of the CSS rule targeting the #mainnav element. This is because the list-style-type property is inherited, so by declaring this property on the `<ul>` element itself, all of its children `<li>` elements will inherit this value.

A value of disc, which is the default for `<ul>` elements, will cause the bullets to return. A value of decimal gives you ordered numbering, beginning with 1, and is the default for `<ol>` elements. In addition to bullets, list markers can also be rendered as squares by declaring the square value. Some of the other possible values for this property are other kinds of numbering systems, including decimal-leading-zero, upper-latin, lower-latin, upper-roman, lower-roman, hebrew, georgian, armenian, hiragana, and katakana, which each cause the marker to be displayed using that numbering system's native glyph. Unfortunately, once again, Internet Explorer does not support the majority of these options (although Internet Explorer 8 is slated to finally add support for them), so in practice you'll usually see only the defaults of decimal or disc used.

The next step in styling the list is to change the way the text appears:

```
#mainnav {
    position: absolute;
    top: 0;
    right: 0;
    margin: 0;
    padding: 0;
    list-style-type: none;
}
#mainnav a {
    color: #FFF;
    font: bold 2em "Myriad Pro", Verdana, Arial, sans-serif;
    text-decoration: none;
}
</style>
```

There's very little new here. The color property declares the text's color to be white, and the font property makes the text bold and sets the font to the same one the designer used in the design document, as well as providing a list of alternatives. It also sets font-size to 2em, which computes to 20 pixels in size.

How did we come up with 20 pixels, though? Well, recall that you originally declared the font size to be 62.5% on the <body> element. Assuming the visitor has set their browser's default text size preference to Medium (the factory default in most cases), this means regular text on the page is calculated to be exactly 10 pixels in size. This value is then inherited by all the elements on the page. The default font-size value for regular text on the page is 1em, which is the same as saying "the same size as the parent element's font-size." Therefore, all the regular text on the page is sized at 10 pixels. When you declare a font-size of 2em, what you're saying is effectively "double the size of the parent element's font-size." Since the parent element's font-size property is calculated to be 10 pixels, doubling that gives you 20 pixels (10 pixels times 2 equals 20 pixels). By the same logic, setting a value of 3em would make the navigation menu text 30 pixels in size, and setting a value of 2.5em would make it 25 pixels in size.

To avoid inconsistencies in the way that many browsers calculate the size of text and render it on the screen, it's important to ensure that all the text on your pages ends up being sized at a precise pixel value. Fractional pixel values can cause some browsers to display your text at a size you didn't intend. Figure 6-14 shows what the header looks like now.

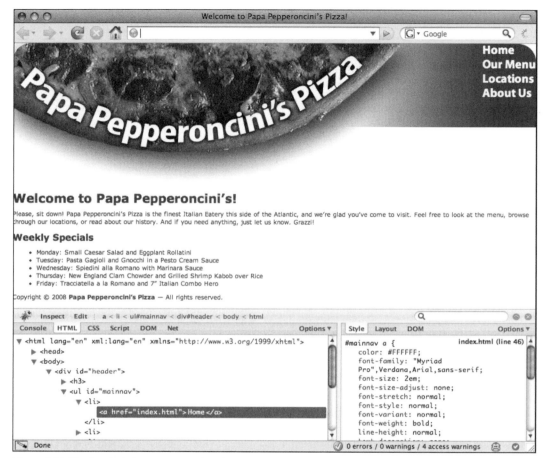

Figure 6-14. The header's fonts are now showing some font styles.

Next, let's get the exact spacing of the text right. In the design document, the navigation menu isn't pressed into the top-right corner like it is on the page. You need to push the text leftward a bit, and you also need to space the individual menu items vertically a bit more. You can use margins, padding, or a combination of both of these CSS box areas to accomplish this. For reasons that will become clear momentarily, let's use padding. Since you're going to need vertical padding as well as horizontal padding, you need to turn the inline boxes generated by the <a> elements into block-level boxes by declaring their display property, too.

```
#mainnav {
    position: absolute;
    top: 0;
    right: 0;
    margin: 0;
    padding: 0;
    list-style-type: none;
}
#mainnav a {
    color: #FFF;
    font: bold 2em "Myriad Pro", Verdana, Arial, sans-serif;
    text-decoration: none;
    display: block;
    padding: 1px 35px 1px 0;
}
</style>
```

That's almost perfect, but the navigation menu is still just a bit too high. To push it down a bit, let's increase the top margin on the list itself:

```
#mainnav {
    position: absolute;
    top: 0;
    right: 0;
    margin: 15px 0 0 0;
    padding: 0;
    list-style-type: none;
}
#mainnav a {
    color: #FFF;
    font: bold 2em "Myriad Pro", Verdana, Arial, sans-serif;
    text-decoration: none;
    display: block;
    padding: 2px 35px 2px 0;
}
</style>
```

Now the navigation menu is spaced just as it is in the design document. Figure 6-15 shows the results of the precise spacing. All that remains to complete it is adding the pizza slice icon that points to the currently selected page. Let's do that next.

Figure 6-15. By adding a little bit of padding, you're able to properly space the navigation menu items apart from each other and from the edges.

Adding interactivity: special styling for selected items and rollovers

The next sets of styles you need to write for the navigation menu are the ones that will add a certain amount of interactivity to the menu. First, you need to extract the pizza slice icons from the design document into a separate image. Since images must be rectangular and the pizza slice icon is decidedly not that shape, you need the image to have a transparent background, so you'll save it as a GIF file. We'll name the file icon. pizza-slice.normal.gif. Figure 6-16 shows the pizza icon image you'll use to highlight the current menu item selected, and Figure 6-17 shows a modified version of the pizza icon image you'll use for a rollover effect.

Figure 6-16. The background image icon for the current menu item is an orange-colored GIF with a transparent background.

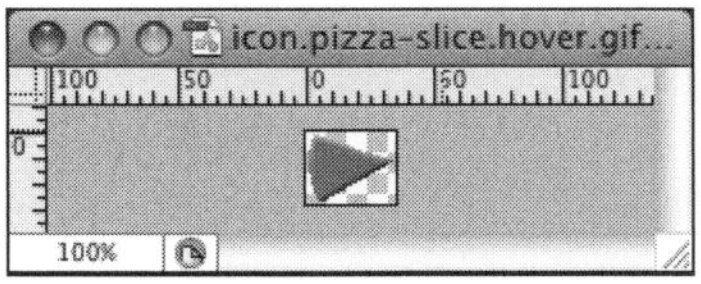

As you can see, we've named the rollover image icon. pizza-slice.hover.gif in keeping with the image file-naming conventions. More specifically, we didn't use "rollover" in the name of the file, because as you'll see in a few moments, CSS calls this rollover state the "hover" state instead.

Figure 6-17. The background image icon for the menu item's rollover state is a blue-colored GIF with a transparent background.

Now that you have the image assets you'll need saved to the images directory, you can begin by adding the normal pizza slice icon to the home page. To do this, you need a way to target just the one navigation menu item of the page that the visitor is currently viewing. The most reliable way to do this is to add an appropriately named class attribute to that particular list item. In this case, this is the home page, so you'll add a class value of selected to the first list item to signify this:

```
<div id="header">
    <h3><a href="index.html">Papa Pepperoncini&rsquo;s Pizza</a></h3>
    <ul id="mainnav">
        <li class="selected"><a href="index.html">Home</a></li>
        <li><a href="menu.html">Our Menu</a></li>
        <li><a href="locations.html">Locations</a></li>
        <li><a href="about.html">About Us</a></li>
    </ul>
</div>
```

Now, you can write a CSS rule that just targets whatever list item has the selected class applied to it. Let's add the normal pizza icon as a background image for the currently selected navigation menu item:

```
#mainnav a {
    color: #FFF;
    font: bold 2em "Myriad Pro", Verdana, Arial, sans-serif;
    text-decoration: none;
    display: block;
    padding: 2px 35px 2px 0;
}
#mainnav .selected a {
    background: url(images/icon.pizza-slice.normal.gif) ➡
                        no-repeat left center;
}
</style>
```

This works, but it places the icon behind the text that reads "Home" instead of next to it. You need to give all the links in the navigation menu a bit of extra space on their left sides. This is no problem; you just need to tweak the padding value in the previous CSS rule. Since the pizza slice icons are exactly 35 pixels wide, you'll increase the left padding value to 45 pixels so you'll have 10 pixels of space between the edge of the icon and the beginning of the anchor text in the link.

```
#mainnav a {
    color: #FFF;
    font: bold 2em "Myriad Pro", Verdana, Arial, sans-serif;
    text-decoration: none;
    display: block;
    padding: 2px 35px 2px 45px;
}
#mainnav .selected a {
    background: url(images/icon.pizza-slice.normal.gif) ➥
                            no-repeat left center;
}
</style>
```

Now let's do the same thing but for the rollover effect:

```
#mainnav a {
    color: #FFF;
    font: bold 2em "Myriad Pro", Verdana, Arial, sans-serif;
    text-decoration: none;
    display: block;
    padding: 2px 35px 2px 45px;
}
#mainnav .selected a {
    background: url(images/icon.pizza-slice.normal.gif) ➥
                            no-repeat left center;
}
#mainnav a:hover {
    background: url(images/icon.pizza-slice.hover.gif) ➥
                            no-repeat left center;
    color: #399;
}
</style>
```

This CSS rule introduces the :hover pseudo-class for the first time, so let's pause momentarily and examine what this means with a little more care.

The dynamic pseudo-classes: :hover, :active, and :focus

You'll recall from the previous chapter that a pseudo-class is a kind of CSS simple selector, which means you can use it to target certain elements on your page. Unlike most other kinds of CSS selectors, though, most pseudo-class selectors—such as the :hover pseudo-class selector—do not target elements that have any particular attribute value or other identifying characteristic. Instead, this pseudo-class selector targets elements that the visitor's cursor is currently hovering (or rolling) over. Since the visitor's cursor can be hovering over any element's CSS box at any given time, the :hover pseudo-class is the cornerstone of CSS-based rollover effects.

The :hover pseudo-class is called a **dynamic** pseudo-class because it describes a dynamic state, which is to say that elements can enter and leave the "hovered" state at the user's whim. In theory, any type of element (not just links) can be placed into this dynamic hovered state. Unfortunately, versions of

Internet Explorer prior to 7 do not support the :hover pseudo-class on anything other than <a> elements, so in practice it's typically only links that get targeted with it.

The latest CSS selector, with its :hover pseudo-class selector, can be read as "when the cursor is hovering over an <a> element that is a child of the #mainnav element." Technically, what's happening is that the <a> element, just like any other element with the cursor hovering over it, enters a new and more specific state. Ordinarily, this fact isn't visually obvious because an element's :hover state inherits its initial values from the values of the element's static state, so there is no change in the visual appearance of the element. The moment you change these values by declaring different values for the element's :hover state, however, the change becomes immediately obvious, visible in the form of a rollover effect.

With the addition of the latest CSS rule, you now have a rollover effect for the navigation menu that shows and hides the teal-colored pizza slice icon, as well as turns the white links a similar color. In fact, it's a little bit too much because all the menu items are changing color on hover, even the currently selected item (Home). This is because you've declared :hover properties for both the selected and unselected items.

To stop the effect from happening on the selected items, you just need to specify the same values for the navigation links' hover states as those of their static state. You already specified a CSS rule for that state, so all you need to do now is add another CSS selector that uses the :hover pseudo-class to that rule and explicitly declare the text link's color.

```
#mainnav .selected a, #mainnav .selected a:hover {
    background: url(images/icon.pizza-slice.normal.gif) ➥
                            no-repeat left center;
    color: #FFF;
}
#mainnav a:hover {
    background: url(images/icon.pizza-slice.hover.gif) ➥
                            no-repeat left center;
    color: #399;
}
</style>
```

With this latest modification, the rollover effect is working just the way you want it to work. Still, there's a little bit more you can do to spruce up the navigation menu effects.

In addition to the :hover pseudo-class, CSS defines two other dynamic pseudo-classes. These are :active and :focus. Like the :hover pseudo-class, these two pseudo-classes apply to elements when they are in a particular state. In the case of the :active pseudo-class, this state is when the element is "being activated," such as between the time the user clicks a link and releases the mouse button. In the case of the :focus pseudo-class, this state is whenever the element has been given "focus," such as when a visitor tabs through the elements on a page. (Most web browsers will outline a focused element with some kind of highlight—Firefox actually uses a box's CSS border area for this, although for some odd reason you can't override this behavior with CSS.)

None of these pseudo-classes is mutually exclusive, which means that an element may be in any number of these states at any given time. For example, clicking a link first brings that element into the hover state (because the mouse cursor needs to be over that element in order to click it) and then

177

gives that element focus *and* activates it at the same time. As you can see, a number of distinct *events* are happening here in quick succession.

We'll discuss more about the different kinds of events that a web browser can expose to you in the next chapter when we cover JavaScript's event-driven programming model. In the meantime, all you need to worry about is how to distinguish different dynamic states from one another using the dynamic pseudo-classes that CSS provides.

Right now, for this design, all you really need is to add another CSS rule to define the look and feel of the navigation links when a user clicks them. Even though the designer hasn't provided a design for this state in the original design document, it would be nice if the text turned red and the pizza-slice icon moved closer to the text itself. Changing the text color is a breeze, and moving the pizza slice icon right without moving the text of the link itself simply requires some careful manipulation of the <a> element's left margin and left padding properties. Since you also don't want this effect applied to the currently selected item, you'll add another selector into the CSS rule that styles the selected navigation item and override the declarations for the properties you add to the CSS rule below it.

```
#mainnav .selected a, ➡
#mainnav .selected a:hover, ➡
#mainnav .selected a:active {
    background: url(images/icon.pizza-slice.normal.gif) ➡
                            no-repeat left center;
    color: #FFF;
    margin-left: 0;
    padding-left: 0;
}
#mainnav a:hover {
    background: url(images/icon.pizza-slice.hover.gif) ➡
                            no-repeat left center;
    color: #399;
}
#mainnav a:active {
    color: red;
    margin-left: 7px;
    padding-left: 38px;
}
</style>
```

What you're doing with this new rule is changing the position of the left padding edge of the <a> element's CSS box relative to the rest of the element's CSS box. Since you know that background images, like the pizza slice icons, are drawn inside a CSS box's padding and content areas, reducing the width of the left padding area effectively moves the pizza slice icon closer to the text.

To be precise, you're moving it exactly 7 pixels closer, since you declared a left padding area width of 45 pixels in an earlier CSS rule and are now changing that width to 38 pixels (45 pixels minus 38 pixels equals 7 pixels). At the same time, you also increase the CSS box's left margin area from zero width to 7 pixels in order to "fill up" the space that you lost by decreasing the width of the padding area so that the CSS box as a whole remains in the same spot in the browser viewport.

As you can see in Figure 6-18, this ensures that the navigation links remain nicely aligned with one another while moving the pizza slice icon toward the text.

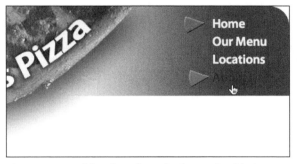

Figure 6-18. Applying the rollover backgrounds with the :hover pseudo-class gives a dynamic rollover effect.

Another way to accomplish the same effect would simply be to change the background-position property so that the background image is moved 7 pixels right from the left edge of the CSS box's padding area.

```
#mainnav .selected a, ➥
#mainnav .selected a:hover, ➥
#mainnav .selected a:active {
    background: url(images/icon.pizza-slice.normal.gif) ➥
                             no-repeat left center;
    color: #FFF;
}
#mainnav a:hover {
    background: url(images/icon.pizza-slice.hover.gif) ➥
                             no-repeat left center;
    color: #399;
}
#mainnav a:active {
    color: red;
    background-position: 7px center;
}
</style>
```

Using this approach, you can also remove the margin-left and padding-left declarations in the CSS rule before this one.

Both approaches are perfectly valid. This example shows that in many situations, you may find yourself with more than one way to accomplish the same thing. The method you choose to use will probably depend largely on your own experience and personal preferences. Sometimes, however, you'll be in a situation where designs dictate your choices a lot more than others. This occurs most often in more complex designs that require you to leverage every feature of CSS you can. In these cases, it's beneficial to be familiar with as many ways of doing things as possible so that you can have the most options available to you.

You'll use the background-position method since that shortens the CSS style sheet by a few lines (and we're lazy typists). Regardless of which method you end up using for the navigation menu, you now have the entire header and navigation menu's designs completed. For the final pièce de résistance, let's add one more declaration to the CSS rule that styles the currently selected navigation menu item:

```
#mainnav .selected a, ➡
#mainnav .selected a:hover, ➡
#mainnav .selected a:active {
    background: url(images/icon.pizza-slice.normal.gif) ➡
                        no-repeat left center;
    color: #FFF;
    cursor: default;
}
```

This final declaration turns the visitor's cursor into whatever the browser's default is, typically an arrow, making it appear as though the currently selected navigation item isn't even a link at all! This often helps prevent the annoying situation where a visitor clicks a link that points to the same page as the one they're currently on and nothing appears to happen. Another way of doing this is by making the cursor appear as though it were a standard text-insertion cursor (often displayed as an I-bar) by using the value text, but this has the drawback that some users may try to select the text of the link and accidentally activate it.

Before you continue laying out the rest of your web page, let's explore what else you can do with links and pseudo-classes.

Styling links using the link pseudo-classes: :link and :visited

The most commonly used pseudo-classes are the :link and :visited pseudo-classes. These two pseudo-classes apply to links based on whether that link has been previously viewed. In other words, the :link pseudo-class is used to define the style of links that a user has yet to click, and the :visited pseudo-class is used to define the style of links that a user has previously clicked.

At first, it may seem a little strange that the name for this pseudo-class is :link since all throughout the rest of this book we've been referring to links as anchor (<a>) elements. However, this abstraction makes much more sense when you remember that you can use CSS to define the styling of *any* markup language, not just XHTML. So, although in XHTML the :link and :visited pseudo-classes simply apply to <a> elements that have been given a value in their href attribute, the :link and :visited pseudo-classes can apply to different elements based on whatever the definition of a "link" is in that other markup language. To put it more succinctly, when you use these pseudo-classes in (X)HTML, the following CSS selectors all target the same elements (albeit with different specificities):

```
a:link { … }
:link { … }
a:visited { … }
:visited { … }
a:link:visited { … }
```

The first two CSS selectors shown in the previous code target all unvisited links, whereas the next three CSS selectors target all visited links. Of special note is the final CSS selector shown in the previous code, a:link:visited, because it demonstrates you can chain pseudo-class selectors just as you can for any other simple selector. Therefore, you can theoretically combine the dynamic pseudo-classes with the link pseudo-classes to create CSS selectors that target links in a particular state. For instance, the following CSS rule creates a rollover effect on visited links that makes them partially see-through:

```
a:visited:hover { opacity: .5; }
```

Sadly, Internet Explorer versions prior to 7 do not understand CSS selectors with multiple chained pseudo-classes such as this, so those browsers read this CSS selector as a:hover { ... }. (As an aside, no current version of Internet Explorer supports the opacity property either, although you can use a proprietary declaration such as filter: alpha(opacity=50); to get similar results as the previous declaration. Beware, however, that using this declaration in your style sheet will cause it not to validate.) The take-away point is that these pseudo-classes are specifically designed to let web designers distinguish between visited and unvisited links.

Since all the pseudo-classes have the same specificity, it's customary to define generic link styles for a design near the top of one's CSS style sheet in the following order:

```
a:link { /* style declarations for regular links */ }
a:visited { /* style declarations for regular visited links */ }
a:hover { /* style declarations for rollover, unvisited links */ }
a:active { /* style declarations for activated (clicked) links */ }
```

By defining these CSS rules in this order at the top of your style sheet, you use the natural CSS cascade to make sure that active link styles always override all the other link styles and that hovered link styles override static link styles. You also ensure that visited link styles override regular link styles. This replicates the default behavior web surfers are accustomed to. Since you've yet to define any link styles, or indeed any links at all, go ahead and add some to the welcome paragraph in this document:

```
<div id="welcome">
    <h1>Welcome to Papa Pepperoncini&rsquo;s!</h1>
    <p>Please, sit down! Papa Pepperoncini&rsquo;s Pizza ➥
            is the finest Italian Eatery this side of the Atlantic, ➥
            and you&rsquo;re glad you&rsquo;ve come to visit. ➥
            Feel free to look at <a href="menu.html">the menu</a>, ➥
            browse through our
            <a href="locations.html">locations</a>, ➥
            or read <a href="about.html">about our history</a>. ➥
            And if you need anything, just let us know.  Grazzi!</p>
</div>
```

Now, let's write some appropriately nice-looking CSS styles for these links. Let's color the regular links a deep blue color so that they stand out a little and the visited links a darker orange color so that they fade away. You'll make all links stand out even more by turning them green when they are hovered and a dark brown when they're clicked.

```
<style type="text/css">
html, body {
    margin: 0;
    padding: 0;
    border: none;
    background: #FFF;
}
body {
    color: #933;
    font: 62.5%/1.3em Verdana, Arial, sans-serif;
}
a:link {
    color: #06F;
}
a:visited {
    color: #906;
}
a:hover {
    color: #393;
}
a:active {
    color: #C60;
}
#header {
    background-image: url(images/logo.cap-right.1028x240.gif);
    position: relative;
}
```

Now, as you can see in Figure 6-19, the regular links in the page will be styled differently based on whether you've followed that particular link before.

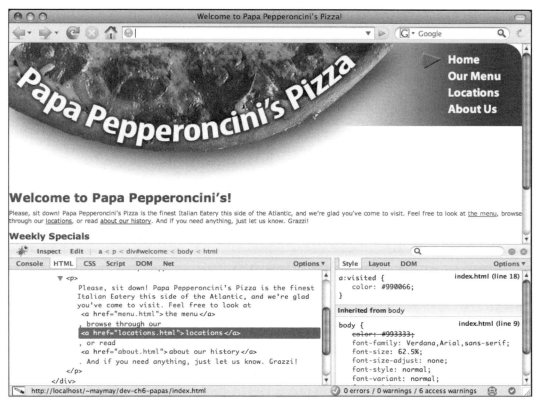

Figure 6-19. Links can be styled differently based on whether the destination of the link is in the web browser's cache. If it is, then the link is visited, as the "locations" and "about our history" links in this figure are. Otherwise, the link is unvisited, like the "the menu" link.

While you're at it, you can improve these links even further by adding a title attribute to each of them. title attributes, as discussed briefly in Chapter 4, allow you to add supplementary information to most elements on a web page. The values of title attributes are usually rendered as tooltips, so they should contain short, helpful descriptions of what will happen when the user activates that element.

title attributes are especially helpful for links that point to the same pages as links in other parts of the page (which may or may not have the same anchor text), such as the links in the welcome paragraph and in the header. To clue the visitor in to the fact that these links actually go to the same destination page, you'll give each pair of links the same title value:

```
<div id="header">
    <h3><a href="index.html" title="Return to home page.">Papa ➥
            Pepperoncini&rsquo;s Pizza</a></h3>
    <ul>
        <li>
            <a href="index.html" title="Return to home page.">Home</a>
        </li>
        <li><a href="menu.html" title="Read our menu online.">Our ➥
```

```
                                    Menu</a></li>
                <li><a href="locations.html" title="Find our nearest ➥
                    restaurant.">Locations</a></li>
                <li><a href="about.html" title="Discover what makes us the ➥
                    best.">About Us</a></li>
            </ul>
        </div>
        <div id="welcome">
            <h1>Welcome to Papa Pepperoncini&rsquo;s!</h1>
            <p>Please, sit down! Papa Pepperoncini&rsquo;s Pizza ➥
                is the finest Italian Eatery this side of the Atlantic, ➥
                and you&rsquo;re glad you&rsquo;ve come to visit. ➥
                Feel free to look at ➥
                <a href="menu.html" title="Read our menu online.">the ➥
                menu</a>, browse through our <a href="locations.html" ➥
                title="Find our nearest restaurant.">locations</a>, ➥
                or read <a href="about.html" ➥
                title="Discover what makes us the best."> ➥
                about our history</a>. And if you need anything, just ➥
                let us know.  Grazzi!</p>
        </div>
```

Since the text of title attributes must be kept pretty short, we've tried to be as direct as possible when writing their values. As you can see, each title attribute uses imperative language to immediately inform the visitor what each link will do for them.

With all the link styling complete, you can next turn your attention to the final layout challenges you face in this design: splitting the welcome and weekly special sections into two vertical columns.

Making columns using floats and margins

In almost every medium, including the Web, designs often split content into multiple columns. There are a number of reasons for this trend. First, the human eye has difficulty scanning very wide lines of text, so splitting content into multiple narrower columns makes reading it easier. Another reason for this is that the human visual system is hardwired to recognize the proximity and alignment of groups of objects as being related to one another, so columns are a good way to distinguish one kind of content from another. Yet another reason is that the amount of physical space that web pages can use to display information to their visitors is limited, so columns also offer a good way to present more information in a smaller space.

The challenge, of course, is that while the human eye looks around a web page in a (mostly) randomized order, the source code of web pages is actually stored in a linear order. Once again, this is another area where properly structured, presentation-free markup used in conjunction with CSS can really shine. Even so, multicolumn layouts can often be very tricky to implement in a cross-browser compatible way.

You can use a couple of techniques to create columns in CSS. One of them is to just use absolutely positioned elements to define each column's location and dimensions. For instance, you might at first try to move the welcome <div> into a left column and the specials <div> into a right column using these CSS rules. Figure 6-20 shows the result of these positioning rules.

```
#welcome, #specials {
    position: absolute;
    top: 250px;
}
#welcome {
    left: 30px;
    width: 275px;
}
#specials {
    left: 375px;
}
```

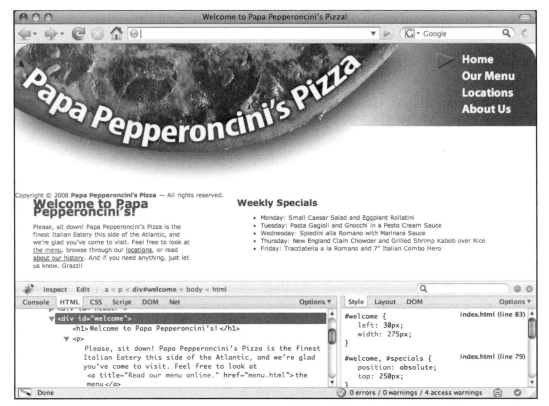

Figure 6-20. Columns using absolutely positioned boxes can be positioned at will, regardless of their source order, but are then stiff and inflexible.

This seems to work rather nicely, and it has the benefit that you can position any piece of content anywhere on the page regardless of where that content appears in your XHTML source document. This method of creating columns does have one big drawback, however. Once the columns are positioned, they are stiff and inflexible because they will each ignore the other's existence.

For example, when you try to position the footer in an appropriately spaced point on the page, you run into the problem of not being able to determine ahead of time how far down the page it should be placed. If you put it too high, then the text in the columns will clobber it when the user increases their font size or when Papa Pepperoncini decides he'd like to add more text to his home page. On the other hand, if you put it too low, then you'll end up with a large amount of (ugly) blank space between the end of the columns and the start of the footer.

Of course, you could just keep tweaking the position of the footer whenever you'd like to make a change (and pray that the user doesn't touch their browser preferences!), but that's obviously not the best solution. Besides, you're a busy person and can't have Papa Pepperoncini calling you whenever he wants to change the text on his website. Clearly, you need to explore other options.

Another way you could separate this content into columns is by using a new property, called float, to move the element that appears first to the left or right content edge of its containing CSS box. In this case, this means you could use the float property with a value of left to move the welcome <div> to the left edge of the browser viewport. Of course, the welcome <div>'s left edge is already at the left edge of the browser viewport, so what good would this do you? Plenty!

Declare the float and width properties on the welcome <div> and see what happens:

```
#mainnav a:active {
    color: red;
    background-position: 7px center;
}
#welcome {
    float: left;
    width: 275px;
}
</style>
```

As you can see in Figure 6-21, this CSS rule has also given you two columns, but the columns are behaving a little bit strangely. The first oddity you're likely to notice is that the bullets in the list of weekly specials are overlapping a bit of the text in the welcome paragraph. For that matter, the entire list isn't even indented anymore, and all of the list items are now aligned with the headline that reads "Weekly Specials." There are actually a few things going on here, so let's take a breather and examine what's happening to each CSS box individually.

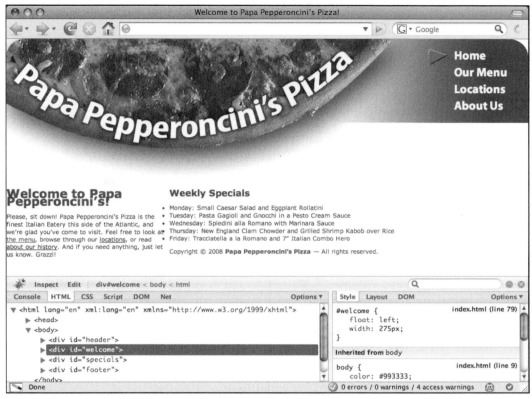

Figure 6-21. Creating columns by using floated layouts keeps the elements within the major document flow but has some limitations of its own.

The many layout effects of floated boxes

When you declare a float value on a CSS box, what you're doing is telling the browser to "take the CSS box this element generates and move, or *float*, it to the left (or right) as far as it can go without bumping into any other CSS box in the same document flow." Once a box is floated, it takes on a number of special behaviors that affect its neighboring CSS boxes in different ways besides simply moving toward the left or right edge of its containing block.

First, whenever you float a box, you implicitly transform the CSS box of the floated element into a block-level box, if the box was not already a block-level box before. Second, the floated box is moved partway out of the normal document flow so that content flows along its right side (for a box floated left) or its left side (for a box floated right). Since it is no longer in the document's normal flow, other block-level boxes appear to "slide upward" on the page in much the same way as you saw happen when you positioned elements absolutely. However, since the floated box is not *entirely* out of the document flow, all inline-level boxes actually wrap around the outer edges of the floated box (honoring the floated box's margins, padding, and border areas, if it has any). Third, if the floated element was previously contained within an inline-level box, the top edge of the floated box will be aligned with the top edge of that box. Otherwise, its top edge will be aligned with the bottom edge of the block-level box that came before it.

187

An example will help clarify this for you. Let's insert a new <div> directly after the welcome headline. We'll identify this <div> as floatbox to make things simple:

```
<div id="welcome">
    <h1>Welcome to Papa Pepperoncini&rsquo;s!</h1>
    <div id="floatbox">I am a floated box.</div>
    <p>Please, sit down! Papa Pepperoncini&rsquo;s Pizza ➥
        is the finest Italian Eatery this side of the Atlantic, ➥
        and you&rsquo;re glad you&rsquo;ve come to visit. ➥
        Feel free to look at ➥
    <a href="menu.html" title="Read our menu online.">the ➥
        menu</a>, browse through our <a href="locations.html" ➥
        title="Find our nearest restaurant.">locations</a>, ➥
        or read <a href="about.html" ➥
        title="Discover what makes us the best."> ➥
        about our history</a>. And if you need anything, just ➥
        let us know.  Grazzi!</p>
</div>
```

Now, let's turn this box into a 60-pixel by 60-pixel square, float it left, and give it a yellow background so you can easily identify its edges. Figure 6-22 shows the resulting display.

```
#floatbox {
    float: left;
    width: 50px;
    height: 50px;
    padding: 10px;
    background-color: yellow;
}
```

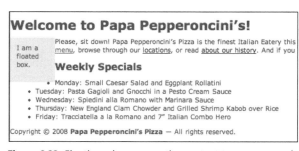

Figure 6-22. Floating a box causes the content to wrap around it at either the left or right sides.

As you can see, the floated box has been vertically aligned with the bottom of the preceding block-level box, which in this case is the <h1> element producing the headline "Welcome to Papa Pepperoncini's." Moreover, the inline boxes containing the text of the welcome paragraph as well as the inline boxes inside the specials <div> are all flowing around the right side of the box. Finally, notice that the floated box actually extends beyond the bottom edge of the welcome <div> in which it is nested in the XHTML source. Figure 6-23, which adds solid backgrounds to the welcome and special <div> elements, shows this more obviously.

```
#floatbox {
    float: left;
    width: 50px;
    height: 50px;
    padding: 10px;
    background-color: yellow;
}
#welcome { background-color: green; }
#specials { background-color: blue; }
```

Figure 6-23. Adding backgrounds to the nearby elements reveals that floated boxes protrude from the bottom of their containing blocks.

This is important: although floated boxes may not be placed *higher* than the point at which their top edge aligns with their containing inline-level box's top edge or the bottom edge of the preceding block-level box, *their bottom edge will protrude beyond the bottom edge of their parent's CSS box*. If you imagine that the yellow floated box were an image, you can see why floated boxes have to stick out of the bottom of their containers; if they couldn't, you wouldn't be able to wrap text around an image that was taller than its paragraph (as many images are).

If you were to float this box to the right instead of to the left, you'll see that the text will now flow around its left edge, as shown in Figure 6-24.

Now that you understand what floated boxes actually do to your layout, let's reexamine what happened when you floated your welcome <div> to the left in order to turn it into a column.

Figure 6-24. Floating a box to the right makes the content nearby it wrap around its left edge.

Spacing your columns

As previously shown, when you floated the welcome <div> left, you created what looked like two columns. In fact, this isn't true. What you actually accomplished was making the content in the specials and footer <div> elements flow around the content in the floated welcome <div>. If you take a second look at the floated welcome <div> (shown in Figure 6-25), this time using background colors to make the specials and footer CSS boxes visible, you'll see that you really still have only one column.

```
#mainnav a:active {
    color: red;
    background-position: 7px center;
}
#welcome {
    float: left;
    width: 275px;
}
#specials { background-color: green; }
#footer { background-color: blue; }
</style>
```

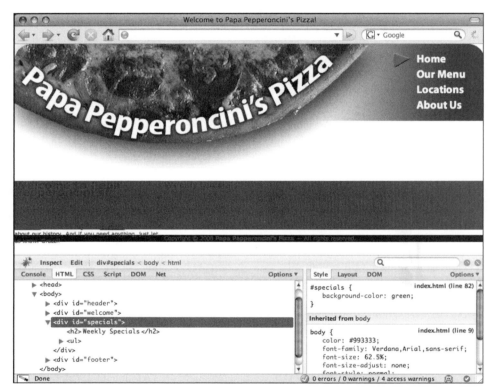

Figure 6-25. Block-level boxes still grow to the width of their containing block, even when they contain floated boxes.

As you can see, both the specials and the footer <div> elements are still in a single wide column that stretches from one edge of the browser viewport to the other. It's merely that all the content, in its inline-level boxes, is wrapping around the floated welcome <div> that makes it appear as though you have two columns.

This also explains why your list of weekly specials no longer appears to be indented; since the block-level boxes that they are inside actually stretch across the entire width of the browser viewport, they *are* indented, but then they need to be moved *even further toward the right* to make room for the 275-pixel-wide floated box. As a result, they appear to lose their indentation since the browser itself has moved them automatically.

To fix this, all you need to do is define a significantly large left margin for the specials <div> so that the left edge of its content area is moved past the right outer edge of the welcome <div>. Since the welcome <div> is currently 275 pixels wide and it begins at the left edge of the browser viewport, any amount greater than 275 pixels will be enough for the left margin of the specials <div> to clear the right edge of the welcome <div>.

```
#mainnav a:active {
    color: red;
    background-position: 7px center;
}
#welcome {
    float: left;
    width: 275px;
}
#specials { margin-left: 375px }
</style>
```

Figure 6-26 shows the result of adding this margin-left declaration (and an additional declaration to color the background green for the sake of example).

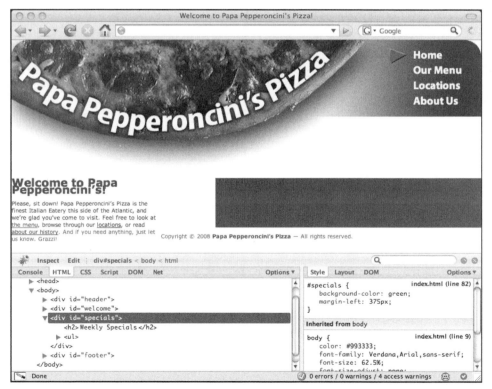

Figure 6-26. Using a combination of a floated box and a significantly high margin property can create the appearance of columns.

191

From here, all it takes is a few more CSS rules to quickly give the columns and their elements proper spacing and font sizing:

```
#welcome {
    float: left;
    width: 275px;
    margin: 0 0 0 30px;
}
#specials { margin: 0 35px 0 375px; }
#welcome h1, #specials h2 {
    font-size: 2.2em;
    line-height: 1.3em;
}
#welcome p, #specials li {
    font-size: 1.4em;
    line-height: 1.5em;
}
#specials h2 { margin-bottom: 0; }
#specials ul {
    list-style-type: none;
    margin: 0;
    padding: 0;
}
</style>
```

This might look like a lot, but it's nothing you haven't seen before. First, you simply set the margins of the welcome <div> to give you 30 pixels of whitespace along the left edge of the viewport. In the next rule, you set the margins of the specials <div> to give you 35 pixels of whitespace on its right side (to avoid having text run into the right edge of the viewport) and 375 pixels of space on its left (to clear the left column).

The rule after that sizes both column's headlines at 22 pixels (2.2em) and increases their line height so that the two lines of text that read "Welcome to Papa's Pepperoncini's!" don't overlap one another. The rule after that does the same for the welcome paragraph and list of weekly specials, only it sets their font size to 14 pixels (1.4em). The next rule removes the default bottom margin of the "Weekly Specials" headline so that, along with the final rule, the list of weekly specials appears to be right underneath the headline without any bullet markers.

Finally, in order to get the first sentence of the welcome paragraph—the one that reads, "Please, sit down!"—to display on its own line, you need to make one last tweak to the XHTML content of your page so that you can target this sentence with another rule. You could use the <span> element, but that doesn't add any additional semantic value to the page. Since the design clearly indicates that this first sentence should be emphasized in some way, you'll use an <em> element so that the semantics of the page more closely resemble the intention of the visual design:

```
<div id="welcome">
    <h1>Welcome to Papa Pepperoncini&rsquo;s!</h1>
    <p><em>Please, sit down!</em> Papa Pepperoncini&rsquo;s Pizza ➥
            is the finest Italian Eatery this side of the Atlantic, ➥
            and you&rsquo;re glad you&rsquo;ve come to visit. ➥
            Feel free to look at ➥
        <a href="menu.html" title="Read our menu online.">the ➥
            menu</a>, browse through our <a href="locations.html" ➥
            title="Find our nearest restaurant.">locations</a>, ➥
            or read <a href="about.html" ➥
            title="Discover what makes us the best."> ➥
            about our history</a>. And if you need anything, just ➥
            let us know.  Grazzi!</p>
</div>
```

Now you can pull this sentence out of its paragraph and display it on its own line by making it generate a block-level box. Figure 6-27 shows the result of all these additions.

```
#welcome {
    float: left;
    width: 275px;
    margin: 0 0 0 30px;
}
#specials { margin: 0 35px 0 375px; }
#welcome h1, #specials h2 {
    font-size: 2.2em;
    line-height: 1.3em;
}
#welcome p, #specials li {
    font-size: 1.4em;
    line-height: 1.5em;
}
#welcome em {
    display: block;
    margin-bottom: 1em;
    font-weight: bold;
}
#specials h2 { margin-bottom: 0; }
#specials ul {
    list-style-type: none;
    margin: 0;
    padding: 0;
}
</style>
```

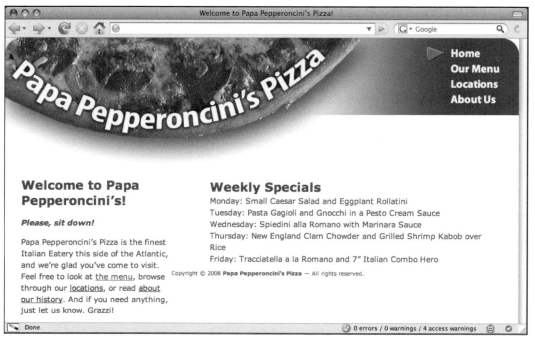

Figure 6-27. Styling the emphasized text as a new paragraph

As you can see, this last group of simple changes has completed the implementation of the main two columns. Better yet, since you didn't take your columns out of the normal document flow by using absolute positioning, both of the columns are now lining up with the end of the header by themselves. This means that if you later shrink the header, the columns will slide up the page along with it.

All you have left to do now is position and style the footer, and you can call your design complete.

Styling the footer: clearing floats and adding borders

The final block of content you need to style to complete Papa Pepperoncini's Pizza website is the footer. The original design didn't actually include a footer, so let's not spend too much time worrying about it. All you really need to do is make sure it always appears at the bottom of the website.

Currently, the footer is flowing around the floated left column right after the <div> listing Papa Pepperoncini's weekly specials in the right column. To ensure that the footer <div> is always beneath both columns, what you need to do is increase the footer's top margin by a significant amount to ensure that it clears the floated left column when the right column doesn't have enough content to push it down beneath the left column on its own. But how can you know how much to increase the top margin of the footer by ahead of time? Thankfully, you don't have to.

By declaring the clear property on the footer <div>, you can tell the browser to automatically adjust its top margin so that element always clears whatever floated boxes precede it in the document flow. In this case, since you want the footer to clear a CSS box that you've floated left, you can use the left value:

```
#specials ul {
    list-style-type: none;
    margin: 0;
    padding: 0;
}
#footer { clear: left; }
</style>
```

However, since you already know that you always want the footer to be at the bottom of the page, you may as well tell it to clear both left and right floated boxes by telling it to clear both.

```
#specials ul {
    list-style-type: none;
    margin: 0;
    padding: 0;
}
#footer { clear: both; }
</style>
```

Now, the footer will always be at the bottom of the page. If the floated left column is taller than the statically positioned right column, the browser will increase the footer's margin on its own so that it clears the floated column. If the right column is taller than the float, then the right column's content itself will ensure that the footer is pushed beneath both columns.

To give the footer a little extra breathing room and a bit of a nicer display, let's center the text, give the footer a top single top border, and push the left and right edges of the footer in from the edges of the browser viewport so that the border you give it will align nicely with the left edge of the left column:

```
#specials ul {
    list-style-type: none;
    margin: 0;
    padding: 0;
}
#footer {
    clear: both;
    text-align: center;
    border-top: 1px solid;
    margin: 0 30px 0;
}
</style>
```

In turn, these three declarations center all the inline-level boxes (the text) inside the footer, apply a 1 pixel solid top border, and finally increase the footer's horizontal margins by 30 pixels. Since you didn't specify a color for the top border, the color of the text will be used by default.

As a finishing touch, to give the design just a touch more whitespace between the ends of the columns and the start of the footer, let's increase the bottom margin on each column by another 30 pixels. You need to use the bottom margins of the columns to do this since you can't rely on the footer's top margin, because you're telling the browser to adjust that for you by itself in some cases. With these last changes, the style sheet—and the web design—is now complete.

```
#welcome {
    float: left;
    width: 275px;
    margin: 0 0 30px 30px;
}
#specials { margin: 0 35px 30px 375px; }
#welcome h1, #specials h2 {
    font-size: 2.2em;
    line-height: 1.3em;
}
```

Figure 6-28 shows the resulting design. Compare it with Figure 6-2 to see how closely you managed to mimic the original design.

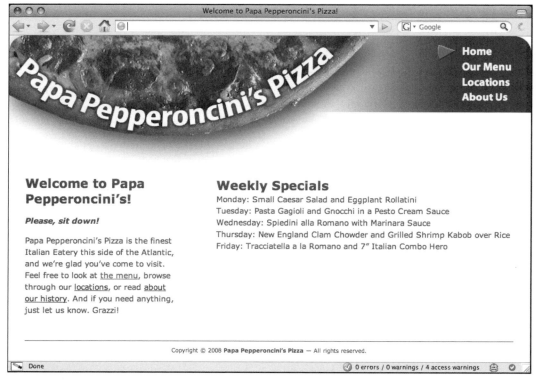

Figure 6-28. The completed CSS-based design

At this point, you have the web page working perfectly in Firefox, but there are a few issues in other, less standards-compliant web browsers such as Internet Explorer. It's now time to return to these issues and mercilessly squash these rendering bugs one by one.

Dealing with nonstandard browsers

Try as it might, today's most popular web browser, Internet Explorer 6 for Windows, just can't cope with a lot of the (very basic) standard CSS-based layout schemes. In addition to its utter lack of support for parts of the CSS specifications, it and its differently versioned cousins sport a litany of rendering bugs that often have seemingly bizarre and completely unpredictable causes and solutions. It is especially notorious for dealing particularly poorly with complicated layouts that make heavy use of floated boxes.

The good news is that, thanks to the work of the web development community, most of these rendering bugs and their solutions have now been documented on websites such as "Big John" Gallant's and Holly Bergevin's Position Is Everything (http://positioniseverything.net/) and Peter-Paul Koch's Quirksmode (http://quirksmode.org/). These sites, among many others discoverable via a simple Google search, are absolutely indispensable resources for learning about the ins and outs of what's happening inside these nonstandard browsers when it seems like nothing is making sense at all.

Some of these bugs are so bad that even with a simple design such as the one you've developed for Papa Pepperoncini's Pizza website, there's bound to be some trouble. Indeed, unfortunately, if you take a look at the web page in Internet Explorer 6, you'll find that you have some (blessedly) minor problems. Figure 6-29 shows what Internet Explorer 6 makes of the code.

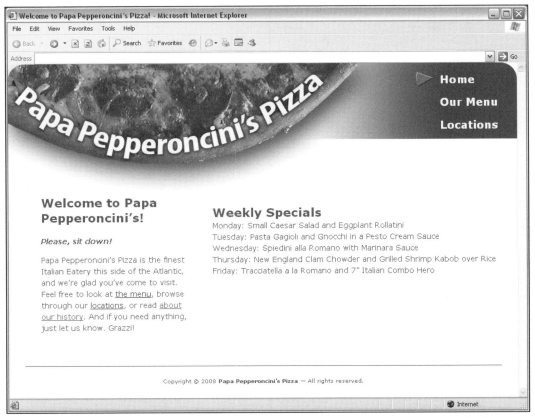

Figure 6-29. Bugs in Internet Explorer 6 cause it to render the page with incorrect spacing in the navigation menu and the right column's headline.

Each navigation menu link is spaced apart from the other ones way more than they should be and . . . yikes! Where'd the fourth navigation menu item go? Since the text of the list items is white, this last one seems to have vanished. In fact, it's actually still there, camouflaged into the white background of the header image. If you hover over it, you can see that it's still there.

However, hovering over the link reveals yet another problem with the navigation menu: only the anchor text of the link itself reveals the link's hover effect. In Firefox (and all other standards-compliant web browsers), the entire block-level box of the <a> element provides space to reveal the rollover.

Though slightly better, even the latest release of Internet Explorer—which is Internet Explorer version 7 as of this writing—has some spacing problems. Figure 6-30 shows the same code in Internet Explorer 7.

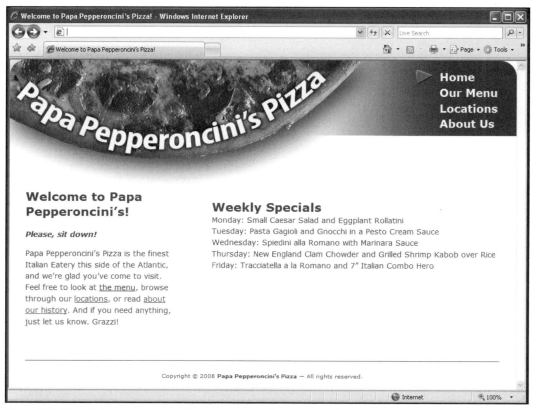

Figure 6-30. Though fewer seem to exist, some rendering bugs still remain even in Internet Explorer 7.

So, how can you wrestle these browsers into compliance? Even though Internet Explorer 8's promised improvements should be quite uplifting, it will still take time for the older versions of the web browser to become obsolete. You have a number of choices, each with their own pros and cons.

Browser-specific style sheets using conditional comments

Of course, one way to deal with browser bugs is to send entirely different style sheets to different web browsers. That's an awful lot of extra work, though, and the work required to maintain these different versions of the style sheets will only increase over time as you try to support more and more web browsers. Besides, even Internet Explorer did manage to get *most* of the rules in the style sheet correct.

Instead of making new style sheets for nonstandard browsers, you can use CSS's own cascading mechanism to write new CSS rules to override just the declarations that these web browsers have trouble with. This way, you won't be duplicating as much of the work you've previously accomplished. In addition, you can segregate the rules you write specifically for buggy browsers into one central place, which many developers find a lot easier to manage.

The most reliable way to apply a browser-specific style sheet to Internet Explorer is by using one of Internet Explorer's own proprietary features called **conditional comments**. (We go into quite a bit more detail on this in Chapter 8.) Briefly, a conditional comment looks exactly like a regular XHTML comment to every browser except Internet Explorer. When Internet Explorer encounters this specially crafted comment, however, it goes ahead and parses the content of the comment as though it were really part of the code. This feature lets web developers write code that only Internet Explorer can see.

If you go down this path, you could create a new embedded style sheet specifically for Internet Explorer that's filled with the CSS rules you want to use to override the problematic ones in the original, standards-based style sheet. Such XHTML code would look like this:

```
<!DOCTYPE html PUBLIC "-//W3C//DTD XHTML 1.0 Strict//EN"
    "http://www.w3.org/TR/xhtml1/DTD/xhtml1-strict.dtd">
<html xmlns="http://www.w3.org/1999/xhtml" xml:lang="en" lang="en">
 <head>
    <meta http-equiv="Content-Type" ➥
                content="text/html; charset=utf-8" />
    <title>Welcome to Papa Pepperoncini&rsquo;s Pizza!</title>
    <style type="text/css">
        /* our original style sheet goes here */
    </style>
    <!--[if IE]><style type="text/css">
        /* special Internet Explorer-only style sheet goes here */
    </style><![endif]-->
 </head>
```

As shown, a conditional comment starts and ends just like a typical XHTML comment, which is why other browsers can't see it. Internet Explorer, on the other hand, evaluates the expression placed within the square brackets (between the [and]> sequences). If the expression evaluates to true, then Internet Explorer will treat everything else up until the trailing <![endif]--> as though it were normal code.

The expression inside a conditional comment can even test to see which version of Internet Explorer is parsing the comment. For instance, here's a conditional comment that only Internet Explorer 6 will see:

```
<!--[if IE 6]> Code for all Internet Explorer 6 ➥
                         could go here. <![endif]-->
```

And here's one that all versions of Internet Explorer prior to (that is, less than) 8 will see:

```
<!--[if IE lt 8]> Code for all versions of Internet Explorer ➥
                         prior to 8 could go here. <![endif]-->
```

Placing CSS style sheets behind conditional comments is arguably the safest method to use for redefining CSS rules specifically for Internet Explorer. Of course, conditional comments won't work for any browser other than Internet Explorer, so unless the problem with the rendering of your page is occurring only in that browser, conditional comments are only part of the potential solution. Additionally, conditional comments can't be placed inside a CSS style sheet, so you're forced to create entirely new style sheets when you want to use a conditional comment, even if that style sheet ends up being just a single CSS rule or two.

Filtering CSS rules with CSS selectors

Another method for tackling browser-specific CSS bugs is to rely on the browser's own failure to support CSS selectors properly. Since you already know that Internet Explorer (and many other, older web browsers) don't support certain CSS selectors, you can hide specific declaration blocks behind such CSS selectors. CSS rules written for this purpose and in this way are typically referred to as CSS **filters**, because they are used to filter CSS declarations away from different browsers.

A common idiom for this is to use the child combinator with the html and body type selectors:

```
html > body /* real selector goes here */ {
    /* CSS declarations for Internet Explorer 6 and below go here */
}
```

Since the <body> element is always a direct child of the html element, prepending this CSS selector to your real CSS selector will always match your real CSS selector. However, since Internet Explorer versions prior to 7 do not understand CSS selectors that use the child combinator, those browsers will completely ignore the CSS declarations inside the declaration block. So, for example, to color the text in an example <div> red in Internet Explorer 5 and 6 but green in Firefox, Safari, and other standards-compliant web browsers, you could use the following series of CSS rules:

```
div#example { color: red; }
html > body div#example { color: green; }
```

The drawback to using a series of CSS rules like this is that if the buggy browser gains support for the CSS selector you used (as Internet Explorer 7 did when it was first released), it will begin to behave like all the other browsers, and it will apply the green coloring to the element. In such a case, if the browser vendor doesn't *also* fix the original display bug, the original rendering error will resurface.

Of course, text coloring isn't used to fix display bugs. Most of the time, these browser-specific declarations will be used to change the dimensions of a CSS box for one browser or another. In this and the upcoming examples, however, I'll use colors simply because they are usually easier to see.

CSS hacks: exploiting one bug to resolve another

Another common idiom to accomplish the same thing as the child selector filter—but that is now considered far safer—exploits a bizarre bug present in Internet Explorer versions prior to 7. Rather than *filtering CSS declarations away from* the browser, however, this CSS selector actually *targets* that browser so that the declarations of the rule apply *only to those browsers*.

For some unexplained reason, Internet Explorer 5 and 6 incorrectly nest the html element inside another phantom element with no name. This unnamed element is what Internet Explorer 5 and 6 consider to be the root element of the page, whereas all other browsers consider the html element to be the root element. As a side effect of this strange behavior, you can actually use a CSS filter that targets browsers based on whether they perceive the html element to be descended from another (mystery) element.

To do this, you need to use the **universal type selector**. This selector, which is represented as an asterisk (*) simply means "any type of element." By combining this selector with a descendant combinator and the html type selector, you can write a CSS hack that is commonly referred to as the **star-html hack**.

```
div#example { color: red; }
* html div#example { color: green; }
```

According to the CSS2.1 specification, backslashes in CSS property names should be ignored. Internet Explorer 5, however, doesn't adhere to this and instead reads CSS property names with backslashes in them as nonexistent properties. You can thus exploit this fact to write a CSS declaration that *only* standards-compliant browsers and Internet Explorer versions 6 and newer will be able to understand. So, to color the text of the example <div> blue in Internet Explorer 5.5 and older, red in Internet Explorer 6, and green in all modern standards-compliant web browsers, you could use this series of rules:

```
div#example {
    color: blue;
    c\olor: red;
}
html > body div#example { color: green; }
```

Internet Explorer 5 for Macintosh has a bug that relates to the way it parses CSS comments. Specifically, if you end a CSS comment with the sequence */ instead of simply */, then the browser will not recognize that the comment is ended and will blissfully ignore any remaining CSS rules until it sees another end-of-comment sequence without the backslash. This bug, which is known to affect only Internet Explorer 5 for Mac, is plainly named the **commented backslash hack** or the **Mac hack**. To exploit this fact and give the text in Internet Explorer 5 for Mac its own color (say, teal), you could write your CSS filters like this:

```
div#example { color: teal; }
/* Start Mac Hack to hide rules from IE5/Mac \*/
div#example {
    color: blue;
    c\olor: red;
}
html > body div#example { color: green; }
/* End Mac Hack to stop hiding rules from IE5/Mac */
```

There's another CSS hack that uses comments, and it filters out Internet Explorer 7. Using it, you could give the example <div>'s text a yellow color only in Internet Explorer 7 without changing the colors for any of the other browsers:

```
div#example { color: teal; }
/* Start Mac Hack to hide rules from IE5/Mac \*/
div#example {
    color: blue;
    c\olor: red;
}
html > body div#example { color: yellow; }
html > /**/ body div#example { color: green; }
/* End Mac Hack to stop hiding rules from IE5/Mac */
```

Quite a number of additional CSS hacks of this kind can filter out or specifically apply CSS rules to other browsers and browser versions, but many of them use CSS syntax that won't validate. Admittedly, CSS hacks can get quite messy quickly! Not only are they confusing, but they aren't always future-proof, so it's often simply best to avoid their use altogether if you can manage it.

In many of the most common cases, you'll find that rendering bugs can be squashed simply by explicitly specifying layout dimensions such as width or height or by changing the positioning scheme certain elements use, such as by using a position value of relative instead of the default of static. So, speaking of squashing CSS rendering bugs, let's get back to Papa Pepperoncini's Pizza and tackle those annoying Internet Explorer bugs.

Fixing your spacing bugs in Internet Explorer 6 and 7

Now that you have a few tools under your belt for dealing with CSS bugs in different browsers, you can use the simplest of these to fix the display problems your CSS code has caused in Internet Explorer 6 and 7. You'll first tackle the strange list item spacing that is pushing the fourth navigation menu item underneath the header. This bug has a name: the **Internet Explorer whitespace bug**.

Though there are quite a few ways you can deal with the Internet Explorer whitespace bug, the most straightforward for these purposes is to create a new CSS rule that overrides the display property and that applies only to Internet Explorer versions 6 and older. A foolproof way to do that is to use the star-html hack.

When you see the star-html hack in a style sheet, you know it's there to specifically fix a rendering bug in Internet Explorer versions older than 7. For this reason, we prefer to keep these hacks right next to the CSS rule they are overriding. If you were to move them into a separate style sheet, you wouldn't be able to easily see what CSS declarations you're overriding.

Use the star-html hack to close the gap between the items in your navigation list:

```
#mainnav a {
    color: #FFF;
    font: bold 2em "Myriad Pro", Verdana, Arial, sans-serif;
    text-decoration: none;
    display: block;
    padding: 2px 35px 2px 45px;
}
* html #mainnav a { display: inline; }
#mainnav .selected a, ➡
#mainnav .selected a:hover, ➡
#mainnav .selected a:active {
    background: url(images/icon.pizza-slice.normal.gif) ➡
                            no-repeat left center;
    color: #FFF;
    cursor: default;
}
```

Simply overriding the display property and setting its value to inline is enough to fix this bug in Internet Explorer 6. With this bug out of the way, turn your attention to the position of the right column's headline.

To deal with this issue, you'll reverse the procedure. Instead of writing a new rule that applies only to the problem browsers, you'll write a new rule that filters them out. To filter out both Internet Explorer 6 and Internet Explorer 7, you can use the CSS filter we showed earlier, a filter we call the **child comment** filter. All you need do is declare a new initial top margin value and then re-declare it for conforming browsers:

```
#specials h2 {
    margin-top: 0; /* IE 6, 7 */
    margin-bottom: 0;
}
html > /**/ body #specials h2 {
    margin-top: .7em; /* conforming browsers */
}
#specials ul {
    list-style-type: none;
    margin: 0;
    padding: 0;
}
```

With these CSS filters in place, the design now renders identically in all the browsers on which you've tested it. Figure 6-31 shows the result in Internet Explorer 6, and Figure 6-32 shows the same code in Internet Explorer 7.

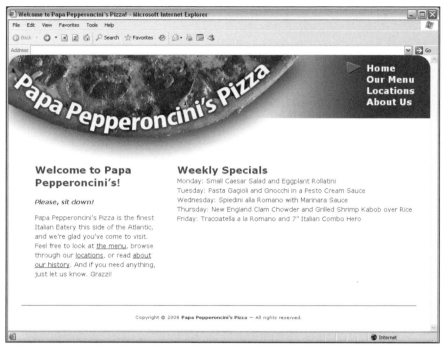

Figure 6-31. The completed design in Internet Explorer 6

Figure 6-32. The completed design in Internet Explorer 7

CSS media types and creating print style sheets

So far, you've seen how you can use CSS to create vivid designs on a computer screen. This is very handy, but CSS can do even more. Since its flexibility comes from the ability to use the same source document and display it in different ways, you can use everything you've just learned to create an entirely new look for the page *when it's printed*. You do this in two steps: first, you create a new style sheet (or an additional portion of your existing style sheet) and declare it as a print style sheet, and then you simply write new CSS rules that restyle your page in an appropriate way for paper.

To define styles specifically for printed media, you need to use CSS's predefined media types. Recall that the original style sheet is embedded in your XHTML document like this:

```
<style type="text/css">
    /* ...CSS rules for Papa Pepperoncini's Pizza are here... */
</style>
```

This style sheet is thus effectively a style sheet for *all* possible media types. One of these media types is screen. Another, as you may have guessed already, is print. So in other words, to the browser, the style sheet element actually looks like this:

```
<style type="text/css" media="all">
    /* ...CSS rules for Papa Pepperoncini's Pizza are here... */
</style>
```

If you wanted to restrict all the CSS rules you wrote to apply only to computer monitors, you could instead define your CSS style sheet like this:

```
<style type="text/css" media="screen">
    /* ...CSS rules for Papa Pepperoncini's Pizza are here... */
</style>
```

In fact, this is probably the simplest way to create a printed version of your page because it will cause the browser to ignore all your CSS rules when the user prints the page and your design will revert to the unstyled look you had before you started. Figure 6-33 shows a preview of how your page will look when printed from Safari.

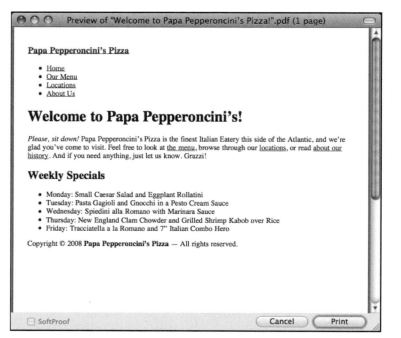

Figure 6-33. The unstyled design as a preview of the printed page

Another way to accomplish this same effect is to nest all the CSS rules inside a special CSS rule whose declaration block can actually contain other CSS rules (including selectors). This CSS rule is called a **media type at-rule** because it "points at a media type." In code, it looks like this:

```
<style type="text/css">
    @media screen {
        /* …CSS rules for Papa Pepperoncini's Pizza are here… */
    }
</style>
```

In both the media attribute for the style element and in an @media CSS rule, you can define more than one media type by listing them in a comma-separated list. For instance, many designs that work well for computer screens also often work well for projection displays, so to declare your styles for both of these types but no other types, you could write your style sheets in either of these two equivalent ways:

```
<style type="text/css" media="screen, projection">
    /* ...CSS rules for Papa Pepperoncini's Pizza are here... */
</style>
<style type="text/css">
    @media screen, projection {
        /* …CSS rules for Papa Pepperoncini's Pizza are here… */
    }
</style>
```

The specificity of CSS rules declared within specific media type targets like this is no different than if the rules were not restricted to a media type. As a result, you can use all the cascading behavior you're now familiar with to define style sheets for different media types one after the other whose rules will override the previous style sheet's rules. In practice, it usually makes more sense to define entirely different style sheets for different media types instead of nesting your CSS rules inside an @media rule because this enables you to more easily "mix and match" simply by changing the order in which you embed (or externally link) your style sheets to your (X)HTML pages.

Let's take advantage of this behavior now to create a new very short print style sheet for Papa Pepperoncini's Pizza that builds on all the work you've already accomplished. While you're developing this style sheet, it will quickly become a nuisance to have to go to the print preview screen every time you want to check the progress of your work. As a workaround, let's *temporarily* simply define your new styles as screen styles *and* print styles, so they become visible in the browser.

With your new style sheet added to the mix, the XHTML header of your page now looks like this:

```
<!DOCTYPE html PUBLIC "-//W3C//DTD XHTML 1.0 Strict//EN"
    "http://www.w3.org/TR/xhtml1/DTD/xhtml1-strict.dtd">
<html xmlns="http://www.w3.org/1999/xhtml" xml:lang="en" lang="en">
  <head>
    <meta http-equiv="Content-Type" ➥
              content="text/html; charset=utf-8" />
    <title>Welcome to Papa Pepperoncini&rsquo;s Pizza!</title>
    <style type="text/css">
        /* ...CSS rules for Papa Pepperoncini's Pizza are here... */
    </style>
    <style type="text/css" media="screen, print">
        /* new CSS print styles will go here */
    </style>
  </head>
```

Now you can start writing new CSS rules to override the rules you already have. Just as you've done before, you'll simply go over design (and its style sheet) from top to bottom changing what you need to and leaving the rest the same. At the top, you have the global rules for the background of the page and the colors of the text and links.

Even though most browsers don't print backgrounds by default, let's turn off all the background colors and images explicitly. This will save some of your visitors some ink, and it's better for the environment, too. Also, since the notion of links is somewhat useless on printed pages, let's make all links look like normal text by turning them black and removing their underlines. After doing this, you can see yet another reason why descriptive anchor text (instead of anchor text such as "click here") is so important.

```
<style type="text/css" media="screen, print">
    html, body { background-color: transparent; }
    body { margin: .25in; }
    body, a:link, a:visited { color: #000; }
    a:link, a:visited { text-decoration: none; }
</style>
```

Notice that these CSS rules are overriding only what you have to from the previous rules, and they are ignoring the declarations that you want to keep. Notice also that there is no CSS rule for the a:hover or a:active styles, since these dynamic pseudo-classes obviously do not apply to printed media. Finally, note that because you are now working on physical media, it makes sense for you to use length values that are native to physical spaces (such as inches).

Next, let's give the nice graphical banner a simpler makeover. You need to explicitly remove the background image, move the negatively indented text back into the browser viewport, and make the text more prominent by increasing its size. Notice that, once again, you're now using a length unit that is native to printed media (points) to size the text.

```
<style type="text/css" media="screen, print">
    html, body { background-color: transparent; }
    body { margin: .25in; }
    body, a:link, a:visited { color: #000; }
    a:link, a:visited { text-decoration: none; }
    #header { background-image: none; }
    #header h3 {
        background-image: none;
        height: auto;
        text-indent: 0;
        text-align: center;
        font-size: 28pt;
    }
</style>
```

Next, you need to completely remove the main navigation menu since, on a printed page, a navigation menu like this makes no sense at all. Doing so is very easy. You could just make the navigation menu invisible by declaring its visibility property with a value of hidden. This works, but doesn't really make sense: the navigation menu will still be there; it just will not be shown. You want to completely remove it from the document (without deleting it from your XHTML, of course), so instead, you declare its display property with a value set to none. This actually does more than simply make the main navigation menu invisible; it *physically removes it from the layout of the page* so that it is no longer in the document flow.

```
#header h3 {
        background-image: none;
        height: auto;
        text-indent: 0;
        text-align: center;
        font-size: 28pt;
    }
    #mainnav { display: none; }
</style>
```

These simple changes are all it took to create a completely restyled page that will be appropriate to be printed. You've retained your two-column layout, your footer, and all the textual elements of the page but removed the graphically intensive banner image and the interactive effects of the links and navigation elements. Figure 6-34 shows the results so far.

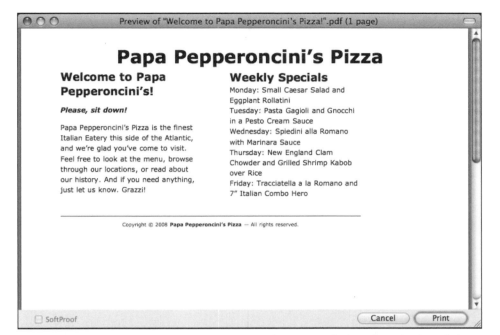

Figure 6-34. Only a few rules are necessary to override the screen styles in order to begin to design a print style sheet.

At this point, you're almost ready to call your print style sheet complete. For the final touches, let's space things out a bit more nicely, turn your page back into a single column, and soften the footer a bit. When that's done, you can remove the screen value from the media attribute of your style element. With these changes, you can declare your print design complete. Figure 6-35 shows the result.

```
<style type="text/css" media="print">
    html, body { background-color: transparent; }
    body { margin: .25in; }
    body, a:link, a:visited { color: #000; }
    a:link, a:visited { text-decoration: none; }
    #header { background-image: none; }
    #header h3 {
        background-image: none;
        height: auto;
        text-indent: 0;
        text-align: center;
        font-size: 28pt;
    }
}
#mainnav { display: none; }
#welcome {
    float: none;
    width: auto;
    margin: 0;
}
```

209

```
#specials { margin: 0; }
#specials h2 { margin-bottom: .75em; }
#specials ul {
    list-style-type: disc;
    margin-left: .5in;
}
#footer {
    margin-top: .5in;
    border: none;
    color: #999;
    text-align: right;
}
</style>
```

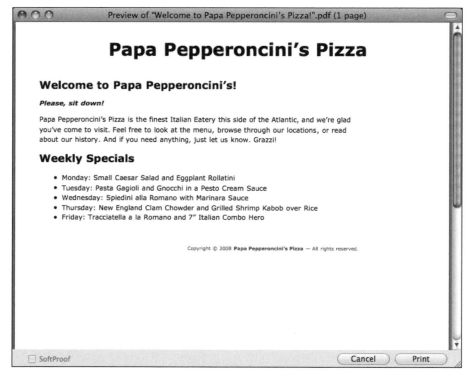

Figure 6-35. A few more additions to the print style sheet give you a nice printer-friendly version of your page.

Now, with both your screen and print style sheets completed, you can easily extract them into external CSS style sheets and link those external style sheets to as many pages as you need to develop for Papa Pepperoncini's Pizza website with minimal fuss.

Designing for other media types and devices

As you can see, creating new style sheets for different media types is fairly painless. All it really requires is an understanding of the destination media and how it works. For printed pages, this should be easy because most if not all of us are intimately familiar with what printed pages can and can't do. It's the other media types, most notably the handheld media type, that become trickier.

The handheld media type is of particular importance because it's used for most handheld devices such as PDAs, smart phones, and other pocket-sized web browsers. Many of these web browsers look through the available style sheets used on a page and opt to use the one declared with the handheld media type, if one exists. If it doesn't, these browsers make a best-effort attempt to restyle the page content on the fly if they have to do so. Sometimes this automatic restyling works well, but other times it makes pages completely unusable. You can use a number of good tools to test your design for handheld browsers, some of which we discuss further in Chapter 8.

Of these devices with handheld browsers, two stand out as important exceptions: Apple's iPhone and iPod touch. These devices use the Mobile Safari browser, a variant of Mac OS X's native web browser, Safari. Mobile Safari actually uses the screen media type and *ignores* style sheets declared with the handheld media type. Thankfully, Apple has done a very good job of supporting the CSS standards in both of its Safari variations, so you needn't be too concerned with the iPhone and iPod touch's compatibility with their websites unless you need certain kinds of advanced interactions (such as drag and drop). Since this is an area of rapid development as of this writing, we suggest you check Apple's documentation to learn more about the iPhone and iPod touch's eccentricities when it comes to developing web pages for them.

Summary

As you've now seen, the implementation of a design in a CSS style sheet is relatively straightforward, but it can be complicated by numerous factors, such as browser bugs or natural differences in the display medium. With the simple design for Papa Pepperoncini's Pizza, you saw numerous examples of how designing for the web page is drastically different from designing for the printed page. You also saw some examples of common techniques used to leverage the flexibility and fluidity of web pages to maximize the usability of your web pages.

By using dynamic pseudo-classes, you added interactivity that would not have been possible on a printed page. By using two different layout techniques—absolute positioning and floated boxes—to lay out the elements of your web page in precise locations, you were able to mirror the designer's original vision for Papa Pepperoncini's Pizza website with a compatible, cross-browser implementation. Finally, you learned how to take the original style sheet and modify it to create a print-ready version of your page in mere minutes.

Clearly, there's plenty you can accomplish just by utilizing what XHTML and CSS have to offer. However, there's much more that the web browser has to offer in terms of creating dynamic effects that far exceed the modicum of interactivity that CSS's dynamic pseudo-classes provide. In the next chapters, you'll see how to harness the full power of JavaScript, a standards-based full-fledged programming language that's embedded directly inside web browsers, to take your web pages to a whole new level.

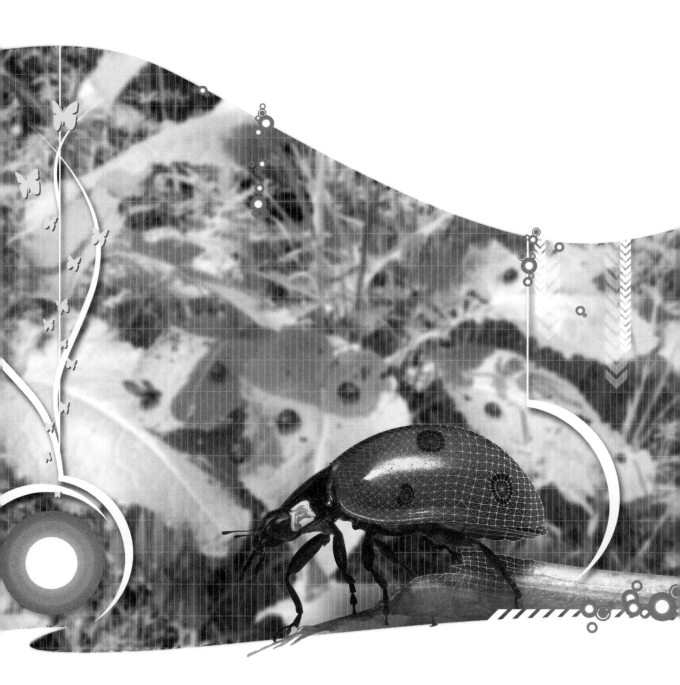

Chapter 7

CREATING INTERACTIVITY WITH JAVASCRIPT

JavaScript is one of the three basic building blocks of the Web. If you think about web technologies as a pyramid, HTML/XHTML is one corner of that pyramid handling the actual content of a page. CSS is another corner, adding style to your pages and allowing you to lay them out in a way that is not only attractive but also adds visual impact. JavaScript is the third corner, allowing pages to do more than just be static documents.

One of the biggest questions amongst those who are new to the Web is, what's the difference between JavaScript and something like PHP? The big difference is that JavaScript is executed on the client side (in the visitors' browsers), whereas PHP runs on the server. So in other words, JavaScript actually makes use of the processor(s) on your end users' computers.

The advantage you get is that things seem to happen instantly in the browser. Using JavaScript, you can make your pages feel more like an application running on the clients' computers. JavaScript operations don't require a round-trip to the server and back; pages aren't submitted, processed, and then returned.

This speed comes with a price, though. Because you're not processing on the server, you don't have access to certain features. You can't, for example, save something to or get something out of a database management system on a remote host using JavaScript. It would be impossible to write a real-time chat application using JavaScript alone, for example. You can't manipulate files or send and receive e-mail.

And individuals have the option to turn JavaScript off in their web browser, meaning you can't do anything with JavaScript at all (so you'd best have a backup plan). You can do some pretty cool things, though, for those people who will let you.

JavaScript basics: origin and background

You can probably guess, based on everything you've read about the history of web standards, that JavaScript hasn't had a smooth journey to where it is today. JavaScript began life as a Netscape development and was initially supported in Netscape Navigator 2 (around the end of 1995). Microsoft quickly fired back with its own implementation, which it called JScript (first supported in Internet Explorer 3 in 1996). Although the two languages were similar, some differences did exist, such as in the way each implementation enabled programmers to find the current date and time.

The dark ages of scripting

JavaScript and JScript really fell from grace with developers for some time because of the differences between browsers. It was one thing to have to write "hacks" in order to get a certain CSS declaration to work properly across browsers; it was something entirely different to have to write multiple versions of your scripts in order to get them to behave consistently. The DOM really was a breakthrough on this front and ushered in the ability for developers to, once again, write a single script that would work everywhere.

Netscape submitted the JavaScript language to the European Computer Manufacturers Association (ECMA), an international standards organization, for standardization in 1996, and it was accepted shortly thereafter. This became the basis of ECMAScript, which is, essentially, a compromise between Microsoft and Netscape on a core set of functions for a scripting language. ECMAScript is the core, and then JavaScript and JScript both extend the functionality.

With the introduction of the DOM recommendation and support from the browser manufacturers, we started to see an upsurge in really innovative web applications being introduced; in fact, it wouldn't be too much of a stretch to credit the entire Web 2.0 technological leap to the introduction of DOM support.

Object-based programming

An **object** is a collection of properties. Those properties may be really simple pieces of data, they may be other objects, or they may be functions (methods). JavaScript has a number of built-in objects, such as an Image object and a Date object, but developers are free to define their own objects as well.

Objects are really useful because they can have global properties that exist in all instances of an object, as well as assign individual properties (or change properties) for certain instances. This is a feature of object-oriented languages called **modularity**; variables and functions can be defined once and then reused in multiple places. Besides the obvious benefit to developers in that they need to write something only once, it also eases maintenance: as new functionality is needed in a particular area, the reusable function being called can be updated, and changes will propagate throughout.

It's probably easiest to illustrate this concept with an example. Say you have a number of download registration forms scattered throughout your website. These forms ask for a variety of information, but one thing they all have in common is that you have to enter an e-mail address. You write a function that can be called when a form is submitted that checks the e-mail field to make sure that it's not left blank. Problem solved.

Three weeks later, you're doing maintenance on your registration database, and you notice a bunch of e-mail addresses that look like asdf and sdfhsdg. It seems that instead of entering an actual e-mail address, people are just punching in some random characters in order to bypass the form and download the file they want. It's easy for you to make a few tweaks to your e-mail address checker function and have it instantly update everywhere on the website, because you've reused that function object throughout.

Another feature of object-oriented programming used by JavaScript is that of **encapsulation**. Encapsulation hides all the steps of a particular function and allows you to simply call that function by its name. This greatly improves the readability of code by simplifying and shortening it.

An example of encapsulation would be with an Ajax function that updates a <div> on a page with the results of a database query when you click a button. So, although you might just have this:

```
<input type="button" onclick="updateDiv('results');" />
```

the actual steps involved in updateDiv() may be to take some value from somewhere, submit it to a program on the server, retrieve data from a database, format that output a particular way, and then display it within the <div> you've specified. Imagine what your code would look like if every time you wanted to have this happen you had to explicitly type this series of commands.

What is the Document Object Model?

The **Document Object Model** (DOM) is a standard way in which web browsers represent HTML and XML documents. It defines a hierarchy amongst elements on a page so that individual page elements can be addressed by your JavaScript code. In other words, the DOM lets you tell your scripts what part of the page to act on. Figure 7-1 shows a representation of a part of the DOM involving a form field.

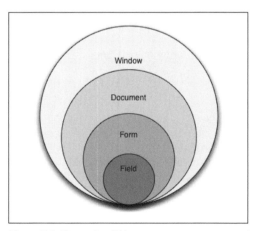

Figure 7-1. Elements within a page are encompassed in a hierarchy known as the Document Object Model.

Standardizing on the DOM API really brought the different JavaScript implementations into greater compatibility with one another. The DOM brought about a standard way for things such as JavaScript to interact with elements encoded in HTML.

getElementById()

One of the really great things that came about with DOM support in browsers is the getElementById() function. Using this function, you can retrieve and change the values of a number of different properties of the various elements on your page. IDs assigned to elements on a web page must be unique (you can't have two <div id="navigation"> elements on your page). As such, you can address elements by their unique ID easily. Here are a few examples of some of the things you can do with a text box:

```
<input type="text" name="FirstName" id="FName" />
<div id="result"></div>
```

You can retrieve the value of that text box and assign it to a variable:

```
var FirstName = document.getElementById('FName').value;
```

You can change the appearance of that text box (for example, to highlight it if the input fails validation):

```
document.getElementById('FName').style.border = "2px solid red";
```

You can easily return the value that was entered in an alert:

```
alert("You just entered " + document.getElementById('FName').value);
```

Or you can take the value from one text box and output it in a <div> (or some other element) on the page:

```
document.getElementById('result').innerHTML = ➡
"My bologna has a first name, it's " + ➡
document.getElementById('FName').value;
```

The point here is that it's really easy to target any element on a page that has an ID.

JavaScript: the basics

As with a number of things on the Web, there's more than one way to do it (which is one of the mottos of Perl, another programming language). You can mix your JavaScript code right in with your HTML markup, or you can separate it completely and store your scripts in separate files. In the following sections, you'll look at three different ways to implement JavaScript within your pages: linking, embedding, or putting code inline. Whenever possible, it's best to try to keep your JavaScript separated from your markup—but sometimes, it may be appropriate to use inline code if you're developing an idea and need to quickly mock something up.

Linking code (separating form from function)

JavaScript files are typically given a `.js` file extension. They are just plain-text files containing any bits of JavaScript code you'd like. These files can then be linked to in either the <head> or <body> of your pages:

```
<script type="text/javascript" src="script.js" />
```

This is definitely the best-practice approach because it creates a clear separation between the content contained in your markup and any interactivity or behaviors that you're including in your pages. Taking this approach, you can then call any functions defined in the `script.js` file on any number of pages (that contain a link to `script.js`) and reuse those functions throughout your entire website.

Embedding JavaScript

Your second option is to embed the actual JavaScript code in your page. This is a less desirable option for a couple of reasons: there is less separation between form and function. You are also throwing away one of the great benefits to JavaScript's object-oriented nature: code reuse.

Let's say you write a function to check to make sure a text box on a form isn't left empty (a common practice when you're validating a form's input). If you embed that function in a page, that function can be called only from within that page. You would have to rewrite it (or at the very least copy and paste it) into any other pages that required similar functionality. This concept might seem familiar to you: it's similar to the way CSS works. If you put your style declarations in a page, as opposed to just linking/importing them from an external file, you'll find yourself doing a lot more typing.

Nevertheless, sometimes when you're working out the bugs of a tricky piece of code, it's handy to have it embedded right in your page so that you do not have to flip between multiple text editors. Here's how you would embed JavaScript into an HTML page:

```
<script type="text/javascript">
    function checkTextBox () {
        /* Some code */
    }
</script>
```

Embedding JavaScript in the <head> and embedding JavaScript in the <body> are no different from one another. It's simply a matter of choice: some developers like to keep related code together, whereas others think that all scripts should be grouped together in the <head> so that you know exactly where to look instead of hunting through markup. If you're going to embed your JavaScript, try to pick one convention and stick to it.

Inline JavaScript

Again, one step down the ladder of properly separating form from function is putting JavaScript inline. This is definitely the worst way to do it, because your code is completely isolated to a particular place and cannot be reused in other places. That said, if you're just trying to work out a functional mock-up of something and you don't want to bother with defining functions and such, a little inline scripting might just do what you need (just be sure to clean it up before you launch the site!).

Here's an example that changes the display property of a `<div>` by clicking a link:

```
<a href="#" onclick="document.getElementById('mydiv') ➥
.style.display='block'; return false;">Click me!</a>
<div id="mydiv" style="display: none;">
    This is sneaky hidden content until the link is clicked.
</div>
```

Commenting your code

There are a couple of ways to put comments in your JavaScript code. You can insert large blocks of comments or put in single-line comments. How much commenting you do is up to you; it's a good rule of thumb to comment your code when needed so that someone of a skill level equal to your own would be able to figure out what you're doing. If you've just written something and you think to yourself that it's not completely obvious how it works, then drop in a short comment.

Don't go overboard on commenting your code. Any comments included in code have to be downloaded by end users, so if you double the length of your page by heavily commenting your code, you're also doubling the size of the file that has to be transferred. If you have a lot to say, include a comment pointing them to a readme file or some other piece of documentation that will bring users up to speed.

Another option is to use a JavaScript "compressor" script that will strip away comments and unnecessary whitespace. The code that these scripts produce is streamlined but difficult to read, so it's a good idea to run them on a copy of your `.js` files and to keep a "readable" copy to which you can make your edits. Packer (http://dean.edwards.name/packer/) is a really good one; CodeTrimmer (http://www.twinhelix.com/javascript/codetrim/demo/) is another pretty good one.

Multiline comments in JavaScript are identical to multiline comments in CSS. A block of comments can be enclosed by a slash-asterisk pair and an asterisk-slash pair to terminate the block. In JavaScript, a single-line comment is indicated by two forward slashes.

```
/* Multiline comments may be surrounded
by a slash-asterisk and asterisk-slash. */

var foo = 1; // Single-line comments are preceded by two slashes.
```

One of the handy things about the "two slash" method of commenting is that those comments can stand alone on a line by themselves, or they can be appended to the end of a line of code. So, you can use them to explain what a particular calculation is doing or what a specific variable is for.

Basic programming features

The following are some basic programming features.

Primitive data types

JavaScript has five primitive data types that are the basics from which more complex data types can be derived. String, number, and Boolean are real data types, which are capable of storing data. The other two data types, null and undefined, come about at specific times.

String data type

The string data type is used to store text (zero or more characters) surrounded by single or double quotation marks. Unlike other programming languages, in JavaScript there is no difference between a single character and a number of characters (they're both just strings). Strings are associated with a string object and can be manipulated using a number of built-in JavaScript methods (for example, `.length()` returns the number of characters in a string).

There are a number of special characters (see Table 7-1) that are represented by special character codes. Because strings are enclosed by quotation marks, for example, you can't just type a quotation mark in your string:

```
var s = "This string would throw a "syntax error" ➡
because the quotes are not escaped";
```

Table 7-1. Common Escape Codes in JavaScript

Escape Code	Character Represented
\t	Tab
\n	New line (line feed)
\r	Carriage return
\"	Double quote
\'	Single quote
\\	Backslash

You can also represent special characters using octal, hexadecimal, or Unicode character codes. For example, the letter e with an acute accent, é (as is commonly used in French), can be represented by \u00E9. A good reference for other Unicode character codes is available at http://unicode.org/charts/.

Number data type

The number data type includes both integer and floating-point values (whole numbers and decimals). JavaScript even supports scientific notation, represented with a lowercase e. These are all valid numbers in JavaScript:

```
17
42.3
47e5
-15.2
.4321e-56
```

As with strings, numbers are associated with a number object, allowing you to use a range of built-in methods for numeric manipulation (toPrecision(), for example, outputs a number rounded to a specified number of decimal places).

You will likely run into the NaN value when working with numbers in JavaScript. If you ever get NaN back from a script you've written, it literally means "not a number." This occurs when you have an undefined operation. You'll commonly see this if your script thinks that one of your numbers is actually a string and then you try to perform math using that value.

Boolean data type

A Boolean is a true or false value. Booleans are commonly used in if/else statements and in while loops. They are also commonly used to define an object's properties. For example, JavaScript has a built-in function that will check whether a variable is not a number (isNaN()). The result of this function will be either true or false.

Undefined and null

The undefined data type is used when a value has not been set. For example, in JavaScript it's completely acceptable to declare a variable without assigning it a value:

```
var noVal;
```

noVal is given the undefined type and value by default. A null data type must be purposefully set but indicates an empty value (nothing):

```
var nullVal = null;
```

However, if you compare the value of a variable with an undefined type and a null type, they will compare equal:

```
var noVal;
var nullVal = null;
if (noVal == null) {
    // this is true
}
if (noVal == nullVal) {
    //this is also true
}
```

Functions

A **function** is a collection of bits of JavaScript code, all packaged together, that can be executed all in one go. Although it's possible to write JavaScript that isn't contained within a function (such as inline), it's a lot easier to reuse your code if all you have to do is call a function by name. Functions allow you to implement a lot of those really useful features we talked about in the earlier "Object-based programming" section.

Before you can call a function, it must be defined (in other words, you have to say what that function does). It doesn't need to be defined physically before it's called (above it on the page), but it does need to be "spelled out":

```
<script type="text/javascript">
    function doSomethingCool(myinput) {
        /* All of the cool stuff this
function does */
    }
</script>
```

Functions can be declared with no parameters, with one parameter (myinput in the previous example), or with multiple parameters separated by commas.

Passing parameters

What good would a function be if it were isolated from the rest of the page? You need to be able to hand information into it so that it can be processed. You can do this in a couple of ways; we covered one way in the earlier discussion of getElementById(), and the other way is that you can pass a parameter (or multiple parameters) to a function.

The advantage of this approach is that on a page that is dynamically generated, you may not know the ID of each and every element. For example, in a shopping cart, you could have any number of items listed. Let's say you have a couple of buttons beside each item that let you increase and decrease the quantity with a click.

From a code cleanliness standpoint, it's better to simply output a line for each item in the cart and pass the item ID to a JavaScript function than it is to dynamically generate separate JavaScript functions for each item, where each function would essentially do the same thing:

```
<input type="button" value="+" onclick="inQuan('item593');" ➡
  id="item593" />
```

If more parameters are passed than expected, the extra parameters are simply ignored. If you pass fewer parameters, those "missing" parameters are given an undefined value. If you're still not satisfied and you want to be able to throw even more data at your function, you can pass arrays as parameters. Arrays are special types of variables that hold multiple values.

If you were already familiar with other programming languages, such as C++, you would expect the parameter passed to be a reference to the original value. Unfortunately, you would be wrong. If you're scratching your head over that previous sentence, we'll use an example to illustrate:

```
<script type="text/javascript">
    var x = 4;
    squareIt (x);
    alert(x);
    function squareIt(value){
     value = value * value;
```

221

```
        }
    </script>
```

Quick quiz: what will be displayed in your alert? If you answered 16, you're wrong. The correct answer is 4. The function received the value of x but did not alter x in any way.

The exception to this is if you pass an object as a parameter. Passing an object actually passes a reference to that object so that any property of that object is available within the function.

Receiving output from

The best relationships are give and take, however. JavaScript would be pretty limited in its usefulness if it was just a big black hole into which data could be passed but no output could be obtained. Let's look at returning values now and how you can get output from JavaScript.

```
function inQuan(itemid) {
    var quan = document.getElementById(itemid).value;
    quan = parseInt(quan) + 1;
    document.getElementById(itemid).value = quan;
    return quan;
}
```

We'll just mention the parseInt() method in the last snippet of code. As we talked about in the earlier discussion of primitive data types, JavaScript needs to be told explicitly that something is a number and not just a string. parseInt(), or parseFloat() for dealing with floating-point numbers, will convert a string to a numerical value.

Now that you have an updated quantity, you'll probably need to do a couple of things. You'll need to update the subtotal, the sales tax calculation, and the total. You can do this really simply:

```
function upSubTot() {
    var newQuan = inQuan(itemid);
     var subTot = newQuan * Price;
    return subTot;
}
```

You can set a variable in the upSubTot() function based on the return value of the inQuan() function. Pretty cool, huh?

Flow control

There will likely come a time when you're going to need to do a little more than just plain mathematics, or string manipulation. You might need to build in some if/then statements in order to handle different scenarios, or you may need to loop over a set of values. Either way, we've got you covered.

If, else if, else

An if statement will check to see whether some condition that you specify is true and will then execute. Let's continue the shopping cart example from earlier in the chapter. Let's say you need to put a limit on the number of a particular item that a single individual can order. Using a simple if statement, you could do this:

```
function inQuan(itemid) {
    var quan = document.getElementById(itemid).value;
    if (quan <= 5) {
        quan = parseInt(quan) + 1;
        document.getElementById(itemid).value = quan;
    }
    return quan;
}
```

Now, the quantity will augment only if it's fewer than or equal to 5 units. You can check multiple criteria by using either && (AND) or || (OR):

```
if ((quan <= 5) || (3 == 2))
```

This is a bit of a bogus example, because the second condition will never evaluate as true, so it does the same thing as the initial example. If you had replaced the || with &&, the code within the if statement would never get executed because 3 will never equal 2 (at least, not in this universe).

One thing worth mentioning is that unlike other programming languages, in JavaScript the assertions in an OR if statement are evaluated in sequence, not simultaneously. So if the first condition evaluates true, the second condition won't even be tested. You're probably thinking "who cares?" but it's actually possible to have functions serve as your assertions in an if statement (as long as those functions return a Boolean). If your function is doing something else, that something else just won't run.

You're probably wondering what will happen if you try to augment it over the 5-unit limit. Well, currently nothing, so let's build in some code to handle that:

```
function inQuan(itemid) {
    var quan = document.getElementById(itemid).value;
    if (quan <= 5) {
        quan = parseInt(quan) + 1;
        document.getElementById(itemid).value = quan;
    } else {
        alert("Hey, limit five per customer buddy!");
    return quan;
}
```

Now, if your customer tries to up the quantity to more than 5 units, they'll receive a JavaScript alert that politely reminds them of your policy. You can go even further, by maybe giving your customer some advance notice of that five-item limit:

```
function inQuan(itemid) {
    var quan = document.getElementById(itemid).value;
    if (quan < 4) {
        quan = parseInt(quan) + 1;
        document.getElementById(itemid).value = quan;
    } else if (quan < 5) {
        quan = parseInt(quan) + 1;
        document.getElementById(itemid).value = quan;
        alert("You can only have one more before we cut ➡
        you off!");
```

```
    } else {
        alert("Hey, limit five per customer buddy!");
    return quan;
}
```

Another way to handle if, else if, and else-type of situations is to use a switch statement:

```
switch(quan) {
case 4:
quan = parseInt(quan) + 1;
    document.getElementById(itemid).value = quan;
    alert("You can only have one more before we cut ➥
    you off!");
    break;
case 5:
    alert("Hey, limit five per customer buddy!");
    break;
default:
    quan = parseInt(quan) + 1;
    document.getElementById(itemid).value = quan;
    break;
}
```

So, you can see the logic changes a little here, but the code is generally the same. You pass the switch statement your quan variable. Each of the case statements is then compared to that variable, so the first one checks to see whether quan is equal to 4. If it is, it delivers the warning message and augments the value. The second case statement checks to see whether the quan variable is already equal to 5. If it is equal to 5, you get the cut-off alert. Finally, the default case is just what happens if neither of the other two cases applies.

Loops

You know what they say; the best way to learn something is through repetition. So, although you're still having trouble with JavaScript, return to the start of this chapter and review the contents. There, you've just created your first while loop! It's pretty much the same thing in JavaScript; the syntax just looks something like this:

```
var understanding = 0;
var mastery = 10;
var reviewChapter = "";
while (understanding < mastery) {
    reviewChapter = reviewChapter + "Chapter reviewed! ";
    understanding = understanding + 1;
}
alert(reviewChapter);
```

A while loop works while the statement contained within the parentheses is true. So if you assume that your understanding of JavaScript is starting off at zero and if you assume that to be considered a master you have to achieve a level of ten, you would end up with an alert box with "Chapter reviewed!" repeated ten times.

Now, we'll show you a couple of shortcuts. Having to increment your understanding by 1 unit is a pretty common undertaking (OK, not just increasing our understanding, but incrementing values in general). Because of that, there is JavaScript shorthand for it:

```
understanding++;
```

This does the same thing as typing understanding = understanding + 1. It's probably pretty easy to guess how you would do the opposite, which is subtract 1 from the value of understanding (understanding--). Another common function is to take a variable and concatenate some value onto the end of it (as in the reviewChapter line).

```
reviewChapter += "Chapter reviewed! ";
```

This will give you the same result; it just saves you a few characters.

But while loops aren't the only game in town; you also have for loops that you can call upon to repeat tasks for you. A for loop takes this general form:

```
for (var understanding=0; understanding < mastery; ➡
understanding++)
```

It essentially encapsulates all the elements you need to make the loop run. It does the same thing as the earlier while loop, just with a little less code (which is a good thing!).

Finally, you have one last option, a do...while loop. It look like this:

```
do {
    understanding++;
}
while (understanding < mastery);
```

We wish we could say definitively that while loops are better or faster or use less memory than for loops, or vice versa, but most of what's out there says that they're pretty equal. Especially today, with client machines running multiple-core processors and RAM measured in the gigabytes, it's extremely hard to declare a winner here. http://www.devpro.it/examples/loopsbench/ presents a series of tests running for and while loops and shows you the "winner" in each. Take it with a grain of salt; we're talking about hundredths or thousandths of seconds here. Use whichever makes sense to you and whichever makes your code more readable.

Arrays

There may come a time when you want to store more than just a single, simple value in a variable. Luckily, JavaScript allows you to create lists of values called **arrays**. Arrays are particularly cool when used in conjunction with loops. For example:

```
var trees = ["Oak","Elm", "Pine"];
var a_tree;
for (var counter = 0; counter < trees.length; \
counter++) {
    a_tree = trees[counter];
    alert(a_tree + " is a tree");
}
```

We'll just dissect a couple of the new things you can see here in this code. For starters, when you create an array, you have to indicate that it's an array and not just a string with a bunch of commas in it. The square brackets take care of that. Second, in the for loop, you've got it looping until the length of trees. In JavaScript, arrays are objects, and all objects have properties. trees.length() will return 3 because you have defined the array with three items. If you needed to retrieve one of these items, though, you would have to use the index value of that item, and JavaScript assigns the first item in an array an index of zero (that's why you start the counter at zero). It's also important to note that the for loop is running only until the value of counter is less than the length of our array (not less than or equal to), because the length property is 3, but the last item in the array is in the second position.

User interaction: alert, confirm, and prompt

Alert, confirm, and prompt are intrusive ways of interacting with your users (but sometimes intrusive is OK). The built-in alert(), confirm(), and prompt() methods in JavaScript will open a dialog box requiring users to click something before they can proceed. Each method is slightly different in what it does, though.

Alert

An alert will open a dialog box with whatever text you specify. You can pass the alert method a variable or a literal value that will then be displayed with an OK button. That button must be clicked before script execution proceeds (blocking action). We talk a little more about alerts later in the "Debugging" section.

```
alert("Warning: Nuclear launch detected");
```

Confirm

The confirm method goes one step further than an alert. It will open a dialog box with both an OK button and a Cancel button. You'll see the confirm method used quite frequently where people are being asked to edit or delete information in a database (as shown in Figure 7-2).

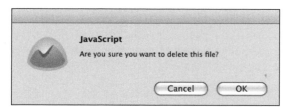

Figure 7-2. JavaScript confirm method. Clicking OK returns a true value, whereas clicking Cancel returns false. This functionality can be used to abort some action that the user may have accidentally initiated (such as accidentally clicking Delete).

Prompt

A **prompt** is similar to an alert and a confirm in that it opens a dialog box requiring input, but it also includes a text box in which some value can be entered. Figure 7-3 shows a JavaScript prompt asking the user to enter their name. Clicking OK returns the value entered, and clicking Cancel returns a null value.

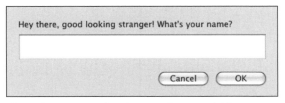

Figure 7-3. A prompt receives text (or numeric) input before the user is allowed to proceed.

Event handlers: executing code

At this point, we've covered how to write scripts that do all kinds of cool things, but we haven't covered how you can actually tell those scripts to run. How can you call the function `impressSiteVisitor()` when that button is clicked? How do you know to check the e-mail address entered into the text field *after* it has been punched in?

Welcome to the world of event handlers. An event handler watches for an event that takes a certain kind of input and executes functions specified by that handler. Let's take a look at a few different options.

"Automatic" execution

The first two event handlers you'll look at don't actually require any user input beyond normal browsing behavior. JavaScript functions can be called onload or onunload, that is, immediately after an element has finished loading or immediately before a page is unloaded (navigated away from). onload is commonly used to preload images. Like if you're planning on swapping an image during a rollover, you don't want someone to mouse over the button and then wait for the image to load; you want it to be instant.

Form-specific handlers

JavaScript is a powerhouse tool at working with forms. As such, a few event handlers are specific to forms (or used primarily in working with forms). onsubmit is a form event handler that gets called when a form is submitted. It is commonly used in order to validate a form's input (check to make sure that text boxes aren't empty, that valid phone numbers were entered, that sort of thing). With the upsurge in Ajax use, JavaScript functions that were previously called using onsubmit are now being called onblur (when a form field loses focus, as previously discussed in Chapter 6: the Tab key is hit, or the next field in the form is clicked).

onblur gives more of an "instant" feel to form validation, and some usability experts have argued that instant feedback is far better than delaying feedback until a form has been completed in its entirety. On some levels, it makes sense: if your form requires a valid US ZIP code (and you've implemented JavaScript validation to check for it), why wait until someone has gone through and filled out all the fields in a form with their mailing information for Canada (Canada's postal codes are a mixture of letters and numbers)? Why not let your customer know at that point that you won't ship outside the United States, rather than after they've completed the entire registration form?

That said, you just can't do certain things with an onblur. Let's say you've written some really sophisticated form validation that will check the area code from the phone number field against the postal code and cross-reference that with the state selected. This type of validation would be better suited to an onsubmit event handler, because you can't be sure that all data will have been entered until the form is submitted. It's not impossible to do with an onblur; you would just have to write a little extra JavaScript to make sure you have all three values before proceeding, though.

A couple of other event handlers might come in handy when working with forms. onchange gets called when the value of an input field is changed. It's commonly used if you're dynamically populating one selection box based on the selection made in another (for example, having a selection box populated with states if United States is selected as the country, with provinces/territories if Canada is selected).

onfocus is the opposite of the onblur event handler. onfocus is executed when an element is clicked or selected using the Tab key. onclick is a common event handler used with buttons and links. onclick fires when the specified element is clicked with the mouse. You can also apply it to radio buttons or check boxes.

Other event handlers

A couple of other event handlers are commonly used today. The onkeyup event handler is called immediately after a key is released. Some of the "search suggestion" functions you see make an Ajax call using the onkeyup event handler, so as input is received, search terms can be suggested (as shown in Figure 7-4).

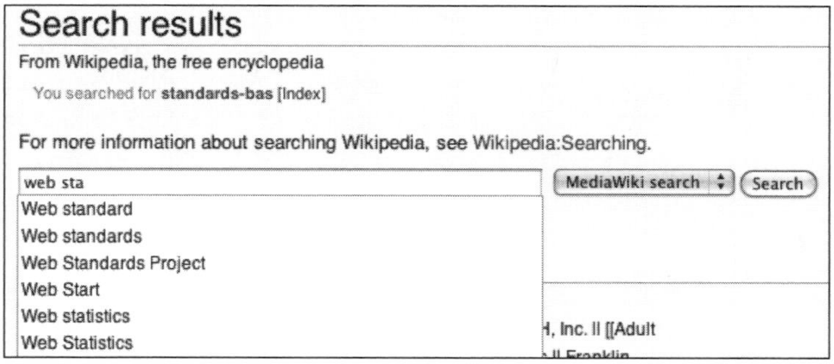

Figure 7-4. "Smart" Ajax-based searches are starting to pop up online. The JavaScript powering these Ajax calls is using the onKeyUp event handler to produce instant feedback.

onmouseover and onmouseout used to be the way to go for performing rollovers on buttons or links, but they've mostly been replaced with CSS-based solutions (as discussed in Chapter 6). You will still see onmouseover and onmouseout used for displaying things such as inline help (tooltips) and for producing really advanced rollover behavior, where multiple elements on the screen are affected.

Tools and practices to debug code

Wouldn't it be great if you could all write perfect code the first time around? It might happen on occasion, but more often than not, something will be slightly off causing either a syntax error, in which case your JavaScript won't run, or a logic error where you won't experience the behavior you were expecting. Luckily, a bunch of free tools are available that help you debug your code.

Alerts

One of the handiest tools in debugging code is the alert method. alert() will open a dialog box with whatever text (or variable) you specify. So, for example, if you're trying to build a basic calculator in JavaScript and you're taking text box A and adding it to text box B but the result is always coming out wrong, you may want to try outputting any intermediate results with an alert():

```
<script type="text/javascript">
    function addVals() {
        var numOne = document.getElementById('txtbox1').value;
        alert(numOne);
        var numTwo = document.getElementById('txtbox2').value;
        alert(numTwo);
        var endResult = numOne + numTwo;
        alert(endResult);
    }
</script>
<form method="post" action="doit.php">
    <fieldset>
    <legend>Numbers to add together</legend>
        <input type="text" name="txtbox1" id="txtbox1" value="4" />
        <input type="text" name="txtbox2" id="txtbox2" value="7" />
        <input type="submit" onclick="addVals();" />
    </fieldset>
</form>
```

We put in some default values here just so that I can explain the example in better detail. We're trying to get these two text boxes to add together, but we keep getting the wrong result. It's so frustrating! What's going on? Is it that the variables aren't being set properly, or is it a problem in the math?

We've dropped in three alerts to give us the value of each variable (numOne, numTwo, and endResult) each step of the way. The first alert tells you 4 (as it should), and the second alert returns 7 (again, as it should). The third alert returns 47 (Figure 7-5). Wait, that's not right! It's just taking the two numbers and treating them like text.

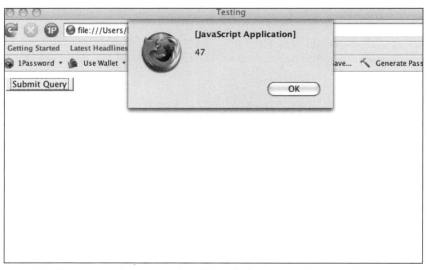

Figure 7-5. The result of the attempted addition, displayed as an alert in Firefox

Clearly, this is where the problem is. The example is pretty simple, but this very code could be just one part of a very complex shopping cart application that automatically calculates totals, taxes, and shipping; in this situation, it may not be as obvious where you have a problem in your code.

We won't keep you in suspense any longer. The problem is that the function thinks that the two variables are strings and not numbers. You have to convert your strings to numbers before you can mathematically add them together. Change the variable declarations for numOne and numTwo in the previous code to the following:

```
var numOne = parseInt(document.getElementById('txtbox1').value);
var numTwo = parseInt(document.getElementById('txtbox2').value);
```

Using the built-in parseInt() function, we're explicitly saying that these values are integers (if you're dealing with decimals, you'll probably want to use parseFloat() instead). Now you're getting the result you would expect (as shown in Figure 7-6).

[JavaScript Application]

11

OK

Figure 7-6. The debugging alert() is now showing the proper value.

230

Debugging tools

You may have noticed (or not) that a lot of the screenshots taken in this chapter show the Firefox browser. We have a small confession to make: Firefox is not actually our browser of choice on the Mac, but the reason why we've used it here is that it has one of the best sets of tools for debugging JavaScript code.

In addition to having a set of debugging tools built right in, Firefox is also easily enhanced through a series of extensions that are available to download and install. We're going to look at a couple of tools that might save you some hair pulling, especially on hard-to-diagnose Ajax scripts.

Safari and Firefox error consoles

One essential tool that is built into Firefox and Safari is the error console. The error console alerts you to any syntax errors in your code, and it tells you roughly where that error occurred. Sometimes the debugging messages are cryptic, and other times they're spot on for where you've messed something up. Figure 7-7 shows the error console with a common error you'll run into when debugging JavaScript (we missed closing the parentheses on a function).

Figure 7-7. The error console saying we've missed closing the parentheses on the alert function on line 14.

Web Developer Toolbar

The Web Developer Toolbar is an essential addition, available as a download from `http://addons.mozilla.org`. It lets you do things like flip JavaScript on and off (so that you can make sure your pages still function, even without JavaScript enabled). It also allows you to flip CSS on and off to make sure your pages make sense, even to a visitor who is visually impaired.

The Web Developer Toolbar will display all kinds of useful information, from the names of IDs and classes inline to the size of various `<div>`s on a page. In terms of useful JavaScript debugging, the Web Developer Toolbar provides a really handy DOM inspector that lets you drill down through the various elements of a page and see the hierarchy of them (as shown in Figure 7-8).

231

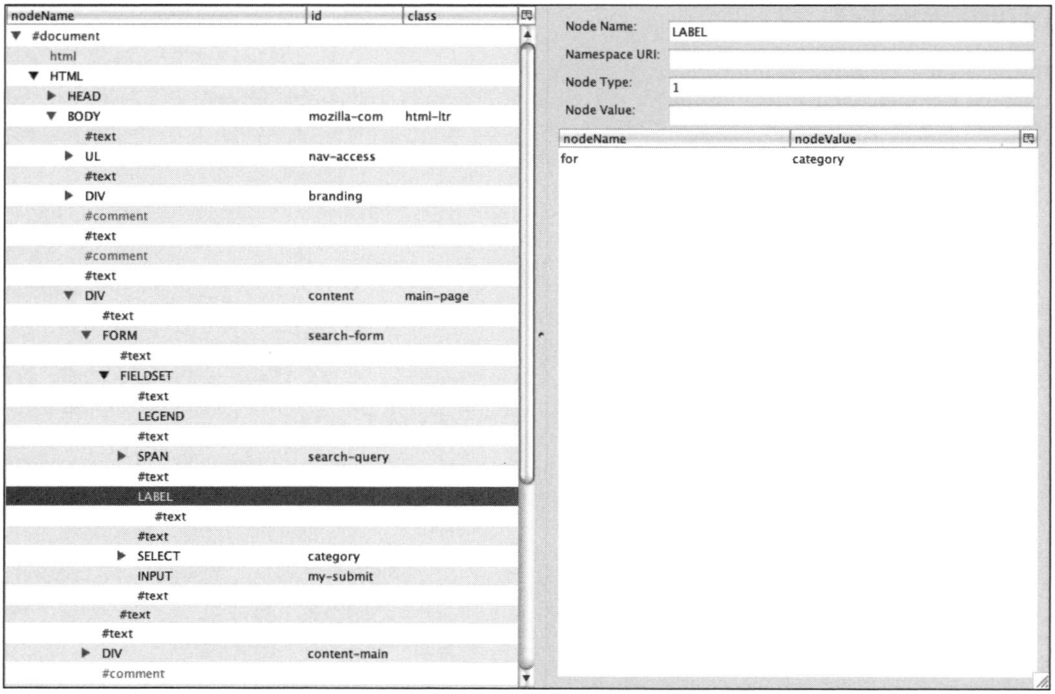

Figure 7-8. The DOM inspector shows you a tree view of the various elements on your page.

All in all, the Web Developer Toolbar is an incredibly handy Swiss Army knife of tools that will help you with everything from visualizing page layout to ensuring that your code validates.

Firebug: Ajax debugging bliss

Debugging an Ajax call can be really tricky. It's hard to tell whether it's the JavaScript, server script, or some problem in your CSS that is causing the trouble. That's where the Firebug extension comes in (it's good for many other things too, such as determining why your page is loading so slowly).

Imagine if you could get a running log file of everything that is taking place on a particular page: what data is being sent to the server, what's being received back, how long each of the files are taking to load, and in what order those files are being loaded. That's exactly what Firebug does for you.

Figure 7-9 shows the Firebug output for a page that makes heavy use of Ajax. This is the Lifestream page of the social networking aggregator, Socialthing (we hope out of beta by the time we go to press). Socialthing does a number of Ajax calls to other websites such as Twitter and Facebook and consolidates all the information it gets back. When so many variables are in play, including a number of different websites, Firebug is an invaluable tool for recognizing bottlenecks.

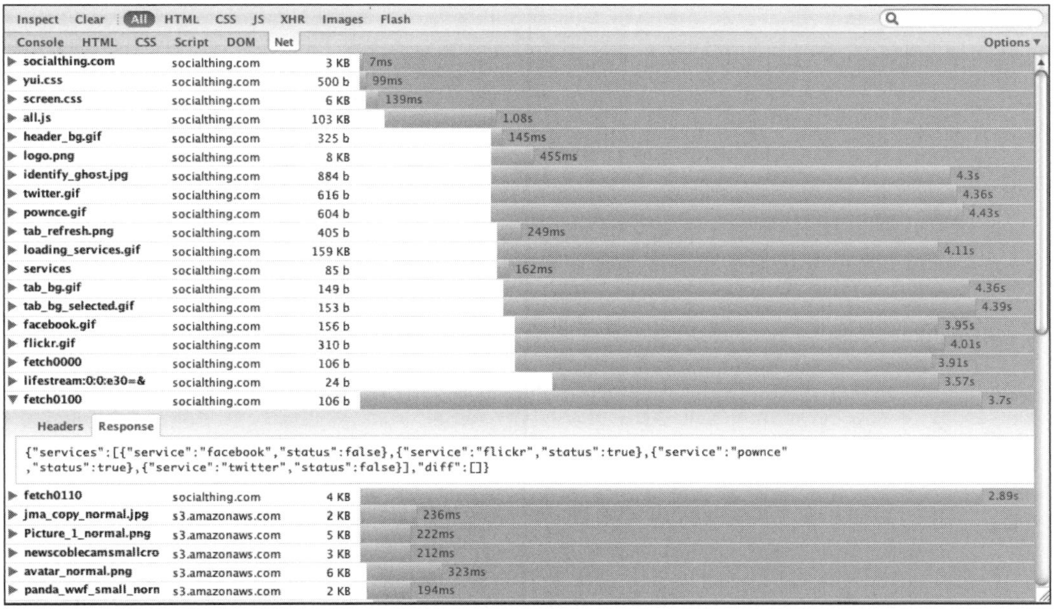

Figure 7-9. Socialthing loads so many files and scripts behind the scenes in order to give you a single, unified view of your social networks. I can't imagine what it would have been like to build an application such as Socialthing without Firebug.

We've covered Firefox-based tools almost exclusively thus far. Opera, makers of the Opera web browser, is working on a set of developer tools that they have code-named Dragonfly. As of this writing, they are currently available as an alpha release at http://www.opera.com/products/dragonfly/, and they offer a lot of the same functionality as the Firefox-based tools we've discussed in this chapter.

The latest release of Safari also features a Develop menu that can be enabled via the Advanced preference pane. Apple has included a Web Inspector (Figure 7-10) that replicates some of the functionality present in the Firefox Firebug extension. Combine this with Drosera (available at http://webkit.org/blog/61/introducing-drosera/), and Safari has a robust set of developer tools available as well.

Even Microsoft Internet Explorer offers some tools to assist developers. There is a developer toolbar available for Internet Explorer 7 at http://msdn.microsoft.com/en-us/ie/, and Microsoft is working on a full stack of developer tools for its upcoming Internet Explorer 8 release.

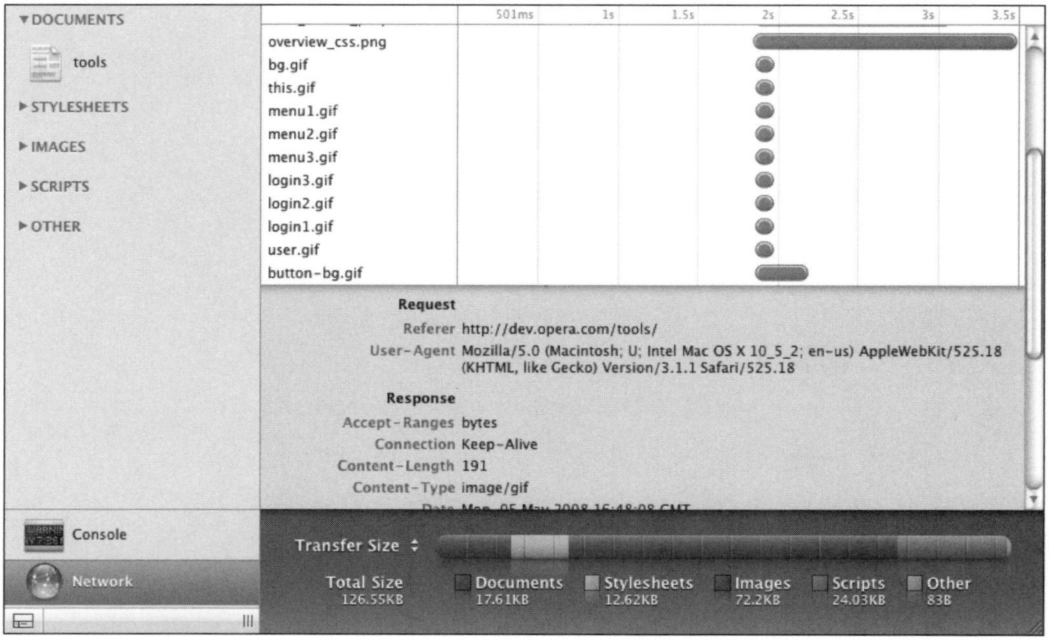

Figure 7-10. The new Web Inspector, present in the latest Safari release, replicates some of the functionality present in the Firefox extensions we covered in this chapter.

JavaScript libraries

Not only do we have a great set of tools for working with JavaScript now, we've also entered an age where a number of really great JavaScript libraries are freely available for your use. We talk a little more about libraries later when we take a look at Ajax in Chapter 9, but they're just such a useful development tool that they're worth mentioning here as well.

You can find JavaScript libraries to help with just about any task you need to perform—from animating page elements to making Ajax calls to adding file-browser and manipulation widgets to your pages.

There could be (and indeed there have been) entire books written about the various JavaScript libraries. We'll recommend Jonathan Snook's book, *Accelerated DOM Scripting with Ajax, APIs, and Libraries*, as a good starting point. Also be sure to check out the websites and documentation for each of the libraries to gauge their strengths and weaknesses in a particular area:

- *Prototype*: prototypejs.org
- *jQuery*: jquery.com
- *Scriptaculous*: script.aculo.us
- *Yahoo YUI*: developer.yahoo.com/yui/
- *ExtJS*: extjs.com

Summary: a little JavaScript goes a long way

JavaScript really is that magic ingredient that makes your pages feel more interactive and more application-like. Used sparingly and where it makes sense, JavaScript can really enhance the user experience. There is nothing you can do to ensure that your end users will have JavaScript enabled, so ensure you always have a backup plan in place, especially where core functionality is at stake. It's great to add some Ajax to your forms to make them submit without a page refresh, but if that's the only mechanism you have in place, you may be shutting out part of your audience. Always make sure that a form can be submitted without using JavaScript (include an `action` attribute in the `<form>` tag), and it's often a good idea to perform a second round of input validation on the server using your scripting language of choice.

Design and develop defensively. Shut off JavaScript in your web browser (either using the Web Developer Toolbar described earlier or using just your browser settings), and try to do all the important things on your website. Can a customer still contact you through your feedback form? Can they still place an order? Can they still navigate and get to your important content? Remember, search engines don't support JavaScript, so if you're relying on it for your website navigation, you will be locking out search engines (unless you provide them with an alternate path).

So, take it easy. Build your website first, and then go back through and ask yourself if a particular function could be improved with a little JavaScript. Keep it tasteful, and keep it accessible.

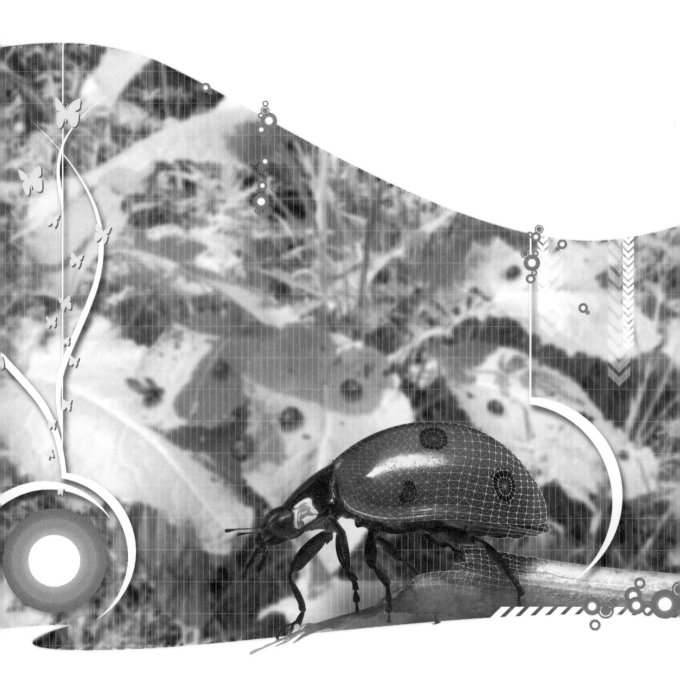

Chapter 8

TESTING, LAUNCHING, AND MAINTAINING

Test early and test often—these are words to live by in web projects. Testing your work can be a frightening, frustrating, and downright maddening experience. But the alternative—not testing—can be an even worse experience. The site that undergoes continual scrutiny and adjustment based on testing and feedback is a site that will differentiate itself greatly from the site that is launched and then left to stagnate. This is a step you will not want to leave out. Customer satisfaction means customer referrals in the future; ensuring the quality of your product helps reinforce your reputation as a professional and ensures that you stay happily employed.

The web development life cycle

When you publish new websites, you are giving rise to an entity that didn't exist before. Your site has life—certainly a measurable birth date. It is therefore helpful for you to consider the **life cycle** that this website will have and think about what will happen to this project before it goes live; how it will serve its functional purpose; how it will mature, refresh, and renew itself as time goes on; and finally how it will be retired and collecting on its 401k.

Considering the web development life cycle up front will help you plan contingencies, help you set goals and milestones, and help you to know what to expect for the future. These practices are the less geeky side of web development, entirely mundane and bureaucratic, and often the first things to be overlooked. And yet, simply following some of the basic premises of these guidelines can ensure that your website remains successful after launch and throughout the site's existence.

It is important when you are composing your project plan to bake in a periodic review of your work as a best practice. Think of it as a maintenance contract—it benefits the customer by making sure you as the site author remain engaged with your product, and it benefits you by ensuring that you know your live examples out there in the wild are lookin' good.

The initial step in adopting a web development life cycle is to begin constructing a plan. Writing this plan down helps you think things through, helps you plan for potential areas for concern, and gives you a road map to refer to as the project progresses. A plan can be as simple or as complex as the project requires, but one thing to remember is that if you want it to be effective, it needs to be readable. That means it needs to be concise and clear. Don't get deeply involved in lengthy process discussions where a sentence or two will suffice. Keep it high level, and leave the details to the trusted professionalism of those working on the project. And at the same time, don't leave out pieces of critical information that you or others will need to get to the next step.

An example of a workflow for a web development project plan might look something like this:

1. Gather initial customer requirements.
2. Research customer assumptions and market conditions.
3. Write up recommendations.
4. Test recommendations by gathering feedback from sample users.
5. Design site information architecture.
6. Test site architecture by gathering feedback from sample users.
7. Develop an initial prototype.
8. Test the prototype (user testing, browser testing, security testing, and so on).
9. Make changes to the prototype.
10. Test the changes (user testing, browser testing, security testing, and so on).
11. Repeat steps 9 and 10 up until the final review date, adding features as you iterate.
12. Conduct a final review with customer.
13. Launch.
14. Test the live site (user testing, browser testing, security testing, and so on) and continue revising.

As you can see, testing comes up a lot in this little example. Having testing cycles placed throughout your web development plan gives you the opportunity to evaluate your assumptions and refine your plans accordingly. Gathering feedback early from even a small sample of potential users can head off many problems before they have time to grow and become deeply rooted in your project. The longer you go down the wrong path, the harder and costlier it is going to be to correct the problem.

Publishing process

Before you begin your web project, it is a good idea to consider what your publishing process is going to be. On the one hand, you might build everything on your personal computer, upload the finished product to your web server, and be done with it. A more professional process establishes a three-tiered environment with a place for development, a place for testing, and a place to deploy your finished product. As the size and scope of projects increase, so does your need to maintain oversight over your files before they go live. Casually deploying your site on a shared hosting service may be perfectly adequate for your local underwater basket-weaving enthusiast's club website. But a major transaction-oriented web service such as a stock-trading operation is surely going to undergo phased development cycles and a careful quality assurance process before being deployed on a locked-down and robust server environment.

Using a three-tiered development environment is a standard pattern in the industry of web development. Many content management systems, code frameworks, and web development methodologies utilize the model of having a development-quality production environment in which to work. Take Ruby on Rails, for example: setting up your garden-variety Rails project by default immediately generates development, test, and production environments for you. Having a delineation between the development, test, and production environments gives you an opportunity to better organize your web development process, routinely pass your work through a place dedicated to the testing process, and keep live changes from occurring on the server before they have had an opportunity to be validated (see Figure 8-1).

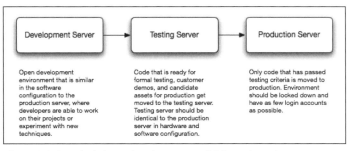

Figure 8-1. A typical three-tiered server model for web projects

Professional web development operations will typically have such a three-tiered environment in place. The **development server** is often a free-for-all—a place where the developer or development team can build away and experiment with ideas here and there. Although the development environment may be chaotic at times, especially in the area of file organization, the goal for such servers is to mimic as closely as possible what the server environment will be like in production. That means a similar edition of the web server, the same plug-ins, the same language support, the same operating system, similar directory structures, and so on. These environments may be vastly different from your local development machines, so it is good to have a playground to work in that has the same baseline configuration as what you can expect when going live.

Similar to a development server, the **testing server** strives to be as close a representation as possible of the production environment. This server, although probably behind a firewall or authentication mechanism, should be a mirror configuration of the production system. It should be set up with the same versions of operating system, web server, languages, frameworks, and the rest of it. The two should have similar security settings, similar directory structures, and even similar CPU and RAM levels.

The testing server is the place where you can stage versions of your code and hit your sites with everything you have: crippled web browsers, disabled JavaScript, screen or Braille readers, and that neighbor of yours down the block who still uses Netscape 4 on an old beige Mac G3 with a dial-up connection. Having a testing server environment is arguably the most important facet of the three-tiered server model, because it gives you a place to do your worst to a site without exposing it to the production world. You can perform security audits, capacity tests, usability tests, and quality assurance activities safely hidden from the judgmental eyes of the public.

In a **production environment**, the system should be locked down for security. Logins may be tightly controlled at this point, preferably with an automated process or with only a few select individuals able to move things to and from production. It is wise to pay attention to what makes it to production and to ensure that you have done an adequate level of testing of new code on the testing environment before going live.

A couple of major differences that may exist on a development server as opposed to a testing or production server might be in the area of directory index listings and server error messages. On a production machine, you would probably not want to allow the user to see the full output of error messages that exist because your database server is down. Similarly, a directory in the web server that is missing a directory index file such as index.html, index.php, or default.htm might show the site visitor a full listing of the directory contents, including any configuration files, archives, and outdated cruft that you may not want the whole world to see. These things, although extremely helpful in a development cycle, should be shut off completely in the production environment. Since the testing server is intended to test things as they would look in the real world before they go to the real world, it is probably best to disable these features here as well.

However you tailor your server infrastructure, be sure to consider carefully how things will move between each point. Keeping backups or using a version control system such as Subversion (http://subversion.tigris.org/) or Git (http://git.or.cz/) will help lessen the risk of realizing that some code changes that you just published are now causing major problems. You don't want to overwrite your only copies of the files on the server. Always leave yourself an escape exit, just in case.

Validating your code

As with any programming practice, your HTML, CSS, and JavaScript code should be well formed, it should use best practices, and it should be validated. Discussions about why you should validate your code have been frequent and ongoing since the beginning of the web standards movement. Suffice it to say, having valid code means your code has embraced the specification in question and adheres to its guidelines fully. This in turn gives your various user agents—be they web browsers, search engine spiders, web services, and the rest of it—a reliable format to expect. Knowing what to expect means they can in turn provide more consistent and functional interpretations of your site code and make better use of your data. Having valid code also means you are moving your web content one step closer to the semantic Web—a state where data contained on one site is interchangeable with data on the next site, and so on and so forth.

Having valid code is not rocket science. In fact, often the simpler your markup is, the greater the chance you have of passing validation. Having a well-formed, semantic, valid, and simple XHTML framework will give you a solid foundation for being successful in implementing an engaging CSS design and highly functional JavaScript behaviors. It is vastly easier to apply CSS and JavaScript to simple markup than it is to complex markup. Keep it simple!

The importance of DTDs

Before you can begin the process of validating your code, it is important to understand Document Type Declarations, often called **doctypes** or **DTDs** for short, which define what type of markup you are using. There are many flavors of HTML and XHTML, and the number of possible varieties of DTDs is unlimited when discussing XML. Web browsers use the presence of a valid DTD to enable "standards mode." In standards mode, the browser will attempt to render your web pages according to the established specifications and not to legacy quirks, at least to the best of its abilities.

To get a flavor for DTDs, try examining a live one in your web browser. The DTD for XHTML 1.0 Strict is as follows:

```
<!DOCTYPE html PUBLIC "-//W3C//DTD XHTML 1.0 Strict//EN"
          "http://www.w3.org/TR/xhtml1/DTD/xhtml1-strict.dtd">
```

If you point your browser to the indicated URL (http://www.w3.org/TR/xhtml1/DTD/xhtml1-strict. dtd), you will come across the XHTML 1.0 specification written in valid DTD syntax. Treated as XML, you could validate your XHTML 1.0 code in an SGML parser against these rules. In a pragmatic sense, you usually will be most concerned with the DTD's effect on enabling a consistent rendering mode for your web pages. Without a proper DTD, your code validator may make unexpected assumptions about what the intended flavor of markup was, or it may simply throw an error or ask for clarification.

For more information on standards mode, please see "Quirks mode and strict mode" at http://www. quirksmode.org/css/quirksmode.html.

For a good introduction to DTDs, we recommend pages 24 through 29 of *Pro PHP XML and Web Services* by Sas Jacobs (Apress, 2006).

Markup validation

In the discussion of markup validation, your first stop should be the W3C validator site at http:// validator.w3.org/. This free resource will validate HTML, XML, and applications of XML such as SVG, MathML, and of course XHTML (see Figure 8-2).

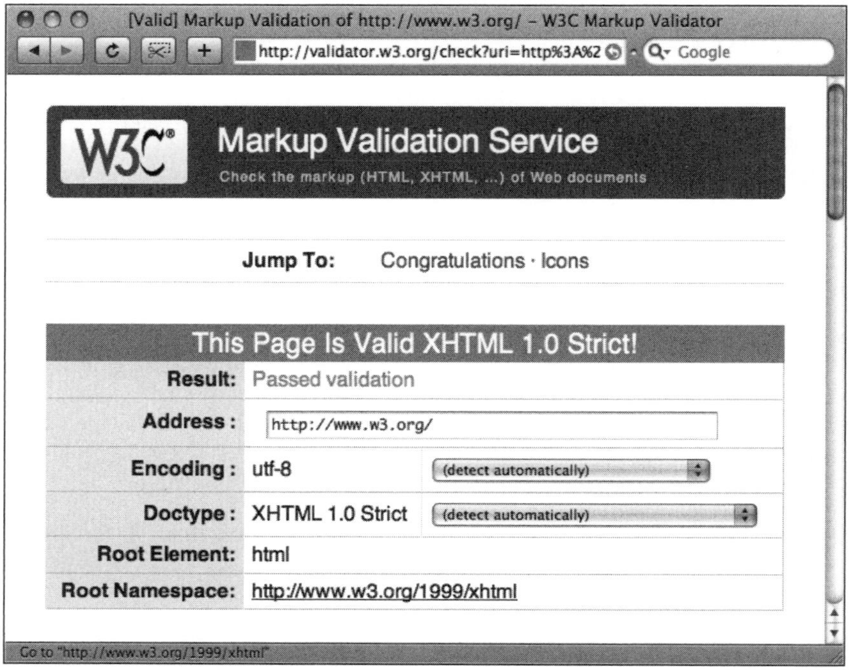

Figure 8-2. The W3C Markup Validation Service

Once you've had a chance to familiarize yourself with the W3C's Markup Validation Service, give it a whirl. Try validating a live URL first and then perhaps an uploaded document, and finally copy and paste something in there. It allows input on all three fronts.

If you are not online, you can use several excellent tools that work equally well while connected to the World Wide Web or while disconnected in a commuter train traversing a long tunnel at the bottom of the San Francisco Bay.

Adobe Dreamweaver features a built-in code validation and tidying feature that is simple to access and use (see Figure 8-3). Choose File ➤ Validate ➤ Markup to pass the current web page or XML document to the validator.

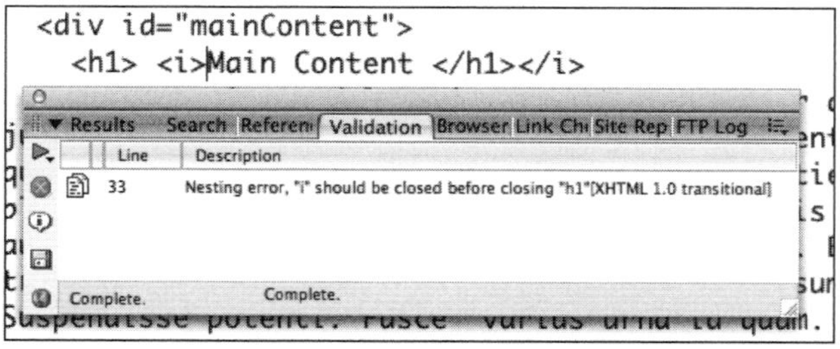

Figure 8-3. Dreamweaver's built-in validation feature

Once you've run your test, you may choose to manually fix any code errors discovered. Or you may want to see how things go if you try to fix everything in one fell swoop. Yes, Dreamweaver has a command for that too. Select Commands ➤ Clean Up XHTML to get the dialog box shown in Figure 8-4.

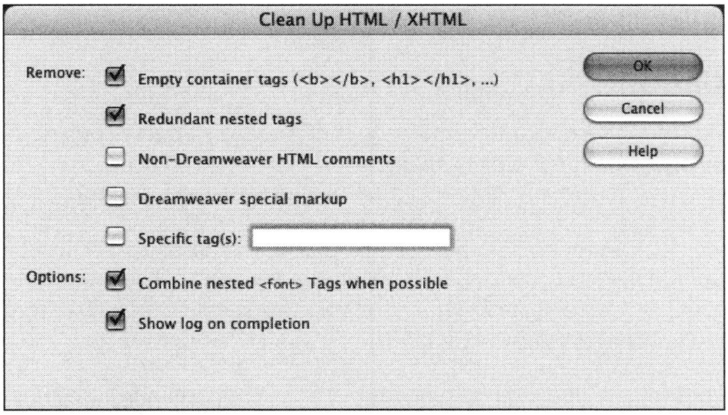

Figure 8-4. Dreamweaver's Clean Up HTML/XHTML dialog box

Another excellent tool to investigate is HTML Tidy. HTML Tidy (we'll call it Tidy for short) is an open source project that you can find at http://tidy.sourceforge.net/. Tidy typically attempts to clean your code, tell you what happened during the process, and warn you of anything it was unable to fix (see Figure 8-5). Many code-editing tools have Tidy built in. For example, the excellent TextMate (http://www.macromates.com) editor for Mac OS X includes a Tidy command. Choose Bundles ➤ HTML ➤ Tidy or Bundles ➤ XML ➤ Tidy to clean up the document on which you're working.

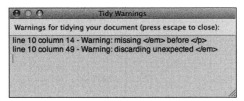

Figure 8-5. Tidy is often included in code editors and provides feedback on errors as well as cleans up the code automatically.

CSS validation

CSS validation is a less critical issue for web developers. Historically, CSS has been less problematic than HTML, and there are numerous CSS tools and techniques that yield pretty good code, at least from a standards perspective.

Nevertheless, it is important to strive for valid code on all fronts, and CSS is no exception. Having a valid style sheet attached to your code helps ensure that future browser developments will continue to render your website as intended.

The W3C CSS validation service (http://jigsaw.w3.org/css-validator/) is likely the most popular tool for CSS validation. As input, it accepts links to URLs containing CSS files or HTML files with CSS embedded, file uploads, and direct input. It has been wrapped into many additional tools around the Web, including code editors such as TextMate, and into browser plug-ins such as the Web Developer Toolbar for Firefox.

JavaScript validation

The use of JavaScript in modern web development continues to gain in popularity. The language was arguably intended for lesser functionality than we are seeing today, with full-scale web apps that replace the functionality of programs you would normally find on the desktop.

With such increased complexity comes the need to follow standards-based processes, for the same reasons you do so with HTML and CSS. Ultimately you want to have well-formed, unobtrusive JavaScript to enhance the functionality of your carefully constructed web pages, and you want to have your JavaScript be maintainable over the long term.

JSLint is one such tool to help you with checking the construction of your JavaScript code. JSLint takes a stricter view of JavaScript than you may be used to, using a subset of the ECMAScript standard, and it steers the developer toward writing more efficient and cleaner code. JSLint is worthy of a bookmark in any web developer's browser: http://www.jslint.com/.

Browser add-ons and features

When it comes to web development plug-ins for our favorite web browser, we web developers have an embarrassment of riches. No discussion of web development tools would be complete without a mention of at least a few of these excellent tools:

- *HTML Validator*: When you are testing pages in a web browser, wouldn't it be spectacular if you could tell in a single glance whether the page was valid? Fortunately, such a tool does exist! Enter the HTML Validator plug-in for Firefox and Mozilla (http://users.skynet.be/mgueury/mozilla/). This free plug-in has to be one of the handiest tools for the standards-conscious web developer. The HTML Validator places a button in Firefox's status bar and instantly provides feedback on whether a page passes validation. In the preferences for this plug-in, you can enable the tool to automatically check WCAG priority levels as well, making it an exceptional tool for your testing process.

- *Web Developer Toolbar*: The Web Developer Toolbar for Firefox, Flock, and SeaMonkey adds a great list of commands and features that work to transform your web browser into a powerful web development tool. This tool contains commands to validate CSS, HTML, RSS feeds, and accessibility; options to disable things such as JavaScript or CSS; the ability to swap between the screen, handheld, and print media types for testing style sheet views; and options to clear out private data such as cache and authentication.

- *Firebug*: Firebug (http://getfirebug.com/) for Firefox picks up where the Web Developer Toolbar leaves off. Firebug gives web developers an incredibly powerful tool for (among other things) inspecting HTML and CSS, graphically examining network activity, inspecting the DOM, and debugging JavaScript. The JavaScript debugging features deserve special mention here, because Firebug features a full-featured JavaScript debugger with conditional breakpoints, a JavaScript console, and a DOM editor.

These are just a few of the browser enhancements and features that exist, and there are many more worth investigating. The Safari browser as of version 3.1 includes a new Develop menu (activated in Preferences), which gives you many great testing tools for disabling browser features, inspecting elements, and monitoring errors and network activity. Microsoft Internet Explorer has a developer toolbar available as well, and as of this writing, the Internet Explorer 8 project is working on a full-featured and integrated developer tools feature.

Browser testing

Beware of site owners that state "Only Internet Explorer users on Windows hit our site." This is essentially advertising that the developers didn't take the time or didn't care to make their work even minimally accessible. Or worse, sometimes a browser detection script will render a sad-faced message along the lines of "You must be using Internet Explorer 6 or newer to enter this site," which really only serves to turn business away. As of this writing in April 2008, Net Applications reports approximately 76 percent of the web browser market share as going to the Internet Explorer family of web browsers, about 17 percent going to Firefox and the related Mozilla crowd, 6 percent going to Safari, and the rest of the remaining couple of percentage points going to everything else. The Web continues to move toward a model of healthy biodiversity in the species of user agents encountered in the wild.

Testing your carefully designed CSS layouts and JavaScript behaviors in a wide variety of browsers is a critical step in deploying your code. Thankfully, the consensus among current browser vendors is to adhere to web standards, even though they all adhere in different ways. For the most part, you can expect that if you follow the CSS 2.1 and HTML 4.01 or higher markup recommendations and the ECMAScript standard of JavaScript and avoid proprietary extensions (or implement them in such a way that they fail over gracefully if not supported), then things should look pretty good across most browsers.

Yes, there *will* be exceptions. No browser has fully, perfectly implemented any of these specifications. Because of the nature of the specifications, there are some differences in interpretation. Most notably, Microsoft Internet Explorer 6 has the weakest support for CSS, but Internet Explorer 7 has cleaned up many of the CSS inconsistencies, and Internet Explorer 8 promises to resolve most JavaScript issues and to support the CSS 2.1 specification.

In addition to browser discrepancies, there will be OS-specific issues to contend with. Perhaps most notably, fonts will be a concern. The reason you need to list such an array of fonts in the font-family CSS rules is because you can never be sure whether font X is going to be installed on a given system. It may not be available; it may have been removed. Providing a font array gives you a reasonable list of best guesses to work with, and then you can always fall back to a default serif, sans-serif, or mono indicator as a worst-case scenario. You will also have to contend with various levels of text antialiasing, letter spacing, and font width discrepancies.

Testing environment

To test your site adequately, you need to define and establish the testing environment. For a professional office-based web development team, you might choose to set up a physical testing lab. This might be a room or a hallway with several machines of varying operating systems, configuration, and horsepower. You might have, for example, a modern Windows Vista machine installed with the latest version of Internet Explorer, Opera, and Firefox and a large display; a Windows 2000 system with

Internet Explorer 6 and a smaller display; a Mac loaded with Safari and Firefox; and a Linux machine with Firefox, Konqueror, and Lynx.

The advantages of having a physical testing lab such as this is that you can really experience how the system will react as people bang around on the site. You might notice text getting clipped off, horizontal scroll bars appearing, and things just not working as you had expected them to work. You can move yourself from machine to machine in order to go through the routine of testing your site in each system. However, the disadvantages of such an environment are that, for starters, you have to maintain a bunch of systems. They take up space, generate heat, and suck up the ol' electricity. And you have to get up out of your chair and walk over there—not very convenient when you're deep in a coding trance or telecommuting.

Perhaps a more flexible environment would be to use virtualization to run multiple operating systems on your desktop. Products such as VMware and Parallels provide you with the ability to install and run several operating systems simultaneously on the same system and at fairly decent speeds these days. This is a popular solution for developers, because you can configure your systems in a very flexible manner—allocate some RAM here, install a few browsers there, launch Linux and Windows XP simultaneously from a MacBook Pro, and finish testing everything during your flight to Albuquerque just in time to make your presentation.

However, virtualization solutions require lots of extra disk space, RAM, and CPU resources. Many of the modern CPUs support virtualization natively, and you can load tons of RAM on most of the higher-end computers these days. If you can afford it, load it up. If you can't shell out those kinds of ducats, you might try a slightly more lightweight option.

If you are on an x86 CPU architecture and a flavor of Unix such as Linux, Mac OS X, or FreeBSD, you may be able to get by with using Wine. Wine (http://www.winehq.com/) is an open source implementation of the Windows API, allowing you to run Windows-only software such as Internet Explorer on your machine without having to purchase, or install, a full Windows system. This method has a bonus in that you can install multiple versions of Internet Explorer with ease. Crossover by CodeWeavers (http://www.codeweavers.com/) is an easy-to-install commercial version of Wine with some nice extra features. The drawback here is that, as of this writing, Internet Explorer 7 will not install in the Wine environment, and the Internet Explorer 8 beta doesn't even appear on the radar.

If you are using Windows, you might be able to get away with simply having a nice array of browsers installed for most of your basic testing. Firefox, Opera, and Safari are all available for Windows and have the same functionality, and you can get a fairly good idea of how things will work across platforms in these browsers. When using a platform-specific approach to testing, keep in mind that there will be occasional discrepancies on other operating systems.

The most lightweight option is using a web service such as Browsershots (http://browsershots.org/). Browsershots excels at giving you a massive set of options for testing your web designs. As of this writing, Browsershots features four operating systems (Linux, Windows, Mac, and FreeBSD) and dozens of browser choices up to and including Internet Explorer 8 and Firefox 3. If all you need to do is test visual design, this is a great way to go regardless of whether you're using a physical lab or virtual machines. The disadvantage is that you get only a screenshot, and if you are using the free version, you will have to wait a while for your jobs to finish and risk them timing out. You also will not have the ability to test forms and behaviors beyond the most basic display items, and you have to feed it one URL at a time.

If you plan on having mobile users, and you should, plan on adding some resources for mobile devices to your testing suite. Nothing beats having a few mobile phones and PDAs lying around. Opera is a popular browser for the mobile set, and it features a small-screen view command that renders things as they'd look on a mobile device, including a switch to the handheld style sheet if it exists (see Figure 8-6). The Web Developer Toolbar for Firefox also includes a menu option to switch rendering to the handheld style sheet for a nice quick preview.

Figure 8-6. Opera in small-screen mode for mobile devices

For Safari/WebKit testing in the iPhone, Android, and Nokia handsets that use it, you can expect it to have a fairly similar rendering behavior to the desktop version of Safari, unless you've done some specific targeting for the smaller screen sizes. Although nothing beats using the actual device, some decent simulators exist, including http://iphonetester.com and iPhoney (http://www.marketcircle.com/iphoney/).

In all cases for your mobile testing plans, remember that the user experience is quite different on an actual handset as compared to viewing these things in emulation from the comfort of your primary development machine; in addition, these devices have control mechanisms that are rare to absent in the desktop world. This includes features such as the iPhone-like touch screens, stylus-based tap screens such as the Treo, and your garden-variety flip-phone with navigation controlled by a rocker dial or the keypad.

Going back and forth fixing browser inconsistencies can be extremely time-consuming and can drive web developers to the brink of madness. It is therefore a good practice to find a testing order for the various browsers in your array and go through testing your designs in an order that warrants the least amount of back-and-forth bug fixing. Typically for us, that means going in descending order of standards compliance and feature support. A sample order might be as detailed in the following sections.

Firefox (Gecko)

With excellent CSS and JavaScript support, coupled with nearly ubiquitous access across operating systems, we generally regard Firefox as the best starting place for testing, and most people we've worked with agree on this point. The sentiment is that if you code your site to standards and get it going in Firefox, the rest of the browser fixes that cascade out of this starting point tend to be easier. Additionally, Firefox has a wonderful plug-in architecture that has been used to create some excellent web development tools, which were mentioned earlier. Many of us find that a good text editor and Firefox with such plug-ins are all we need for web development.

Firefox is based on the Gecko rendering engine. Gecko is used in several other web browsers such as Camino, SeaMonkey, Flock, and the now-discontinued Netscape Navigator.

Safari (WebKit)

As of version 3, Apple's Safari web browser is available for Mac OS and Windows. And because it has outstanding support for CSS, Safari makes a compelling second step for your testing cycle. WebKit is the underlying open source rendering engine that drives Safari. WebKit and Gecko have typically had good parity in CSS support, although you may find that some of the more advanced features such as text-shadow and the <canvas> tag that are implemented in Safari or WebKit nightly builds are not available yet in other browsers. Remember to adhere to the principles of graceful failover, and you should have little cause for concern.

WebKit is widely deployed in many other browsers and frameworks, including iCab, Adobe AIR, and OmniWeb. For mobile handsets, this platform is rapidly gaining in popularity: the Nokia Web Browser for S60, Google's Web Browser for Android, and of course the iPhone are all using WebKit by default.

Internet Explorer 8 (Trident)

As of this writing, Microsoft Internet Explorer 8 is in beta, and by the time you read this, it may very well already be in production. If we were betting folk, we'd bet that Internet Explorer 8 is going to quickly leapfrog Internet Explorer 6 and Internet Explorer 7 in terms of market share, thanks to its vastly improved support for web standards. Since it is too early to predict, we are placing Internet Explorer 8 at the third spot in the testing cycle just on principle, although if the final version delivers as much on web standards as Microsoft says it will, you may want to move this one up to the second spot. But then again, by the time Internet Explorer 8 is available, there will likely be new versions of Firefox and Safari with greater standards compliance, as well.

Opera

The Opera browser has excellent standards support, with some interesting additional features and a large presence in the mobile browser world. Its small-screen mode emulates handheld devices, has default support for the handheld media type for mobile devices, and includes Opera Show, which enables presentation-like functionality using the projection media type.

Using Opera's small-screen mode is excellent for getting an idea of how things are going to look in the palm of your hand, but remember that the proof is in the pudding. Until you see this in the actual mobile device in question, you won't really know what sorts of issues might arise in the areas of design and usability. If you have any intent to target handheld devices for your site, Opera is an essential tool.

Internet Explorer 7

Internet Explorer 7 improved CSS support in many areas, and those fixes are outlined on the IEBlog at http://blogs.msdn.com/ie/archive/2006/08/22/712830.aspx. Although this browser still doesn't adhere fully to W3C specifications, Internet Explorer 7 makes great improvements over the preceding version.

At this time, it is probably wise to mention the availability of conditional comments in the Internet Explorer line for versions 5 and newer. A **conditional comment** allows you to target a specific piece of HTML code to your audience based on some versions of Internet Explorer while hiding it from older versions. To show a linked style sheet to Internet Explorer 7 only, you might write the following:

```
<!--[if IE 7]>
<link rel="stylesheet" href="ie7.css" type="text/css"
    media="screen" title="IE7 Styles" charset="utf-8" />
<![endif]-->
```

Or suppose you wanted to hide it from Internet Explorer 7 but show everyone else a particular set of styles. In that case, place an exclamation point (aka the not operator) in front of IE:

```
<!--[if !IE 7]>
<link rel="stylesheet" href="not_ie7.css" type="text/css"
    media="screen" title="Not IE7 Styles" charset="utf-8" />
<![endif]-->
```

You can even use less than (lt), less than or equal to (lte), greater than (gt), and greater than or equal to (gte) operators, and (&), and or (|) operators. Here are a few more examples:

```
<!--[if lt IE 7]>
<link rel="stylesheet" href="less_than_ie7.css" type="text/css"
    media="screen" title="Styles for IE less than version 7" />
<![endif]-->
```

```
<!--[if gte IE 7]>
<link rel="stylesheet" href="greater_than_or_equal_to_ie7.css"
    type="text/css" media="screen"
    title="Styles for IE less than or equal to version 7" />
<![endif]-->
```

```
<!--[if (gte IE 5.5)&(lte IE 7) ]>
<link rel="stylesheet" href="ie_transition_styles.css" type="text/css"
    media="screen" title="Styles for IE versions from 5.5 and 7" />
<![endif]-->
```

```
<!--[if (gte IE 8)|(IE5)]>
<link rel="stylesheet" href="gte_ie8_or_ie5.css"
    type="text/css" media="screen"
    title="Styles for IE8 and greater, with a nod to IE5 for fun." />
<![endif]-->
```

For more information on conditional comments, check out the entry on the Microsoft Developer Network at http://msdn.microsoft.com/library/default.asp?url=/workshop/author/dhtml/overview/ccomment_ovw.asp, or visit Peter Paul Kotch's article on the subject at http://quirksmode.org/css/condcom.html.

Internet Explorer 6

OK, take a deep breath, because here we go. The bane of every web developer's existence in the modern era is Internet Explorer 6. Thankfully now that Internet Explorer 8 is in beta with its multiple web standards improvements, we can only hope that Internet Explorer 6 will become obsolete very soon.

Still, this is the dominant browser on the Internet as of this writing and the one that you need to make sure looks respectable for the sake of your customers. With Internet Explorer 6 controlling the largest chunk of market share, coupled with the large number of unsupported or broken CSS and JavaScript items, you will likely spend the majority of your time fixing Internet Explorer 6 inconsistencies in your project above all other browsers.

However, that's OK. You've gotten this far. Don't throw up your arms just because everything has been going so smoothly so far and all of a sudden the whole thing is broken in Internet Explorer 6. The issues you will encounter are largely known and well documented. Some of the excellent resources that cover browser compatibility issues include Position Is Everything (http://www.positioniseverything.net/) and QuirksMode (http://quirksmode.org/).

Mobile devices

In February 2008, Google announced at a conference in Barcelona that searches from the iPhone were 50 times greater in volume than searches coming from any other mobile device. The open source WebKit is available for mobile device manufacturers and is already used in the Nokia S60 platform and Google Android. Expect that more and more users will be showing up on your sites, and expect browser manufacturers to follow suit in improving usability.

The main browsers to pay attention to are of course Safari/WebKit, Opera Mobile, and Internet Explorer Mobile. You will also see Treo users on the Blazer browser, and expect to see Mozilla-based mobile clients appearing soon.

The trick with mobile devices is that, for the most part, users won't upgrade as often, if at all (iPhone users excepted). That means you may have some obsolete user agents appearing in this space. Don't expect things to be there that you might take for granted, such as fonts, plug-ins, and basic things such as RAM. Screen real estate will be limited and will vary wildly between browsers.

Different mobile browsers have different rules with regard to how they intend to handle things like CSS. For most mobile browsers, the handheld media type is supported. The notable exception is Safari/WebKit, which notably (and controversially) ignores the handheld media type and shows the screen media type instead. The Amazon Kindle simply disregards CSS altogether and shows the user raw HTML. If you expect a significant presence on mobile devices, and you should consider this as a growing trend, then expect to find an incredibly wide array of conflicting issues that will make designing for the desktop look like a walk in the park on a sunny spring day.

Text-only browsers

There is an argument to test your site in a text-only browser first, before you apply even so much as a stitch of CSS or JavaScript to your site, in order to experience the semantic structure and content format of your HTML code. If you have a solid markup foundation, then you can expect greater understanding of your content from site visitors, a greater life span from your code, and an easier time applying styles and behaviors as you go along.

The easiest way to examine your site this way is to disable styles and behaviors in the source code and see how things look. Comment out your links to your external CSS and JavaScript files as well as any such code embedded in the page and see what happens. However, it is important to note that every web browser comes with a certain default style sheet and will apply some basic formatting to features such as headings, paragraphs, list items, and inline elements such as <em> and <strong>. You can find a shortcut to achieve this sort of view in your web browsers in Firefox's Web Developer Toolbar extension. To disable JavaScript, choose Disable ➤ JavaScript ➤ All JavaScript. Then disable CSS by choosing CSS ➤ Disable Styles ➤ All Styles. Finally, you will want to disable images, so select Images ➤ Hide Images. The result is a good representation of your semantic document output.

Perhaps an even better method is to switch to a dedicated text-only web browser such as Lynx. Lynx is a command-line utility that has the capability to render text only; navigation is achieved via the keyboard. This represents a new usability challenge and removes the mouse from the equation. If things "look good" in Lynx—that is, things are readable and make sense—then you know that your document markup stands on its own.

Putting your site into Lynx also puts you into "machine mode," where you can start to visualize what the experience will be for a text-crawling search engine or a semantic web service (see Figure 8-7). Remember that some of your site visitors are machines—Google, Yahoo, and the rest of the search engines will show up to index your site content from time to time. Having a navigable and well-formed semantic structure to your markup that is free of presentational cruft means that search engines will have all the better time indexing and understanding your content.

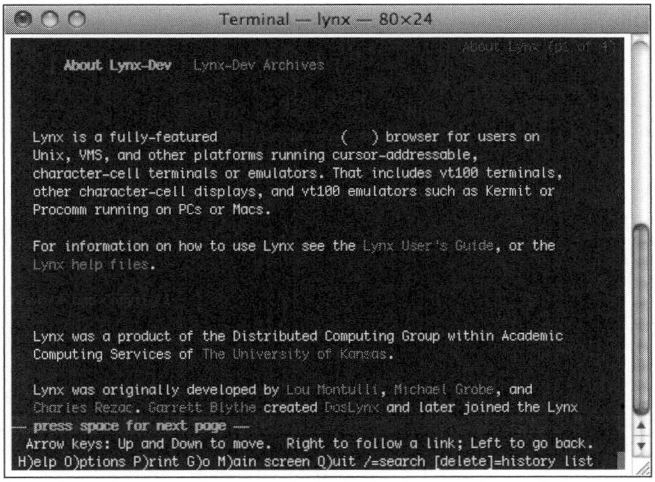

Figure 8-7. The Lynx web browser provides a text-only output and requires keyboard navigation.

Obsolete browsers

On those rare occasions when it is necessary, test your site in old versions of Internet Explorer 5 on Mac or Windows, Netscape Navigator 4, and the rest of it. If you have any users presenting these outdated browsers to your website, chances are the numbers will be miniscule. If you hide JavaScript and CSS from these folks and show obsolete browsers a text-only experience, we are willing to bet they will be plenty happy. If someone is still using one of these browsers, chances are they are used to sites breaking on them or locking them out, and they know they are on obsolete equipment and are really interested in just obtaining the content they need. In the rare case where the customer insists on it, work the additional testing into your timeline and budget.

Thoughts on browser testing

The issue of browser testing has been discussed and debated at length. It is an ongoing debate that will continue to evolve over time as browsers, operating systems, specifications, and user patterns change. Don't be afraid to modify, experiment with, and fine-tune whatever process you come up with—just be sure you do have a process and are in fact performing testing. For additional discussion on the subject, please visit the following articles:

- "Browser testing order" by Andy Clarke at http://www.stuffandnonsense.co.uk/archives/css_browser_testing_order.html. Andy covers a simple and pragmatic model for testing Cascading Style Sheets layouts in various modern browsers, with some good arguments about what to do with obsolete browsers such as Internet Explorer 5 on Mac and Internet Explorer 5.5 on Windows.

- "Browser testing CSS and JavaScript" by Roger Johannson at http://www.456bereastreet.com/archive/200702/browser_testing_css_and_javascript/. This is an excellent write-up building on Andy Clarke's post that includes JavaScript consideration.

- "W3C DOM Compatibility Tables" by Peter Paul Koch at http://www.quirksmode.org/dom/compatibility.html. PPK keeps an excellent resource for looking up DOM support between browsers.

- Position Is Everything by Big John and Holly Bergevin at http://www.positioniseverything.net. This site digs deep into many of the common CSS problems that are to be expected among the various browser editions.

Virtualization is a trend in computing that has been rapidly increasing in importance in recent years. For us as web developers, this affords us an opportunity to run multiple OS configurations on a single computer for testing purposes, each with widely varying environments. The improvements in virtualization over the past few years have been significant, giving you the ability to run virtual machines at near native speeds and with fairly seamless integration between environments.

Finally, screen width is an ongoing issue for web developers. Up until the iPhone was released, it was arguable that optimization for a layout to fit within an 800×600 screen was safe and 1024×768 optimization would not be unheard of. But now we are seeing an emerging trend for even smaller screens to appear at our sites by way of mobile devices, with the iPhone leading the charge. So, what are you to do now?

For the issue of screen optimization, the best way to make an informed decision is to know your site visitors. Running a log analysis tool or analytics program such as Mint (http://haveamint.com/), WebTrends (http://www.webtrends.com/), or Google Analytics (http://www.google.com/analytics/) can give you an excellent idea of how many of your visitors show up at the various resolutions. Ultimately the best solution is going to be the one that caters to the widest number of visitors, and going with flexible widths that scale down to almost arbitrarily small screen resolutions may make the point moot.

Security testing: how much is enough?

Although a discussion of how to perform an extensive security audit is beyond the scope of this book, the subject is worth a mention in the context of the testing process. Here is the one question every site developer needs to answer before dismissing security concerns entirely: does your site accept any form of user input in the shape of a form or a query string in a URL? If so, then you are exposed to vulnerabilities and should perform some level of security testing. Really, if your site does anything in the form of server-side processing, you have potential application-level exposure.

When dealing with any sort of exposure in the form of user input, there is a simple thing to remember: do not trust your users. Sorry, we know we'd all like to believe the better nature in humankind, but when it comes to web forms, it really seems to bring out the mischief in people. Quite a number of attacks could potentially arise simply by placing a single-field input form into a web page. And yes, even URL parameters should be considered user input. If your URL looks like this:

```
http://some.random.website.com/form?pageID=873
```

then right away you have alerted the public to the fact that you probably have a field in your database called pageID that accepts integers. What if someone types pageID=0? What if that page ID does not exist? Or worse, what if that is the admin page? If the site is coded well, it will display an error message—something along the lines of "page not found" or "access denied"—and we hope in a way that uses a more user-friendly language. In a worst-case scenario, it might display things you might not want the public to see, such as an administrator interface or a set of error messages giving away details about your site that you'd rather not divulge to the world. This is an overly simplistic case and far worse scenarios are possible, but this should get the point across.

So, what's a web developer to do if their own precious users cannot be trusted? We of course mean that in a figurative sense—we don't mean *all* users, just the one or two users who wish your website harm. The motivations for hacking a site are many, but they generally fall into these categories:

- *Curiosity*: This kind will rarely do any actual damage—they just want to see what would happen if they poke around a bit.
- *Bragging rights and vandals*: These folks will almost always leave you a little present in the form of an altered image, web page copy, or just missing files. They might be just looking for bragging rights whether they defaced your site or not, or they might be activists looking to publicize their cause at your website's expense.
- *Theft, fraud, and espionage*: These types typically have the goal of stealing information, manipulating records (such as academic grades or employment data), or stealing money.

The basic things to remember for any situation where your scripts take user input and have that affect how things operate with your site is to ensure that data is validated as it is entered and escaped as it is redisplayed to the browser and, where appropriate, that you properly authenticate and encrypt your transactions. For larger projects, you will likely want to hire a security professional to audit your site before going live and periodically thereafter as your site and known threats continue to evolve.

User testing

When you design websites, you need to do so with the needs and goals of the end users in mind. User testing is the process of determining whether your website is usable and makes sense to your potential and intended visitors. Early in your project, you should bounce ideas off potential persons who would use the site in question. You can do this as a formal survey with random sampling and scientific processes, or you can do this by grabbing some people you know and asking them some questions about your site or having them look at some sketches or diagrams. Don't wait: as soon as you have a set of initial requirements together, get some feedback.

Defining usability

When testing for usability, you are asking whether your site visitors and application users can get what they need out of the site. Can they find the information they need? Is it intuitive for them to find their way around the various parts of the site? Are they finding the things you want them to find? Do they get stuck anywhere, and can that particular area of concern be improved at all? Are you getting your message across? When designing your site, you are assuming you are addressing these needs. Now you need to test your assumptions and analyze the resulting data so that you can determine whether this effort has been successful.

Formal usability testing can be quite involved. Typically the usability team will requisition a special room equipped with eye-tracking equipment and video equipment for viewing and recording behavior, and they will hire a proctor to administer the test in a neutral and bias-free way. This can be expensive and often includes paying subjects for their time. Each subject is presented with a script or set of options or goals to try to accomplish during a fixed time period. Data from such exercises is analyzed and reviewed against the design objectives for the project, and recommendations are made as to how to improve the design or alter the project plan based on the findings. It's all very scientific and rational, and if you have the budget to perform such studies, it may well be worthwhile.

However, there is a not-so-well-kept industry secret that can achieve similar results with much less money and formality. Simply do informal testing with a few people off the street (or even people you know). Show them the part of the site you are working on, and have them use it while you watch. Give them some parameters: write up a script or set of tasks to accomplish, and have them talk through their experiences. Write down things as they talk, or grab an inexpensive video camcorder and tripod to record the event. For a fraction of the budget, you can come away with much of the benefit you'd get from a more expensive and formal usability study. As usability experts such as Steve Krug and Jakob Nielsen have argued in the past, you don't need a lot of subjects to get an adequate amount of feedback. Even just one test subject is better than performing no usability analysis at all, and Nielsen argues that five users per test is the practical upper limit of subjects for any given usability test (Alertbox, March 2000). If you do small usability tests frequently throughout the life cycle of your web project, you will come away with a far more refined product with a far greater chance of success than if you just build it and put it out there.

Accessibility testing

When launching a website into the public domain, you are opening up your business to a wide range of people out there on the Web. Some will be on Windows, some on Mac, and some on Linux. Some will be using desktop computers; others might be visiting on a handheld device such as a Blackberry or an iPhone. Perhaps most important, some of your users may require special preference settings or varying types of assistive technologies to overcome the disabilities they may live with. With adoption of solid accessibility guidelines in your web development practices, you can open your website's arms to the widest possible number of visitors and provide everyone with an enriching and informative experience.

Although accessibility may be considered a universal issue that covers browsers, devices, operating systems, and whatnot, we'll now take a moment to consider site visitors with disabilities and what that means for us as web designers and developers.

Disabilities come in many flavors, and the most obvious one for you to consider for the purposes of web development are the vision-impaired users. These users include the blind as well as those with color blindness and low vision (to the point where the issue is beyond the assistance of what corrective lenses could provide). Deafness is another consideration, especially obvious if your site content includes aural cues, audio clips, or video. Users with limited motor ability form another category for consideration—imagine the experience of trying to show up to work with your arm in a cast and not being able to grab the mouse or type beyond one-handed pecking at the keyboard. This group includes such users, users with neurological conditions that prevent proper hand and eye coordination or control, and amputees. Finally, we have the cognitive disabilities—those with learning disabilities such as memory problems, ADHD, and so on.

Accessibility recommendations: WCAG

In 1999, the W3C published a Recommendation entitled Web Content Accessibility Guidelines 1.0 (WCAG), which you can find at `http://www.w3.org/TR/WAI-WEBCONTENT/`. It gave developers a common set of guidelines to aim for when targeting accessibility and a benchmark to measure things by. The stated target for this document is for users with disabilities, but it also states that all user agents, including PDAs, text browsers, and mobile phones should benefit from following these practices.

The WCAG breaks down accessibility into three levels:

- **Priority 1** covers items that *must* be met. Failure to do so means that there will be groups of users that will be unable to access your content.

- **Priority 2** covers items that *should* be met. Meeting these guidelines will remove the most significant barriers for accessing your content.

- **Priority 3** covers items that may be met. Although these items are optional in most cases, taking care of them means you've substantially eased accessibility for your content.

Each checkpoint in the WCAG document is assigned a priority—1, 2, or 3. For example, providing text equivalents for nontext elements such as `alt` text within your image tags would be a priority 1 checkpoint. Properly using heading tags such as `<h1>` and `<h2>` in a hierarchical fashion to denote document structure would be a priority 2 checkpoint. Expanding the full text representation of an acronym within the `title` attribute of a tag, such as `<abbr title="Web Content Accessibility Guidelines">WCAG</abbr>` would be considered a priority 3 checkpoint. It is recommended that you read the WCAG guidelines to become familiar with the concepts and keep the site bookmarked in your web browser for future reference.

Accessibility law

In the context of web accessibility, **Section 508** refers to an amendment to the US Rehabilitation Act of 1973, which is legislation that expands the requirements for federal and related agencies to provide equal access to electronic resources to those with disabilities. All federal websites are potentially subject to this requirement, and many nonfederal organizations are subject to these policies as well. The law is designed to provide access for disabled employees as well as members of the public. Section 508 is one of the most often referred to legal precedents when discussing web accessibility law.

The W3C Web Accessibility Initiative maintains a list of laws broken down by country at http://www. w3.org/WAI/Policy/. Although it maintains that "this page is not a comprehensive or definitive resource for all applicable laws and policies regarding Web accessibility," it is a great place to start researching accessibility law in your country.

For your web project, be sure you understand what legal obligations you may have with regard to accessibility, and develop a process for checking your work to make sure you have everything covered.

Accessibility basics

To work toward an accessible web infrastructure, there are some basic guidelines to keep in mind:

Images Use the alt attribute to describe the image in question. The alt attribute descriptions should be concise and clear. For example, a photo of a grizzly bear might have the alt attribute "Photo of a grizzly bear catching salmon in a mountain stream". A logo image for a corporation might have the alt attribute "Acme Incorporated Corporate Logo". If you are able to use the <object> tag for images, you may provide information about the image between the <object> tags. For example:

```
<img src="lincoln.jpg" alt="Portrait of Abraham Lincoln." />
```

Or for example:

```
<object data="lincoln.jpg" type="image/gif" >
      Portrait of Abraham Lincoln.
</object>
```

Image maps If you are using image maps, be sure they are of the client-side variety and have text equivalent information for hotspots. You can do this by using the alt attribute within <area> tags, like this:

```
<map id="labmap" name="labmap">
<area shape="rect" coords="0,0,55,55" href="patients.html"
    alt="Patient Information" />
<area shape="rect" coords="60,60,100,100" href="doctors.html"
    alt="Doctor Information" />

</map>
```

Including text-based alternate links (for example, <a href="patients.html">Patients</a> | <a href="doctors.html">Doctors</a>) in context with these image map URLs would satisfy an optional but useful WAI priority 3 checkpoint.

Video Any video being served from your site should contain subtitles, include closed captioning, or have a text transcript.

Hyperlinks Ensure that the text you wrap inside your anchor tags makes sense for the target content. Avoid using text like "click here." Try to use descriptive title attributes as much as possible to provide additional information about the links. Most browsers will render a tooltip when using the mouse to hover over the link.

Tables You're using tables only for tabular data, right? Avoid using table layouts and instead ensure that your display layer is CSS-based. If for some reason you must, please do your vision-impaired site visitors a favor and make *absolutely certain* that an empty summary attribute is included in the table:

```
<table summary="">
```

Screen readers that encounter tables with empty summary attributes will skip going through the annoying process of announcing the table, giving your vision-impaired users a far smoother experience.

Tables when formed properly have constructs for great amounts of information. The <table> element allows for a summary attribute, which can be used to describe the basis for the data you are representing. The <caption> element provides a text caption for the table. The <th> element is provided to indicate table headings. Use these features for your accessibility advantage.

Here is an example of a simple well-formed table with accessible representations of the content:

```
<table summary="This table lists goldfish lengths for project 6.">
    <caption>Goldfish Lengths</caption>
    <tr>
<th>Fish ID</th>
<th>Length</th>
    </tr>
    <tr>
        <td>23</td>
        <td>321mm</td>
    </tr>
    <tr>
        <td>24</td>
        <td>402mm</td>
    </tr>
    <tr>
        <td>25</td>
        <td>376mm</td>
    </tr>
</table>
```

Document structure Use properly nested heading tags that denote the hierarchical structure of your content. An <h1> tag might represent a primary heading with possibly one or more subheadings represented by the <h2> element. In turn, an <h2> might have one or more subheadings represented by <h3> elements. But an <h3> would never appear higher up in the semantic hierarchy than an <h2> or an <h1>. Use paragraph tags to denote paragraphs and the appropriate lists (ordered, unordered, and definition) to denote the types of lists you are representing.

Each HTML tag was created to represent a specific type of content. Chances are, there is one available for the item you are trying to represent. Markup should as much as possible represent the semantic *meaning* of the content. Resist the urge to insert presentational markup and inline style information.

Graphs and charts These are usually images, but the information they contain is usually more complex than what a typical `alt` text description can provide. Use the `longdesc` attribute to point to a full-text description of the data represented within the graphic, as shown:

```
<img src="2007sales.gif" alt="2007 Sales Chart"
    longdesc="2007salesreport.html" />
```

The resulting page should be as many paragraphs as required to describe the data in your graphic in a way that adequately conveys the meaning of the data represented.

Unfortunately, many browsers do not support the `longdesc` attribute. In addition to using the `longdesc` attribute, provide a simple text-based hyperlink pointing to the same resource.

JavaScript Do not expect JavaScript to be available to all of your users. Use the Document Object Model to direct JavaScript behavior and externalize all your JavaScript in separate files. Make sure all intended behaviors have a graceful failover mechanism, such as directing the user to a standard HTML form with a submit button in lieu of an Ajax behavior.

For more information on best practices and useful techniques of using JavaScript against the Document Object Model, check out the excellent book by Jeremy Keith titled *DOM Scripting* (friends of ED, 2005; `http://domscripting.com/book/`).

Anything that requires a plug-in Adobe Flash is probably the most ubiquitous plug-in found in browsers today. Adobe currently claims 98 percent of U.S. web users have Flash enabled. But for that remaining 2 percent, and specifically those users who are unable to use Flash for whatever reason, there needs to be some consideration as to their user experience.

Flash is a best-case scenario. Flash has made great strides in accessibility features, but that still leaves some users out of the loop—either because the plug-in isn't available to them or because accessibility has not been implemented for the given SWF file. Other plug-ins have far slimmer market share, so as a general rule of thumb, you should never count on any given plug-in being available. Provide alternative text-based content for these instances.

PDF Adobe's Portable Document Format is excellent for providing accurate print-ready representations of your content. However, if you are wrapping up your content in PDF files when the text content of such could be represented in HTML, you are not doing your site visitors much of a favor. Provide PDF content in the context of being a printer-ready representation of an accessible HTML document.

For further reading on the issues concerning PDF and accessibility, please check out the A List Apart article "Facts and Opinions About PDF Accessibility" by Joe Clark at `http://www.alistapart.com/articles/pdf_accessibility`.

Frames Frames can complicate accessibility, and it is considered best to avoid them whenever possible. If you must use frames, use meaningful frame titles and a `<noframes>` content section for when this feature is unsupported. Support for frames is dropped in XHTML 1.1, so it may be best to just avoid frames altogether.

Valid markup Not all valid web pages are accessible, but all accessible web pages are valid. Be sure to strive for validity in your XHTML code and test validity regularly.

Assistive technologies

Making your website accessible to users who require assistive technologies is the right thing to do. Assistive technologies help certain types of users navigate your web content to retrieve the information they need and achieve the tasks they need to accomplish. This includes screen readers, Braille readers, text enlargers, alternatives to mouse input such as foot pedals, keyboards, eye motion trackers, and much more. For the purposes of this discussion, let's include providing subtitles and text transcripts as part of the assistive technologies discussion.

If you are really in tune with accessibility, you will test the user experience for yourself using some of various assistive technologies. Testing your sites in a text-only browser such as Lynx goes a long way, but there is really nothing like putting yourself in the driver's seat and feeling what it is really like to, oh, say complete one module of an online course in ancient Roman history using nothing but a screen reader and keyboard input. Try it once: turn on a screen reader. (JAWS allows an unlimited trial that can be used up to 40 minutes per session, and users of Mac OS X 10.4 and newer have a free excellent reader called VoiceOver as part of the Universal Access suite.) Turn off your computer screen, put on a blindfold, or turn out the lights. Unplug your mouse, and go! Try navigating a good site first, such as WebAIM (http://www.webaim.org/). Then hit something really bad—something, oh, circa the year 1999 or 2000 or so—a ripe example of table layouts, text baked right into images (no `alt` attributes of course!), plug-ins galore, and a side helping of invalid markup. Then let us know how it works out.

Now imagine having to put up with this every day. Imagine trying to attend college like this, trying to go to work, or just trying the simple act of going online to check e-mail or surf the Web. For sites that have horrific markup, it just doesn't work. This is the cyber equivalent of opening a business in a busy part of town and not building a wheelchair ramp.

Although it may be time-consuming and cost prohibitive to test every page of your site using these sorts of assistive technologies, it might be entirely feasible to just spot-check things here and there. If you are using a markup template that retains good control over how your XHTML foundation is constructed, then you should remain in good shape. At the very least, it wouldn't hurt to try this little experiment to gain some experience and appreciation for accessibility issues. Having this sort of experience helps you appreciate well-formed, semantic, accessible code so much more.

Accessibility checklist

To keep in step with whatever your legal, corporate, or project requirements may be, it is a good idea to develop a checklist against which to test your site. It does not have to be complicated—it could be anywhere from a formal checklist to a mental note if you feel that confident about your skills, but don't skip the step. A sample checklist for accessibility might look like this:

- Markup has been validated against the indicated DTD, Schema, or X/HTML specification indicated in the doctype.
- All nontext elements have text equivalents (`alt` text for images, `longdesc` for charts, and so on).
- JavaScript behaviors use DOM best practices, are unobtrusive, and fail over gracefully with alternative content or functionality.

- Plug-in-based content has alternative content provided.

- Video captions or text-based transcripts have been provided.

- Tables have summary content provided and are semantically constructed.

- The site is free of presentational markup, inline styles, and embedded behaviors.

- The site elements have proper hierarchical order and semantic representation of the content.

For things that might be fuzzy or not representable as absolutes, you might even rate the level of quality. For instance, you could say that the hierarchical and semantic document markup structure is rated "fair" but could be better. Record this as something to improve upon on at a later date.

Accessibility resources

The following are accessibility resources:

- WebAIM (http://www.webaim.org) is one of the finest resources for accessibility available today. WebAIM offers plenty of articles on accessibility issues, a site evaluation tool called WAVE at http://wave.webaim.org/, and professional services.

- The HiSoftware Cynthia Says Portal at http://www.cynthiasays.com/ is another great resource for learning about accessibility. The site allows you to test pages and generate reports using Section 508 or WCAG priority levels, and it offers a suite of commercial products that provide more extensive functionality.

- The U.S. Government has established a website covering the laws and applicability of Section 508, which can be found at http://www.section508.gov/. In addition to this resource, WebAIM has created a helpful checklist for evaluating your site for Section 508 compliance, which you can find at http://www.webaim.org/standards/508/checklist.

- The Web Accessibility Tools Consortium (WAT-C) maintains a list of free tools for developers to assist in producing accessible sites; you can find WAT-C at http://www.wat-c.org/.

- The WCAG Samurai (http://WCAGSamurai.org/) is a group of developers led by web accessibility guru Joe Clark that publishes corrections and extensions to the Web Content Accessibility Guidelines. The WCAG Samurai project was formed in response to a feeling that the WCAG 2.0 guidelines effort was not headed in the right direction, and it opts to publish errata for version 1.0 of the WCAG instead. It takes a decisive and opinionated stance on many of the issues, where the WCAG merely provides "recommendations." For background on this initiative, we recommend reading the A List Apart article titled "To Hell with WCAG 2," which you can find at http://alistapart.com/articles/tohellwithwcag2.

Launching your site: the big milestone

After you've thoroughly tested your site, there's only one thing left to do—launch it! And since we are discussing *professional* web development, you should think of the site launch as the most important milestone of your project. It is an event to be treated with some respect and care. All too often we see haphazard management of the launch process—just upload it and go. Are you sure everything is working? If something breaks during a particular release, are you going to shut users out of your site or otherwise alienate your customer base?

To avoid surprises, it is a good idea to come up with a production checklist—something to verify in your web development process that you have gone through at least a basic level of quality control and are confident that what you are about to launch is production quality. Here's the checklist we use:

- All copy has been approved by marketing.
- The site has been reviewed for branding and design.
- The site has passed in all required browser checks.
- All the required accessibility checkpoints have been reviewed and approved.
- All the markup and CSS passes W3C validation.
- The site has passed the required security evaluation.
- A backup of the old version has been made (or source code versioning has been verified).
- The customer has signed off on this release.
- All the documentation has been recorded and archived.

There—once you pass your production checklist, now you can flip the switch! Be aware that this is just a sample. Your checklist might be simpler or far more complex. Whatever meets your needs is best, just as long as you give some adequate consideration to the publishing process.

Having a production checklist works well with a three-tiered server environment as mentioned earlier. Once the site is approved, you might set up your process so that the production person—such as a capable server admin, knowledgeable developer, or just yourself putting on the appropriate hat—receives the production request, verifies that the checklist and any other required artifacts have been taken care of, and then proceeds to perform the launch.

Ongoing maintenance: beyond launch

Launching your site can sometimes feel anticlimactic. After you've done all this work building and testing and testing again, the final step after the customer signs off on it is really just to flip the switch in whatever publishing process you have established. But wait—what's next? You've built the best website you know how to build. You've tested it for validity, functionality, usability, and so on. Everything is perfect; how do you know it is going to stay that way? Enter the web development life cycle: plan periodic checks on your site.

When you launch a website, you are giving rise to a new entity on the Internet—something that people will continue to interact with on a daily basis—and you hope something that will grow over time. It is therefore a good practice to plan on how you will maintain this site ahead of time. Will you and your team check in on it from time to time? Will there be a site manager to continually review and maintain the content? Or have you designed the site so that the client can do all the maintenance, meaning that your role is over until there's a need to enhance or expand the site? In the last case, it might be a good idea to set an expiration date and plan for taking it down. This is especially important on intranet projects where outdated information can be left just sitting there getting indexed by search engines when such data has long outgrown its usefulness or has become an information security liability.

261

Embedding ownership of your work into your original proposal is perhaps the most important step to take in keeping up with your site. Even if it is just an annual review with a proposed recommendation write-up, you should always try to bake this into your proposals up front and plan on checking in from time to time.

Content management

Now the trick is that once you've launched your site, what is to stop the content owners (who know just enough HTML to be dangerous) from breaking your beautifully architected and well-formed markup? Chances are it is unlikely most of these sorts of folks are going to want to take the time to learn how to construct semantic markup and validate their code. The way to do this is to plan on implementing some sort of content management solution.

A good content management solution can help ease the entry of content into the ongoing management of a website, but it can also be used to set up constraints that enforce your information architecture and your markup design and keep things neat and tidy.

For static content websites, setting up the content owners with a tool such as Adobe Contribute can assist in achieving both aims of easing content management and controlling your source code. You can assign roles in Contribute that handle specific tasks—for example, a Contributor role for the majority of those who write or input copy, an Editor role for approving and publishing content, and an Administrator role with full access to architect and define how things work. The default roles are User and Administrator, with User having typical edit and publish access, and this may be just fine for many small to medium-sized projects. Role settings in Contribute allow for control over the types of files that can be edited, how styles are applied, and accessibility and markup controls. To administer roles in Contribute CS3, follow these steps:

1. Choose Contribute ➤ Administer Websites on Mac or Edit ➤ Administer Websites on Windows, and elect the site you want to make changes to.

2. Select Users and Roles from the left menu.

3. Select the role you want to edit from the Users who have connected box. The Users role might be a good place to start if you're using the default configuration.

4. Click the Edit Role Settings button.

5. In the resulting dialog box, set the options that make the best sense. For instance, you may want to ensure that your content editors don't touch your dynamic code, only use image assets already stored on the server, are prompted to enter alt text for any images they insert, and use <em> and <strong> instead of the deprecated <b> and <i> tags, as shown in Figure 8-8.

The alternative to static content is serving your content via a database-driven system. There are dozens of viable options to choose from. Delving into the finite details for such systems is far beyond the scope of this book, but we'll highlight some of the basic things to be aware of.

Database-driven content management systems (CMSs) can be purchased, adapted from solutions in the open source community, or developed entirely from scratch. There are pros and cons to each.

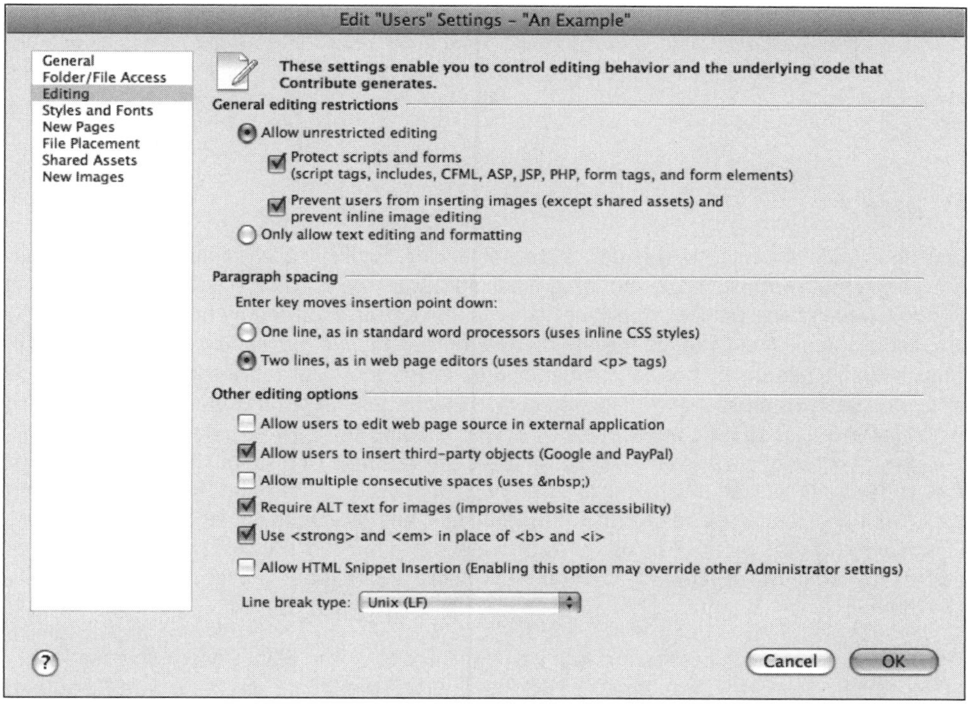

Figure 8-8. Contribute gives you several options for controlling how content is edited by a site editor.

Purchased Commercial off-the-shelf (COTS) systems can be feature-rich and tie in with your existing enterprise infrastructure. They should have all the i's dotted and the t's crossed when it comes to enterprise requirements, and enterprise decision makers often seem to like the idea of a large corporate entity backing the software that is being deployed. On the downside, these systems can be bulky, can use proprietary and non-standards-compliant code, and can often be a bit behind the times in terms of modern features and functionality. And they can be expensive both to purchase and to maintain. Be sure to evaluate such systems with web standards in mind. If the product claims support for only a limited number of specific browsers and has no mention of standards compliance or accessibility, keep looking around. You don't want to shackle your customers to a particular platform for years to come and lock out their potential customers.

Open source This option has become much more popular for a number of reasons. Open source systems are free, they are fully featured, and they tend to be quite robust and effective. Blogs, wikis, and the rest of the buzzword-laden vectors of Web 2.0 are mostly just specialized variances of content management solutions, and in many ways this diversity addresses the specialization required when discussing CMS. There is no one-size-fits-all solution, and whatever you choose from the preexisting software world is going to mean some compromises to make with regard to your site.

Custom developed Custom CMS solutions are those that you or your development team create from scratch. The benefit here is that you can program things to work exactly the way you need them to—no extra cruft, no distracting features—and it fits your business needs as designed. And of course the obvious drawback is the effort required to develop such a system. If expertise in server-side languages such as PHP, Perl, or Ruby on Rails is lacking, then this is probably not going to be a cost-effective solution. (On the other hand, it is a great way to learn!) But if the requirements are simple, a custom solution might be a far better choice than trying to fit a square CMS peg into a round website infrastructure hole.

Summary

In this chapter, we discussed many issues relating to testing, publishing, and maintaining your websites in a development/test/production model. We talked about the idea of a website management life cycle and how engraving certain important issues can be better managed by baking these things right into the project plan. We discussed the importance of maintaining the validity of your code by keeping tabs on it throughout the project span and some of the tools out there that make the process of checking validation a simple task. You looked at testing your sites in different web browsers and examined some of the ways to ease the process of developing and testing your code across the vast array of user agents that your sites might encounter. We discussed how to test your design assumptions for usability with potential users. We got into some of the details of accessibility, including assistive technologies, the user experience for those with disabilities, and strategies for helping ensure your sites are open to the widest number of users. And finally, we discussed the launch process and keeping your sites in shape by developing maintenance plans and adopting a philosophy of continued improvement.

When it comes to testing and managing your work, the first step is to plan. Once you've made the conscious decision to do so, the next step is to act. Set yourself reminders and mark dates in your calendar when you need to take care of things so you don't forget. If you make sure you have provided for testing and maintenance in your development plans and follow through on these issues, you can be sure that the quality of your work will be greatly improved, and your customers and users will be thankful.

> *With the high level of importance we place on our online information resources, it is often surprising for web professionals to see what a low level of regard people have for the web profession outside of our industry. This is in part because of the wonderful simplicity and low learning curve of HTML, coupled with the prevalence of WYSIWYG web production tools that completely shield the amateur from the responsibility or understanding of what semantic, accessible web page creation is all about. Their only goal is to copy and paste information into the thing, publish it, and be done with it. But what you pay for is what you get. To produce quality web infrastructures, the process itself must be nobly regarded.*
>
> *The cyclical process of testing and revising your work should be a basic premise for every professional web developer. Although all of the recommendations outlined in this chapter may be more trouble than they are worth for many cases, adopting even just some of these premises will be beneficial to your web development process and will yield a higher quality of work. Don't leave things to chance—take some care in how you produce code, assign some level of quality control to your work, and treat it with some reverence and care.*

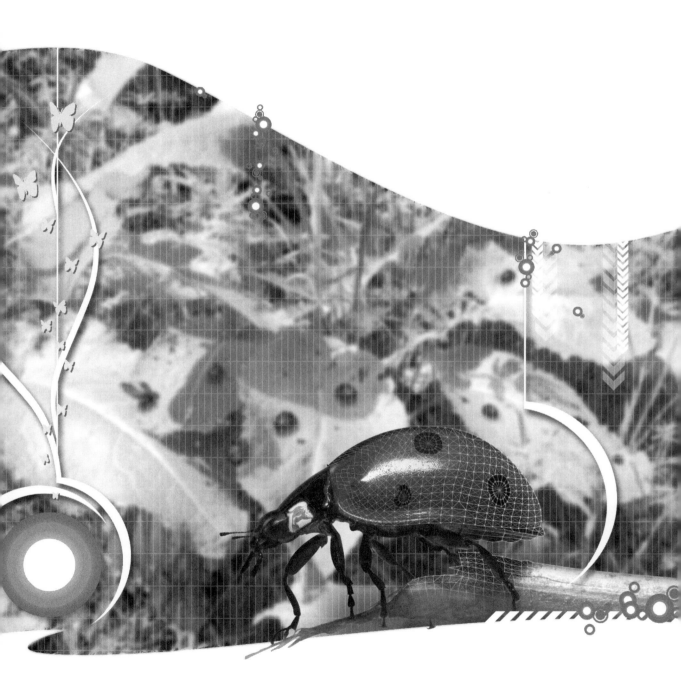

Chapter 9

WEB 2.0: USING AJAX AND SOCIAL SOFTWARE

The Internet has already gone through a boom and bust cycle. Some would argue that we're now seeing an upswing once again (which will be followed by an inevitable crash). The late 1990s saw the first bottoming out of the Internet industry. Funding for really neat and innovative services (but unfortunately not-so-profitable services) dried up, and a good number of companies went out of business. After that, it took some time for investors to regain confidence in web-based businesses, and by about 2004, investors started looking at "dot-coms" once again.

Around this time, the term **Web 2.0** started to appear. Just as with software, version 2.0 of a product is a major milestone, introducing new features and fixing a lot of bugs. In the case of the Web, version 2.0 brought in a number of advances in business, in technology, and even in philosophy. It fixed the major "bug" of Internet companies thinking that they didn't have to actually make money to be successful. Web 2.0 is still an open book, but a number of signs are pointing to it being far better business-wise than the early days. While version 1.0 of the Web was largely about capturing users (page views), version 2.0 is mostly about producing profits.

Companies have come to realize that the major advantage of a global network is that information can be made freely available and shared openly. Locking users into your technology and walling yourself off from others is counterintuitive. People want their applications to work together, and this includes the web applications they use. On the technology front, user experience is paramount; if you can't produce something that people want and are willing to pay for, then it just doesn't matter whose server is bigger.

Some of the biggest leaps forward on the Web, in technology and business, happen when somebody fixes an existing problem using existing tools: "reinventing the wheel" so to speak. Web standards are constantly evolving, and new features are being implemented in browsers as they're rolled out, but the problems of today need solutions today, and waiting for XHTML 2 and CSS 3 to be widely supported by the major web browsers just isn't an option.

The concepts of openness, cooperation, and "mashing up" what we have to work with are what is fueling the Web 2.0 movement. The overall philosophy has changed from one of information silos and walled gardens to one of producing something really good and then sharing it. Don't get us wrong; the key to Web 2.0 isn't to give everything away. On the contrary, profitability is more important now, particularly with investors, than ever before. Web 2.0 is about giving back, because chances are that you've used somebody else's contributions to get where you are today.

That said, a number of technologies and concepts have emerged and helped move things along for Web 2.0. In this chapter, you'll learn about some of these transformative technologies and how they have had a profound effect on the Web today.

The Web isn't application-like

Right around 2003, the Web seemed to have hit a bit of a wall. There were still new websites and new web applications being introduced, but they lacked any serious innovation. Web standards had taken hold amongst a number of developers, but they were receiving a good deal of criticism because what they were developing wasn't as interactive as websites developed in Flash. Indeed, there was a bit of a return to simplicity, because the really advanced features offered by CSS weren't fully implemented in all major browsers, and developers shied away from JavaScript because of browser incompatibilities. Flash had a major advantage in that its applications often felt faster because data could be sent back and forth from the server without having to reload the page. Flash allowed for animation and a level of interactivity that felt more familiar, more like a desktop application than anything else available on the Web.

Things like Dynamic HTML (DHTML) had been around for some time, giving developers the ability to add some "wow" factor to a page, but most of this was superficial client-side "tricks" to make pages feel more real-time than they actually were. Additionally, DHTML was onerous to develop, often involving hundreds of lines of code in JavaScript, and then had to be debugged and, in some cases, completely rewritten from one browser to the next.

This was an unsustainable route, and more often than not, developers just wouldn't bother. There was still a longing for all of the semantic (and search-engine-friendly) benefits of standards-based development over Flash, but there was no good way to compete with the glitz being offered. Fortunately, web-developers are industrious types, and instead of simply admitting defeat, a number of breakthroughs were introduced at this point into the mainstream. Some will argue that these weren't breakthroughs at all but merely a repackaging of existing techniques. That goes to show you how important packaging can be, we guess.

Ajax was born

Asynchronous JavaScript and XML (Ajax) was a term coined by Jesse James Garrett of Adaptive Path in 2005; it describes a technique that lets web pages interact with servers in near real time using existing (and thus widely supported) technologies. In fact, the underlying ideas behind Ajax date back to 1996 when Microsoft proposed a technique of using a hidden frame to pass data back and forth between the client and server. This technique never really caught on, however, because it had some browser-specific components to it (it worked only in Internet Explorer).

By and large, prior to Ajax's official introduction, if you wanted to send data to a server, you would submit a form (which would cause the page to reload). If you wanted to receive data back and display it, you would have to wait for a page load. People who are new to the Web would have trouble with this concept. If you do a search using the e-mail software on my computer, the results come back instantly. Why do they have to click a button on the Web and wait?

Ajax allows developers to write code that interacts behind the scenes with a web server, passing information back and forth without having to refresh/submit a page. Using Ajax, parts of a page can be updated while the visitor is still there. One of the first implementations of Ajax came from Google Maps (Figure 9-1) where visitors could drag around and zoom in and out of a section of map on the fly. Previously, web-based mapping products were extremely slow to use, requiring a page reload every time you wanted to shift the view in any compass direction or zoom in/zoom out on a map.

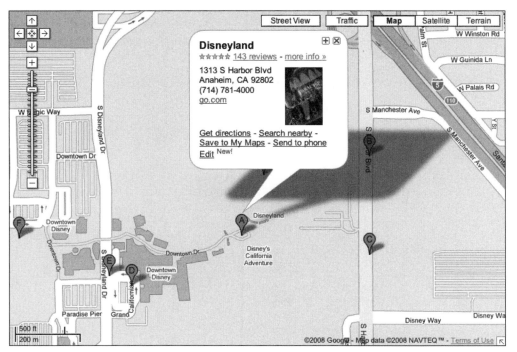

Figure 9-1. Google Maps was revolutionary when it was introduced. People could pan and zoom around maps without having to repeatedly reload web pages in their browser.

This has a number of advantages over the traditional request/response mode. Web pages now start to act more like desktop applications in that visitors no longer have to do something, wait, do something else, and wait as communication is taking place over the network. Similar to desktop applications, data can be exchanged behind the scenes, freeing users from the latency of web-based applications. Additionally, if implemented properly, Ajax implementations can save significant amounts of bandwidth because only the data parts of a document are sent back and forth between the client and the server. So, for example, instead of returning an entire record set from a database, the web app may load only the first three records and then request additional information later, and only if required.

With all good things, there are some drawbacks. Depending on the implementation, some of these disadvantages can be major usability problems and in other cases may be entirely negligible. One of the major concerns with Ajax when used for dynamically generating pages (pulling the content of a page in on the fly) is that it "breaks" the web browser's Back button.

Web browsers expect content to be separated into discreet chunks and maintain a history of these chunks. Users can then browse back and forward through the pages stored in their history using the Forward and Back buttons. However, if a new page is not loaded, and rather just a section of a page changes, this does not get recorded in the history. For the same reason, it's difficult to bookmark the exact information you want on a page that is using Ajax.

The second possible problem emerges when network connections are slow (or drop out all together). Similar to a desktop application freezing, if your web browser sends out an Ajax request, it expects to receive a response. If the developer hasn't built in a timeout or some sort of feedback for the end user, it can be quite frustrating when pages just appear to stop responding. If you want to see this in practice, go to a page that uses Ajax, such as the one shown in Figure 9-2, and just before you're about to submit your request, unplug your Internet connection.

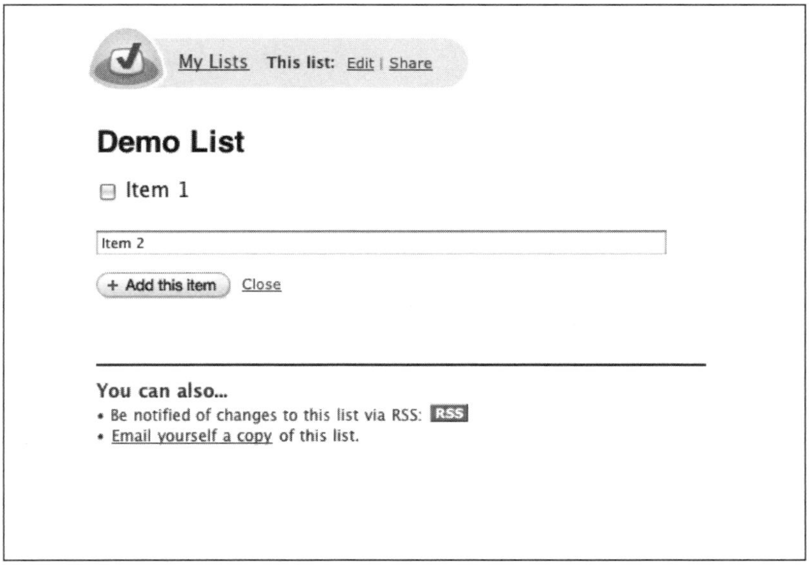

Figure 9-2. An example from a to-do list application, Ta-da Lists. Here, we've selected to add a new item to our list, entered it, and hit Add this item. Because we've lost our network connection, nothing happens, and the page just sits there.

The loading behavior in Ajax happens because of JavaScript, which is not executed by search engines. Therefore, if you have data being dynamically loaded into a page through Ajax, it's not going to get indexed by a search engine. This drawback is quite simple to work around, however, by simply providing a set of static pages that can be easily indexed by search and used by any browsers that don't support/have JavaScript turned on (screen readers for the visually impaired, for example). Additionally, it's easy to build your forms first, have them submit normally, and then add Ajax so that the advanced functionality will degrade gracefully in browsers that are less capable (as in the following example).

A simple Ajax example

You are probably wondering what the heck the code looks like for working with Ajax. We'll cover the basics of it here, and then later, we'll recommend that you check out some of the JavaScript libraries we talk about. They make the process of implementing really advanced effects reasonably simple.

First, we'll talk about the workhorse that makes everything go: JavaScript. Using JavaScript, you could do a number of things. Essentially, it takes some input (such as from a text box) and sends it to a PHP page on the server. Based on the input, this page could carry out a number of tasks such as perform a database query or, in this case, present a guessing game. The results of the PHP code are then returned and placed inside a <div> on the page.

```
<script type="text/javascript">
    function createRequest() {
        var req;
        var browser = navigator.appName;
        if(browser == "Microsoft Internet Explorer") {
            req = new ActiveXObject("Microsoft.XMLHTTP");
        }else{
            req = new XMLHttpRequest();
        }
            return req;
    }
    var reqObj = createRequest();
    function sendReq(query) {
        reqObj.open('GET', 'ajax_script.php?query='+query);
        reqObj.onreadystatechange = handleResponse;
        reqObj.send(null);
    }
    function handleResponse() {
        if(reqObj.readyState == 4) {
            var response = reqObj.responseText;
            document.getElementById('searchresult'). ➥
      innerHTML = response;
        }
    }
</script>
```

Drop that script into the <head> of your page, or preferably, include it as a .js file in the <head> of your page, and place the following form in the <body>. The HTML that accompanies this JavaScript is really simple. All you really need is a text box and a <div> (with the appropriate ID):

271

```
<p>I like to eat, eat Apples and...</p>
    <form action="ajax_script.php" method="get">
        <p><input type="text" name="query"  ➥
      onblur="sendReq(this.value);" /></p>
        <p><input type="submit" value="Take a guess" /></p>
    </form>
<hr />
<div id="searchresult"></div>
```

We have the text box using an onblur event to call the JavaScript function sendReq(). This means that when the text box loses focus (the user hits Tab or clicks outside the box with their mouse), the JavaScript will run. Optionally, you could use an onkeyup event, which will call the JavaScript function with each character entered in the text box—this can add a little extra load to the server because it has to execute the PHP file repeatedly, but it gives you the appearance of immediate results in the searchresult <div>.

There's one other thing we want to mention about this code. We've actually set up the form action to be the PHP page and set the method to GET for the form. The reason we did that is for folks who don't have JavaScript enabled. They're still able to submit their guess and receive confirmation as to whether they guessed right (it's just not as attractive).

Here's what the really simple PHP code looks like:

```
switch($_REQUEST['query']) {
    case 'bananas':
        echo "Bananas is the right answer!";
        break;
}
```

As you may have gathered from this example, the "x" in Ajax is optional. The server doesn't have to return XML at all. The server could return HTML, XML, plain text, or even some type of file (but sending a big file to the client could slow things down quite a bit). Figure 9-3 shows our example displayed in a web browser.

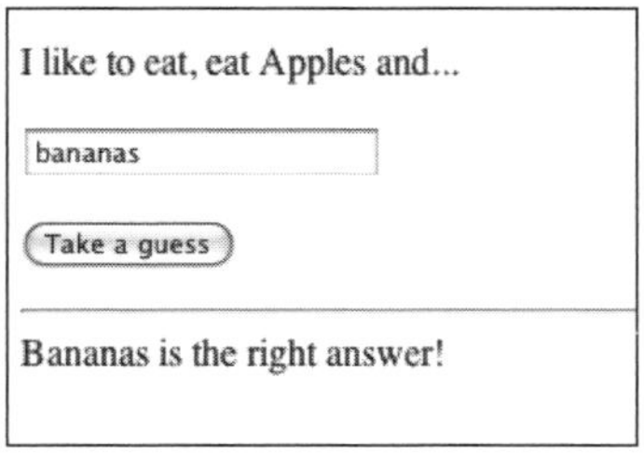

Figure 9-3. The completed application lets you know when you've guessed the right word, all without actually having to submit the form.

This example is absolutely bare-bones as it sits. The beauty of Ajax, however, is that the client-side functionality is pretty much done with your code. All you would really need to do now is spruce up your PHP (or whatever server-side language you choose) to handle anything additional you want to throw at it. (For example, wrong guesses return nothing; also, *bananas* is case sensitive, so if someone types *BANANAS*, it's the wrong answer.) You could also add a little CSS in order to style things nicely so that a correct answer is greeted with a big check mark whereas an incorrect answer receives a great big X.

The "j" in Ajax

Now that you've gotten a gentle introduction to how Ajax works and you've gone through how to put together a really simple Ajax application, let's step things up a notch. As we mentioned in the previous section, a number of JavaScript libraries are available that simplify Ajax and DHTML development. Let's take a look at a couple of them.

Instead of having to write scripts themselves, developers simply have to include a particular .js file in their page, and they can do all sorts of really advanced animation effects and Ajax interactions. Although this has dramatically lowered the bar for amateurs wanting to get started in development, it has also massively shortened development time for professionals who previously had to write the same routines over and over again. As a general rule, programmers are an efficient bunch, and the less time they can spend solving one particular problem, the better.

script.aculo.us

When it comes to developing web-based user interfaces, script.aculo.us is a dream come true. It's now possible to easily implement really cool features such as drag-and-drop reordering of lists and fade-in/fade-out animations using only a couple of lines of programming. script.aculo.us is based on another library, Prototype, that is very capable of handling Ajax requests and that adds a number of really interesting (and useful) features.

Instead of trying to describe in detail what script.aculo.us does, we'll simply refer you to the website (just add an http:// in front of the name) where you can see examples in action.

jQuery

Although both script.aculo.us and jQuery can both do animation and simplify handling Ajax requests, we've found that jQuery is just a little bit better at the data manipulation side of things. Instead of having to write all the JavaScript code over and over again to handle the mechanics of the Ajax request, wouldn't it be nice to be able to focus on the user interactions instead?

We'll now show you what the example would look like using jQuery instead of our bare-bones hand-coded example. This example assumes you've downloaded a copy of the freely available jQuery library from http://www.jquery.com/ and saved it to a directory called scripts in the root of your website. Here's the JavaScript:

```
<script type="text/javascript">
$(document).ready(function() {
    $('#query').blur(function(){
        $.get("ajax_script.php", {
            query: $('#query').val()
        }, function(response){
        $('#searchresult').fadeOut();
        setTimeout("finishAjax('searchresult', ➥
```

```
            '"+escape(response)+"')", 400);
        });
            return false;
        });
    });
    function finishAjax(id, response) {
        $('#'+id).html(unescape(response));
        $('#'+id).fadeIn();
    }
    </script>
```

The HTML is pretty similar with just a couple of subtle differences (adding an id to the text field and removing the onblur event handler):

```
<p>I like to eat, eat Apples and...</p>
        <form action="ajax_script.php" method="get">
            <p><input type="text" id="query" name="query" /></p>
            <p><input type="submit" value="Take a guess" /></p>
        </form>
        <hr />
        <div id="searchresult"></div>
```

Although it doesn't look like significantly less JavaScript than the previous example, it does have quite a few advantages. First, jQuery has added some nice eye candy. The result will slowly fade in as opposed to just appearing. Second, you can use this same snippet of code over and over again throughout the entire website—all you would have to do is change the ids for the <div> elements and (optionally) the name/location of the PHP file doing the server-side processing. Using jQuery, you have completely separated the form from the function of the page; in the previous example, you had to embed some functionality in order to call the onblur event.

As with script.aculo.us, it's better to see what can be done with jQuery, instead of having us describe it to you. The website provides great documentation and examples of what can be done. One final advantage to jQuery: it can accept plug-ins, meaning that all kinds of people have been writing additional code to add even more functionality (such as image viewers, form validation, and page tabs).

Design characteristics of Web 2.0

A number of design trends started to emerge with Web 2.0. The most refreshing trend was a movement toward cleaner and simpler design. We're making some generalizations here, but interfaces were becoming increasingly cluttered and complex near the end of the 1990s (see Figure 9-4 as an example). A lot of companies seemed to believe that company size was a function of the number of pages on their website (or the number of links on their home page). Search engines were some of the worst offenders, having their home page filled with ads, links to auxiliary services, and news snippets. It was occasionally difficult to find the search box.

Figure 9-4. AltaVista (February 2000) was one of the most popular search engines pre-Google. Its home page is typical of what a number of search engines did at the time.

Lickable interfaces

The Web 2.0 backlash to this cluttered design situation was to produce almost minimal interfaces with brightly colored, highly visible elements. Gradients are a common sight, as are bright starbursts to draw attention to key elements. Figure 9-5 shows some of these elements in use on current websites.

Figure 9-5. Some of the graphical elements, taken from an example on Web Design from Scratch, are so bright and shiny they're likened to candy—something you just want to taste.

You can find a great overview of Web 2.0 design trends at Web Design from Scratch (http://webdesignfromscratch.com/current-style.cfm). It lists nine areas that are considered "trademark" Web 2.0 design. Check out the website for examples of each:

- Simple layout
- Centered orientation
- Designed content, not pages (focus on styling page elements, not the background)
- 3D effects, used sparingly
- Soft, neutral background colors
- Strong color, used sparingly
- Cute icons, used sparingly
- Plenty of whitespace
- Nice big text

Web 2.0 is more than just Ajax

Technological advances are exciting and tangible. If you're doing something new such as implementing drag and drop to add products to your shopping cart, you can see that and interact with it. It's something new, above and beyond what you used to do in the 1990s with Add to Cart and Check Out buttons (which are still widely used today—we're not knocking them). However, there is an intangible philosophical switch that's been welcomed in with Web 2.0, one of openness and sharing between companies, each other, and their users. This philosophy is, in turn, fueled by a number of technology advances such as blogs and wikis.

The desire to collaborate with others exposed a hole in current product offerings. People had been publishing personal websites with their own articles and opinions online for some time; however, for the most part, these people were just creating static pages. Something more was needed to allow for the level of dialogue that was desired. If you wanted to engage your website visitors in a dialogue, you would have to develop some kind of custom setup to do so.

A somewhat new trend started to emerge offering hosted applications so that even people with little technical knowledge could take advantage of the new applications. Some of these services (such as Blogger by Pyra Labs, now owned by Google) and "do-it-yourself" solutions (such as Moveable Type by Six Apart) hit the scenes allowing people to very easily set up their own weblog, complete with database back-end. The hosted services caught on with individuals who had very little technical knowledge but just wanted to publish their work. Moveable Type, and later WordPress (Figure 9-6), took hold amongst individuals with some technical knowledge and organizations that needed to host their own weblogs.

The market space for these applications became very intense as companies worked hard and quickly to release their products first. One of the big clichés of Web 2.0 was that every new service would launch with a "beta badge," a graphic in the corner touting that the product was still being tested, and users should proceed at their own risk. If you weren't "in beta," then clearly you had been around too long, and your idea just wasn't fresh enough. More often than not, these badges were superfluous, and the services themselves were perfectly stable and complete.

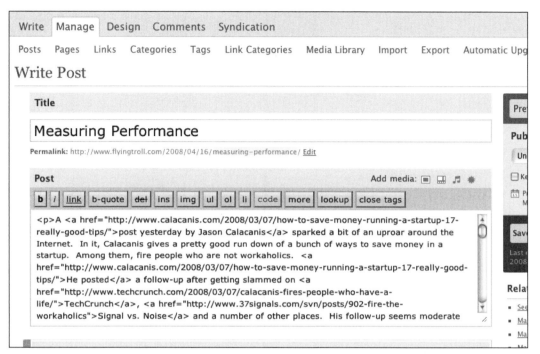

Figure 9-6. WordPress offers an easy-to-use administrative interface that allows users to very easily publish whatever they like online. Posts are displayed in reverse chronological order, are searchable, and are organized into categories or with tags.

Today, the "News" section on a number of corporate websites has been replaced by weblogs where employees post product updates and receive feedback instantly from their customers. Instead of formal press releases, a number of companies have opted for a much less formal route of simply blogging about company milestones or even opening up the product development process and letting customers interact at all stages of a product life cycle.

We've found it so incredibly easy to set up and customize a WordPress weblog that we'll often use one in any situation where we need to get a website online really quickly. If we've just registered a new domain but we're not ready to put the "real" website up yet, we'll drop in a WordPress installation just so that we can start communicating with visitors about what the eventual website will be. This serves a couple of purposes: visitors are presented with useful information upon arrival, and search engines can begin indexing the content of the website so that when the actual website or web app launches, it's already findable in Google.

Implications of social software

Social software, such as blogs and wikis, have brought about an era of collaboration online that was previously unheard of. In the 1990s, if you had suggested to anyone that they put up a website where anyone could come along and make an edit (which would be instantly published online), they would probably have laughed at you. Some organizations would have even balked at the idea of their own employees publicly publishing without some sort of editorial process. Today, however, entire websites exist that have been created by the community.

Wikipedia (Figure 9-7) is a prime example, where a community of users come together to post and edit articles about anything and everything. Wikipedia's goal is to "crowd-source" an alternative to the often very expensive encyclopedias available (which are frequently out-of-date in terms of current events by the time they go to press). Although the jury is still out in some circles, some preliminary studies have been conducted showing that Wikipedia is certainly more complete than any encyclopedia available and, in most cases, just as accurate.

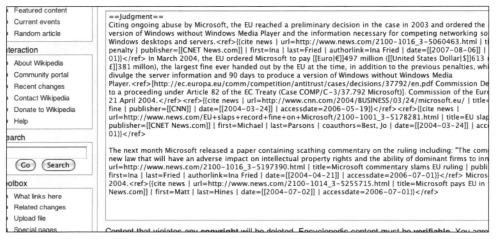
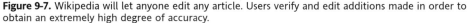

Figure 9-7. Wikipedia will let anyone edit any article. Users verify and edit additions made in order to obtain an extremely high degree of accuracy.

In business, social applications are being rolled out internally and externally throughout major corporations. A lot of companies have followed Wikipedia's example and have rolled their own internal wikis where company information is stored. They've found it to be the most efficient way to keep employees up-to-date on the latest company news, as well as changes to policies and procedures.

Another excellent example of a public social application is Digg.com, a website where the user community submits links and summaries to news stories, which are then voted on by the community. Through this system, the user community is able to tailor Digg.com to profile only the stories they find most interesting. This was not a completely original idea; the technology news site Slashdot.org had been doing something similar for a number of years prior to Digg.com's creation, but Digg.com took the idea mainstream.

Web 2.0 has sparked a craze as web developers scramble to add social features to their existing and new product offerings. There is no shortage of social networks that have emerged, allowing individuals with similar interests to connect with one another and share information within their interest-based communities. In fact, some would say that the idea of social networks has been overimplemented at this time, with niche communities popping up for everything.

APIs and syndication

For there to be a true openness, software has to work together and share data back and forth. One of the best features of weblogs, wikis, and a slew of other Web 2.0 applications is that along with publishing the content in HTML for people to absorb, they simultaneously publish an XML feed. These

Really Simple Syndication (RSS) feeds strip away all the formatting in a story and add a little more metadata to make things really easy for another computer to understand. Because of their structure, these feeds can then be consumed by other websites, remixed, and republished, making it easy for end users to receive all the information that interests them in one place (this type of setup is commonly referred to as an **aggregator**).

Not only does an XML feed of content make it easy to exchange information between applications, but it also makes information highly searchable. An XML feed contains highly concentrated information, which search engines love. In fact, once blogging started to really take off, Google had to adjust its page-ranking algorithm in order to balance out content in blogs with that published on other websites (blogs just started taking over).

Application programming interfaces (APIs) take things one step further by not only exposing the information of one website to another, but actually exposing the functionality. The big implication in this is that now information can flow both ways, instead of it just becoming a one-way producer/consumer type of setup. What this means is that now web applications can be written to work together, just like desktop applications. Data in one application can be created, modified, or deleted by another application. A great example, which has been done extensively, is to use the Google Maps API to tie maps in with street addresses or to generate directions from one location to another on the fly, based on data stored in an address book.

Building products based on products

APIs present an interesting opportunity to developers. They will actually let you build upon an existing product, giving you access to the underlying functionality of that product. So now, instead of rebuilding something from scratch, developers have the option of simply extending existing projects to suit their needs or the needs of their customers.

On the business side, there has been some work done in this arena with regard to project management/time tracking and invoicing applications. One product we discussed in Chapter 2, Basecamp, has an excellent API that a number of other products have tied into. Using the API, for example, you can import your clients and projects into other applications and create an invoice from a particular project's time tracking data (for example).

The possibilities really are limitless when you start looking at what you can accomplish. Instead of relying on a company to build in all of the features into a product that you could ever need, you can now take it upon yourself to extend products on your own. Products no longer need to be everything to everyone; instead, people can extend them to suit their own needs. External forms can be created for reporting bugs, uploading files, or tracking time.

We'll further illustrate what can be done with a project of our own that ties into Basecamp using its API. (Basecamp isn't the only product that offers an API, as you'll see in a second; it's just quite commonly used amongst business products.) We had become frustrated with the lack of a certain piece of functionality in Basecamp, and after poking around the 37signals (the company that makes Basecamp) forums, we discovered that we weren't the only ones.

Mailmanagr (http://mailmanagr.com) is an e-mail interface for Basecamp. It allows users to send e-mail to special addresses, which will then post content to the designated area of their Basecamp project. So, for example, a message can be added to the messages section of a Basecamp project by sending an e-mail to google-design-msg@mailmanagr.com.

This project emerged out of a function we needed (or wanted) as a Basecamp user. We have some clients who just prefer to use e-mail for communication, instead of logging into Basecamp to add messages and to-dos. In the past, we would have to take these messages and copy and paste them into Basecamp so that we could keep track of them—something that we didn't find to be a very efficient use of time.

From a mobile perspective, we find it far easier (and efficient) to send a mail message than to browse a website on a phone (even with an iPhone). We actually started to build an entire replacement for Basecamp that would address these shortcomings, before we stopped and realized that we could just add it. We're completely satisfied with everything else in this product, so why try to reproduce it just to add one feature? Instead of wasting our time rebuilding everything we were happy with, we could just take a shortcut and build this little piece.

At the time of this writing, Mailmanagr is still in development, but it should (at least) be available in beta by the time this book is published. Because so much of the work has already been done, we're finding it one of the easiest projects we've ever worked on—there is very little code that we actually have to write.

Increasingly, we're seeing a higher level of integration between products. This is a really exciting trend, because you'll see integration between web apps that you didn't always see between desktop applications. Because there are a set of standards to follow, web applications can all be made to speak the same language, breaking down barriers to interoperability and improving the user experience overall.

Blame Facebook

We'll be frank; as of late, we've been pretty unimpressed with Facebook because of its lack of interoperability with outside applications. It seems to be taking a very Web 1.0 approach of trying to get everyone to use "their Internet"; that is, if it doesn't exist within Facebook, it's not worth doing. That said, Facebook does have a very mature and well-documented API, probably one of the best online.

APIs existed long before Facebook, but the announcement of the Facebook Platform (Figure 9-8) really brought it to the forefront in the web community. Entire products and companies have been started in order to build Facebook applications—applications that could not exist without the underlying functionality provided by Facebook. Because Facebook has such a large user base, there is automatically a group of potential users to market to.

All of a sudden, aspiring social application developers, game developers, and companies looking to increase their exposure started developing Facebook applications as either stand-alone entities or to integrate with some external website. Box.net is a great example: it offers online file storage and sharing. Box.net developed a Box.net Facebook application to allow people to share files within their friend network. Not only is that a useful idea for users, but it increased Box.net's market share in a pretty competitive area (online file sharing).

While application developers are flocking to Facebook, we don't think that many are making much money. Facebook allows application developers to embed advertising within their apps but doesn't provide for a great way to target those ads (see the next section) and restricts things such as the type of JavaScript needed to use Google ads.

Figure 9-8. Facebook provides the documentation and the users; you provide the idea and programming savvy. Instant web application!

The mobile Web

Web 2.0 has also brought about a realistic mobile Web. During the 1990s, some attempts were made at producing handheld devices that could handle e-mail and web browsing, but for the most part, the bandwidth and device limitations at the time killed any chance of success. It isn't until very recently that the mobile Web has been brought to the forefront and people have gotten serious about developing applications that work well for cell phone/PDA users.

Research in Motion's BlackBerry did wonders for wireless e-mail, but it had little impact on the Web. The BlackBerry, as well as various devices from Palm, was equipped with a web browser that had such poor standards support (it couldn't handle JavaScript, for example) that doing anything other than basic browsing of content was nearly impossible. For this reason, the mobile market has been effectively ignored, especially amongst Flash websites and websites that degrade poorly in browsers with no JavaScript support. The two companies that have made huge progress in this space and have massively improved on browsers for mobile devices are Opera and Apple with the iPhone and mobile Safari.

Opera (Figure 9-9) supports a wide range of devices, from cell phones with tiny screens all the way to BlackBerry devices and desktop browsers. Opera has long been known for its excellent support of web standards and its work to promote interoperability. As we discussed in the introduction to this book, they have been relegated to a niche market on the desktop but have recently made huge in-roads by providing an exceptional web browser for nondesktop devices.

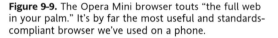

Figure 9-9. The Opera Mini browser touts "the full web in your palm." It's by far the most useful and standards-compliant browser we've used on a phone.

Apple flipped the entire mobile data market on its head by introducing a package that offered not only one of the best mobile web browsers available but also a device with a beautiful high-resolution screen and an easy-to-use interface.

Web 2.0 means business

As mentioned earlier, Web 2.0 ushered in a renewed focus on business, or, more specifically, on profitability. The "we'll make money from advertising by driving a ton of traffic to our website" model of Web 1.0 just didn't work out. Was the Web a complete failure as an advertising medium?

Targeted and contextual advertising

A lot of people think that Google has become what it is today because it's so successful at providing search. Although its search engine is an excellent application, it doesn't generate much money by itself (you can buy Google search to use within your company for private documents, but that business hasn't made Google billions of dollars). What's made Google so successful financially is its introduction of targeted and contextual advertising online.

If you, once again, take a step back into the 1990s, advertisers were quickly losing faith in the Web as an advertising medium. They just weren't making any sales off the leads that web ads were generating, combined with the fact that people were increasingly ignoring ads or installing software to block online advertising. The solution that developers proposed was to make ads larger and more intrusive—let's use Flash and have it open full screen in a new window!

As you can imagine, this only frustrated Internet users more, and an arms race began between online advertisers and web users (a race that really did nothing to improve the bottom line). Similar to the earlier discussion of design, search engines became the worst offenders, paving the way for Google to take over. What made search engines so bad was that anytime someone would search for a particular topic, search engines would insert random advertising throughout search results, occasionally disguised as relevant search results. Although this increased the number of "click-throughs" they would get for a particular advertiser, people weren't very inclined to buy anything once they got there.

Google turned this all around by eliminating the annoying, in-your-face advertising techniques and insisting instead on using text ads (Figure 9-10). What improved the effectiveness for Google was that it targeted its advertising based on search queries, or the content of a particular web page. Now, if people were searching for cars, they would be presented with ads relevant to purchasing a car (or at least automobile accessories). As you can imagine, having an ad that is relevant to what an individual is looking for at the time is far more effective in making a sale than just a random "in-your-face" pop-up.

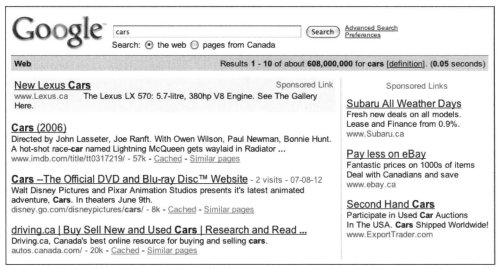

Figure 9-10. Searching for cars gives you ads for Subaru, Lexus, and a couple of websites advertising used car sales.

The long tail

One of the major business concepts introduced in Web 2.0 is that of "the long tail." Chris Anderson, editor-in-chief at *Wired* magazine, wrote an entire book on the topic (and coined the term). The gist of the long tail is that there is huge demand for what's hot at the moment, but that demand tapers off as new fads are introduced. In the past, that would mean sales would just die off for a certain product, and it would stop being produced. Eventually, people would forget it existed as they moved on to newer and more readily available things.

The long tail describes the shape of a graph as you plot sales on the vertical vs. time on the horizontal. Sales of a recording artist's new album, for example, will be really strong as their record label invests a lot of time and money into promoting them. Over time, however, those sales will drop off

283

until they reach almost zero. It's unlikely that they'll ever completely bottom out, because there is such a large consumer base with such varied tastes that someone will still be buying their music 50 years from now.

Music is a really interesting and relevant example of the long tail, because in the past, the continued sales of a particular artist depended heavily on whether music stores were willing to devote shelf space to those artists, even though they may sell only a couple of copies a month. With the introduction of online stores such as Apple iTunes, shelf space is no longer a consideration. An artist can remain in stock forever. It's thought that a number of "knowledge-based" products will eventually move this way. We're starting to see an increasing number of e-books available, as well as online movie and TV rentals.

Social features in business

Availability is just one piece of the puzzle, though. People still need a way to discover this content. One of the greatest boons to online business has been the creation of recommendation systems, also known as **personalization** systems, fueled by customer data mining. The basic idea behind this is that one customer may buy an album from the group Nickelback and also purchase an album from the group Theory of a Dead Man. Because it's generally assumed that people have somewhat specific preferences (most people aren't nuts about gangster rap, heavy metal, and opera, for example), it can be assumed these two music acts are somehow related. Based on sales data that websites such as Amazon build up about you and about people who make purchases similar to the ones you've made, it can then personalize your shopping experience by offering you products in which you may be interested.

When these albums are both purchased by the same person, a linkage is made between them so that the next person who visits the online store, who knows only about Nickelback (and not Theory of a Dead Man), will be presented with the information that "People who bought this album (Nickelback) also bought this album (Theory of a Dead Man)." That will likely tweak their curiosity, and they'll be inclined to try Theory of a Dead Man as well.

Try it for yourself! Head over to Amazon.com and try searching for one of your favorite recording artists. Click through to the product page of one of their albums and check out the "People who bought this album" section to see whether you recognize any of the other acts listed. If none of them is familiar to you, you may want to check them out; go listen to the previews of some of their songs at the iTunes music store. We'd be willing to bet that you discover a new artist (or two) that you like.

What does the future hold?

Really, the sky is the limit. There is some discussion taking place right now as to whether web applications are likely to replace desktop applications entirely. Wireless Internet access is becoming more widely available, and storing your documents on some central server gives you additional peace of mind if your computer is ever lost, damaged, or stolen. In storing information centrally, it's easier to share with other people and keep everyone up-to-date on the latest developments.

A number of companies are working on solutions so that their online applications can also be used offline for a period of time. Google has recently rolled out the ability to work on Google Documents offline and then sync up any changes you've made when you next reconnect to the Internet. A number of blog clients have existed for some time allowing bloggers to author posts offline and then publish them once they are next online.

A short time ago, common consensus was that it's completely reasonable to expect applications such as word processors and spreadsheets to move off the desktop and to go online. It was thought that there would always need to be desktop applications for things such as image editing, movie editing, and 3D rendering. However, even today, inroads are being made into each of those areas.

In terms of social features, the next logical step we see is for Google (or one of its competitors) to release personalized search based on a recommendation system similar to those you find on e-commerce websites. Google already maintains a history of what you search for when you're logged in (unless you turn it off). It's a small step to start tracking the links you visit and then to start displaying more links like that near the top of your search results. Tie this in with a social network to harness the data of your friends/associates, and you're looking at a really interesting (or privacy-invading) application.

Profiling Professions: Chris Messina

Chris Messina is one of those people who could write the book on collaboration. In fact, the mission of his San Francisco–based company, Citizen Agency, is to "change the world through empowering individuals. We believe in architecting for collaboration, not merely participation."

Citizen Agency helps companies build communities around their offerings and play an active role in those communities. Chris, personally, is involved in advocating for the use of open technologies, open standards, and interoperability.

Lane: What is your role at Citizen Agency, and what does that translate to in terms of day-to-day activities?

Messina: Well, I'm the owner of the company, but there's only two of us, so we split up our duties accordingly. My background and experience lends itself to strategy and product development; Tara tends toward research and marketing. In terms of day-to-day stuff, well, it's a lot of teasing out what's going on out in the wild and seeing opportunities for clients, for making connections, for seeing bigger pictures that we can get involved with and help shape. There's a lot of instinct involved, not a whole lot of science. This industry is changing constantly, so we've gotta keep on our toes!

Lane: Citizen Agency is about collaboration and developing communities. Could you walk us through an example project (or a hypothetical project) and what your involvement would be?

Messina: Hmm. Well, an example might be Songbird, an open source media browser. We've worked with them for some time to consider how they both get themselves out there but, more important, how they join existing conversations. Or where those conversations need stoking, we light a fire.

Consider the Open Media Web initiative (http://openmediaweb.org). We had no idea what CEO Rob Lord was talking about and felt that a wider audience would have even less an idea of what he was so excited about . . . so we kicked off a conversation with a series of meetups and interviews and have been working on building up awareness of the topic, essentially asking people what it means to them, in their own words, so that as we move forward. It's not just a marketing pitch but something that people actually care about and identify with.

Our work is bringing people together, framing the discussion, bringing in the right experienced folks, and then rebroadcasting to expand the number of folks involved in the Big Idea.

Lane: What is your background (education, work/volunteer experience) that led you to what you're doing today?

Messina: Personally my background is communication design—a fancy kind of graphic design where computers and humans are involved. But I also did some volunteer work at the ACLU in Pittsburgh helping out as a volunteer observer and watching interactions between police and protesters. It's not that that was a formative experience or anything, but democracy, as represented through *accessible* forms of technology, is important to me.

Lane: If there were one thing about the Internet that you could change (or add/remove), what would it be?

Messina: Spam. Then again, the human body is made stronger through susceptibility to the common cold, so I'm somewhat reluctant to say even that.

Lane: You were heavily involved with Spread Firefox. Could you share with us some of the considerations and process you went through when working on that project?

Messina: Man, well, first of all, I had no idea what I was doing or what the stakes were, but I knew that Firefox was important and that, as a web designer, web standards were important. I knew that I certainly couldn't speak for everyone (or even most people), so we instead focused on giving people the mouthpieces to speak for themselves. I've continued with that tradition in trying to find ways to allow individuals to feel more direct ownership of the projects I'm involved in . . . typically in simple or small ways, but that end up being very effective.

Otherwise, it was just building focal points through which we pushed the massive amount of energy being generated by the grassroots Firefox community looking to bash the f**k out of Internet Explorer.

Don't mess with the Internet, or you'll get screwed!

Lane: You're one of the biggest advocates around of open source, open formats, and working with standards. Why do you think that using existing standards and formats is so important, and what advantage is there over developing your own?

Messina: I don't think I'm the biggest, but it is important to me. And I think that's because I recognize the enormous amount of privilege that I've grown up with as a white male in America. No really—open data, open formats . . . all the rest are ideally a way of pushing for the distribution of opportunity and allowing people to get involved or to innovate without paying the incumbents a tax. It keeps us honest, and it leads to distributed innovation. Given how far technology has to go before it's generally usable by regular folks, I think that's a good thing!

Lane: How do you keep up with industry news and advances? Any favorite sources of information you'd like to share?

Messina: I hate to say this, but Techmeme. I left it awhile back because of the echo-chamber effect, but damn, it's good to know what's going on. Otherwise, it's all about Twitter.

Lane: What advice do you have for people just getting started in working with the Web today?

Messina: Hmm. Well, I guess I'd say pursue things that you're passionate about and that you can talk about nonstop, 24/7. If you're just trying to get famous or make a lot of money, you'll probably fail. If you can infect other people and help make them care, you have a shot, so starting with your passion is key.

Lane: What do you see as the biggest advantage and the biggest disadvantage to working with the Web?

Messina: Being online all the time is pretty amazing. The kind of access you have to people is enormous, new, and powerful. At the same time, you're online all the time. I'm struggling to find that ripe balance between being on and off, and it's "effin" hard with an iPhone, with wifi, with e-mail everywhere . . . so I'm reminding myself of what's important and that disconnecting every now and then is actually a good thing—if not an obligatory thing to make time for.

Lane: Where do you see things going with the Web in the next couple of years? What are you most excited about?

Messina: Well, I think distributed social networking and a "middle class" of web applications is going to grow up and grow into mainstream adoption. This requires a clearer sense and provisioning of identity on the Web, so we're hard at work at that. But as far as I'm concerned, it's not OpenSocial and it's not Facebook; it's the open Web striking its revenge on closed or semiopen but proprietary systems.

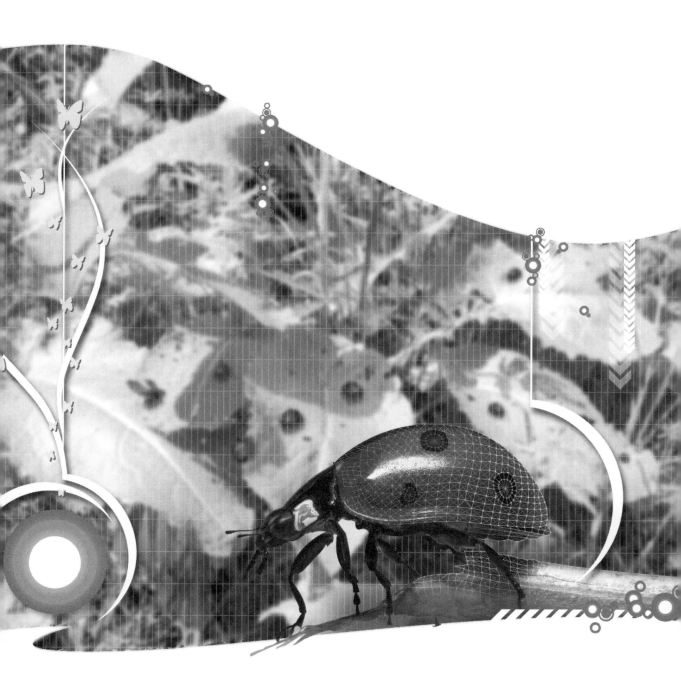

Chapter 10

USING SERVER-SIDE TECHNOLOGIES

It's pretty hard to find a website these days that doesn't use some kind of server-side scripting and database. So many different options are available, from commercial products to open source products, that it can be really daunting to decide which direction you want to go. In the case of web servers, web scripting languages, and databases, the open source alternatives are just as good (and in some cases even better than) the commercial options.

This chapter isn't going to walk you through the syntax of each of the various languages, and it isn't an instruction manual about how to set up and configure your servers. It is a guide to some of the different options available, as well as an explanation of the differences between the various products.

Occasionally, you'll have your choice of server technologies, and other times you will be required to use what's already in place. A lot of web scripting languages are reasonably easy to pick up for technically minded individuals. The best thing you can do is get some background in software design and programming (any introduction to programming course will do) just so that you know the basics of if-then-else, functions, and loops.

The server side removes barriers

In the early days of the World Wide Web, there was the saying that "content is king." Although that's still true today, visitors expect more from the Web than just a passive experience. Putting up a static page with some interesting text and a pretty picture just isn't enough anymore; end users expect interaction. News websites are a prime example of this evolution: readers are encouraged to discuss topics inline with the stories. Client-side scripting (JavaScript) just isn't enough anymore. To store input and interact with diverse data sources, websites have turned to server-side technologies.

JavaScript is limited in what it can accomplish, largely because of security concerns. Would you feel safe running an application on the Web that had free reign of your hard drive? How would you like a website that's capable of reading and writing any file on your hard drive? Some people think that JavaScript already has too much power, so the option exists within browsers to disable it. As a developer, you need to have confidence that what you've built will be able to run for everyone.

Web servers: dishing out hypertext

The web server along with the web browsers are the bare essentials of the World Wide Web. Web servers are computers that are constantly (we hope!) connected to the Internet, and they host websites. They respond to HTTP requests from browsers, serving a whole host of different types of files that reside online. Web servers are the front line in any website, handling requests by either filling them or passing them off to a web application server to dish up dynamic content.

As with everything in this chapter, you have a whole host of options available in web servers, and the best part is that most of them are free. Some servers are designed for specific purposes: lighttpd is a speed demon that is great at serving static content. Mongrel was developed specifically for serving Ruby on Rails applications. Others, like Apache, are generalists that can be easily extended through a series of modules.

Apache HTTP server

Apache is the reigning champion online and has been since 1996. It is an extremely popular web server that runs on virtually every operating system imaginable. (You can even run Apache on an iPhone!) There are a number of reasons for its success, but probably paramount is that it's reasonably fast, secure, and extensible.

Apache supports a module architecture where functionality can be added by loading new modules when the server starts . Because of this functionality, things like PHP are easy to add; instead of having to run a separate application server, PHP can be parsed directly through Apache, which makes things faster and easier to administer.

Microsoft Internet Information Services (IIS)

If Apache is the reigning champion, then Microsoft IIS is the first runner-up. Microsoft introduced its web server running on the Windows operating system in the mid-1990s. It gained popularity primarily because it was easy to configure and set up in comparison to Apache's command line and text file configuration mechanism (for some strange reason, people like their graphical user interfaces). IIS got quite a bad reputation in the beginning because early versions were full of security holes, opening up the entire machine to an industrious hacker and even launching self-propagating worms, which could then attack other IIS servers. One of the most notorious, Code Red, at its peak infected an estimated 360,000 IIS web servers and caused a noticeable degradation in network speed worldwide.

IIS has been growing in popularity as it's matured into a more secure and stable hosting environment. Today, it's estimated that IIS serves just less than 50 percent of the websites online today. Microsoft has bundled in its scripting language, Active Server Pages (ASP), into IIS, making it really easy to develop dynamic websites on the Windows platform.

lighttpd

A few years ago, Apache and IIS would be the only two web servers worth mentioning in terms of market share, but lately there have been some new servers that have seen increased use. One of the big players is lighttpd (Figure 10-1), which is a super-streamlined web server used for serving really large files. It doesn't have the flexibility of Apache or IIS, but it has discovered a niche in that it can serve data at much higher speeds.

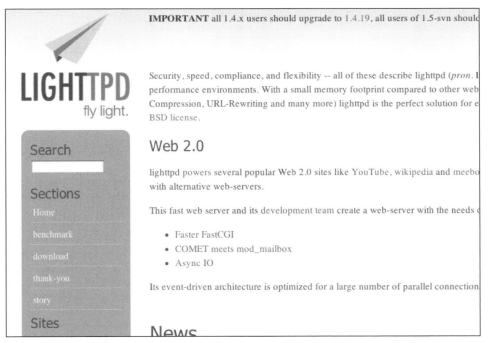

Figure 10-1. lighttpd is gaining a foothold in Web 2.0 as larger, more flexible servers are traded in for smaller, faster, single-purpose servers.

Websites such as YouTube use lighttpd to serve their movie files, and some of the largest BitTorrent tracker websites (including the infamous The Pirate Bay) use lighttpd for serving up their static content (such as `.torrent` files).

Web servers rarely ever do the heavy lifting on a dynamic website or web application. That job is usually handled by a web application server, which handles the process of talking to databases and constructing content on the fly.

Mongrel

A little later in this chapter, you'll read about frameworks and why they're taking off in popularity. Leading the framework pack is Ruby on Rails, and Mongrel is a web server developed specifically for dishing out Rails applications. Mongrel is the uncontested leader in terms of speed, scalability, and stability in serving Rails applications, because it supports Ruby natively; other web servers deal with it via a module that executes Ruby code as a common gateway interface (CGI) script.

A wide range of hosting options

We're at a really great time for web development right now. The cost to host a website is falling, and it's easier than ever to outsource your hosting needs to a third party. If you're working for a big organization, chances are that they'll be running their own servers for web hosting. Smaller organizations and individuals will often opt for a hosting company, though. Running a server takes a lot of skill and resources: it has to be connected to the Internet with a fast connection (that DSL line you have at home just won't cut it), it should be backed up regularly, and it should be kept in a secure place, especially if you're storing customers' personal or financial information in a database. Not to mention, how many people have a diesel backup generator in case of power failure?

You should look at a number of different options when you're picking a company to host your website. Obviously, the features/application support will be a big one; if you've written a Ruby on Rails application, you'll need a server that supports Rails. Other considerations to take into account are bandwidth, disk space, machine specs, technical support, and an uptime guarantee.

Most hosting plans will give you a set amount of bandwidth every month. This is usually measured in the gigabytes of data transferred, but larger-capacity hosting plans may offer terabytes of bandwidth (1,000 gigabytes). You'll see a few different options in terms of types of plans offered, ranging from shared hosting to dedicated hosts. A shared host is exactly that: you're sharing the machine that hosts your website with other customers. If one of those other customers has a particularly high-traffic website or does something that locks up the server, your website will also be affected. Although that's not the end of the world for your personal weblog, a company that conducts business online may have a lower tolerance for frequent or extended outages.

The next step up from a shared host is a virtual machine. Virtualization software is special software that will let you run multiple operating systems, or multiple copies of the same operating system, off a single machine. If you're on a Mac and have ever used VMware Fusion or Parallels to run Windows, you're using virtualization software. The big advantage to a virtual machine over shared hosting is that each hosting account is housed within its own container. So although all customers on a single machine are sharing that machine's resources, each container is isolated from each other. If customer X does something that locks up their virtual machine, none of the other virtual machines on that computer will be affected. The added benefit from this is that because customers are isolated from one another, hosting companies are often willing to let customers have more control over their own account, such as install software and reconfigure system and server settings to optimize performance.

The final option is dedicated hosting where you get your own machine, hosted by some other company. This has all the advantages of virtual machine hosting, plus you don't have to worry about sharing resources (RAM, CPU, bandwidth) with other customers. Shared hosting is by far the cheapest option, whereas dedicated hosting will cost you a few hundred dollars a month (or more).

Picking the level of plan isn't that hard. Start with the least that you think you can get away with and then upgrade as you go. Most hosting companies are more than happy to let you upgrade your plan at any time; it means they get to charge a higher monthly premium! There's no point buying dedicated hosting for that application you're developing if you're not sure whether you're ever going to have more than a dozen users.

Picking a host can be really difficult, though. If you just look at ratings and reviews online, you'll never be able to find one. Every host has glowingly positive reviews and absolute horror stories posted about them. Your best bet is to ask around to friends, co-workers, and other professionals to see whether they have any recommendations for you.

Databases for web geeks

We recently posted a question on a blog asking people how they would describe a database to some-body who has absolutely no knowledge of computers. The common consensus was that people would use the analogy of a file cabinet, with database tables being file folders and the individual papers within those folders being records. It's not a bad analogy until you try to explain all the other parts associated with a database setup—things such as primary keys, foreign keys, relationships, and, of course, Structured Query Language (SQL).

Terminology

The field of database management systems is rife with all kinds of technical terms and acronyms. Here's a quick guide to some of the most common terms:

- A **database** is a collection of data structured into records within tables. It might help to think of the difference between a relational database management system (RDBMS) and a database in these terms: the RDBMS is similar to a web server, whereas a database is similar to all the pages available on that server (except in a far more structured way).

- A **field**, sometimes also referred to as a **column**, is a single piece of information contained within a record. Mary's phone number would be stored in a field in a database. All records within a single table will have identical fields.

- A **foreign key** is the special piece of information that relates a record in one table to a record in another table. The foreign key in one table will refer to the primary key in another table.

- A **primary key** is a special field within a table that uniquely identifies a record. In its most basic form, this could be a simple integer that increments by one for every record added. The rea-son tables have primary keys is so that each record can be uniquely addressed if changes need to be made to it. For example, I might have a table that contains a log of people buying things on a gift card. This log might list that "Ron" bought "1 cup coffee" every day for a month. If that's all it lists and (for some reason) you have to go in and say that he didn't, in fact, buy every seventh cup of coffee, you would have no way of addressing those particular records.

- A **record**, sometimes also referred to as a **row**, is a grouping of similar pieces of data. So for example, a set of contact information for your friend Mary would be a single record.

- A **relational database** is a database system in which information stored in different tables can be related to each other. You might use this if, for example, you were storing business contacts. Chances are that you know a few different people at a single company; instead of storing that company name 3, 10, or 50 different times in the record for each person, you could create a companies table and then just relate each person to the appropriate row in the companies table. The big advantage here is if the company gets bought out and changes its name from Acme Corp. to Wonderwhizz Inc., you need to change that name in a single location only.

- **Relational database management systems** are applications such as MySQL and Oracle, which are commonly (and incorrectly) referred to as *databases*. These applications are actually RDBMSs, the software that interacts with a database.

- A **schema** is the structure of the database, including the tables, fields, and any relations between tables.

- **Structured Query Language (SQL)** is a standardized language developed specifically for interacting with relational databases. SQL lets you add, remove, update, and query data. There are small variations in SQL syntax from one database system to the next; but for the most part, once you have the basics of SQL mastered, you'll be able to work with practically any database system out there.

- A **table** is a collection of records within a database. For example, you might have a table for "contact information" in which you list the addresses and phone numbers of a number of different people.

The world outside relational databases

A lot of the terminology covered previously is specific to relational databases. Most DBMSs available today are relational, because it's frequently advantageous to design your database schema in a relational manner in order to avoid duplication of information. But RDBMSs aren't the only game in town. There are a couple of other types of databases that you may run into online, so it's worth mentioning them here.

Object databases

Object databases aren't too common outside of very specific scientific applications. There is a very common and popular content management framework called Zope that uses an object database, however. The Zope Object Database (ZODB) is ideal in its application because it supports versioning natively, allowing someone to undo a change made on the website.

XML databases

XML is widely used online for data exchange between websites/web applications, but it's also an effective way of storing data. Occasionally this term will be used for referring to XML data stored within an RDBMS, but there are native XML databases that exist.

The biggest advantage to storing data in XML format is that XML is widely used for data exchange. Because of this, there doesn't need to be any conversion of data to/from XML, which saves on processing "costs" (that is, the server doesn't have a bunch of extra operations to perform).

XML databases store data in nodes, which is the correct term for data arranged within a hierarchical structure of XML tags. Instead of using SQL to query an XML database, two forms of querying syntax are widely in use: XPath and XQuery (which is just an extension of XPath). Each provides a way to extract data from an XML database by providing a syntax for addressing each of the databases' nodes.

Relational databases

A relational database simply means that data in one table can be joined (or related) to data in another table through the use of keys. Relational databases strive to normalize data, that is, to eliminate any duplication of data. Normalized data is a good thing: if there is duplication of data within a database, the chance exists for there to be a data anomaly, that is, when the two pieces of data become out of sync.

For example, if you were developing an online store with a series of products, chances are you would have a table listing each of those products along with their price and description. Occasionally, you want to be able to offer certain items on sale by marking them down 15 percent. Instead of creating a table of sale items and duplicating the product names, descriptions, and prices there, you would simply relate to the original products table. That way, if a product's price changes, it needs to be updated in only one place.

Structured Query Language (SQL)

There are four main types of interactions you'll have with databases using SQL: SELECTs for getting data out of a database, INSERTs for adding data to a database, UPDATEs for changing data in a database, and DELETEs for removing data.

Getting data out

What good is creating a database of information if you can never get anything out of it? If you return to the original file cabinet analogy, being able to find specific data within a database is the single biggest advantage over the old paper-based alternative.

How often have you looked at a big stack of papers and thought to yourself "Gee, I wish I could just run Google on that"? (OK, so it might just be us.) If you boil it down, though, search engines are really just great big databases full of information about the information on the Web. Every time you run a search on Google, you're running a query on a database.

In SQL terms, that query looks something like this:

```
SELECT url
FROM websites
WHERE content = "that thing I'm looking for"
```

If you dissect that statement, it's actually pretty easy to read. You're asking for the URL field from the websites table. Instead of just returning all the URLs stored in the table, you're narrowing the search down and getting only the URLs where the content field has that thing I'm looking for as the value.

There are a bunch of other options we could throw in here, such as an ORDER BY to sort the results or an INNER JOIN in order to relate the data from this table to the data stored in another table.

Putting data in

Your database would get stale pretty quickly if you couldn't add new information as it became available. SQL uses an INSERT to do this:

```
INSERT INTO websites (url, content)
VALUES ("http://www.amazon.com", ➡
"A really big store that sells a bunch of stuff")
```

Again, breaking this down, you're adding a record to the websites table. We've specified two fields in this table, url and content, and given them both values. Depending on how the table is set up, there may be other fields in the table that you haven't specified, but when you're creating a table, you have to go out of your way to specify that a field can have a NULL value; otherwise, running this SQL will give you an error.

Changing data

Shoot, that last addition we made makes it sound like Amazon is actually a store, located somewhere. We had better change the content field to clear that up:

```
UPDATE websites SET
content = "A e-commerce website that sells a wide range of products"
WHERE url = "http://www.amazon.com"
```

The first part of this SQL statement should speak for itself at this point. You're updating the websites table and setting the content field to have a better description. The last part (after WHERE) is the interesting part. You need to have some way to tell the RDBMS which record you want to update. In this case, you've done that with the URL field, but this could backfire on you. If there were more than one record with http://www.amazon.com listed as the URL, all those records would be updated as well. The flip side is that you may have specified that the URL, in fact, is the primary key, in which case there could not be multiple Amazon.com records listed. You would get an error if you tried to insert another one.

Removing data

Websites come and go. Although it's not likely that you'll be removing Amazon from your database for that reason, you have noticed that your favorite store for buying lawn gnomes is now offline. You had best keep things up-to-date:

```
DELETE FROM websites
WHERE url = "http://www.ultimatelawngnomes.com"
```

It's a nice, simple statement to remove ultimatelawngnomes.com from the database. The same caution applies with deleting records as does with updating records. You should try, whenever possible, to specify the primary key in the WHERE statement so as to limit your deletes to the actual record you intend to delete. In this example, it would be OK, because even if you had multiple records for ultimatelawngnomes.com and the site really had gone offline, you would probably want to eliminate all records. On the other hand, going into the HR database of a large company and running a DELETE on all records where the last name of the person is Smith may not be the best idea (that's why a lot of companies have employee ID numbers).

Your best bet for learning more about SQL is to check out http://www.w3schools.com/sql/. The site has a pretty good set of introductory lessons to SQL. If you get further into databases, be sure to check out the documentation specific to your RDBMS because it might have some specific functions that can save you time and significantly speed up your website.

A look at the RDBMS players

There are literally hundreds of different database systems, all great at different things. The ones listed in the following sections are the most common, so you're likely to run into them at some point when developing a website. We have limited the field here to database servers, so applications such as Microsoft Access didn't make the cut; although you could use Microsoft Access as the back-end for a website (we have before), it doesn't scale really well because it doesn't handle concurrent users all that efficiently. If you're comfortable with Microsoft products, you're better off upgrading to Microsoft Access's big brother—Microsoft SQL Server.

Oracle

The longtime heavyweight in the database world and reigning champ is definitely Oracle. Chances are really good that if you have a large organization running a database, that database will be Oracle. Having been around since the late 1970s, Oracle is a tested and proven solution for storing and retrieving large quantities of data (it's also the most expensive option available). Oracle is well known for its ability to handle extremely large data sets and to work with them in a fairly efficient manner (meaning running a query on a million records isn't a daylong activity).

Microsoft SQL Server (MSSQL)

Microsoft introduced a commercial RDBMS to try to compete with Oracle. Early on, it just wasn't up to snuff at handling large amounts of data, and it experienced a few security vulnerabilities. It's fair to say that because of its rocky start, Microsoft hasn't really made a dent in the market that Oracle addresses (really big databases/applications), but it's still a pretty big player in medium-sized applications. Those customers who need an Oracle-sized system will still buy Oracle. Those who think that would be overkill will generally either go with Microsoft or go with one of the open source alternatives.

MySQL

MySQL is the most popular open source database system available. It gained a great deal of popularity early on because it was really fast compared to PostgreSQL and it worked amazingly well for web applications. A number of large Internet companies have skipped the Oracle bandwagon altogether and have invested heavily in MySQL as their primary RDBMS.

Even though the software is open source, there is still a commercial company behind MySQL so that if a company wants to use it, they'll have someone to lean on for support. MySQL AB (the company behind MySQL) was recently purchased by Sun Microsystems, a hardware and software company that has been around for quite some time.

One of the big reasons for MySQL's popularity amongst open source RDBMSs is that a number of excellent front-ends are available. phpMyAdmin is an interface written entirely in PHP, and it's hosted online, which allows developers to create, delete, and modify databases and tables within MySQL.

MySQL AB has released a number of GUI tools for Windows, Linux, and Mac OS X that eases development and server administration. Figure 10-2 shows an excellent commercially available front-end editor, Navicat.

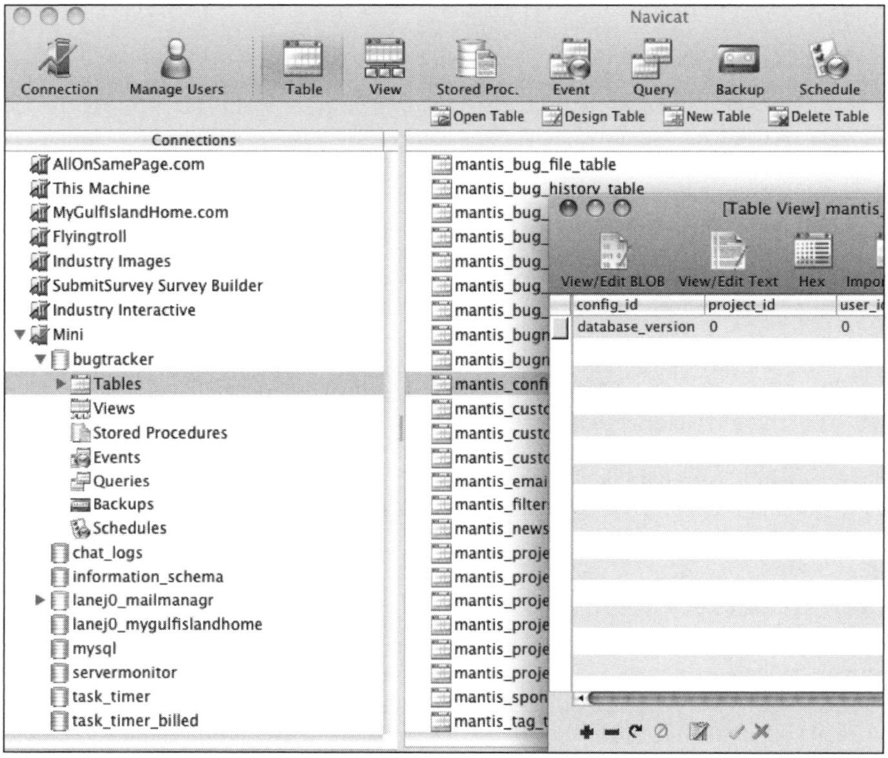

Figure 10-2. Navicat is another popular, commercially available front-end for MySQL that enables developers to quickly build and modify databases.

PostgreSQL

PostgreSQL is another excellent open source RDBMS that is completely driven and maintained by the user community. A couple of companies provide commercial support for PostgreSQL, but they are only peripherally involved in the continued development and evolution of the software (they're members of the user community, just like everybody else).

PostgreSQL's biggest selling point is that it's quite Oracle-like in the way it works and in its syntax subtleties. Therefore, companies that are looking for open source alternatives to try to rid themselves of the burden of high Oracle licensing fees will often look to PostgreSQL because it's the path of least resistance.

Other data sources

We talked a lot in the previous chapter about interoperability and sharing data between different websites and web applications. This is generally accomplished using XML, but there's a couple of other terms and acronyms that you should probably be aware of when discussing data exchange:

- **Web services** are software systems that allow for computer-to-computer interaction over the Web (not necessarily involving the interaction of a person). It's a general term that can be used to refer to something as complex as an API or something as simple as an RSS feed from a weblog.

- **SOAP** is a protocol for exchanging XML messages over the Web (using HTTP or HTTPS).

- A **remote procedure call (RPC)** is a way of having one computer initiate a procedure on another computer without having the details of this interaction explicitly programmed. So, in other words, RPC is a way of getting another computer on the network to do something and return a result to your computer. Most commonly on the World Wide Web, RPC will be used in conjunction with XML for data exchange between machines (XML-RPC).

- An **application programming interface (API)** is a series of "hooks" built in to an application that allows external access to the application's data and functionality.

One of the best things about developing applications for the Web is that there is already a wide array of data repositories available to tie in to your application. It's easy to integrate input from your users with map data available from Google and housing information stored in a database, as some realtors are now doing.

Web application languages

Similar to this look at databases, you'll find a world of options in web application languages. These are commonly called **scripting languages**, or **server-side scripting languages** to be more precise. Each of the options uses a different syntax, but at the end of the day, they all pretty much do the same thing. Some may have certain strengths over others, but when it comes to small to medium-sized web applications, you really won't notice a huge difference in performance between any of the players.

If you're just starting out and you're not sure what language is best to pick up, we recommend sticking to PHP. It's free and is widely used, and PHP hosting plans are offered for next to nothing from a wide range of companies. Whatever you pick, don't sweat your decision too much. We have one friend who's a brilliant Python programmer and complains a great deal about the lack of job postings for Python developers. The fact of the matter is that knowing Python, he can easily pick up any number of other languages and be proficient in a matter of weeks (and he has for various projects).

PHP

By far the most popular scripting language on the Web amongst developers is PHP, which is free and is often installed with the Apache web server (the most common web server on the Web). PHP was designed to be a scripting language for the Web, so it focuses a great deal on the needs of web developers.

Chances are that if you've downloaded an open source web application (such as WordPress, Drupal, or PHPBB), the tool is written in PHP. PHP is widely used amongst open source web application developers, because it is often self-contained; end users don't have to install a bunch of other software in order to get things working. To install a PHP application, it's usually as easy as uploading the files to your web host, creating a database, and editing a configuration file (of course, depending on the application, your mileage may vary). Organizations of all sizes have rolled out PHP-based applications in some capacity (Figure 10-3).

Figure 10-3. Drupal is an excellent open source content management system built with PHP. Even big companies such as SonyBMG are starting to see the benefits of using free software for their online applications.

PHP is a great starting point for people wanting to learn web application development. Because it's free, anyone can download a copy and install it on their own web server (if you don't feel like spending a few bucks for a hosting plan). PHP got a bit of a reputation for having security problems early on, which has prevented its adoption in a lot of large organizations, but that's definitely starting to change. Organizations we know that had previously never touched PHP are rolling out redesigns of their corporate websites using PHP-based content management systems.

Ruby

Ruby is a computer language that has been around since 1993, but it previously was not considered a strong contender for developing web applications. It's only with the introduction of the Ruby on Rails framework (discussed in a moment) that Ruby has joined the mainstream for web application development.

The jury is still out on whether Ruby is ready for the mainstream Web. Personally, we think that its use in some very large-scale applications (Basecamp, Twitter, Yellowpages.com) speaks for itself. Ruby, when used in Ruby on Rails, is the fastest growing web-programming language of the past three years. Developers are tired of having to repeatedly develop the same "type" of application and have turned to Ruby on Rails to streamline the process.

You'll probably see Ruby on Rails slowly sneak into big companies as developers try it and develop internal applications with it. We can't see Rails' use decreasing any time soon, and it's more than likely to continue to steal market share as companies search for faster, more agile ways to develop web applications.

Python

Python, similar to Ruby, has been in existence since the early 1990s, but it's not until recently that it has been adopted as a web application language in the mainstream. Zope, which is an excellent open source web application server intended for content management purposes, is the largest user of Python.

Python is a little bit of an odd-man-out in web application development. It's a great, fully featured language, but for whatever reason, it's not really in the mainstream. It has gotten a little traction lately amongst small web startups because it doesn't have the bad reputation brought about by PHP's security issues early on.

ASP (.NET)

Active Server Pages is the Microsoft-centric solution to web application development. The biggest advantage to ASP is that it integrates well with other Microsoft offerings; users can be authenticated off Active Directory servers easily, for example. ASP has been around for quite some time and is available not only on Microsoft IIS servers. Sun Microsystems makes a server product that allows ASP to run on a variety of different operating systems including its own Solaris and Linux.

Java/JSP

Java/JavaServer Pages (JSP) were quite popular during the first web boom in the 1990s and have somewhat died off since. Java was a quite common skill for developers during the dot-com boom but is pretty onerous to use for developing web applications. JSP didn't die out because it lacked functionality or because it was inferior technology, but rather because development cycles took too long. We don't mean for it to sound like we're ringing the death bell for JSP—it's still used in a number of enterprises, but you don't see many startups choosing JSP for their applications these days.

ColdFusion

ColdFusion is a commercial web application server produced by Adobe. It has a syntax that is similar to HTML, and it uses CFML tags and attributes to specify functionality. It's because of this that we've found ColdFusion to be extremely easy to learn and an excellent starting point for people wanting to learn web application development. There is excellent documentation and books available to get you up to speed quickly.

ColdFusion has, historically, been widely used in commercial websites but has seen a decline in recent years as open source scripting languages have increased in quality and popularity. It's hard to justify spending $1,000 for a web application server when you can have the same functionality for free using one of the many alternatives. ColdFusion is used heavily still in intranet development because it has built-in support for a wide array of database management systems as well as products such as Microsoft Exchange (which is used for e-mail/calendaring in a number of large corporations).

Frameworks

A framework is one step above a web application language. Frameworks are a collection of functions and libraries that make web development easier by automating some of the common (and tedious) tasks in developing a website. Things such as user login/logout and access control are used in a lot of different web applications, so why would you want to write code to manage that function over and over again? Similarly, a lot of web applications use a database on the back-end to do adds, updates, deletes, and listings; wouldn't it be nice if there were a simple way to build a basic page to add a record to the database, without having to rewrite SQL repeatedly?

Why bother with frameworks?

Frameworks aren't a new idea, but they really seem to have taken off in popularity recently. Everyone seems to have an idea about how best to implement a framework: some people prefer flexibility to efficiency; others just want to keep things simple. Most of the major frameworks all support similar features; they just take a different approach to how they do it. Most frameworks are language-specific; however, there are a few that have been ported between languages.

For the most part, you need to learn the language before you become proficient with a framework. Once you do reach that point, however, frameworks can save you a great deal of time and really allow you to focus on the big picture instead of worrying about writing code to interact with your database (as one example). There is no right or wrong time to use a framework; if you are comfortable working in a particular language, it might be a good time to branch out and explore the frameworks available to you. Big project or small project, they will save you time.

A few popular candidates

Frameworks are available for every language and every purpose. We've limited the discussion to three here, all based on popular open source languages. If you're not into Ruby, PHP, or Python, however, just run a search for *<language> framework*, and we guarantee you'll get at least two or three solid results.

Ruby on Rails

Ruby on Rails (RoR) is a great example of a web development framework. An enterprising developer, David Heinemeier Hansson, created Ruby on Rails when he was working on a project management web application. He grew bored of always having to rewrite the same code over and over again and realized that some of the process could be automated.

Frameworks can be great boosts to productivity but can also impose constraints upon your development process. For example, Ruby on Rails applies a "convention over configuration" philosophy to development: if you follow certain conventions, the code will write itself; otherwise, you'll end up rewriting a bunch of stuff by hand. One example of this is if you create a class called product (meant to add/delete/edit products in your database), Ruby on Rails will assume that the table in your database storing product information will be called products. It's not a big deal, but some organizations may have a strict naming scheme in place for database tables, such as you have to put the name of the department before your table name. In cases like that, you're going to have to do a little extra legwork (you don't have to write off Rails; you'll just need to spend a little extra time configuring things instead of using some of the built-in functionality).

Another feature of Rails (and several other frameworks for that matter) that's worth mentioning is its extensive implementation of the Model-View-Controller (MVC) architecture (Figure 10-4). We talked about separating content from form from function using XHTML, CSS, and JavaScript. MVC is sort of like an implementation of this in server-side development.

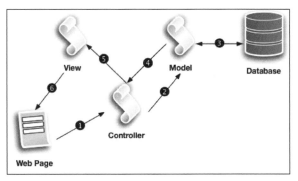

Figure 10-4. MVC request/response loop. 1) The browser initiates a request to the controller, and 2) the controller interacts with the model, which 3) may or may not interact with a database. 4) The model returns a result to the controller, which 5) invokes a view that is 6) returned to the browser.

The model handles all the data and logic in an application. It isn't directly responsible for data storage. Although we've focused on databases in this chapter, there are certainly other ways of storing data, such as a flat text file or as an XML file. The model is more interested in "working data," such as the total for this person's cart is $99.95 or that Friday is three days from today.

The view is the presentation layer. Any sort of user interface rendering is handled through the view, from the colors used on a page to the placement of check boxes and input fields in a form. The view will often generate the UI on the fly based on information from the model.

The controller is responsible for handling input, interacting with the model, and returning output back to the view. All of the application legwork is done in the controller.

CakePHP

If Ruby on Rails isn't your thing or if you're already a whiz at PHP but you love the idea of what a framework has to offer, you're in luck. There is a pretty long list of frameworks available for PHP, and most of them implement MVC architecture. CakePHP is one such framework for PHP that has grown in popularity since its invention in 2005. Although it shares a number of features of Ruby on Rails, it's been written from the ground up as its own distinct and powerful framework.

One of the big advantages of CakePHP is its ease of use and excellent documentation. If you're new to PHP, you may just want to skip all the groundwork and dive right into CakePHP—chances are you'll be able to accomplish 95 percent of what you set out to do with it right out of the box.

Django

The Python developers out there need not feel left out either—or the ColdFusion developers, ASP developers, or pretty much anyone else; there is a framework for any web application language. Django offers similar features to the other frameworks we've covered and has been used on a few high-profile Web 2.0 web applications (such as Revver and Pownce).

Of special note, Google recently announced its Google App Engine application platform (Figure 10-5), where you can essentially host your web application with Google. Google App Engine has built-in Python support, and developers appear to be using Django quite extensively in the early applications that have been built. It's definitely a great boost for the Python programming language and the Django framework.

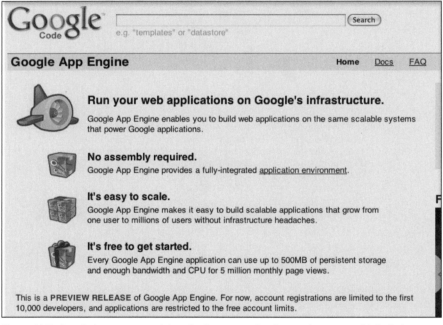

Figure 10-5. Google has announced App Engine, an application environment with built-in support for Python developers. Now, you can build an application that runs off Google's infrastructure and has the same scalability.

Summary

As we mentioned in this chapter, it doesn't really matter what application server, language, or framework you choose (if you even have the choice). They're all mature enough products that they are equally capable in their feature sets. If you're new to the area, pick something open source because they're the easiest and least expensive to learn on.

It's easy to get bogged down in language/database/framework discussions on projects. If you're going to be doing the technical development, you should ultimately be the one making the decision on what to use. Developers have to be confident in the tools they use; if the back-end architecture is being dictated to you but it's something you've never worked with, be sure to either get some help or allow extra time for learning. End users can tell whether there are problems in a site's construction.

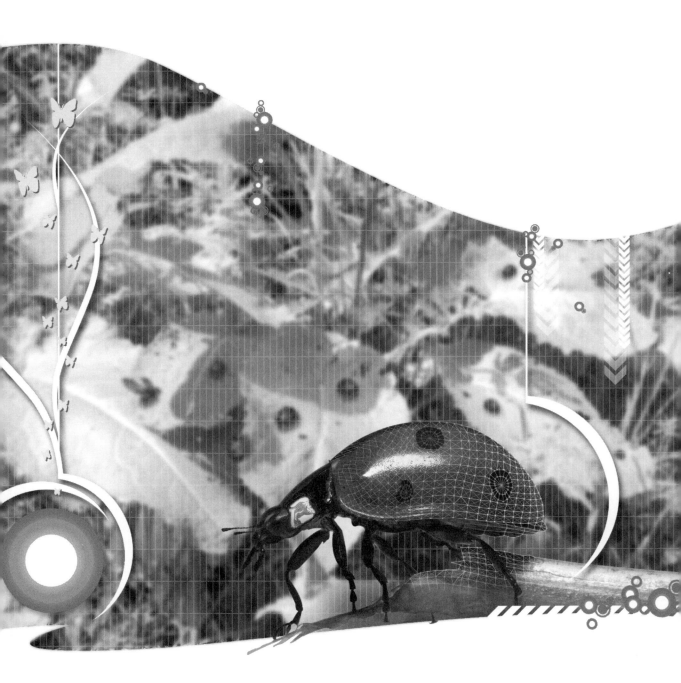

Afterword

THE BUSINESS OF THE WEB

This afterword will look at a few different areas on how to best conduct business as it relates to the Web. We've known brilliant designers who weren't very adept at billing. We've known excellent developers who have had trouble getting paid because they didn't work out the terms of an agreement before starting work. Freelancing is a very popular option among people working on the Web. We don't know whether it's the nature of the industry or just the personality type of the people who work online, but based on conversations we've had at conferences with others working in the field, there seems to be a really high occurrence of people doing side work for themselves amongst those employed at larger organizations (it was true for us for a number of years). It's not uncommon to find individuals who work in completely different fields such as print design or photography, or even a couple of licensed electricians who we've met, to occasionally work in web development.

This afterword will most apply to freelancers, or people in business for themselves. If you're working for a company, you will likely have other people who will handle things such as invoicing, setting your rates, and collecting payment (consider yourself lucky).

Basic needs of the freelance web professional

You have skills and a love for what you do. To turn that into a business, however, you're going to need a little bit more. If all you want is to build websites for the love of creating something, best wishes to you, and feel free to skip this chapter. If, on the other hand, you want to make a living at what you're doing, you will need to handle the business side of things too. The good news is that as far as businesses go, web design/development is one of the easier ones to be in. You don't have to worry about inventory, shipping, or accepting returns, and you can outsource things like web hosting to any number of commercial web hosts.

You do need to have a way to find clients, convince them that they should have you do the work for them, and then actually ensure that you get paid for the work you do. It's only intimidating when you put it in terms like "accounts receivable," "nondisclosure agreement," and "payment schedule." These terms all translate to plain English just as HTML, CSS, and JavaScript do for you now.

We think that the biggest shift you need to make is to get into the mind-set that you're running a business. Even if your livelihood doesn't depend on the income you're getting from contract work, pretend that it does (it's not as easy as it sounds). Your attitude and approach toward watching your finances and interacting with clients/prospective clients completely change.

Being legally well informed

We'll preface this section with the common Internet disclaimer of "we are not lawyers." Even if we were, it would be impossible for us to write legal advice that would be common across all countries, states, provinces, or even cities. If you're in doubt about anything, we encourage you to seek competent legal advice. With that in mind, there are some basics that we can talk about, such as types of businesses, and we can offer you some of the best practices in the industry.

Freelancing on the side

We can't think of a single designer or developer we know employed full-time who doesn't freelance. Most employers are completely fine with it as long as it isn't done on company time or using company resources (equipment, bandwidth, server space, and so on). Freelancing on the side is a great way to get started if you're eventually planning on going solo; it allows you to build a client base while still having the security of a salary and medical benefits.

The flip side is that if you become successful, you could find yourself with very little free time. It's pretty difficult to find motivation to work on client projects after having spent eight hours at the office, especially if your full-time job is working with the Web too. When we were working in this situation, we would always be up front with new clients about the situation. We wouldn't try to pretend that we were working full-time on their project; we told them that it was a side business.

Making the transition

One of the most common questions is "how do I know when to quit my full-time job and freelance full-time?" (if that's your ultimate goal). There is no hard rule on when you're safe to leave a regular paycheck, but you definitely need to start thinking about some savings if that's the direction you're headed.

Every case is different; if you already have a defined client base that you're working for and you're earning a good, consistent monthly income from your side work, you're probably safe to drop out of full-time work with three or four months worth of expenses in savings. If you're starting from scratch and need to build up your client base, you shouldn't even consider going solo until you have at least six months worth of living expenses tucked away. Reaching a break-even point isn't that glamorous, but it's the single greatest feeling you'll experience early on in your freelancing career.

Think of it this way: even if you have a number of big jobs lined up, it may be months before you start seeing payment on any of them (depending on the terms you've worked out with your client). One of the things we'll look at later in this chapter is the concept of cash flow—having enough money to live on now. You may have contracts that are promising to pay you thousands of dollars when they're finished, but if your account balance is zero and you still have weeks worth of work to do on each, you'd better start asking your friends for dinner invitations.

One idea, if you're moving in the full-time freelance direction, is to see whether your current employer will let you drop down to working part-time. That way, you'll still have the security of a regular paycheck (although diminished), but with more free time, especially within regular business hours, to build your client base and spend with existing clients.

More information

One of the best resources we found when making the switch is the Freelance Switch website (http://freelanceswitch.com). This site is a great source of information for everything from pricing your services to advertising and finding clients.

Business types

In Canada, there are three routes you can go for setting up a business; the United States adds one other option that's worth exploring. We're listing them in order of simplicity from what you can do today with no paperwork/setup to the most complex setup involving setting up a board and figuring out shareholders.

The good news is that no matter what route you decide to go, you can handle most of your incorporation/business setup needs from the comfort of your own home. The final filing of the papers (depending on where you live) may have to be done in person, but all of the forms and name searches (if you want to use a cool trade name like Google—wait, we think that's taken) can all be done online.

Sole proprietorship

The first, and simplest option, is a sole proprietorship—going into business for yourself. The majority of people we know who do "side work" operate a sole proprietorship in which they are the only owner and operator and they get paid directly for any work they do. Come tax time, any income you've made freelancing is included on your tax return (no need to file separately for the company). Customers pay you directly, and payments can be deposited directly into your personal bank account. Any sort of legal agreements, such as contracts or nondisclosure agreements, are between you and the client directly. If you decide to try for a bank loan to grow your operation, you'll be using your own personal assets as collateral.

The major benefit to this arrangement is that it's simple; there's really nothing special to set up. You can (in certain places) file paperwork with the government in order to secure a trade name (or "doing business as" name, sometimes abbreviated to DBA name). The drawback is that if something goes sideways with a client or with the bank, your personal assets are on the hook. For example, if you're contracted to build an e-commerce website that subsequently gets hacked and ends up costing your client their business (don't get scared; although it's a possibility, it's not likely), then that client could choose to sue you. If you lose in court because you left some major security hole in the code, you will be personally responsible to pay what the court awards.

Partnership

A partnership is similar to a sole proprietorship in that the profits don't go to a company and then get paid to employees; the profits flow directly through to the partners of a company according to the division identified in a partnership agreement. There is no need to file a separate tax return for the company; any income is reported directly by the partners on their individual returns.

So, let's say you and a friend of yours decide to start a company. She's brilliant with HTML and CSS, whereas you've always been a killer designer and can produce graphics like nobody's business. You're working part-time for the local newspaper, though, and don't want to give that up at this point, so you decide that you'll be able to devote only 50 percent of your time to the company. It wouldn't be fair to split the profits 50/50 in a case like this, so you opt for a 75/25 split because your friend will be devoting all of her time to running the business, selling to potential clients, handling the accounting, and doing all the coding on website projects.

Being friends and all, you may be tempted to just start working together based on this verbal agreement. It's probably a good idea to go one step further, though, and put some things in writing. In certain places, partnerships are required to register a partnership agreement with a government office; other jurisdictions are far more lax (this is something you'll want to check on). Regardless of whether you need to have a formal partnership agreement in place and registered, you should probably draft up something that answers a few basic questions:

- Who are the partners?
- How will money be divided amongst partners?
- Who will look after what parts of the business?
- How will decisions be made about the business (vote, certain people handle certain decisions, one person has authority)?
- What happens if one of the partners wants to leave the partnership? What if one of the partners dies?
- What happens if one of the partners wants to increase their stake (such as if you decide to quit your job with the newspaper and go full-time)?
- What happens to any assets if you decide to end the partnership (dissolve the company)?

It doesn't have to be complicated and written in heavy legalese. Just put something in writing that everyone agrees to and signs off on so that you have something to reference in case any of these situations arises. We're not trying to say that lawyers are useless here; in fact, if you have the money (usually a few hundred dollars), have a lawyer write up your partnership agreement for you; it could remove any ambiguity in future interpretations.

Limited Liability Company (in the United States)

An LLC isn't unique to the United States; it's also available in certain European countries (usually under a different name). The gist of an LLC is that it gives you all the simplicity of a sole proprietorship/partnership in terms of taxation, with some of the legal protection of a corporation. An LLC's profits can "flow through" to its owner/partners, so there is no need to file a separate tax return. LLCs can have shareholders, but they aren't required to hold annual shareholder meetings.

Corporation

Strictly speaking, an LLC is a form of a corporation. We mentioned it separately, though, because it's not available in all places, and it's probably your best bet if it is available to you. The most complicated route to forming a business is incorporating. In the United States (not in Canada), you have the option of either forming an S corporation (which has a lot of similar benefits to an LLC) or forming a C corporation, which is what most major companies are (like Microsoft or Dell). The differences between S and C corporations are pretty complex and have mostly to do with structure and taxation—so if this is the route you're going to go, talk to an accountant.

The single biggest benefit to incorporating, instead of going any of the other routes, is that you have a tremendous amount of flexibility in how many/what types of shares you can offer. In general, if you plan on trying to raise investment money later or if your plan is to grow your business and then sell it off, incorporating may be the best route for you.

Contracts

Contracts are a funny thing. Depending on who you talk to, the answer will be either "never start work without a signed contract in hand" or "don't worry about contracts; a verbal agreement is fine." We take the middle road in this discussion: sometimes you need a contract, sometimes you don't.

Let us qualify that a bit: if it's a repeat customer or someone we're really familiar with, we're usually OK with just a verbal agreement (unless they have a history of not paying us!). Standard practice is to accept a deposit up front for work, get another payment at the 50 percent point, and then get final payment on completion. We'll even waive this practice if it's a serial-repeat customer (we have a few of those). On the other hand, there's nothing wrong with asking a client to sign a contract or being asked to sign a contract by a client. What's important is that you both agree on the terms.

Usually a contract will cover a lot of the things we talked about in Chapter 2: time, money, and scope. If that sentence made you sit up a little straighter, thanks for having read and bought in to what we said about project management: how can you define scope in the contract when you're not sure what the project will look like?

You can define it generally (you're going to be doing the website, but not a logo, business card, and three-panel brochure for the company) and then put in a statement about how things will be revised as the project progresses. This informal, up-front contract can sometimes be called a *statement of work* (SOW); it just provides a written record of some of the things that both you and your client understand about the project.

Do you need a lawyer?

Maybe/eventually. When you're just starting out, lawyer fees can be a bit daunting. Most lawyers charge hundreds of dollars per hour, which usually translates to a lot of billable hours for a new freelancer. Chances are that most of your clients when you're starting out will be reasonably small and you'll be able to work really closely with them. That goes a long way toward avoiding potential legal hassles, leading to one person suing the other. For the work you're doing in the beginning, the costs to sue/defend a lawsuit will be way higher than just completely refunding your client (not that you should immediately offer that option if there is some disagreement).

What we're getting at is that you should in the beginning skip the lawyer. You can find contract templates and other legal forms online or offline in a lot of business-supply stores and bookstores. You can then customize these templates to your own needs. It really isn't until you start to get into projects that are worth tens of thousands of dollars that you should get concerned about the legal system. Even then, keep your head down, do good work, and everything will work out in your favor.

Resources

Here are some resources:

- http://www.designerstoolbox.com/: Buy individual templates that you can then customize.
- http://www.nolo.com/: Good, general legal advice on all kinds of things.
- http://www.mynewcompany.com/: Good resource for new businesses—how to incorporate, and so on.

Nondisclosure/noncompete

You're not likely to have to deal with either of these early on (we have yet to see one from a client), but in the event that you do, it's good to know what you're getting into. Normally, a nondisclosure agreement is pretty harmless; it's just there to make sure you keep anything you learn from your client to yourself. Your client/employer may ask you to sign one of these if you're going to be exposed to some sensitive company material. Generally, these agreements are there to prevent you from learning everything about a client's business and then taking that and marketing it to one of their competitors.

The only thing to watch out for is if the nondisclosure you're asked to sign also has a noncompete clause. What that means is that you may be legally prevented from taking on certain clients for a period of time. So, if you went to work for Pepsi and were asked to sign an NDA with a noncompete that had a five-year term, you couldn't then, two years later, go and work for Coca-Cola.

The two factors to look at are the length of the term and how general the clause is. We're not saying to refuse to ever sign an NDA with a noncompete clause. You just need to be sure to read it before signing and to decide whether the benefits outweigh the costs. If you take the Pepsi/Coke example and add that your practice specializes in food and beverage manufacturer websites and that the clause actually applies to all beverage manufacturers (not just Coca-Cola), you're effectively reducing your potential client base for the next five years.

If the contract with Pepsi is profitable enough (either financially or in terms of prestige) and if your practice is general enough that you'll have no trouble finding clients outside of the industry, then go for it.

Making money: financial survival

You probably want to make a little money, so looking after your finances is a good idea. There are a few terms and concepts you should be familiar with in order to ensure your financial well being. Although you hear a great deal about revenue and profits when you're watching business news, a more important concept for new business people to learn is about cash flow.

Staying in business

Yes, it's important to make money (revenue). Yes, it's important to turn a profit (bring in more money than you spend), but both of these concepts are secondary in the early stages as you're just struggling to survive. Cash flow is more of a big-picture concept where you look at how much money you're starting out with (if any), how much you're going to make every month (if any), and what your expenses are every month. In the early stages of starting your freelancing career, don't expect to be pulling in profits hand over fist. In fact, if you're making enough money to cover your own living expenses, you're doing great!

Let's look at a quick example of cash flow. We'll assume that you're starting out with some savings and that you're the only source of income for your household (you aren't, for example, living rent-free in your parent's basement). You've just quit your job and are starting up your own freelancing practice. You've managed to put away $5,000 in savings in addition to already owning your own equipment. Figure A-1 shows what your cash flow might look like for the next 12 months.

	January	February	March	April	May	June	July	August	September	October	November	December
Expenses												
Rent	$500.00	$500.00	$500.00	$500.00	$500.00	$500.00	$500.00	$500.00	$500.00	$500.00	$500.00	$500.00
Insurance	$100.00	$100.00	$100.00	$100.00	$100.00	$100.00	$100.00	$100.00	$100.00	$100.00	$100.00	$100.00
Advertising		$500.00							$500.00			
Phone	$30.00	$30.00	$30.00	$30.00	$30.00	$30.00	$30.00	$30.00	$30.00	$30.00	$30.00	$30.00
Internet	$40.00	$40.00	$40.00	$40.00	$40.00	$40.00	$40.00	$40.00	$40.00	$40.00	$40.00	$40.00
Utilities	$100.00	$100.00	$100.00	$100.00	$100.00	$100.00	$100.00	$100.00	$100.00	$100.00	$100.00	$100.00
Transportation	$70.00	$70.00	$70.00	$70.00	$70.00	$70.00	$70.00	$70.00	$70.00	$70.00	$70.00	$70.00
Food	$300.00	$300.00	$300.00	$300.00	$300.00	$300.00	$300.00	$300.00	$300.00	$300.00	$300.00	$300.00
Hosting	$50.00	$50.00	$50.00	$50.00	$50.00	$50.00	$50.00	$50.00	$50.00	$50.00	$50.00	$50.00
Computer Repair					$400.00							
Income												
Joe's Pizza	$0.00	$0.00	$1,000.00	$0.00	$0.00	$300.00	$0.00	$0.00	$0.00	$0.00	$0.00	$0.00
Scrapbook store	$0.00	$0.00	$0.00	$2,000.00	$2,000.00	$0.00	$0.00	$0.00	$0.00	$0.00	$300.00	$0.00
Web Startup X	$0.00	$0.00	$0.00	$0.00	$0.00	$2,000.00	$1,000.00	$1,000.00	$1,000.00	$1,000.00	$2,000.00	$0.00
Savings												
Savings Account	$5,000.00	$3,810.00	$2,120.00	$1,930.00	$2,740.00	$3,150.00	$4,260.00	$4,070.00	$3,380.00	$3,190.00	$3,000.00	$4,110.00
Results												
Profit/Loss	$ (1,190)	(1,690) $	(190) $	810 $	810 $	1,110 $	(190) $	(690) $	(190) $	(190) $	1,110 $	(1,190)

Figure A-1. Example cash flow for the first 12 months of business. It's OK that we're not showing a profit every month because we have a cushion in our savings. All in all, we haven't lost that much during our first year of business.

Getting paid (aka accounts receivable)

Standard practice in the web design and development world is to accept a down payment at the start of any work, one at the halfway point, and then payment of the remaining balance upon completion of the project. If you're doing fixed-price work (quoting a total for the project up front as opposed to working hourly), normal practice is to divide your payments into 50:25:25 percent (feel free to adjust however you like; these are just guidelines).

The reasoning behind taking a majority payment up front is that it commits your client to the project. Although that might seem like a silly statement to make, it's not uncommon to get hired by a client asking to have a project developed, for you to put in a bunch of work in developing a prototype or design for them, and then have them drop off the face of the earth because they get busy with other things. If they aren't committed enough to pay you half of the total contract up front, chances are they aren't committed enough to follow through until completion. We'll reiterate here what's been said a million times in this book: developing a website is a collaborative process; you are going to need your client to work with you throughout the process.

As with everything, take it on a case-by-case basis, but with new clients who you've never worked with before, a substantial deposit is your only insurance they'll stay engaged.

Tracking time and invoicing

If you're billing hourly, keeping track of the time you spend on individual projects is essential. It's completely within your clients' rights to ask to see an accounting of the time you've spent on their project if you're billing them by the hour. If you're billing a flat rate or if you're working on other things, such as your portfolio/promotional website, we recommend you still keep track of the hours you're spending. It's the only source of data that you'll have if you get into financial trouble and need to try to figure out why you aren't making money (it might not always be obvious, but if you have a log of the time you spent over the past few months, you'll at least be able to see whether the problem is that you haven't been putting in enough billable hours or whether your rate is set too low).

Thousands of different applications will run on a Mac, a Windows machine, or even a number of really good web-based products that will let you track your hours. A lot of these products are integrated with some type of invoicing software, so once you've tracked the number of hours you put in on a project, you can then automatically generate an invoice to send off to your client. Speaking from experience, a client is far less likely to question the hours on an invoice if it contains a good amount of detail. Handing someone a piece of paper that says "10 hours: $300" just won't cut it. Break it out into individual work periods (Mar. 2: two hours, Mar. 5: two hours, and so on), and provide a short description of what you were working on during that time.

We use an excellent web-based product called Blinksale (blinksale.com) for all our invoicing (see Figure A-2). It doesn't have a built-in timer function, but we've hacked together something that allows us to export hours from a desktop application we use for timing with Blinksale.

Qty	Description	Price	Total
3.0 Hours	Updates (October 05)	$30.00	$90.00
2.0 Hours	Site Updates (August 05)	$30.00	$60.00
2.0 Hours	Site Updates (September 05)	$30.00	$60.00
		Subtotal:	$210.00
		Late Fee:	$2.10
		Paid:	$212.10
		Total Due:	$0.00

Figure A-2. Blinksale has a nice, clean interface and offers a free trial that lets you send up to three invoices per month. (That doesn't sounds like much, but really, how often are you going to be invoicing more than three different clients in a single month?)

Do you need an accountant?

Although we stayed pretty noncommittal about the need for a lawyer, we will highly recommend that you talk to an accountant early on in your freelancing career. An accountant will tell you what you need to keep track of come tax time and will be able to help you immensely (save you money) if you decide to set up a corporation.

If you're really determined to save the expense, you can forego getting things set up professionally. Just bear in mind that it may end up costing you a little extra come tax time. Either hire yourself an accountant or save a little extra money from every invoice (just in case). Taxation varies a great deal from country to country, state to state, province to province, and in some cases city to city. If you decide to go it alone, without seeking the advice of a professional, then at least look for information that's specific to your locale. Assuming that advice from the United States will apply in Canada (and vice versa) is foolish.

Resources

Here are some resources:

- `http://cpadirectory.com/`: Directory of certified public accountants (in the United States)
- `http://www.accountants-4u.ca/`: Directory of Canadian accountants

Advertising and promotion

The best, and least expensive, way to gain exposure is to do really good work. If you build up a solid reputation as someone who produces high-quality work and is reliable in meeting time and budgets, you'll receive a ton of business through word-of-mouth referrals. What better way to find more good clients than having your current good clients recommend you to their associates?

If your specialty is in design, build up a great portfolio. If you're having trouble landing those first few clients because you have nothing to show them, make some stuff up. Just because the "Bank of Steve" doesn't actually exist doesn't mean that they don't need a website. Similarly, the "Antarctic Beach Resort" is just crying out for a solid online presence; it's way more fun making up your own clients with their own bizarre requirements than having to explain real-life examples most of the time anyway.

No client is too big or too small to be showcased. No client is too real or too imaginary.

Getting the word out

But hey, producing a great product is not enough. You have to shout it from the rooftops once it's done. The best way to do that is to build up your reputation online. The only way to build reputation is to get out there and communicate. It's just like you'll be telling your clients. It's not enough to have a really great website; people have to know about it and visit it too.

There are a few ways you can drive traffic to your website. You could go out and buy some advertising, but if money is tight, it might be more useful to look at some free alternatives:

- *Participate*: Comment on blogs, join threads in discussion groups, and write your own blog; do anything to get your name out there. It used to be said that there's no such thing as bad publicity. That's certainly not true online. If you're out there stating your opinion and joining the discussion, don't be a jerk. Nobody wants to work with a jerk.

- *Write*: Offer to write an article or two for an industry-specific website. Websites like A List Apart (alistapart.com), as shown in Figure A-3, take submissions from their readers all the time. Your article will need to be well thought out and pretty innovative, but if you manage to get published, you'll get an instant jump in prestige out of it.

- *Design*: Developers have it rough. It's really hard to get anyone (other than another developer) excited about code you've written. We have yet to hear anyone exclaim "Wow! Look how efficiently it parses that text string!" Designers, on the other hand, are constantly producing beautiful work that's easy to show off. Similar to A List Apart, if you're a designer, get your work featured on CSS Zen Garden (csszengarden.com) or CSS Vault (cssvault.com), and a number of other people in the industry will get to see it.

- *Develop*: Join an open source project, and get involved in the community. If you're pretty good with PHP, Ruby on Rails, Python, or any number of other languages, there are all kinds of open source projects to choose from. Pick one and start looking at the code. Fix up/improve on it, and submit it; it won't be long until other developers start noticing your work. Designers, this works for you too. Many open source projects suffer from very poor visual design; pick one and clean it up.

Figure A-3. A List Apart gets upwards of 3 million page views every month. Having your article published there certainly can't hurt your chances of improving name recognition amongst your peers.

All of these activities will give you name recognition, and chances are people will start to link to your website. Although you're making your mark primarily within the community (you're not really getting exposure with potential clients), when you're starting out, a lot of your work may come as a subcontractor to someone else or as a referral from someone who's just too busy and was really impressed with your work.

Finding work to pay the bills

Following the steps in advertising and promotion (discussed earlier) will eventually get you the clients that you've always dreamed of. It's really a wonderful feeling once clients start coming to you in sufficient quantities that you can pick and choose who you want to work for, but that doesn't happen overnight. Sometimes, you'll just need to pay the bills.

You have two options for finding work right out of the gates. You can go local and try to drum up work in your city or town, or you can go online to a number of job sites that post contract jobs. There are advantages and disadvantages to each approach; let's look at each individually.

Working locally

Depending on your locale, this may be a viable option for you. If you're in an urban center, flush with businesses looking to build an online identity, then you have a viable source of work. If you live in a rural setting, where you have to drive an hour to the nearest supermarket, chances are lower (but not nonexistent). The biggest single advantage to working with local clients is that you have access to them. If you're developing a website for Acme Hotels down the street and you want feedback on what you've done, all you need to do is go for a short walk.

Recruiting these types of clients can be much easier as well (at least we've found this to be the case). It's hard to convince someone that you're the right person for the job using only e-mail and phone calls. Meeting with someone in person to discuss their needs and expectations and to talk with them about work you've done is often a far easier way to sell yourself. In general, people will first look at whether you'll be good/easy to work with, before they look extensively through your portfolio of work. That doesn't mean you don't have to produce quality projects, but small-business owners, in particular, like working with other small-business owners.

Working locally also has its challenges. The same advantage that access to people gives you during development can turn into a challenge if you land a client who is needy and believes that every problem is a disaster (you know the type). Another disadvantage, again depending on your locale, is that local projects may be smaller (in terms of budget), or the local mind-set may be that web development services are worth little.

We previously lived in a primarily agricultural center. Although there was work to be had locally, the budgets for local projects were often no higher than a couple of thousand dollars (and that was for fairly complex projects). People in this center just didn't realize the amount of work that goes into certain things, and they truly believed that technical skills are a very cheap commodity. Your mileage may definitely vary on this factor, however.

Finding work online

Finding work online has become increasingly difficult. There are a huge variety of job sites allowing employers to post contract gigs (see Figure A-4). You aren't limited by geography; assuming the client

319

is comfortable working at a distance, you can bid on projects nationally or even internationally. It can take some practice to produce projects completely online; not being able to schedule a face-to-face meeting if something goes wrong is a bit of a detriment. Also, it can make it harder to enforce contracts/collect payment, especially from clients in other countries. If you do decide to go this route, be diligent about getting a deposit up front.

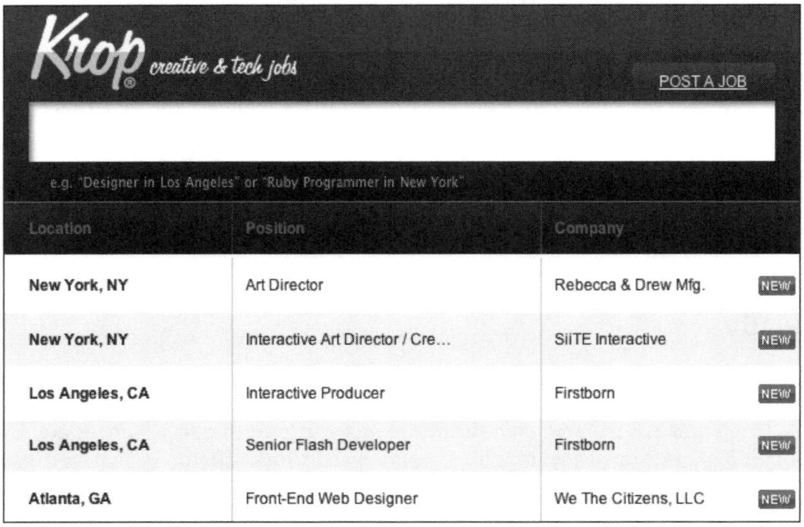

Figure A-4. Krop is just one of several websites listing both full-time and contract web work. Some positions require you to be on-site (in the office), and others will allow you to work from anywhere.

The major downside, of course, is that your competition isn't limited by geography either. You'll often find yourself bidding against folks from countries where the cost of living is significantly lower than it is in North America. Some clients won't care and will simply go for the lowest bidder. Others will be hesitant to work with individuals where language may be a barrier to success. The only thing you can do here is stand behind your work; if you have a great portfolio, you'll win over those clients who have enough budget to pay you. Just make sure you're not cutting your rate to compete with individuals in India or Vietnam.

There's a fairly comprehensive list of online job boards available at http://freelanceswitch.com/finding/the-monster-list-of-freelancing-job-sites/.

Finding good resources: people

You've survived the startup, and your client base and the corresponding workload have increased to the point where you need some help. It's time to hire, or subcontract, or partner. There's a bunch of options here, and they're all appropriate in various circumstances.

Hiring: finding the right skills and personality

Hiring is one of the most intimidating and difficult decisions for a new freelancer to make. It's the point where you decide that you are making enough money to not only support yourself but also to support someone else. You have to be sure that you're not just enjoying a temporary spike in business but that you've seen a steady growth and that you can now sustain two (or more) people.

All of that aside, you have to make sure to find the right person(s) for your business. Not only do they need the right mix of skills and interests, but they also need to be able to fit in culturally. As the only employee up until this point, you've set the culture of the company. If you value alone time and being able to work through a problem on your own from start to finish, hiring someone who needs to constantly collaborate to solve problems may not be the best bet (or maybe they are, and you can offload all your client-facing work to them, leaving you to work behind the scenes). Hiring someone who believes in a strict development cycle will certainly go crazy working for a firm that practices agile development.

We've sat through countless interviews and hired quite a few people to join our team in the past. Hands down, the people who have worked out best were those individuals who fit in culturally, well above those individuals who looked really good "on paper." Skills can be learned, but the right attitude toward the work you do is something that only certain people will bring to the table.

Where do you find candidates?

The best hires we've ever made have been people we found out about through referrals. If a friend of a friend is looking for a job, we're usually very interested. The main reason is that it's difficult to recommend someone for a job. If a friend of ours refers somebody and that person is a complete disaster, we won't even consider going to that friend for a referral ever again. Likewise, if we're ever asked to refer somebody, we will draw upon only the very small pool of individuals who we've worked with, and we know will be able to accomplish what needs to get done.

If you're having trouble finding candidates for what you're looking for, re-think what you're looking for. We live on an island with 900 other people. The chances of us finding someone local who can develop websites, configure web servers, and work directly with clients on projects is slim. Expecting a local candidate, or even expecting that someone would be willing to relocate here to work for us will severely limit our pool of candidates.

Likewise, you shrink that pool considerably when you advertise a job using the shotgun approach. Monster.com is horrible for job ads that request candidates be expert PHP programmers, Photoshop masters, Flash developers, and certified project managers. Although it may be true that what you really need is a generalist, most people don't categorize themselves as such. Most people will say that they are a really strong designer, so listing "PHP expert" will immediately have them self-disqualify.

If you have to resort to posting a job ad, try Craigslist first. We're not sure what it is; it's probably just the type of person who frequents Craigslist, but in general, applicants to well-written Craigslist ads seem to be of a higher quality. The only real drawback is that you do have to target the ad geographically, so if local/remote work doesn't bother you, you will have a difficult time reaching all potential candidates.

Finding temporary help: subcontracting

Subcontracting is pretty common in the web industry. The major advantage to hiring subcontractors is that the labor is available to pick up the slack when you're busy, but you don't have an ongoing commitment to feed those individuals work. The biggest drawback to subcontracting is that the people you're working with aren't your employees, so they may be busy when you need them. Also, identifying reliable individuals who are easy to work with can be difficult.

There are some key things to keep in mind when subcontracting work:

- Subcontractors work for you. They are not partners; they don't work for your client. If your client decides they aren't going to pay you for a project that you've already completed with the help of subcontractor(s), you're still on the hook to pay your subcontractor(s). This is another great reason why you should get partial payment up front on a job.

- Subcontractors are responsible for their own equipment. You aren't required to buy them a computer or a piece of software to complete a job. The price they quote you to do a job is just like the price you quote your client, all-inclusive.

- You don't need to deduct tax or provide benefits to a subcontractor. They'll take care of their own tax when they report the income at tax time. They aren't an employee, so they get treated differently.

- Expect to pay a higher hourly rate for a subcontractor than you would an employee (of the same quality). Subcontractors are just like you; they're trying to make a living. They need to provide for themselves all the overhead (office space, Internet connection, computer equipment) that you would normally provide for an employee. As such, contractors will typically charge a premium for their services over what you would pay an employee with a similar skill set/level of experience.

Partnering with others to complement skill sets

We talked about partnerships earlier, but in a different sense you may encounter people or organizations with which you want to partner. This makes complete sense if you each have a set of skills that is unique or if you both address a similar market. Joining forces will allow you to do more while sharing all the risks and benefits that go with that partnership.

Similar to hiring, however, make sure there is compatibility in company culture if you plan on working closely. A number of web designers and developers will either officially or unofficially partner with a hosting provider. It's difficult and expensive to run a server and to keep it online 24/7. Usually, freelancers don't have the resources to do it themselves (your home DSL line just won't cut it for bandwidth).

A simple example of partnering is that most hosting companies will offer a reseller discount. So if you sign one of your clients up for web hosting with them, they will charge you 10 percent less than the normal rate. You can then turn around and charge your client the full rate and pocket that profit. There's an advantage to the hosting company as you're bringing them business, and they're happy to reciprocate by throwing a little money your way in return. It sure beats buying a really expensive server, high-quality bandwidth, and better backups; hiring a systems administrator; and possibly even colocating your server depending on your needed uptime.

Growing your practice and increasing capacity

Don't fear growth, but at the same time, don't rush toward it foolishly. If you need additional people or equipment or servers to host your clients, then get them, but don't do it in response to a "what if" scenario. What if your hosting plan doesn't have enough disk space to accommodate this new website? Wait and see; soon enough, you'll find out whether you need more disk space. Don't upgrade to the next most expensive hosting plan in advance out of fear that you'll run out of space. Don't hire that new employee now because you think you'll have enough work for them to do in the future. If you have enough for them to do now, hire them; if not, subcontract it, or just juggle your schedule.

Growth is the single greatest thing and, at the same time, the biggest challenge to any team. You'll hear that you need to grow to survive; that's hogwash. If you have a good, diverse client base, you're making enough money to cover your expenses (and feel free to increase those expenses as you become more successful) and you're happy with what you're currently doing, you have no obligation to grow beyond where you're at currently. For some bizarre reason, there is a mentality in the business world that you have to constantly grow and expand, turning higher profits every year and hiring more employees. Why?

Bear in mind that there will be additional overhead in growing your team. What that means is that if your workload, for some strange reason, doubles overnight and you have enough work for two of you to do, hiring someone will not automatically solve the problem. Generally, when someone new comes on, they will need some time to get up to speed with company policies and practices, they will need to become familiar with your clients, and more than likely, you will have to be the one to bring them up to speed. So although you shouldn't hire early to deal with an anticipated workload, you shouldn't wait until the last minute either, expecting a new hire to come in and save the day.

Training to stay current and competitive

The last topic we'll cover is training. As a web professional, you have an obligation to yourself and to your clients to keep your skills up-to-date. Thankfully, the very medium you work in is also one of the greatest sources of information about your profession. It's really easy to keep up on things by reading various online sources of information.

Books are another good option, but the thing with books is that the information becomes out-of-date at some point (we appreciate the irony of you reading this in a book). That's not to say that books don't have their place; books are generally highly concentrated sources of information that are professionally organized and presented. A good book can really give you a leg up and jump-start your understanding of a particular topic.

There are also a number of really good industry conferences that take place every year at various locations. The cost to attend these conferences can be quite high, but we have never regretted a decision because of the great information and networking opportunities offered. Without fail, when we return from a conference, we always have a flood of new ideas and creative energy, even if the actual speakers contributed little actual new knowledge.

The bottom line is that training consumes resources, both in time and in money, but it's essential. If you don't keep current on industry trends, you will lose your competitive edge in this business as clients look for designers and developers who can provide the latest solutions.

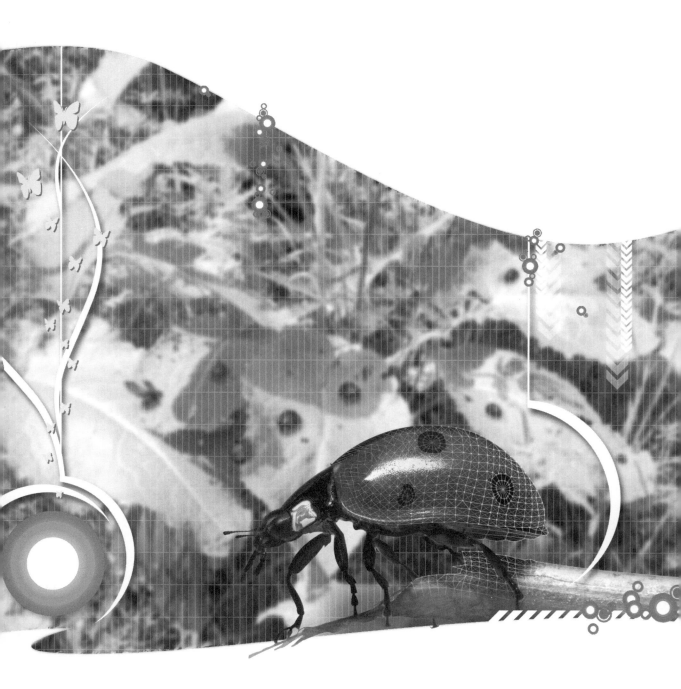

INDEX

XML for Flash	**Actionscript Animation**	**Flash 8**	**ASP.NET 2.0 for Flash**	**Flash 8 Video**
1-59059-543-2 $39.99 [US]	1-59059-518-1 $39.99 [US]	1-59059-542-4 $36.99 [US]	1-59059-517-3 $39.99 [US]	1-59059-651-X $44.99 [U

EXPERIENCE THE DESIGNER TO DESIGNER™ DIFFERENCE

Flash Applications for Mobile Devices	**New Masters of Flash**	**New Masters of Photoshop**
1-59059-558-0 $49.99 [US]	1-59059-314-6 $59.99 [US]	1-59059-315-4 $59.99 [US

Object-Oriented ActionScript for Flash 8	**Extending Flash MX 2004**	**Apache Essentials**	**Dreamweaver MX 2004 Design, Projects**	**From After Effects to Flash**
1-59059-619-6 $44.99 [US]	1-59059-304-9 $49.99 [US]	1-59059-355-3 $24.99 [US]	1-59059-409-6 $39.99 [US]	1-59059-748-6 $49.99 [US

AdvancED ActionScript Components	**AdvancED Flash Interface Design**	**DOM Scripting**	**Web Accessibility**	**HTML Mastery**
1-59059-593-9 $49.99 [US]	1-59059-555-6 $44.99 [US]	1-59059-533-5 $34.99 [US]	1-59059-638-2 $49.99 [US]	1-59059-765-6 $34.99 [US

Blog Design Solutions	**CSS Mastery**	**Flash Application Design Solutions**	**Web Standards Solutions**	**Podcast Solutions**
1-59059-581-5 $39.99 [US]	1-59059-614-5 $34.99 [US]	1-59059-594-7 $39.99 [US]	1-59059-381-2 $34.99 [US]	1-59059-554-8 $24.99 [US